MW00807204

STATS™ 1997 DIAMOND CHRONICLES

Don Zminda, Editor

Ethan D. Cooperson, Kevin Fullam, Jim Henzler, Chuck Miller, Tony Nistler and Mat Olkin, Assistant Editors

Published by STATS Publishing

A division of Sports Team Analysis & Tracking Systems, Inc.

Cover photo by Tony Inzerillo, The Sporting Views

First Edition: March, 1997

ISBN 1-884064-41-8

Acknowledgments

There's one thing about this book that you just can't miss: it was a real team effort. Just about everyone here at STATS, Inc. put in their two cents' worth at some point in the conversation.

John Dewan, our President and CEO, was never too busy to get involved in the dialogue. Under his leadership, STATS has become one of the most visible and productive suppliers of sports books and information. He always takes the time to ensure that every STATS product—including the *STATS Diamond Chronicles*—is of the highest quality from cover to cover.

Don Zminda, STATS' Vice President of Publications, organized and supervised the production of the book every step of the way. In addition to his frequent contributions to the discussion, you'll also find excerpts from his column, the "Zee-Man Reports," which appears on our baseball area on America Online.

Along the way, you'll get the opportunity to sample the work of our other columnists, Steve Moyer ("Baseball Babble-On"), Scott McDevitt ("Online Baseball Abstract") and yours truly, Mat Olkin ("The Fantasy Baseball Advisor"). Tony Nistler and John Sasman each produced a couple of columns as well, and Tony, Don, Ethan Cooperson, Kevin Fullam, Jim Henzler, Mike Mittleman, Craig Wright and myself contributed essays to the "Favorite Games" section.

One of the great things about working at STATS, Inc. is the opportunity to solicit opinions from one of the most respected authorities in the field of baseball research and analysis, Bill James. His insights on a variety of subjects—originally circulated on the STATS office E-mail system—are yours to share on the following pages.

Special thanks go to Chuck Miller, who took the raw material, ran it through our publications software, and somehow produced a book. We still can't understand how he found the time or the patience.

The rest of the employees at STATS helped to create this book, both through their participation in the debates and through their professional efforts. We'll start with our managers: Art Ashley, Mike Canter and Sue Dewan (Systems); Doug Abel (Operations); Bob Meyerhoff (Vice President of Finance and Human Resources); Stephanie Seburn (Marketing Support and Administration); and Jim Capuano (Vice President of National Sales).

Thanks also to staff members Kristen Beauregard, Grant Blair, Dave Carlson, Jeff Chernow, Marty Couvillon, Marc Elman, Drew Faust, Ron Freer, Ken Gilbert, Ginny Hamill, Mike Hammer, Tiffany Heingarten, Mark Hong, Jason Kinsey, Dave Klotz, Stefan Kretschmann, Mike Mittleman, Betty Moy, Jim Musso, Jim Osborne, Brent Osland, Oscar Palacios, Dean Peterson, David Pinto, Pat Quinn, Jeff Schinski, Heather Schwarze, Matt Senter, Leena Sheth, John Sickels, Lori Smith, Allan Spear, Kevin Thomas, Mike Wenz and Peter Woelflein. Finally, we thank former staff members Jim Guthrie, Dave Mundo, Rob Neyer, Kenn Ruby and Ross Schaufelberger.

— Mat Olkin

**This book is dedicated to Laura Brooks Aust,
the woman who makes my life complete.**

—Mat Olkin

Table of Contents

Introduction

If there's anything in the world that's half as fun as a whole season's worth of baseball, it's the discussion that surrounds it. Here at STATS, Inc., our office is the home away from home for some of the most serious sports fans around. When something of interest occurs in the world of sports, it's sure to be analyzed, dissected and digested within these walls. It's a treat to be part of the give-and-take, and we thought you might like to observe the debate as well—comfortably above the fray. Hence this book.

The first annual *STATS Diamond Chronicles* is, in essence, a diary of the 1996 baseball season, from start to finish. It's Bill James defending Marge Schott's right to make a sorry spectacle of herself. It's Don Zminda reminding us that the sport of baseball is *not* shriveling up and dying. It's Steve Moyer bemoaning the level of ineptitude in baseball's front offices. It's Bill James and I getting into a knock-'em-down, drag-'em-out argument over the proper utilization of one Jose Offerman. It's insightful analysis, sarcastic remarks and heated debates. Above all, it's *baseball*, and it's fun.

We present all the discussions that took place over STATS office E-mail as the season unfolded. The participants include a group of dedicated baseball-watchers both inside and out of our office, ensuring that every topic is attacked from about 17 different angles. A frequent member of the discussion is the man who re-defined the way a whole generation of fans view the game of baseball, Bill James. We run through all the major events of the season, from spring training of 1996 right through to February of 1997. Along the way, we include excerpts from the essays our columnists wrote for our baseball area on America Online. You'll get the best from Don Zminda's "Zee-Man Reports," Scott McDevitt's "Online Baseball Abstracts," Steve Moyer's "Baseball Babble-On," and my "Fantasy Baseball Advisor." Good stuff (mine too, from time to time).

We wrap it up with both a look forward and a look backward. First we let our baseball experts present their picks for the 1997 baseball season. Can the White Sox edge out the Indians this year? We happen to have several opinions on that. We also pick this year's award winners. MVP? Rookie of the Year? How far out on a limb will we go? (Mark Lemke for MVP? Well, maybe not *that* far.)

We continue with a trip into the past. . . back to our favorite baseball game of all time. Several of us penned essays on the best nine innings we've ever had the pleasure to witness.

We conclude with "A World Series Journal," an essay by Craig Wright about a trip to the 1996 World Series with a STATS press box reporter named Stan Reynolds. It's an inspirational story about a very courageous individual. Don't miss it.

One final word. There are a lot of candid opinions expressed here—some of them by people who work for STATS, some by our baseball friends outside the office. The opinions expressed here are not necessarily those of STATS, Inc. (and quite often are not). But a good give-and-take adds to any discussion, and that's what you'll see in this book. Enjoy.

—Mat Olkin

Dramatis Personae

(in alphabetical order)

The following people contributed their opinions, insights, observations and analysis throughout this book:

Kristen Beauregard	Matt Greenberger	Dave Mundo	John Sasman
Mike Canter	Jim Guthrie	Rob Neyer	Jeff Schinski
Jeff Chernow	Jim Henzler	Tony Nistler	Stephanie Seburn
Ethan D. Cooperson	Bill James	Mat Olkin	Ross Schaufelberger
Marty Couvillon	Stefan Kretcshmann	Jim Osborne	John Sickels
John Dewan	Scott McDevitt	Brent Osland	Allan Spear
Marc Elman	Bob Meyerhoff	Oscar Palacios	Mike Wenz
Drew Faust	Chuck Miller	Dave Pinto	Peter Woelflein
Ron Freer	Mike Mittleman	Pat Quinn	Don Zminda
Kevin Fullam	Steve Moyer	Kenn Ruby	

In addition, Scott McDevitt, Steve Moyer, Mat Olkin and Don Zminda contributed numerous columns and essays, many of which can be found in the STATS Baseball area on America Online (keyword: STATS). These columns and essays are indicated throughout this text by dates and titles which are italicized. Look for their fresh perspectives throughout the 1997 season on AOL.

2

1996 Preseason

February 15, 1996—Can Canseco and McGwire Be Far Behind?

MOYER: The Cardinals signed "possibly the worst 132 innings of pitching in one season"—Mike Moore—to a minor league contract.

SICKELS: I wonder if Carney Lansford is looking for a contract. . .

ZMINDA: Don't forget Ron Darling.

RUBY: New starting rotation for St. Louis:

Steve McCatty, Mike Norris, Rick Langford, Matt Keough

SICKELS: Let's see. . . the Cardinals need pitching. . . I think LaMarr Hoyt is out of jail now. They also need power. . . how 'bout Ron Kittle.

ZMINDA: And Dave Stewart says the snap is back in his forkball.

MILLER: Don't forget to add Brian Kingman to that awesome staff!!!

DEWAN: Lansford might not have a contract, but it appears that Juan Disgosto, er, Agosto does!! He's listed with California in our system. I think he's 67 years old, but he can still *see* left-handed hitters when they come to the plate.

MOYER: This is semi-repeated from my AOL column, but I am certain the Cardinals will be way, way overrated in the preseason and end up being a huge disappointment during the regular season. For some reason, the media seems to love to pick the Cards high. Even last year, when they were simply wretched (and it was pretty apparent in the preseason already) they were picked to win that division fairly frequently. This year, guaranteed, they will be picked to win a lot, maybe more than any other team. As I see it, the Cards improved from wretched to OK. I think they've got a ways to go before they're good.

PINTO: I really don't see anyone beating the Astros in that division (unless, of course, Bagwell breaks his hand again).

JAMES: The Cardinals look pretty decent to me. Benes is a tremendous pitcher, although few people realize it, and Stottlemyre has turned a corner. I think they're the best 1-2 pitching punch in that division.

I bet they win 85-90 games. That could be enough.

COOPERSON: I think that with Jim Hart and Terry Metcalf, the St. Louis Cardinals will be unstoppable this year.

NEYER: Gotta disagree about both Benes and Stottlemyre. My spies tell me that Benes has lost three or four miles off his fastball since he came up. And I honestly don't understand the optimism regarding Stottlemyre. Yes, he went 14-7 and struck out a career-high 205 hitters. But his ERA was also 4.55, just the sixth-best of his career. I remember after his 1991 season (15-8, 3.78), people were saying he turned the corner then, too. He's OK as a number-three or -four starter.

MOYER: All Stottlemyre has done is learn to K people. Maybe that's such a great step forward that it constitutes "turning a corner." What I see is that he still gives up lots of hits and walks per IP, gives up lots of homers, and has an ERA a little better than league average. His seventh-best in the A.L. run support (6.48) allowed him to win 14 and lose seven. The Ks are a great thing that not everybody can do and usually are necessary to be a real dominant pitcher, so I wouldn't be shocked if he turns in a great year, but I wouldn't expect it. I've tagged along on Benes' coattails for all these years as much as anyone, telling everyone to watch out for the great year he's going to have. He just never has it. We'll see, I guess. I want to know who's going to hit besides Lankford and Gant?

SICKELS: Let's look at the Cardinals.

The outfield of Gant-Lankford-Jordan looks pretty good to me.

The infield is more unsettled. Gaetti had a great year last year, but I wouldn't trust him to repeat it. Clayton at short is an OK player. David Bell at second is pretty good. I've never liked John Mabry much. Pagnozzi is pretty decent if he is hitting .270, but if he is hitting .215 like last year that's not too hot. Rotation: Andy Benes, Stottlemyre, Osborne, Mike Morgan, Alan Benes. . . that's not bad, but Morgan and Osborne aren't exactly durable. Eck in the bullpen. . . well, who knows? He's not an elite closer anymore. To me, the Cardinals look like an 85-win team. . . if they get lucky they could win 90, but if they are unlucky and get hurt they could win 75. The Astros look better to me.

MOYER: The only thing I see that's really pretty good about Bell is that he's 23 and could get "pretty-gooder." If he stays what he is, he's mediocre. I think the best thing that could happen to the Cards is for Geronimo Pena to finally stay healthy for a year. That could help a lot.

SICKELS: Given a full shot in the majors, Bell would hit around .270 with 6-12 homers and solid defense. That's not bad for a 23-year-old second baseman.

In his limited time at second base in the majors last year, Bell made too many errors and fielded .967, but his range factor was quite good. I think he can handle the position if given sufficient patience on the part of La Russa.

WOELFLEIN: Future Cardinals pitcher Dave Stewart turns 39 today. Happy Birthday Stew. He fits right in with their youth movement. "He's a veteran pitcher who knows how to win. He'll give us 200+ innings and he has championship experience. We're lucky to get a guy like Stew." (Fill in name of Cardinals executive here).

February 21—Seeing Red

NEYER: Noted while rooting around in *Baseball Weekly*. . .

The Reds are supposedly hoping that Vince Coleman and Eric Davis win starting jobs this spring training. 'Nuff said.

JAMES: What happened? They didn't fire Davey Johnson, did they?

SICKELS: *Baseball Weekly* is a very useful publication, since the baseball suicide of the *Sporting News* a few years back. But sometimes they say really stupid things. Item:

Headline on page 42 of most recent issue, regarding Vince Coleman and the Reds: "Coleman could help offense in a hurry." Help it do what? Collapse? Combine with Eric Davis to steal at-bats from young players? Teach Curtis Goodwin how to throw firecrackers? Help Thomas Howard reduce his on-base percentage?

COOPERSON: The Reds would have done better to keep Mariano Duncan than to sign Coleman and Davis.

PINTO: Absolutely! I have no doubt that by the end of the season, someone is going to ask me for biggest Reds collapses from one year to the next.

COOPERSON: Wouldn't that be the '81 Reds to the '82 Reds? If you go by winning percentage, the dropoff was huge.

MOYER: It's funny that you voice your preference for *BBW* over *TSN*, since I've discovered, in my opinion, just the opposite over the past six months or so. Even though *TSN* is always outdated, at least they have some fun stuff (Fly, especially) and their reporters and editorialists voice opinions (mostly stupid, but so what) which are totally avoided in *BBW* for the blandest, boringest, mamby-pambiest baseball reporting on the planet. They also succeed in wasting so many pages on totally useless garbage (how many different ways can you take up 10 pages reprinting last year's final totals), I usually find myself able to finish a *BBW* in about a half hour.

Anyway, as a challenge to "Coleman could help offense in a hurry," I'll offer this, from the new *BBA*: from "baseball guru" Peter Gammons, "Outfielder Luis Polonia was a terrific cheap signing for a turf team, because while his five-year .343 on-base percentage isn't great, he hustles and he can run." Right on the money, Peter. Polonia's probably almost as good as Coleman.

MILLER: I was talking to Chris Welsh (one of the Reds' TV announcers) the other day and I asked him who the Reds planned to get to add some power to their lineup and to fill in in left field considering they've lost two left fielders in two years (Kevin Mitchell and Ron Gant). He said they had about 15 guys they were going to have go head-to-head and whoever was left standing at the end of spring training would be the starter. He said probably Vince Coleman. He said they didn't have enough money to go after any big free agents, so their power would be limited. I told him that since the Reds launch fireworks behind the center-field scoreboard when a Red homers that if Coleman didn't fit into their left-field plans, he could always play center and launch the fireworks.

MOYER: Greene was always the Reds' third baseman of the future for no more than 50 at-bats. When he didn't hit then, he was dumped. "Chris Sabo could help this offense in a hurry."

February 22—Spring Reports

NEYER: More *Baseball Weekly* fun [brief excerpts from various articles in the February 27 issue]. . .

"Lance Johnson, signed as a free agent, is the leadoff hitter the Mets have been missing since Vince Coleman left."

"Tim Wallach is coming back from knee surgery and Jack Howell from four years in Japan, and the Angels open camp expecting the veterans to platoon at third base."

"[Mets] Rookie shortstop Rey Ordonez—barring a total offensive outage in spring training—appears to be a lock to make the team." [Ordonez hit .214 with no secondary skills in Triple-A last year.]

"Another reason the Phillies think Jefferies could have a big year is that he's been reunited with Todd Zeile. Both had their best seasons when hitting 3-4 in the Cardinals' lineup in 1993 and 1994." [What???]

"If we can use Coleman at leadoff and use Curtis Goodwin in center and bat him second, we might set a record for stolen bases by one team in a season." [—Jim Bowden; Coleman's lifetime OBP is .326, Goodwin's .301 in 89 games. True tablesetters, those guys.]

"The Pirates don't have an established veteran pitcher, although they've brought 40-year-old Danny Darwin to camp to see what he has left." [6.96 ERA, 1994-95]

PINTO: I've heard the Jefferies/Zeile thing is actually based on the fact that the two are real good friends. Zeile gives Jefferies an outlet for his immaturity, so he doesn't feel alone and isolated on a team.

FAUST: You're right—Ordonez is terrible. Where's Kevin Elster these days?

NEYER: Call me a skeptic, but the Jefferies/Zeile thing sounds like one of those things sportswriters write about because they don't have time to get any actual information. I'll bet you this: Their 1996 numbers will be closer to their 1996 projections than to their 1993-1994 numbers.

PINTO: I'm sure you are right. But it's a harder explanation to argue with than the 3/4 thing.

ZMINDA: The optimism over Ordonez is based on the fact that he finished second in the league in hitting in the Puerto Rican winter league (Roberto Alomar was first). He's only had two seasons of American professional ball, so I think it's premature to say he *can't* make it. Just look at Ozzie Smith's first four major league seasons (though Smith obviously had a much better knowledge of the strike zone compared to Ordonez even back then).

Ordonez will almost certainly be a very weak offensive player, but if his defense is as good as they say, they're gonna play him for a couple of years, at least.

JAMES: On *Baseball Weekly*, etc.

It is unfair to blame a) sportswriters, or b) *Baseball Weekly* because baseball men are often locked into Neanderthal thinking patterns. What do you expect sportswriters to do, if the Mets tell them Rey Ordonez is going to make the team? Not report it? Report it but immediately tell the public the Mets are idiots?

Even if they were, for example, to tell the public that the Mets think that Ordonez can play, wink wink, the effect of this in very short order would be that the lines of communication would short out even worse.

February 22—Who Am I?

NEYER: Which major league closer am I?

Year	Saves	ERA
1990	43	2.56
1991	7	5.54
1992	36	1.85
1993	26	4.54
1994	27	2.17
1995	22	5.01

Give up? I'm Doug Jones, and Rob Neyer wants to know what the chances are that I'll rebound *again* in 1996.

OSBORNE: Jones will never be the closer he once was, now that his moustache has eaten his mouth.

MOYER: I have a feeling Jones will be toast in Wrigley. The Cubs should pray for Duane Ward's arm, I think.

February 22—Nearly Useless Trivia

SPEAR: This is from the SABR Biographical Committee Newsletter. . .

The 1995 Rookie Class produced:

- The only teenager to play was Karim Garcia.

- Todd Hollandsworth and Steve Wojciechowski tied the ML record for longest last name, with 13 letters.

- Arquimedez Pozo's first name scores 31 points on a Scrabble (TM) board, outdistancing the previous record-holder Alozjy Bejma.

- Two players (Paul Douglas Creek & Chad Everett Fonville) were named after actors, while one (Derek Sanderson Jeter) was named after a hockey player.

- Ugueth Urtain Urbina became the first major leaguer with the initials UUU.

PINTO: The 31 scrabble points (for Pozo) is just the tile aggregate of the letters. Since there are 10 letters in the name, you would almost certainly need to use all seven letters in your hand to finish the word, which would result in a 50 point bonus. It's also possible to have the word land on two triple letter scores, making the upper limit of the word well over 300 points.

Of course, proper names can't be used, so the whole question is moot.

MOYER: I think it's cool that, when Ugie Urbina comes into a game, fans could chant, "You, you, you, you. . ."

February 22—Turf Talk

SPEAR: Did you see that the Cardinals are offering big chunks of their old turf field for fans to buy?

NEYER: I'll take 200 square feet.

Seriously, that's kind of weird. As you know, Allan, the Royals sold smaller pieces of their turf for 15 or 20 bucks, albeit with a neat little lucite & wood display case.

Anyway, I *will* take a few square feet, just in case any of my relatives—nearly all of them Cardinals fans—want some. BTW, can you ask the guy during which seasons the turf was in use?

ZMINDA: Can I get the two square inches once patrolled by Ken Reitz?

February 27—Tony Phillips Retrospective

MOYER: The fax I just pulled from our machine:

Tony Phillips Decides To Retire

"I talked to Tony last night and he told me at this point he wants to retire," said Ron Schueler. "I tried to talk him out of it, but he said his family means more to him than playing baseball."

Wow.

PINTO: That is pretty amazing. He's one of the best leadoff men in the majors, and I'm sure he'd be getting a good salary. I'm going to miss him.

DEWAN: Sayonara, White Sox.

SICKELS: *Wow*. . . that is weird news. Well, I guess Lyle Mouton is going to have a job after all. If he doesn't hit or gets hurt, watch for Jeff Abbott. . . career average in the minors: .357.

COOPERSON: He retired to pursue a minor league basketball career.

SICKELS: Let's put his career in context:

If Tony Phillips entered the Classic Game tomorrow, what should he cost? 60K? 70K? He would be a 2B-3B-SS-OF. . . with a 1,600 game career. . . great OBP. . . where does he fit? How much would you be willing to pay?

We could play the same game with some recent retirees. . . John Kruk. . . a 50K first baseman? Mike Moore (assuming his career is finished). . . 45K?

JAMES: Tony Phillips' retirement reminds me of one time when I was in the army, we had this soldier who had brought his wife and baby daughter to Korea, and although he was a very talented man and a very likable man, he wasn't getting much done. We were talking about what his problem was one day, and a man named Lt. Williams volunteered that his problem was that "he cares more about his wife and his daughter than he does about doing his job." He said this with precisely the same expression one would use to say he cared more about drugs and parties than he did his job, as in "What in the world is this younger generation coming to."

Tony's worth more than 65K. . . I'd say 80, maybe 85. Eddie Stanky started out at 58, as I recall, and has been bid up to 79, and I just purchased him at 79, so his value may not have peaked yet. I would think Phillips was a little ahead of Stanky, wouldn't you? So maybe 90, 95. . .

SICKELS: I'd pay 80K for Phillips. . . I don't know about 90. Well, maybe I *would* pay 90K. . . he is (was) damn good.

February 27—Size vs. Offense

KRETSCHMANN: This splits 1995 stats by a ratio of person's height to his weight.

Anyway the number of ABs is the total, the rest are just the rate multiplied by a 502 PA season. (Batters only)

	AB	R	2B	HR	RBI	SB	BB	K	AVG	OBP	SLG
Light	9408	62	19	6	42	17	40	70	.263	.326	.364
Light-Average	22638	63	23	10	53	11	42	75	.266	.332	.399
Average	102806	63	22	12	57	10	45	77	.269	.340	.414
Heavy-Average	18306	64	22	16	66	8	50	83	.270	.347	.444
Heavy	13332	66	22	20	75	5	48	86	.280	.353	.476

The cut-off's were:

Light (K−.015) = Lance Johnson/Otis Nixon

Light-Average (K−.015 K−.0075) = Kenny Lofton/Mark Grace

Average (K−.0075 K+.0075) = Barry Bonds/Albert Belle

Heavy-Average (K+.0075 K+.015) = Eddie Murray/Tim Salmon

Heavy (K+.015) = Dante Bichette/Jose Canseco/Cecil Fielder

(K=(4 x Weight)/Height^2). BTW, the K for 1995 Batters was .1468

PINTO: The bigger you are, the harder you hit. This is great stuff.

February 28—Bichette & Veterans

ZMINDA: Quote of the day: "I base most of my style on what Ted [Williams] teaches." — Dante Bichette.

NEYER: The new *Baseball Weekly* has a box on the Veterans Committee vote coming up next week. Among non-Negro Leaguers, they list the following as top candidates. . .

Infielders: Nellie Fox, Bill Mazeroski, Harvey Kuenn, Maury Wills, Gil Hodges, Cecil Travis, Joe Gordon.

Outfielders: Larry Doby, Dom DiMaggio, Roger Maris.

Pitchers: Jim Bunning, Allie Reynolds, Don Newcombe, Mel Harder.

If you ask me, only four of these guys are legit. In rough order: Gordon, Mazeroski, Bunning, Fox. The rest are pretty much jokes, especially when you contrast them with the guys the BBWAA is refusing to put in these days.

On the other hand, most of these guys have as strong a case as Vic Willis.

MOYER: On my Classic Game team, Joe Gordon could only manage to bat .275 with 19 doubles, 26 homers, 79 runs scored, and 97 RBI at Coors Field with teammates like Ralph Kiner, Dick Allen, John McGraw and Wally Post for a full season. If Gordon's a Hall of Famer, then Bichette's Babe Ruth.

JAMES: No, Bichette is Ted Williams, not Babe Ruth. Didn't you see that quote?

ZMINDA: Don Sutton is hoping that his strong showing as a CG call-up will help get him some more HOF votes next year. . .

It'll be interesting to see if the Veterans vote in Bunning, who won 224 games in his career, in the same year in which the writers felt that two 300-game winners couldn't cut the mustard. Not that I think Bunning is a bad choice. . .

I have a feeling that this is Nellie Fox' year, however. I believe that he and Bunning came closer to making the Hall in the writers' balloting without getting in than any other players in history. If the old timers ignore both Fox and Bunning and vote in Dom DiMaggio or somebody instead, I'm going to vomit all over my BBWAA card.

MILLER: If Dom DiMaggio gets voted in, and after we clean up Don's mess, I'll begin my campaign to get another famous brother into the Hall.

Tommie Aaron, where are you?

DEWAN: I firmly believe that the reason Nellie Fox is not in the hall is because Al Lopez never liked him. And Lopez makes it clear he didn't like him. Now that Lopez is getting closer to that big baseball diamond in the sky, Fox's chances should get better and better. It all depends on how many of Lopez' old cronies are still on the Veterans Committee.

ZMINDA: I've heard the same story about Lopez not liking Fox and actually working against Fox getting into the Hall of Fame. Which is one of the evils of having a small committee like this making the decisions. It's like the football HOF keeping out Al Davis and John Mackey all those years, just because a few spiteful people had it in for them. As maddening as the baseball writers can be in *their* voting, having 400 people voting tends to eliminate that particular sort of pettiness.

NEYER: Well, I guess I'll play the devil's advocate. . .

It seems to me that of all the guys on the Veterans Committee, Lopez is the one *most* qualified to pass judgment on Nellie Fox. After all, he managed the guy for seven seasons. How many men alive today saw Fox play more? Is it possible that Lopez simply doesn't think Fox is a Hall of Fame-caliber player? It just seems a little strange to be saying, "Well, just wait until the guy's manager dies. *Then* we'll get Nellie in."

Fox isn't a bad candidate, obviously. He's got those 2,600 hits going for him. Mazeroski barely topped 2,000, and Gordon has only 1,500. It won't be an injustice either way, but I don't think I'd vote for any of the "top candidates."

By the way, that article didn't mention any of them, but there has to be a list of 19th century candidates, too. Go, George Davis and Bill Dahlen and Bid McPhee!

ZMINDA: Yeah, Rob's right. We should forget Fox' MVP award. We should forget that he led his team to the only pennant they've won in the last 76 years. We should forget the four times he led the American League in hits, the 10 times he led in putouts by a second baseman, the six times he led in assists, the seven times he led in fielding average, the nine times he had the most chances at second base, the five times he led in double plays, his American league record for the most DPs by a second baseman in a career, the 798 consecutive games he played (most ever by a second baseman), the 11 times he had the fewest strikeouts in the league, the eight times he led in games played, the three Gold Gloves he won (it would have been many more, but they didn't exist until he'd been in the league for eight years), the 12 years he made the All-Star team. . . we should forget all that, and *leave it to Al Lopez!!!!* because he managed Fox. And by God, no major league manager would *ever* feel jealous of his best player for being more popular than he was.

How could I have been so blind?

OSBORNE: Gee, Don, why don't you tell us how you *really* feel?

DEWAN: I concur that Fox is a marginal candidate. I also agree that Lopez should be a good judge of talent and should have a more informed opinion on Fox' qualifications. However, it's been very clear that Lopez' opinions on Fox go well beyond qualifications into the realm of a personal thing. I've heard Lopez talk about this and it's really rather amazing.

NEYER: Makes sense. Personally, I know nothing about Lopez' vendetta, though I wish I did. This kind of reminds me of Leo Durocher and Ernie Banks, another great manager/middle infielder combination. As those of you who have read Durocher's book know, he spends about three pages ripping Banks. And I had the same impression of that relationship that Don gives to Lopez/Fox: Durocher resented Banks for being the bigger star of the two.

By the way, my first message listed my four serious candidates in the following order:

Gordon, Mazeroski, Bunning, Fox

I have to say that a quick look at the numbers makes me feel silly, if only because of the vast difference in the career totals between the three second basemen. I'd now rate them like this:

Fox, Maz, Gor, Bun

Still don't know if I'd vote for any of them. If you trust the fielding stats, you might have to put Mazeroski on top.

JAMES: Analyzed in traditional ways, Fox has the most impressive Hall of Fame-type credentials of the three. As a player, Joe Gordon was better.

[*Editor's Note*: The *Chicago Sun-Times* reported on March 4, 1997 that "Nellie Fox' chances for the Hall of Fame might improve now that his manager, Al Lopez, is off the Veterans Committee and Ted Williams is on." The *Sun-Times* went on to say that "Lopez maintained that Fox was slow. . . and only the fifth-best player on his 1959 A.L. championship team." Williams was always impressed with Fox' ability to throw Williams out at first base all the way from right-center field when the shift was on.

After just missing election in 1996, Fox was finally elected to the Hall of Fame on March 5, 1997 by the Veterans Committee.]

February 29—Phillips Returning

RUBY: The Score is reporting that Tony Phillips has "solved his family problems" and is coming back to the Sox. Their source was Ron Schueler.

SICKELS: So, he is "unretiring"? Is this the quickest unretirement ever?

March 1—Lofton or Williams?

QUINN: The AOL message boards have had a spirited discussion comparing Lofton to Williams. What do you guys think, which of them is more valuable in 1996?

ZMINDA: I like Bernie Williams, but I think Lofton is a much more valuable player.

PINTO: Lofton by far. He's a better center fielder and a much better basestealer.

JAMES: Lofton should rate ahead of Williams, but it's close. Lofton is like 5-10% better than Williams.

Lofton is perceived as being much better than Williams for several reasons—

1) He got good sooner.

2) People overrate both of Lofton's central skills—speed and batting average.

3) Lofton is a better Rotisserie player.

4) The Indians were in the World Series.

5) It's the nature of the game that the very best players get all the publicity, and the second-best players don't. Lofton's not Griffey, of course, but he is an all-star.

But Bernie's a good player.

March 9-22—Random Comments

SICKELS: Mike Moore pitched two innings a couple of days ago, allowing seven hits and seven runs for a nifty 31.50 ERA. Somehow, I don't think this reclamation project is going to last much longer. . .

STEPHANIE: Best BJFB team name. . . Someone is still disgusted about the strike. He named his team the Vastly Overpaid Prima Donnas!

COOPERSON: Two former Phillies, along with three other pitchers, threw a combined no-hitter for the Angels.

Almost as thrilling as when Neyer (I believe it was Neyer) managed a no-hitter during simulated play in 1994.

PINTO: Not that it means much, but it looks like the Angel offense is really pounding the ball. Unfortunately, it looks like their pitchers are getting equally pounded. Must be that dry Arizona air.

I was just doing notes on the Cardinals, and I expect the Cardinals believe that Ron Gant can deliver 30 home runs this year. But since 1966, only two Cardinals have had 30 HR seasons: Jack Clark with 35 in 1987 and Dick Allen with 34 in 1970.

COOPERSON: From Bill Conlin of the Philadelphia Daily News:

"Jim Fregosi is about to run the Indianapolis 500 with a fleet of Pintos. Pintos, like the pitchers assembled [in Clearwater], were cheap transportation vehicles that broke down often and had a nasty habit of going up in flames when rear-ended."

ZMINDA: I'm sure he didn't mean that personally, Dave.

March 22—Baseball Babble-On

USA Today went back to box scores and got rid of those nasty line scores they were printing for a couple of days. They must've been scared by my scathing review.

If you're feeling down this weekend, here's a quote by Felipe Alou about David "most overrated player in baseball" Segui that'll make you laugh your head off: "David's going to hit even if he doesn't want to hit, that's how good he is. He's a contact guy, and he gives good protection for Moises."

Apparently, Davey Johnson has blessed B.J. Surhoff as his starting 3B. They would've been better off with Leo Gomez, honest. Good luck to all the folks who are expecting the O's to be the only challenge Cleveland sees.

USA reported today that Lee Smith will be ready for Opening Day as the Angel closer. Good luck to all the fantasy players who paid mondo dinero for Troy Percival.

Another blessed one, Met SS Rey Ordonez, could contend with Segui for that "most overrated" title this year. That is, if he lasts long enough. If he's hitting .200 by mid-May, I'll be pretty shocked. Why is the media so in love with slick fielders, whether they can hit or not? Ordonez will be lucky if he develops into Rafael Belliard.

TSN rips the Rockies for trading prospects to get Bret Saberhagen. These are exactly the same kind of guys that would rag on a team for not going out and spending money for big guns down the stretch. I hate to use cliches, but the old "hindsight is always 20/20" certainly applies here.

TSN also rips Rockie starter Kevin Ritz, who had, I think, the most overlooked starting pitcher season in 1995. He was decent at Coors (an unbelievable feat in itself) and untouchable on the road. Yeah, I used to think he was a bum with the Tigers too, but he's a different pitcher now. If he'd get unloaded to another park, look out.

TSN's Fly blames Mark McGwire's constant troubles to "when he got heavy into heavy liftin'" after the '91 season." Ho hum. Weightlifting, just another new-fangled taboo for the old farts of baseball to whine about. How the frick do you get nagging heel troubles from weightlifting? Does that make any sense to any of you?

— Steve Moyer

1996 Season

April 4—Random Thoughts

Some random thoughts four days into the baseball season:

1. What the hell were the Mets thinking about with Bill Pulsipher? In 1994, at the age of 20, they had him working 201 innings in Double-A ball—the most for *any* pitcher in Double- or Triple-A, regardless of age. In 1995, at 21, they had him pitch 218.1 innings between Triple-A and the majors, which is more than all but two major league pitchers worked last year (David Cone and Mike Mussina). Now Pully's blown out his elbow. Big surprise. If this is how the Mets are going to handle the arms of their great young pitching prospects, they'll all be washed up by the time they're 26.

2. Transaction of the week: the Yankees sent Rich Monteleone to the minors, while releasing Paul Gibson. Talk about a gut-wrenching choice. If Gibby comes back and pitches some team to the pennant, heads are gonna roll in the Bronx!

3. I love stats which show how ludicrous Coors Field is. A STATS publications fan named John Sasman sent me some great ones. Using the park factors in our Major League Handbook, he came up with the following home run totals for these 1995 sluggers, assuming they had played half their games in Colorado and received the normal "Coors boost": Albert Belle, 81 (!!!!) homers. Frank Thomas, 70. Mo Vaughn, 66. Mark McGwire 63 (including all that time missed with injuries!).

And that's in the strike-shortened season. I love it. The only reason people haven't quite grasped what a joke Coors is, is that a *real* home run hitter hasn't played half his games there yet. But of course, you're free to continue thinking Vinny Castilla is a great slugger. . .

4. I hate the way Terry Bevington manages the White Sox. He's the type of "strategist" who brings in a lefty to pitch to one left-handed hitter in the fifth inning. No wonder they play all those four-hour games. Fortunately for me, the Sox will have a new manager by the All-Star break.

5. Hideo Nomo got shelled yesterday, mostly because he kept walking people. I wouldn't be surprised if this keeps happening all year. He still has great stuff, but I think the umps are going to be squeezing him.

6. Did you see where Jack Howell hit a pinch home run on Opening Night? Hey, I told you 10 years ago he was a great young prospect!

7. By the time you read this, Jimmy Key will have made his first start of the year. Don't get too excited even if he pitches great; the key (get it?) will be how his arm is holding up come June.

8. My favorite quote of the spring was the one in which Lance Johnson told a reporter he gave the Mets the sort of leadoff man they haven't had since Mookie Wilson. Exactly! I know just what Joe McIlvaine was thinking this winter: "Here's what we need to turn this team around. . . a leadoff hitter who's going to get me 30 walks a year. Where can I find

another Mookster?" Of course, McIlvaine was also the guy responsible for the care of Pulsipher's arm.

9. Willie Greene got his annual two at-bat trial yesterday. He struck out both times, so Ray Knight switched to Spuds Sabo. I love a team that shows its commitment to a young player.

10. News report: Disney's planning to rename the Angels. Some possible choices:

A. Orange County Goofies (perfect, when you think about it).

B. Disneyland Dumbos.

C. Anaheim Annette Funicellos.

D. Southern California Sons of Flubber.

— Don Zminda

April 4—You Can Run, But You Can't Manage

Ray Knight is a madman. I haven't seen anything like this in years. Sure, he warned us about it all spring, but now that it's actually happening, it can be avoided no longer. Wake the kids, batten down the hatches, stockpile the power hitters: *the stolen base is back*.

And it's back in a big way, at least in Cincinnati. I know it's early, but it's already clear: Knight is crazy. The man has gone completely nuts. He's got his team trying to steal every base in sight. He's sending runners he doesn't even have. He's giving the green light to complete strangers on the street. The Reds look like they're playing Whiteyball on four cups of coffee.

Allright, it *is* early, and maybe I'm overreacting. Maybe the Reds will end up with a nice, reasonable stolen base total. More than last year's league-leading total of 190, certainly; let's say 220, just to be conservative. But it doesn't look like it's going to work out that way.

No, it looks like Ray Knight is going to make the stolen base his central philosophy in life. Through Tuesday's game (the one where the Reds swiped seven bases against the Mets), the Reds were running at a rate that can only be called alarming.

Alarming? Am I being an alarmist? (I hope not; I greatly prefer my snooze bar.) Well, decide for yourself. Let's review one basic rule of scoring: in order to steal a base, you must first *get on base* (unless, of course, you happen to be Herb Washington). The point is that the number of stolen base opportunities you get depends on the number of men you can put on base—*first* base, mostly. It's simple. You only have so many runners to send. Most managers feel constrained by this fundamental truth.

The average team will send around 10 percent of the runners it puts on first base. The Reds were a little extreme last year: they sent between 15 and 20 percent of their runners, leading the league by a comfortable margin. This year, Knight's upped the ante. . . Heck, he's betting the darned farm. The Reds have sent about a *third* of the runners they have put on first base, almost twice the rate of any other team.

Whitey never took it *that* far. Even Billy Martin managed to restrain himself, to a point. To find a team that ran that often, you have to go back to the '76 Oakland A's, the team that stole 341 bases (that's 38 per lineup position, catcher, first base and DH included). Yes, if Ray Knight keeps this up, Cincy is going to be the Woodstock of stolen bases.

—Mat Olkin

April 6—Frank Thomas/Complete Games

JAMES: 1) What do you all think of the chance that, by the time he retires, Frank Thomas will replace Lou Gehrig as the first baseman on the all-time team? It seems possible to me.

2) Will we, in our lifetimes, ever see a season in which there are *no* complete games in the major leagues?

Without checking data, I think that when I was a kid the record for fewest complete games by a team in a season was like 25 or something. Last year the major league average was less than 10 complete games per team, and we have been working our way steadily toward the first complete season with no complete games by a team. Two years ago San Francisco had only two complete games, and last year Colorado had only one.

Very soon, we will have a complete season by a team with no complete games—then we will have two such teams in a season, then three, etc. This leaves two questions:

1) Will this trend continue until there are *no* complete games?

2) If so, when will it get there?

Anybody want to start a lottery? Pick the year. . . 2005, or 2025?

DEWAN: 1) He has a ways to go, but I think the Big Hurt could replace Lou as the all-time first baseman. Anyone notice that Frank is taking far fewer walks this year, both in pre-season and the first few games of the season? I hope all the talk about being too patient isn't getting to him. It doesn't appear to have affected his overall hitting—he's really ripping the ball, even though the stats don't yet show it. He hit a line drive to left field in last night's game that took all of .0001 seconds to reach Garret Anderson after it left his bat. Anderson almost fell over after he caught the ball.

2) Adios, complete game. A league season without a CG? As long as there's a least one manager who was around in the 60s, we won't see it. However, it's a consistent trend over, at least, the last four decades. It's probably a trend that spans the entire history of baseball, especially considering that in the 1800s virually all games were completed by the starter.

April 8-10—Unabomber & Hardball

JAMES: Why is it that nobody has commented on the fact that the alleged Unabomber played major league baseball? I guess that's what happens to you when you have a career average of .217, with a slugging percentage of .299. . .

Ted Kazanski, of course. [*Editor's Note*: the alleged Unabomber's name is Theodore Kaczynski, who has no connection with ex-major leaguer Ted Kazanski.]

FAUST: An $8,000 second baseman in the Classic Game, but I'm sure his price will jump. Does he have a special injury coding for "suspended during bombing investigation"? And how quickly would the justice system move? Two to three weeks?

MILLER: I agree with Drew Faust about the fact he will miss time. However, I think his description of the missing time is too explicit. I think it would show up on the weekly report more like this:

"Out 2-3 weeks: Bomb."

FAUST: Vince Coleman will someday be "Out 1-3 weeks: Firecracker."

This could be fun.

JAMES: You could platoon Coleman with Len Koenecke. Koenecke's injury report would be "Out for rest of season: Fire Extinguisher."

ZMINDA: How soon before someone names their team the Montana Unabombers and picks Ted Kazanski to be their second baseman?

OLKIN: Vince Coleman would have to be the left fielder; you might say he's an explosive leadoff man in more ways than one.

ZMINDA: Montana Unabombers starting lineup:

C	Cracker Schalk
1B	Boomer Wells
2B	Ted Kazanski
3B	Steve (Psycho) Lyons
SS	Jimmy Piersall
LF	Vince Coleman
CF	Wildfire Schulte
RF	Carlos May (think about it)
SP	Boom Boom Beck
SP	Urban Shocker
RP	Tom (The Terminator) Henke

OLKIN: Looks like the only pitcher that could cool off that lineup would be Virgil "Fire" Trucks. . . still, I could see him losing on a dramatic pinch-hit home run by Bombo Rivera.

JAMES: How about Joe KMAK. Jimmy Outlaw? Would Rube Waddell leave the mound to be a camp follower? Could we use Silver Flint to ignite the offense?

Harmon (Killer) Killebrew?

MUNDO: Three Finger Brown.

He shouldn't have played with firecrackers.

JAMES: Let's not forget Steve Sparks. They might get some moral support from Marvin Freeman. . .

ZMINDA: More additions to the roster:

Paul (The Igniter) Molitor

Travis Fry-man

If we're allowed to switch sports, you could use Edgar (Special Delivery) Jones of the old Cleveland Browns. . .

MILLER: If only. . .

Karl Malone played baseball, then we'd have someone to deliver the final blow to the opponents of the Montana Unabombers.

MUNDO: Manager: Sparky Anderson

JAMES: The 10 best starting pitchers in baseball so far this year:

1	Al Leiter	55.3
2	Sterling Hitchcock	54.2
3	David Cone	54.1
4	Roger Pavlik	53.5
5	Kevin Brown	53.4
6	Allen Watson	53.2
7	Ben McDonald	53.2
8	Sid Fernandez	53.1
9	Mike Hampton	53.0
9	Mike Mussina	53.0
9	Tom Glavine	53.0
	Bottom man	
	Todd Van Poppel	43.7

FAUST: Gee, Al Leiter might find a spot on the Unabomber team. . .

OSBORNE: Who would be favored if the Unabomber team was facing the Bronx Bombers?

OLKIN: I can see the papers the next day: Unabomber claims, "You gotta fight fire with fire."

MOYER: I didn't think the lameness of Rod "The Joker" Beaton's Chan "HoHoKam" Park joke in today's *USA Today* could be topped, but I'm starting to wonder. I prefer Benito Santiago's quote (also in today's *USA Today*) about Philly cheesesteaks: "They are very good." Please no follow-ups linking cooking cheesesteaks to fire to firecrackers to Unabomber, etc.

Hey Mike Canter, does Dave Mundo have enough work to do?

April 10—Tickets/Events

RUBY: White Sox tickets

I just called the White Sox. Their voice mail states that tickets are still available for yesterday's opener, in case you wanted to go. I'd love to get tickets to the '59 World Series. Think any are available?

April 11—Baseball Chatter

MOYER: Boston game today:

They are clearing the field of snow right now and the game, scheduled for 12:05 our time will start around 1:30 our time. Now you don't have to ask.

QUINN: Dan Wilson has three HRs today!

I think Chuck told me somebody froze Dan Wilson in BJFB, maybe that owner is smarter than you.

DEWAN: Dan Wilson has three HRs today?

We must have an over-zealous reporter with wishful thinking!

April 12—Piazza Power Outage

FAUST: Mike Piazza

He is now hitting .413 (19-for-46) without any extra base hits, and just one run scored. He has five RBI.

COOPERSON: Seemed like he got a bunch of weakly hit singles last weekend.

MOYER: He'd be Vince Coleman, if Vince Coleman hit .413.

April 12-17—More Random Chatter

CANTER: Tonight on "Unsolved Mysteries":

"Amnesia doubles a baseball player's batting average." 7:00PM—NBC

I don't know what this means, but that's what's actually on. Isn't this some kind of true crime show?

COOPERSON: Bob Tewksbury

Had a slightly subpar outing in that he gave up one walk in his five innings. Other than that, I think he was vintage Tewksbury, and the fact that he has such great control continues to distinguish him as the quality pitcher he is.

MUNDO: Worst Pitcher in Baseball.

Any nominees? I'll offer up the Rockies' Bryan Rekar. Future Hall-of-Famer.

April 15—Baseball Babble-On

It's too bad the Astros can't see that John Cangelosi is a real player who doesn't look like one and James Mouton and Derrick May are pretenders who do. Nevertheless, the Cangy man has been forcing his way into the lineup more and more lately.

I'm hoping Terry Adams (he's on both my LABR league and my other league teams) pitched his way out of a trip to Triple-A Iowa. Adams has been a marked man ever since Dave Magadan got hurt and Steve Trachsel was sent down early until a fifth starter is needed. I really don't know why the Cubs would keep Rod Myers instead.

My big sleeper, Steve Montgomery, is now sleeping in the minor leagues.

It looks like Leo Gomez might get a shot at some 3B playing time for the Cubs. He'll hit 20 homers playing half his time at Wrigley if he gets 350 ABs.

— Steve Moyer

April 16—Trying to Reason with Ray

(To receptionist: Please send in Mr. Knight.)

(Note to the reader: Look, I promised to take it easy on Ray, and. . . well, I'll try.)

Hello Ray, have a seat.

Ray, *what the hell* are you doing with Pete Schourek?

OK, OK, Ray, it's all right, I'm just a little worked up here, please Ray. Sit back down, please.

Good. Thanks.

There's something I need to discuss with you here.

Ray, Schourek can't handle what you're giving him. He can't. You simply have to face that. Look, I know that going to your bullpen can be a traumatic thing sometimes. That Moore kid's wilder than Ryne Duren on greenies, Brantley shouldn't even be pitching yet, and Carrasco's been throwing napalm.

But you've gotta bite the bullet, Ray. Schourek's your ace, and if you want to have him in September, you've gotta use your hook.

I know it doesn't seem like you're working him that hard, but you are. He's thrown more pitches per start than anyone in the league.

Yes, he has. I looked it up. That's my job.

And he's never been the workhorse type anyway. He's averaged 116 pitches per start this year. In the past three years, do you know how many times he's even *thrown*116 pitches in a game? *Once*. One time. Uno. Until this year, that is.

Just take it easy on him. You know his arm was hanging in the playoffs last year—and all it took was 98 pitches per start to do that do him.

So this is all I'm saying: you need Pete. Start acting like it.

Shut the door behind you. Thanks.

(You see, Ray's not such a bad guy. I kind of like him, personally. He just does some things that bug the hell out of me. Sorry you had to hear all that. I'd talk to Lasorda too, but you know, I doubt it would do any good.)

—Mat Olkin

April 17—Dan Wilson Debates

MILLER: Dan Wilson

Needs only four more homers in Seattle's final 148 games to tie his career-high of nine homers that he set last year.

ZMINDA: Two more three-homer games, and he *shatters* the record!

MOYER: Dan Wilson is more like:

A) Mike Stanley—1993

or

B) Chad Kreuter—1993

I'm interested to know what you guys think.

ZMINDA: I don't think Wilson's a total fluke like Kreuter in '93; he did hit nine HR in 399 AB last year. I could see him developing into a 15-HR guy, but not into a really *good* hitter like Stanley.

OLKIN: I'll take C) Tuffy Rhodes, 1994.

QUINN: Steve, here's what John Benson wrote on Friday about Dan Wilson for his AOL article:

DAN WILSON, MARINERS C: Wilson didn't look like much of a hitter when he first reached the majors, hitting .224 in a 1993 callup and .216 in his first full season in 1994. Wilson collected only four home runs in his first 400 major league at-bats, and never had more than four homers in a minor league season. Things changed, however. Seattle manager Lou Piniella had seen Wilson go 9-for-25 in a brief 1992 stint with the Reds, when Piniella was managing in Cincinnati. Wilson and pitcher Bobby Ayala followed Piniella to Seattle in a trade for Bret Boone and Erik Hanson in 1993. Under Piniella's tutelage, Wilson reached a .278 average with nine homers in 1995, not bad for a catcher and not bad for a 26 year old.

The Wilson case hinges on age. He got to the major leagues early because of his defensive prowess. If he had been an outfielder, those .216 and .224 performances would have landed him back in the minors, but Wilson had the precious abilities to handle pitchers and throw out baserunners. He was regarded as a major league asset even while he matured as a hitter. Wilson is likely to reach new highs across the board in 1996 hitting stats. Just don't expect any more three-homer games; he isn't Mike Piazza.

GUTHRIE: No, Dan Wilson is definitely not a Mike Piazza. Wilson has actually got some extra-base hits this year whereas it appears Piazza has become a pure singles hitter.

FAUST: Speaking of catchers. . .

What about Rick Wilkins? He had quite a 1993 season (.303, 30 HR) that looked like a fluke after the last two years. But I remember Gammons in some preseason notes mentioning that Wilkins was finally over the neck problems that had bothered him the past few years. I doubt he'll hit .300 with 30 homers, partly because he's now in the Astrodome and not Wrigley, but what will he do?

He's off to a great start—14-for-33 with two doubles and two homers. Heck, he's been intentionally walked three times.

We project him to hit .243 with 10 HRs, but I wouldn't be surprised by .270 with 20 HRs.

OLKIN: Actually, the move to the Dome may end up helping him. If I remember correctly, he has some sort of vision problem that makes it difficult for him to pick up the ball in day games. If you check, I think you'll find that he actually didn't hit very well in the Wrigley sun. The move indoors should help.

JAMES: 1) Let's not leave Scott Servais out of this discussion. . . who would your rather have on a BFJB team—Dan Wilson or Scott Servais? What about a real team?

2) According to Wayne Larrivee, Vince Coleman made five outs yesterday (0-for-5) on just six pitches.

MILLER: Vince Coleman 4/16/96

First inning—bunted first pitch for an out (catcher to first)

Third inning—hit first pitch for groundout (second to first)

Fifth inning—hit first pitch for groundout (third to first)

Seventh inning—took first pitch for strike, hit second pitch for groundout (first unassisted)

Ninth inning—hit first pitch for groundout (first unassisted)

Coleman led off the game and ended it in his first and fifth at-bats respectively. Wayne Larrivee seems to know his stuff. However, Ray Knight may need a leadoff hitter who sees more than two pitches per at-bat.

ZMINDA: Let's support Vince in his efforts to help speed up the games!

SPEAR: Wayne Larrivee (who celebrated a birthday today, by the way) is correct. Vince Coleman did indeed go 0-for-5 on six pitches, from the leadoff spot no less.

But to show how versatile he is, Coleman went 0-for-5 again today, but he looked at 16 pitches from the #8 spot.

April 20/22—A.L. East Pennant Race Over?

MOYER: Goodbye, buy-everyone-available Orioles. So long, Yankees and your proven loser manager. Dan Duquette got Wil Cordero for nothing and will now undoubtedly kick your butts. It was a good race while it lasted.

JAMES: Thank you, Steve.

PINTO: Yeah, right. Cleveland, with the smarts to sign all its players young, kicks everyone's butt. Steve, you obivously haven't watched the Red Sox actually play. They are awful. They're 10 DHs trying to field.

MOYER: Call me "Red Sox Braveheart."

My response to my weekend attackers is in my "Baseball Babble-On" that goes into AOL tonight, in case anyone cares.

April 22—Save Our Sox

My Red Sox and I were personally attacked by a couple of the STATS baseball heavies over the weekend. I'll share my answer here with you:

1) The Red Sox' team OBP is .307 and their team slugging percentage is .351. If you want to swallow all the media horse manure about the Red Sox losing because of their defense, I hope it tastes good.

2) The Red Sox are 0-7 against the Cleveland Indians. As I recall, the Indians were supposed to be a pretty damn tough team to beat, for anyone, going into this season. The Sox have also played three games each against the Rangers and Orioles, pretty fair teams themselves. Granted, they've lost to the KC pansies and the better-than-hopeless-they're-supposed-to-be Twinks, but they must've played the toughest schedule so far in the American League.

3) I was going to say the Red Sox have played 12 games on the road and only six at home, but I'll take that back because the Sox actually had a better record (44-28) on the road last year than they did at home (42-30). But if they end up playing better at home than on the road this year, as is normal, their schedule so far was even tougher.

Things will get better. A lot better. I'm kind of ashamed of these guys for doing what everyone else in the country does and magnifying the first small chunk of the season tenfold. 3-15 *is* pretty horrendous, but if it happened in July instead of April it wouldn't seem nearly so bad. I just hope the team doesn't panic, but I'm starting to read things suggesting they will.

And if things don't get a lot better, I'll tell you, I'm going to lose lots of my faith in sabermetrics. The Red Sox batting lineup has to be one of the best, sabermetrically, that we've seen in a long time. Now, if they'd lost most of their games by Sunday's 11-7 score, I'd say, yes, everything's in order, but their pitching and/or defense is just so bad that they can't win. However, that's not the case at all. The hitters just aren't hitting. It reminds me very much of a few of my STATS Classic Game teams that I put on the field. (In the Classic Game you choose old-time players and the games are played via the most sophisticated simulation around.) I base my teams on scoring runs and keeping the inning alive (my current Atlantis Association team is *not* one of these, in case you were wondering) and they don't win. And it's not always that the pitching and defense are so horrible either. They just don't club other teams over the head as much as they should. I used to think the game had it out for me, but I'm starting to think that maybe it is a prophet. Maybe having good hitters isn't as important as it's supposed to be. Maybe good pitching does stop good hitting, etc. etc. Please, God, don't let it be. Make the Red Sox win.

— Steve Moyer

April 23—No Defense for Boston

Did the Red Sox really win the division last year? I must have dreamt it; this team couldn't beat the Elks Club right now. What the heck is going on up there?

This is what we have so far. They got a guy from Montreal who couldn't play shortstop, Wil Cordero, and put him at second base, a position he'd never played. In spring training, before

Cordero had even had a chance to try to turn a double play in a Grapefruit League game, they released their real second baseman, Luis Alicea. So you've got a non-shortstop at second.

Next, they tried to make DH Jose Canseco their right fielder. Canseco gave it a whirl, but found that it required him to do unpleasant things—like running. So he pulled the plug on the idea. Undaunted, they signed up Kevin Mitchell, and they actually have been playing him in right field. Now, as you know, right field in Fenway is one of the bigger right fields in the majors. . . actually, I guess that's only appropriate, because Kevin Mitchell certainly must be one of the bigger right fielders himself. But can he play the position? Last time I saw him, he covered about as much ground as his shadow.

It's bad enough having Mitch out there in the first place, but when he lumbers out to right field, it pushes Troy O'Leary over to center. Hey, Troy's a good hitter, but as an outfielder, he's. . . a good hitter. He's not a center fielder.

So, at times, they have been trotting out a defense with a second baseman who isn't a second baseman, a right fielder who isn't, and a center fielder who isn't. These guys are just. . . what are they? Can we call them "figureheads"? They have these titles—"right fielder"—titles that have nothing to do with what they actually do, titles that they haven't earned. Cordero just woke up one day and somebody had *anointed* him second baseman.

So when their moves didn't work, the Sox didn't have any options left. If Cordero can't play second, you can't move him because 1) with a million other DHs on the club, there's nowhere for him to go, and 2) they don't have anyone else to play second. Same thing with Mitchell: if he can't work himself up to a trot, and can only DH, how are you going to get him into the lineup?

So when they started kicking away games left and right, the Sox were hamstrung—they couldn't address the problem directly. But they felt they had to do *something,* so they did.

Their reaction to the problem was most revealing: *they took Dwayne Hosey down to South Station and put him on the first train to Pawtucket.*

Yes, Hosey, their one true outfielder, one of the few guys who could cover center field for them, one of the few guys on the club who had played errorless ball. "I've been disappointed with his defense," lamented manager Kevin Kennedy.

Folks, if Dwayne Hosey's defense is the real problem with this team, then the Germans lost WWII because they failed to conquer Sweden.

—Mat Olkin

April 24—Names

JAMES: There have been 153 major league pitchers who have started games so far this year. The most common first name for a major league starting pitcher is "Mark", of which there have been eight. . . (Langston, Thompson, Petkovsek, Clark, Leiter, Gubicza, Gardner and Portugal. Actually, one or two of these may be "Marc", I'm not sure). Anyway, after Mark comes Kevin (7), Jason (5), Mike (5) and Paul (5), followed by Andy, Greg, John, Steve and Tom, 4 each. There are seven variations of "James"—one James, two Jamie's, two Jim's, and two Jimmy's.

April 24—Offensive Explosions

ZMINDA: Twins-Tigers

The Twinkies scored at least three runs in six of the nine innings today. Has that ever happened since we started keeping records?

Actually, the most interesting thing about this game to me (24-11 Twins, in case you haven't heard) is that Dan Naulty of the Twins worked three shutout hitless innings in the middle of all this carnage. They could have given him credit for the win, as the Twins starter (Rodriguez) lasted only two innings. But they didn't. Hey, maybe *that's* the most amazing thing about this game.

KRETSCHMANN: The Mets had six three run innings against the Cubs (at Wrigley) on 8/16/1987.

Inning	Runs
1	3
4	3
5	3
6	7
7	3
8	3

MOYER: Did you ever see so many "Hot Players" after one game?

OLKIN: So that's why the windows were rattling!

It's been confirmed now: the 35-run outburst in Detroit was the highest-scoring game in 10 years. Stefan's research reveals that from 1987-on, only four games have produced as many as 33 runs—and one of those games was the Rangers' 26-7 thrashing of Baltimore last week. Next time you go to the park, bring your helmet.

April 25—Breaking the HR Record

JAMES: 1) If somebody takes the home run record away from Roger Redneck, will those idiots who think Maris belongs in the Hall of Fame finally shut up? Or will they just switch gears?

2) I never liked Maris, and he's not a good enough player to hold one of baseball's major records, so I don't really see how anybody can be disappointed to have his miserable memory

wiped out of the books. If Frank Thomas breaks the record, that's great—Frank, or Ken Griffey, or Juan Gonzalez, or Matt Williams.

But if Albert Belle breaks the record, what about that? Do you root for Albert to break that record, or not? What about Cecil Fatso? What about Klesko? Klesko seems like a good guy, but wouldn't it cast the rest of his career into shadow if he does something like this now, and then spends the rest of his career explaining why he's not going to hit 60 homers this year?

PINTO: I'd like to know why you don't like Roger Maris? Does it have to do with his personal life or his baseball career?

I see Maris as a tragic figure of baseball. He wins the MVP in 1960, then hits 61 HR in 1961 as a follow up, but is destroyed by it rather than elevated to superstardom. I find it very sad.

I agree he doesn't belong in the Hall of Fame. The feat belongs there, just like Clemens' 20-K game does. But he did not do enough in his career to get into the Hall.

I'm rooting for three or four of the above to break the record, especially Griffey and Belle. Sixty HR by Griffey would bring him back to a decent lead over Aaron at the same age, and a real good shot at the 755 record, which is what I'm really pulling for. I really like players like Belle, jerks that are really good, and don't care that they don't conform to the public's perception of what a player should be. (Rickey and Reggie fall into this category, although neither is as bad as Albert). Jose Canseco does not fit into this category, because Jose does not care about winning. I probably would have liked Ty Cobb, had I been living in the teens.

Frankly, with more expansion coming, and what is passing as ML pitching these days (did you see the Detroit-Twins game yesterday???), 70 may be reachable.

OLKIN: If the trends of the last few years continue, the only thing Klesko will have to explain is why he hit "only" 62 HRs in 1996.

MOYER: Geez, Dave, I never thought of you as one who liked "jerks that are really good, and don't care that they don't conform to the public's perception of what a player should be." Viva-la Belle! Screw Sandberg and Ripken!

PINTO: I actually like Ripken. He's nuts, he's intense, and he likes to win. He's also a great player.

You really need both Belle and Ripken to balance each other. I like them both.

OLKIN: Balance each other? You mean Belle would throw balls at Ripken's hands and Cal would just play through the pain?

PINTO: Exactly. He'd also make a perfect throw to first.

SICKELS: Maris doesn't belong in the hall. As for Albert Belle being a jerk, well, yes, he is a jerk. But it would still be neat to break the record, because he is a genuinely great player, as opposed to Maris, who wasn't a great player. Here's a question: If Kirby Puckett's career is over due to the glaucoma, does he go in the Hall?

April 25—Will Puckett Make the Hall?

ZMINDA: It looks like Kirby Puckett's career is over because of eye problems. What do people think of his Hall of Fame chances?

RUBY: No doubt in my mind that Kirby is a Hall of Famer. Add to his two World Series rings, enormous popularity and All-Star appearances, as well as very good career numbers, how could you not vote him in? Of course I was one of the few that said last year that Don Mattingly deserved to be in too. . .

FAUST: Mattingly/Puckett

These are really similar cases! On Mattingly's similarity score list, Puckett is number five (I don't know Puckett's list). Both of these guys are as well-liked as they come, whatever that counts for, and both would be sure inductees if not for injuries. Mattingly struggled through some mediocre years at the end of his career with a bad back, and Puckett's career may end prematurely with this injury. If he comes back full speed anytime soon, Puckett could still make a run at 3,000 hits (and certain induction into the Hall).

OLKIN: True, Drew, but Mattingly only put in six Hall-of-Famer-type seasons. After that, he was just a "great clubhouse presence" who played good defense. Kirby's working on a string of 10 straight excellent years.

FAUST: Sure, there are differences, and arguments can be made for and against both of these guys.

I think in Mattingly's best years, he was better. Yes, I'm biased, but he was awesome from '84 to '86—probably the best player in baseball over that stretch. Batting crown in '84, RBI in '85, slugging in '86, and he led the league in doubles each year.

Bill did some analysis on players who were good over a longer stretch, and players being great for a shorter stretch. He put them on average teams and showed that the "great player" teams won a slightly higher percentage of pennants.

Bill—I hope I didn't butcher your work. I think that's the general idea.

SICKELS: A comparison that came to mind for Kirby was Tony Oliva. Their career totals are similar. . . extremely similar if the difference in eras is taken into account. Both lost (may lose in Kirby's case) 3,000 hits due to injury. Both are nice guys.

OLKIN: Actually, Oliva's career reminds me more of Mattingly's. Both brilliant early, and then increasingly ordinary as injuries slowed them.

SICKELS: Well, Mattingly had what, five mediocre seasons? Oliva really only had three, 73-75, after the last bad injury. He may have been good longer than Mattingly was. . .

FAUST: Right, but at the same time, was he ever great like Mattingly? I'm not familiar with his career, but looking at the numbers, I didn't see any season that popped out as great. Did he ever win the MVP?

HENZLER: Here are the 10 (actually 11) most similar players to Kirby Puckett, along with their similarity scores. . .

Don Mattingly	883
Cecil Cooper	880
Tony Oliva	871
Kiki Cuyler	867
Carl Furillo	861
Minnie Minoso	859
Cesar Cedeno	852
Cy Williams	851
Fred Lynn	845
Joe Medwick	844
Bing Miller	844

Of those eligible, only Cuyler and Medwick are in the Hall.

Please be aware that due to database limitations, all pre-modern outfielders are considered right fielders (the middle factor in outfield position adjustments). Lynn, one of the modern guys, is considered a center fielder. Kirby has played more games in center also, so he's a center fielder, too.

OLKIN: To me, Oliva was a better player than Mattingly for a longer time. I'd take his 1964-71 years over Mattingly's peak. Oliva was consistently among the leader in hits, doubles and RBI, and he won three batting crowns in eight years. If he played today, he'd be a consistent .340 hitter, with power. And they'd probably scope his knees and he'd play until he was 45.

ZMINDA: If his career is over, Puckettt will make the Hall with no problem. A few reasons:

1. His stats are genuinely impressive. He's never had anything resembling a bad year.

2. He's played his whole career with the same small-market club. Voters love players like this.

3. He's one of the most popular players in history.

4. He was a key player on two underdog World Champions.

What more do you want—a few years hitting .280 so he can "qualify" as a HOFer because he has 3,000 hits? He doesn't need that. And if his career is over because of the glaucoma, he'll get additional sympathy votes.

Puckett has exactly the package of gifts, baseball—and otherwise—that makes people tend to overrate a player. But I think he's a Hall of Famer.

April 26—Who's the Best Closer Ever?

FAUST: A little while ago, Bill mentioned that Frank Thomas could pass Lou Gehrig and become the best first baseman ever. It got me thinking about who the best ever at each position is, and I got stuck on closers. Obviously, there's been quite some change in how bullpens and relief pitching is managed over the history of baseball. Is Lee Smith the best because he has the most saves? Is it Eckersley?

MOYER: Percival's 1995 was phenomenal. Our *Scoreboard* confirms this and concludes that he'll be hard-pressed to repeat in '96. I know it's early, but he's doing it again. And if the Angels give that big fatso baby his closer sucker back at Percival's expense, they truly deserve to lose. I don't know who's the best of all time now, but converted catcher Percival's sure headed down that road.

FAUST: I'd use Percival as a closer, but what do they do with Smith? I heard that he's said he'd retire rather than be a set-up man. Maybe they'll give him some saves in the next few months and try to trade him to a team trying to make a playoff run without a veteran closer.

Or maybe the Cubs could use him. He did spend the first half of his career with them.

OLKIN: Best Closer? Good question. I guess the answer would depend on how much weight you would give to longevity. Career length seems to be the greatest variable. If you only require a good five-year run, I'd have to say that the three best would be Sutter (77-82), Quiz (80-85) and Eck (88-92). I'm probably missing someone, but it's Friday, dammit. If you cut it to three years, it could be just about anybody—Radatz, Bill Campbell, Mike Marshall. . . But if you're talking about 10 years, it's a short list: Gossage, Fingers, Reardon, Lee Smith. . . there aren't many. What about guys like Wilhelm and Tekulve who weren't always used as closers?

MOYER: The Angels could trade Smith back to the Cubs for a big happy homecoming. I just don't think Wendell's good enough to last very long. (I'm not sure the Cubs do either as his shortest save was 1.2 IP and he pitched mop-up yesterday.)

PINTO: I hear they would rather use Percival for up to two innings to get to Smith.

JAMES: 1) The best season ever by a closer was by John Wetteland in 1993.

2) For all-time closers, I stick with Hoyt Wilhelm. He had more remarkable seasons than anybody else.

3) To say that Wilhelm or Face doesn't qualify because he wasn't used as a modern reliever seems to imply that we accept that the modern use of the reliever is the most effective use of the reliever, that the relief ace used in this way has more impact on the games than a relief ace used in some other way. This seems to me a debatable proposition at best.

I wonder how many of us here really belief that the most effective use of a relief ace is to let him pitch 70 innings a year and see how many saves you can get him in those 70 innings. It never has made a lot of sense to me.

COOPERSON: Does Tug McGraw's 1980 compare to Wetteland's 1993?

OLKIN: Best single season ever by a closer:

Eck, 1990. 0.61 ERA. Five earned runs all year. 48-for-50 in saves. 73 Ks, three unintentional walks. Didn't even end up with a trophy! He won the Cy Young, but *he won it for Bob Welch.*

April 26—MVP Points

With several big names nearing the end of the line, I thought it would be interesting to see how some of them have stacked up in MVP voting over the course of their careers.

To do so, I devised a simple system, giving each player a certain number of points (consistent with the current MVP voting system) based on his finish in each year's MVP race. First place was worth 14 points (as it is in the real voting), second place worth nine. . . all the way down to 10th place, which was worth one (finishes outside the top 10 get you nothing). Here are the active leaders using the system, including those players who played in 1995 but not this season (Winfield, Mattingly, etc).

Player	Points	Player	Points
Barry Bonds	58	Dennis Eckersley	31
Eddie Murray	51	Will Clark	28
Kirby Puckett	42	Ryne Sandberg	28
Frank Thomas	42	Darryl Strawberry	24
Andre Dawson	36	Roger Clemens	23
Cal Ripken	36	Terry Pendleton	23
Rickey Henderson	35	Tony Gwynn	22
Don Mattingly	33	Fred McGriff	22
Dave Winfield	33		

With three first-place finishes (1990, 1992 and 1993), one second-place finish (1991) and one fourth-place finish (1994), it's not surprising that Barry Bonds is on top of the list. Here's how we compute Bonds' point total:

First place (three times)
3 x 14 = 42

Second place (once)
1 x 9 = 9

Fourth place (once)
1 x 7 = 7

Total
58

Now for a few comments on each player, particularly their Hall-of-Fame chances.

Barry Bonds (58)—Bonds is a no-brainer for the Hall of Fame and will push his 58-point total considerably higher before he's done. He's arguably the best all-around player of his generation. Let me give you something to think about. Bonds was named National League MVP in 1990, 1992 and 1993. He finished a close second (274 to 259) to Atlanta's Terry Pendleton in 1991, and might have won the award in 1994 had there been a full season. Houston's Jeff Bagwell won the award that year, but broke his wrist shortly before the strike. Bonds was rolling at the time, with 16 homers and 32 RBI in his final 36 games. Think about that. Bonds wasn't too far away from *five* straight MVP Awards.

Eddie Murray (51)—Murray's 51 points is very impressive considering he never won an MVP Award. He finished second in the balloting twice (1982 and 1983), fourth once (1984), fifth three times (1981, 1985 and 1990), sixth once (1980) and eighth once (1978)—eight finishes in the top 10. Has there ever been a player in major league history more consistent than Murray was over the first half of his career? He's easily a first-ballot Hall of Famer.

Kirby Puckett (42)—With his current vision problems, Kirby's career might be over at age 35—which could hurt his Hall-of-Fame chances (he's 696 hits away from 3,000). A .318 lifetime average and two World Series rings might get him in anyway. His popularity with both the fans and the media won't hurt either. Right now, I'd say he's a borderline case.

Frank Thomas (42)—He's in the Hall of Fame right now, no questions asked. By the time he's done he'll go down with Babe Ruth and Ted Williams as one of the three greatest hitters who ever lived. Thomas already has two MVP Awards (1993 and 1994) to his credit, one third-place finish (1991) and two eighth-place finishes (1992 and 1995). Not bad for a player who turns 28 years old tomorrow. It's frightening to think how high his numbers could go.

Andre Dawson (36)—His combination of power and speed will certainly get him in, but I'll doubt he'll receive the same recognition as Murray or Winfield. Dawson's best seasons came in Montreal—hardly the center of the baseball media world. It looks like he'll retire without ever having played in the World Series.

Cal Ripken (36)—Of course he's in. It's somewhat interesting that Ripken has only three top-10 MVP finishes in his career, but two were firsts (1983 and 1991). The only question is whether or not his selection will be unanimous.

Rickey Henderson (35)—The greatest leadoff man of all time—period. Baseball's stolen-base king has also shown remarkable power and plate discipline over the course of his career. This guy finished second in the A.L. in slugging percentage in 1990 (.577) while hitting *leadoff*. Think that'll ever happen again?

Don Mattingly (33)—Despite his credentials, I really don't think Mattingly will make the Hall of Fame. He basically packed his whole career into a six-year span (1984-1989) and never played in a World Series. He's a great player, but I expect him to fall short of Cooperstown. Don will be happy to know that I celebrated my first job offer (I eventually accepted) in his "Mattingly's 23" restaurant in Evansville, Indiana. Great buffalo wings, Don.

Dave Winfield (33)—I was a little surprised that Winfield's point total wasn't higher, considering the length of his career. He never won an MVP Award, finishing six times in the top 10 but only once in the top three (1979). He's headed for Cooperstown anyway.

Dennis Eckersley (31)—He's perhaps the most interesting Hall-of-Fame case in baseball history. It's one thing to be an effective reliever, but it's another to be completely dominating—and that's what Eckersley was from 1988 to 1992. His strikeout-to-walk ratio over that span is phenomenal. I think he'll make the Hall of Fame, as he should.

Will Clark (28)—He's put up a career very similar to Keith Hernandez. Like Hernandez, I don't expect him to make the Hall of Fame. With so many slugging first baseman around, it's very hard for a player at that position to distinguish himself. He's quietly built an outstanding career.

Ryne Sandberg (28)—He's clearly among the handful of baseball's greatest second basemen and should waltz into Cooperstown without question. Only one active player (Ripken) earned an MVP before Sandberg, who turns 37 this September.

Darryl Strawberry (24)—With Tony Gwynn's attitude, Strawberry could have been Willie Mays. Instead, he's. . . well, I don't know *what* he is anymore. He literally threw away a Hall-of-Fame career, and it's truly sad. He had 108 home runs and a World Series ring before the age of 25.

Roger Clemens (23)—I'm really afraid he might be going through the "Don Mattingly syndrome"—packing all of his monster years into a short span and nothing big after it. It seems ridiculous to think that any player with three Cy Young Awards wouldn't make the Hall of Fame, but Clemens has little to show for his last three-plus seasons. Another 20-win season would likely ice things for him, but that seems a lot to ask for at this point in his career. I bet he gets in anyway.

Terry Pendleton (23)—He's had a unique career, highlighted by his MVP Award in 1991 and second-place finish in 1992. He's obviously not headed for the Hall of Fame, and it's a shame he's never gotten a World Series ring as consolation. Pendleton fell short with the Cardinals in 1985 and 1987 (both seven-game Series) and the Braves in 1991 (seven games) and 1992 (six).

Tony Gwynn (22)—Six batting titles? I think we can find some room for him in the Hall. Gwynn's highest finish in the MVP balloting was third in 1984. He somehow finished seventh in 1994, despite batting .394. He now has a .337 lifetime batting average, three points better than Wade Boggs.

Fred McGriff (22)—He's a lot like his A.L. twin, Toronto's Joe Carter. With 291 lifetime home runs, McGriff is certainly building a strong Hall-of-Fame case, but he might need to make it to 500 in order to get in. Again, it's very tough for first basemen to distinguish themselves. He's always been one of the most underrated players in baseball.

— Scott McDevitt

April 28—Carlos Delgado/Jeff Suppan Fan Clubs Reunite. . .

MOYER: How many years was Carlos Delgado the old "guy who can't hit the major league curveball"? Now, he's hitting the crap out of the ball and no one's noticing.

I guess it shows two things:

1) How far the Blue Jays have fallen,

2) You just don't bury a minor league monster at 26.

MOYER: As Jim Henzler kindly pointed out, Delgado's birthdate is 6/25/72, which makes him almost 24, not 26. (Sorry, I can't add this early in the morning.) Which proves two things:

1) You don't bury a minor league monster at 26,

2) You don't bury a minor league monster at 23, either.

PINTO: Delgado's gotten off to a good start early before. If he's hitting like this at the end of May, I'll believe it.

SICKELS: Jeff Suppan, Red Sox pitching prospect, has a 28/3 K/BB ratio at Pawtucket. How much longer will the Boxsox go with Wakefield?

PINTO: Wakefield has pitched better in his last couple of starts. They really need to get rid of Tom Gordon. I don't know what the Red Sox saw in him. As a KC area resident, maybe you can fill us in.

April 30—Brave New World

So how do you like our new sport, *Hyperball*? It's far more exciting than our stodgy old former National Pastime, baseball. Yeah, baseball was nice, and I'll always treasure the memories, but it was just getting so darn slow. . . remember? Sometimes a team wouldn't even score for a whole inning. The strike zone—remember the old zone?—it must have been the size of my *torso*, for goodness sake.

—Mat Olkin

April 30—Random Notes

OLKIN: The Steve Moyer "Annoying Quote of the Week"

From Mel Antonen's column in Tuesday's *USA Today*:

"The Tigers don't plan to call up any of their Triple-A pitchers. . . until at least June 1 because they don't want to rush the prospects."

You can use your own punch-line, or feel free to select one from the following wise-aleck remarks:

1. "It must have been obvious to the Tigers' coaching staff that those young arms would need at least four more weeks before they would be ready."

2. "The Tigers have *prospects*?!?"

3. "When your closer is Brian Williams, and your rotation consists of Keagle, Lira, Gohr, Aldred and Sodowsky, what do you need another Triple-A pitcher for?"

4. "The call-ups won't be necessary because Greg Olson will solve all of the Tigers' pitching problems."

COOPERSON: First Inning Scoring

I'm looking at the linescores today, and it looks like MLB is trying to set a record for most runs scored in the first inning throughout baseball. Not to mention, Toronto scored two runs in the "first" inning of the suspended game resumption!

SICKELS: On another note. . .

Since Matt Lawton was sent to the minors, Rich Becker has gone 5-for-10, with a double, two homers, and two walks.

Raising his average from .070-something to .164.

Tom Kelly, master of psychology?

MOYER: Moyer Scoops Rod Beaton

Who says Rockie pitchers stink at Coors Field? Kevin Ritz' complete game yesterday was the first ever by a Rockie starter at Coors.

OLKIN: Beaton indeed

Oh, the delicious irony. Baylor opted *not* to lift Ritz with two outs in the ninth (with Leskanic warming), and Ritz responded by surrendering a game-tying two-run HR to Conine. Sure, they pulled it out in the bottom of the inning, but the bottom line remains: they got the complete game, but it almost cost them the ballgame.

May 2—Will Barry Make Us Proud?

Quote of the Week I (*Baseball Weekly*, 5/7)—"The guy has talent, unbelievable talent. He could be as good as he wants to be. It all depends on how much he's willing to push himself, how far he's willing to go." Who are we talking about here. . . Johnny Damon, maybe? Derek Jeter? Paul Wilson? No, it's Andre Dawson, talking about that promising young player, Barry Bonds. Well, let's hope that, one of these days, Barry will stop settling for all those MVP awards and really start applying himself; maybe he'll finally make us proud of him.

Quote of the Week II (*USA Today*, 5/1, from a story on the early season offensive surge by Chuck Johnson)—"Pitching has been distinctly better in the National League. . . But with a league-wide 4.23 ERA, NL pitchers have not fared much better than the league's all-time high ERA of 4.97 in 1930." Sure, Chuck. . . 4.23, 4.97, just about the same. Greg Maddux won 19 games last year, not much different than Denny McLain's 31 wins in 1968. Dante Bichette drove in 128 runs, not much worse than Hack Wilson's 190 ribbies in 1930. You get my drift. . .

It's Not the Park, Dante's Just a Great Hitter Dept.: Through Sunday's games, the Rockies were hitting .321 and averaging 6.3 runs per game at Coors field; on the road, they were hitting .227 and averaging 3.8 runs. All hitters, Rockies and opponents, are batting .329 at Coors this year; those same players are hitting .230 in Colorado road games. The Rockies and their opponents are averaging twice as many homers in games played at Coors (3.08 per game) than they are in Colorado road games (1.55). The *average* score of a game at Coors this year has been Opponents 9, Rockies 6. Dante's hitting .414 with 14 RBI at home (13 games), .222 with 8 RBI on the road (12 games).

Did you know that Ryne Sandberg has come to the plate 94 times this year (through 4/30) and swung at the first pitch exactly once? Whereas Vinny Castilla and our boy Dante have each swung at the first pitch 55 percent of the time. Hey, maybe *that's* why Vinny and Dante are such great hitters!

— Don Zminda

May 4—Grand Slams Off Maddux: To Be or Not To Be?

COOPERSON: As you may know, yesterday's Benito Santiago blast was the first ever slam Maddux gave up. The *Atlanta Journal-Constitution* called wondering if we had anything on how long a pitcher has ever gone without giving one up. I don't know if anyone would be interested in programming/researching this, but I wouldn't be surprised if other people call with the same question.

QUINN: My understanding is that is *not* the first ever grand slam versus Maddux. He gave one to Will Clark in the 1989 playoffs when he was a Cub. I realize this is the playoffs and not regular season, but is seems wrong to say "first ever." I am not criticizing Ethan for not being specific, because *everyone* is reporting it as "first ever" (AP, Baseball Tonight, apparently the *Atlanta Journal-Constitution*, as well). Preseason may not count, but it seems some comment should be made about game one of the 1989 NLCS. Is this just "baseball tradition"? or an error?

DEWAN: Pat, if you're right, it's quite significant.

PINTO: Postseason and regular season statistics are kept separately. Babe Ruth's 714 HRs do not count postseason stats. Winning streaks do not count playoff victories. So the fact that Maddux has never given up a grand slam is correct, but it should also be noted that it was only during the regular season.

JAMES: Jim Palmer never gave up a grand slam home run in his major league career, although he did give up one in spring training, to, as I recall, Freddie Patek. This fact is fairly well known. . . I'm sure the Orioles can confirm.

COOPERSON: Isn't it wrong not to mention playoff stats? . . .

I wholeheartedly agree with Pat. Postseason games are the most important games of the year; why should their numbers be disregarded?

PINTO: They aren't disregarded, they are just kept separately.

JAMES: Postseason stats are recorded separately. The question is, how do you translate this into English?

I personally would have trouble with the statement that this was the first major league grand slam Maddux had ever allowed, for the simple reason that it isn't. If you say that this is the first GS Maddux has allowed in the regular season, it's technically true, but I think you need to add a statement about the playoff if you don't want to risk misleading the public.

COOPERSON: Ah, the delicate balance of numbers and semantics. This all becomes especially significant in sports like basketball & hockey, where a player might play, in his career, enough postseason games to equal two extra full seasons played!

April 30—Bad is Good

All right, it's gut-check time. No, not for *you*—for *me. How* far am I willing to go to help you win? How willing am I to compromise—or even destroy—my precious credibility? Well, here's your answer.

You see, I'm not just going out on a limb for you here, folks. No, I'm absolutely hanging by a twig. By my teeth.

Bear with me. I can do this.

The recommendation I am about to make goes against every instinct in my being. I've been playing Fantasy Baseball for years, and I like to think I've learned a thing or two from my experiences. Now there *are* a lot of things that I'm still not quite sure about, but I *have* discovered that there are some absolute laws to playing the game. Not rules; *laws.*

The first one, above all else, is to *stay the hell away from Jose Offerman.* It doesn't matter if he's a free agent in your league; it doesn't matter if some other owner offers him to you for one-tenth of his value; it doesn't matter if you bump into Offerman himself in the airport and he wants to autograph your luggage. *It doesn't matter*. In any conceivable situation, your response to Offerman must be exactly the same: *you get as far away from him as possible*.

That's all there is to it. If this needs any explanation at all, then welcome to earth.

But now I find myself having to do something so absurd, so heretical, so absolutely *wrong*, that it pains me in a way that can't be expressed in words. However strongly obligated I may be to follow Offerman's Law, even more absolute is my duty to adhere to the Prime Directive: I must Help You Win. As such, I hereby do recommend to you, on this day, in this time, that you *get Jose Offerman*.

Now you are more than entitled to ask me "why"; in fact, if you have any sense, you'll want to ask me that while you crack me on the side of the head with a beer stein. So before you shake my nerves and rattle my brain, let me try to formulate a coherent explanation.

S$R^B: TYysxbv545hrn4cofih786'^~5^.

OK. Let me try again.

Ahem.

Jose Offerman can help your team. (This *still* doesn't feel right). He qualifies at shortstop, and since Bob Boone has moved him to first base, it's a whole new ballgame. Now in real life, playing Jose Offerman at first base is akin to building a shark tank out of tinkertoys and saran wrap, but hey, this is Fantasy Baseball we're playing here—emphasis on "Fantasy."

Check this out: since Offerman's been moved away from the position where he's had to think about catching and throwing the ball without screwing up, something amazing has happened: he's relaxed. Yes, for quite possibly the first time in his major league career, he has stopped pressing—both in the field and at the plate. The results have been incredible: 10 games at short, five errors, .200 batting average; 13 games at first base, no errors, .395 average. Could you use a guy who qualifies at short and hits .395? OK, so he won't hit .395, but you've got to admit that he's always had the talent to hit .320. All he ever needed was to relax, and now he has. So *do* it: break the law. Go get him.

—Mat Olkin

May 7—Trivia Time

QUINN: Which active player has the second longest consecutive game streak?

OSBORNE: Jeff Conine? Brett Butler?

OLKIN: Molitor?

OSBORNE: Sosa???? Thomas???

WOELFLEIN: Frank Thomas.

QUINN: The Answer is. . .

Frank Thomas with 288 games.

Peter was the first person to get it right on the first try.

DEWAN: That was my guess. Why didn't I e-mail you?

WOELFLEIN: That's why they call me the baseball coordinator.

MILLER: Speaking of Ripken's understudy, who will play SS for Baltimore should Ripken (gasp) get injured or retire? Is there anyone in their farm system capable of filling the spot, or would it take a trade or free agency?

May 7—The Great Marge Schott Battle

OLKIN: You know, I may get killed for saying this, but Marge Schott actually was a pretty good owner in the beginning—but then she just went too far.

WOELFLEIN: She was even a better owner when she was serving her suspension.

MOYER: I finally found someone else who subscribes to my thinking that Marge isn't any much different than most ladies her age. WAIF (must be an Reds radio station) talk-show host Rob Ervin says in *USA Today*, "If Marge didn't own a team she would just be an eccentric old lady who lives at the end of the street and shoots a shotgun full of sugar at the neighbors' cats and won't give the kids their ball back when it goes into her yard." Robin Quivers (who's black, by the way), Howard Stern's sidekick said this morning, "Why can't people just leave racist old ladies alone?"

SICKELS: I don't know. . . I know a few old ladies, and most of them aren't particularly sympathetic to Hitler. Richard Nixon, yes, but not Hitler.

ZMINDA: "Pretty good at the beginning. But then he just went too far."

Hey, that's what they used to say at the post office!

JAMES: Am I the only one who is really offended by the idea of punishing Marge Schott for her comments? Somehow, I thought the idea of free speech was that other people had the right to express their own opinions, no matter how stupid. Since when did historical ignorance become a punishable offense?

I mean, my father used to say chyt like this all the time. He didn't know anything about history, either. It wasn't a prerequisite for having opinions in his generation. To me, the idea of censuring Marge Schott because she doesn't have a firm grip on the history of the Third Reich is a great deal more offensive than anything she said.

CANTER: Her comments certainly aren't punishable by law, etc., but (and I'm not sure about this) I think she made the comments while doing an interview as the owner of the Cincinnati Reds, not as just some strange old woman. She is a representative of the Reds and also of Major League Baseball. If Don Zminda goes on a radio talk show to give the stat of the week, and made similar comments, I suspect STATS would want to censor him, too.

She has the right to speak freely about whatever she wants, but while representing her team and the league, they have the right to ensure they are represented the way they'd like. No?

On the other hand, if in her free time she goes to skinhead rallies, and wears white hoods, or whatever, that's her business. I suspect MLB would try to punish her anyway, though.

FREER: I suppose that MLB trying to punish Schott for a poor understanding of history, racism, etc., is no different than, say, punishing the athletes for "conduct detrimental to the league." To understand this point of view, see Vince Coleman about firecrackers, Pete Rose about wagering, or the Doc for drug use/abuse. While some of these incidents included the involvement of law enforcement, it was nonetheless the decision of the league to go above and beyond the decision(s) of the U.S. justice system, and enforce it's own penalties. It's nice to have power!

PINTO: Baseball isn't going to punish her, for the very reasons you state above. However, if I were a fan, I'd have a hard time supporting the team this woman owns. I grew up a Yankee fan, and the offensiveness of Steinbrenner over the years has turned me off to that team. I never remember him doing anything like this, however. She's free to say what she wants, and we are free to be offended by it, and free not to buy Reds tickets and merchandise. The fans of Cincinnati should stay away from the ballpark until she's gone.

BEAUREGARD: Her words are protected under the First Amendment and the others' actions are illegal. There's a big difference. Even if her comments were made in an interview, and thus reflective of her, and the Reds possibly—although that's a stretch—you can not compare them to the illegal activities of Coleman, et al.

ZMINDA: I agree with Bill. I was watching this stupid tabloid show with my parents last night, and they had a 900 number to call so people could express their opinions on whether or not Marge should be thrown out of baseball. For what. . . being stupid and ignorant? If you had to have intelligence to get a job in baseball, a lot of people would be out of work.

MOYER: I agree with Bill too. Sorry, but I think Marge Schott is a funny old lady with funny old lady opinions that get heard by the public more than any other funny old lady. There's a big "Here's Exactly What You'd Expect The Exactly-What-You'd-Expect *USA Today* To Say" editorial in today's paper saying, "There is very little that is harmless or entertaining about a wheezebag like Marge Schott." Well sorry, but I think she's pretty damn harmless and equally she's pretty damn entertaining, actually.

FREER: I think you missed my point. Above and beyond the legal implications of any of the aforementioned incidents, pro sports leagues have always taken it upon themselves to enforce their own brand of justice. The reason: to protect the "image" of the league. Perhaps Schott herself is the best example of my point. I recall, not so long ago, when MLB decided to toss her from the game for an extended period of time (one year?). This suspension was for her use of racist terminology. She did not face criminal charges for this usage (i.e., protected by the First Amendment), but still felt the wrath of a league which does not condone such "free speech." With regard to the other incidents, my point was that Coleman, Rose, Doc Gooden, and my personal favorite, Steve Howe, faced criminal prosecution. They then faced the league's justice system, above and beyond their civil matters (if any).

PINTO: Marge is not a funny old lady. My parents sometimes say things like this, and old ladies I know say things like this, and I don't think they are funny. I especially get upset when they say things like this in front of my daughter.

Like it or not, Marge Schott, being a public figure, has influence on people. It would be just if she eventually lost this team because enough fans were disgusted by her to drive her out of business.

I agree with Freer on the image issue, although Selig is such a wimp he'll only slap her on the wrist.

JAMES: Freer's comments are a very fundamental abnegation of the concept of freedom of speech. Yes, I know he's trying to tell us that baseball has the right to take extra legal actions against persons involved in the game, and I agree with that and support that—but on the way to getting there, he also tells us that "erroneous speech" is essentially the same as criminal conduct. Well, what a despicable idea.

The idea of this country—the most fundamental idea—is that everybody has a right to think and say whatever they hell they want to. No one's speech is deemed "too wrong" to be tolerated, either by the law or by the culture. You're naive beyond belief if you think that we can continue to draw up lines of culturally acceptable speech, without ultimately codifying those barriers into law.

And what she said *isn't* that offensive—I mean, I'm sorry, David, but if you're deeply offended by these comments, you need some reality therapy. She said that Hitler started out to do good, but just went too far. This is offensive to Jewish people, because it sounds as if what she is saying is that he went too far in slaughtering six million Jews, but if he had only killed a couple of hundred thousand that would have been keen. But that's not what she said. She didn't *mention* Jews or the holocaust in any way, and I will absolutely guarantee you that she wasn't *thinking* about Jews in any way. She was thinking about Hitler without any reference to the Jewish question, which is stupid and thoughtless, but that's all it is.

We live in a society in which offensive behavior is commonplace. I can walk two blocks from my office, and find 500 things that offend me—obscenities spray-painted on the sides of buildings, homeless people begging for money, posters of naked women hanging in the windows of music stores where anybody of any age can see them. It's offensive, but it's America; we put up with it. How in the world, in such a society, do people choose to be deeply offended by some essentially innocuous comments by a daffy old woman a thousand miles away? It's crazy. I mean, is this *really* what is offensive in our society? Isn't Geraldo a lot *more* offensive?

Sure, STATS would censure Don Zminda if he spoke glowingly about Mussolini, but Don is an *employee*. Marge Schott is not an employee of organized baseball. She's a *participant*. She's a citizen. The principle that citizens may be punished for inappropriate speech is the road to hell.

PINTO: Bill, I do agree with you on the freedom of speech issue. I'm not arguing her right to say it. I'm talking about appropriate action.

Daffy old women (or daffy old men) should not be in positions of authority, because their daffiness can do real harm; they can cost people jobs by making bad decisions for example. In government we vote, in business we vote by buying products. Do you frequent establishments where you see the offensive things you mentioned above? If you do, you are voting for their continuation. If you don't, you're voting for their removal. If enough people vote for removal, the establisment goes out of business and the offensive material is removed. No infringement on freedom of speech, just capitalism working.

I'm sorry, I'm going to continue to be offended by people who can't bother to learn history, who are openly racist and drink too much. That's my right.

OLKIN: Bill—I don't see the issue that way. The way I see it, the issue is not whether a private citizen can be punished for saying something that offends others. The real issue here is what the sport is entitled to do when one of its participants says or does something that diminishes the game's credibility in the eyes of the public.

I think that under such circumstances, the leagues are perfectly entitled to respond with some sort of punishment. Let's look at it this way: what is the single most important virtue that the sport needs in order to survive? It's *credibility*, isn't it? If the public doesn't buy it—in both the literal and the figurative sense—there will be no baseball.

When Landis threw out the Black Sox, what was he doing? He was showing the public that the only players who would be allowed to play were the ones who were trying to win. (The Black Sox broke no laws either, apparently. You will recall that they were acquitted in a court of law.) The same with Rose—the public needed to know that managers didn't have money riding on the outcomes of the games they were managing.

And I think the same principle should apply here. Minority employment in baseball—as both athletes and executives—has been an issue since the game's inception. In order to maintain credibility with the public, it must be shown—now more than ever—that the teams are *not* run by bigots and racists.

Marge Schott's freedom of speech is not the issue here. Of course she can say whatever she wants. But when she says things that injure the credibility of the entire sport (a sport that she profits from nicely, and an enterprise that is—need I say it?—much more important to our society than she is), then I think that baseball is entitled to do something about it.

MEYERHOFF: Bill, it is impossible to know what was on Marge Schott's mind. I would not be so generous as to suspect she has committed "erroneous speech" given her racist comments in the past. I would guess that her comments about Hitler starting out to do good were further expressions of her racist beliefs.

Nonetheless, we would all probably agree that as a citizen Marge is entitled to say what she has said in the recent past. I suppose it would take a franchise law attorney to determine whether MLB is entitled to censure her for her remarks given that she is an owner and not an employee of a MLB franchise.

If she owned a McDonald's franchise and was in the national press as somebody who was clearly associated with McDonald's and she said to McDonald's customers everywhere that Hitler started out as a good guy, it would be reasonable to expect McDonald's to determine how it could protect its image.

Baseball influences children and Marge Schott espouses racism. Why shouldn't MLB exercise its rights with regard to a franchise owner if MLB sees harm coming to the game from the remarks Marge Schott has made?

If I thought my children might adopt her point of view I would consider trying to distance them from the game with which she is associated. It seems to me MLB has a legitimate interest here and should be able to act within its franchisor, franchisee relationship.

MOYER: If you can show me *one* child whose life will be affected or influenced one iota by what Marge Schott says, I'll start worrying about her opinions. Kids have a hard enough time listening to and respecting their parents these days (geez, that sounds a lot like Hal Bodley, there), much less some old lady who owns a baseball team.

DEWAN: I'm not Jewish and I don't live in Cincinnati, but if that were the case, I would have to consider not giving any more of my business to the Reds. The powers that be in MLB (whatever that is right now) should definitely consider, in evaluating the business implications of her comments, that others would feel this way. Then the lawyers can figure out what action can be taken.

Neverthess, it's clear that living in America gives her the right to say what she said.

JAMES: To withold your business from an enterprise because the owner is a jerk and/or a racist jerk is legitimate. To *punish* her for what she says, whether by law or by civil action, is reprehensible.

Voltaire said that "I may disagree with what you say, but I will defend until death your right to say it." What are we saying here? I may disagree with what you have to say, but I will only punish you for saying it by civil action and civil penalties, as opposed to criminal penalties? This is not an argument about *how* we should punish people who express opinions that we disagree with. It is an argument about *whether* we should punish people who express opinions we disagree with. I have learned, in middle age, that I have a far different concept of what it means to be a liberal than does most of our society. To me, liberal means "tolerant." Liberalism is not grounded in sensitivity, which is the determination to say or do nothing which might give offense; rather, liberalism is grounded in *tolerance*, which is the determination not to *take* offense.

The idea that we should punish people for expressing erroneous ideas is a million times more dangerous than the idea that Adolph Hitler was good in the beginning.

Would I patronize a restaurant run by someone who made offensive remarks about tall bearded statisticians? If it was a good restaurant, absolutely.

Why? Because there is much more to be said for forgiveness and tolerance than there is to be said for self-righteousness and hypocrisy. Which of us has no bigotry in our soul, no dark pockets of unvented anger? So Marge is a little stupider than the rest of us, so what? Give the lady a break. You'll need it yourself someday.

PINTO: Yes, you are right. Forgiveness is a very tough thing, but it should be given.

OLKIN: Bill's just hit on it, right there. It's the fundamental oxymoron that underlies the entire argument: must we be tolerant of those who are intolerant?

MEYERHOFF: The more a person's intolerant views influence others to act with intolerance, the more fuss needs to be made in opposing those views.

Another irony is that the press picked up her remarks. In some ways that forces the fuss against her and soon the matter takes on a life of its own. It is funny to look at Marge's picture and read "dangerous person" in the caption.

Does that somehow take the conversation back to the Unabomber?

MOYER: *Much* more entertaining than Marge Schott is Butch Hobson's "why I had the cocaine" story. O.J. probably believes him. (For some *real* racism, I wonder if the coke was found on Darryl or Doc Gooden, if the *USA's* Hobson-favored slant on the story would be the same. But of course, Hobson was a good white boy who always hustled, so maybe someone did just mail him cocaine instead of money and he didn't really know what else to do with it but put it in his toiletry bag.)

May 10—Back to Baseball Blather

SICKELS: I am not making this up. The Reds Media Guide tells you if the player owns a dog. Like this, "Joe Slabotnik is married to Groupia. They have three kids (Joe Jr, Sam, Tiffany) and a dog (cocker spaniel) named Spot"

Dog owners: Eric Anthony, Andre King, Eric Owens, Roger Salkeld, Gabe White, Aaron Boone, Eric Davis, Bryan Hickerson, Brett Tomko (1995 draft pick). This may explain why Willie Greene can't get a job. He doesn't have a dog.

SPEAR: A Few Words from the President of the Olerud Fan Club

Has anyone noticed (besides me) that Olerud is hitting .341 over his last 11 games? He also got *two* SportsCenter highlights last night.

Not only that, but yesterday afternoon I purchased his 1996 Donruss baseball card, bringing my OleCard collection to 157.

SCHAUFELBERGER: Did you read where Barry Bonds got in "a shoving match" with Rod Beaton? Couldn't have been much of a match. Bonds apparently took issue with Beaton's loitering and told him "Don't be hanging around my house." The exchange resulted in Bonds shoving Beaton.

MOYER: "Beaton's loitering"—That makes the whole thing more hilarious.

May 14—Maris' Record Falls; No One Notices

Well, it happened. No one seemed to have caught it, but it did. Yep, we can all pack it in and go home. The chase is over.

Whaddaya mean you didn't catch it? Well, I guess I can understand, since none of the newspapers noticed it either. And I guess you would expect to hear all about something like this on ESPN, but no, they let it go without comment as well.

I'm talking about Maris' record here. Awake now?

Belle broke it.

Yeah, it was pretty dramatic, even if you didn't have a clue about what was really going on. What ESPN viewers saw was Troy Percival coming on to face the heart of the Indians order Sunday night in the ninth inning of a tie game. Percival punched a couple of 93 MPH fastballs past him on the outside corner. Then he got one in a little too far, and Albert jumped all over it, sending it into the left field seats for the eventual game-winner.

Here's what you didn't hear: over Belle's last 162 games, that homer was his *62nd*. Take *that*, Maris!

Now, before the ghost of Ford Frick comes down and beans me with a giant asterisk, let me explain a few things. First, it obviously happened over the course of two seasons, so the record books won't be rewritten. And nitpickers also would point out that Cleveland had actually played 163 games over that span, since Belle sat out a meaningless game against the Royals last September 24th.

Well, I'd respond by saying that there's no way Belle would have sat out that game if he had been chasing the record in the *conventional* sense. While it's true that the games took place over the course of two seasons, I think the real significance here is that it illustrates how easily Maris' record could be broken.

In his last 127 games of last year, Belle launched a total of 48 moon shots. That's a nice pace; in fact, it projects to 61 over a full season. But still, it was not a full season's worth of games. In order to get 62 dingers over that span, what he needed to do this year was to hit 14 in his first 35 games (a 65-HR pace). And he did it. He kept up the Maris beat, and on the last at-bat of game #162, against possibly the toughest pitcher to hit in all of baseball, he got the pseudo-record-breaking homer.

—Mat Olkin

May 15—Gooden's No-Hitter

FAUST: His last four starts. Hey, this guy is only 31.

Daily pitching log for Gooden, Dwight:

Date	Opp	W	L	Sv	SvOp	GS	CG	SHO	GF	IP	H	R	ER	HR	TBB	SO
4/27/96	Min	0	0	0		0	1	0	0	0	6.0	5	1	1	0	0	7
5/03/96	ChA	0	0	0		0	1	0	0	0	6.0	3	0	0	0	6	4
5/08/96	Det	1	0	0		0	1	0	0	0	8.0	2	3	3	0	2	8
5/14/96	Sea	1	0	0		0	1	1	1	0	9.0	0	0	0	0	6	5
TOTALS																

ERA		G	W	L	Sv	SvOp	GS	CG	ShO	GF	IP	H	R	ER	HR	TBB	SO
1.24		4	2	0	0	0	4	1	1	0	29.0	10	4	4	0	14	24

FREER: Is Dwight For Real?

My early recommendation for the cover of STATS *Batter Versus Pitcher Match-Ups!*

SICKELS: I don't see any reason why he can't be for real. He's not old, he still throws hard. His control is a little wobbly, but that's probably rust. If his personal problems are behind him, he could last six or seven more years, hell, maybe longer. I think it would be better for him if he wasn't pitching for New York. . . maybe the less-pressure filled environment of Milwaukee or Minnesota would be better. Heck, he may even end up in Tampa in 1998.

FAUST: Seattle's Revenge

Well, they made up for being no-hit last night. The M's pounded out 19 hits tonight versus the Yankees. Could that be a record for most hits by a team the game after being no-hit?

COOPERSON: Amaral singled for Seattle on the first pitch of the game!

May 16—Do Top Hurlers Have "The Look" of Dominance?

MOYER: Hot News:

Amaury Telemaco was just called up for the Cubs and Kevin Foster sent down. Telemaco gets a B+ from Sickels, and has pitched great at Iowa so far this year. Jim Capuano will update us on how Harry will pronounce his name.

SICKELS: Telemaco is one of the best pitching prospects in baseball, although he has been somewhat underappreciated by the press. I gave him a B+ in my book, which after his excellent start at Iowa this year I would raise to an A–. The only real concern I have about him is his long-term durability. . . he has had a sore shoulder several times in the past. Anyhow, he throws hard and he throws strikes.

The most impressive thing about Telemaco's debut isn't his stuff or his pitching instincts, although these are very impressive. It's his eyes, his expressions. He's magnetic, very enthusiastic but not in an obnoxious Pascual Perez way, wide smile, bright eyes, obviously very intelligent and clever. If he stays healthy he will be an excellent pitcher.

COOPERSON: "Magnetic?" Randy Johnson fans might suggest that looks, magnetic or otherwise, don't count for much!

JAMES: You're kidding, right? Nobody is more magnetic on the mound than Randy. He's ugly, but he's beautiful when he gets on the mound.

SICKELS: I'm not talking about aesthetics. . . I was talking about concentration and confidence. Johnson has that, even if he is an ugly SOB. My point about Telemaco was that he had poise, confidence, concentration. Sorry if I didn't make that clear.

COOPERSON: I have a hard time buying that you can see all that in a guy's face. Carlton, with all the facial contortions and twitching he did on the hill, looked anything but confident. Steve Rogers practically talked to the ball, and he got a few people out. Not that this guy doesn't have all of those qualities necessarily, but can you really see in his face? I'm skeptical.

OLKIN: My friend Terese told me that Tim Salmon has a nice butt. I really hadn't noticed.

WOELFLEIN: Jason Bere looks like he has ice water for blood he is so cool. I'm skeptical too.

May 17—Run Support

My fantasy baseball team, the Evansville LaLooshes (named in honor of fictional Durham Bulls flamethrower Ebby Calvin "Nuke" LaLoosh), has had a rough go of things early on in the 1996 season—typified by the tale of pitcher Kevin Brown.

I was anticipating big things out of Brown in his first season in a Florida Marlins uniform, and he's done his best to deliver. Through his first nine starts, Brown has posted a sparkling 2.24 ERA. . . and has a 2-4 record to show for it. The problem, of course, is lack of run support. The Marlins have averaged just 2.54 runs per nine innings with Brown on the mound—the third-lowest figure in the majors behind Rich Robertson (2.31) of the Twins and Frank Castillo (2.52) of the Cubs. That once again got my mind churning on the value of run support. Believe me, its importance can't be overstated.

In the 1996 STATS *Baseball Scoreboard*, we took a look at the plight of Dodgers knuckleballer Tom Candiotti—seemingly a perennial victim of lack of run support. The Dodgers scored just 3.45 runs per nine innings for Candiotti last season, the worst support in the majors. Take a look at Candiotti's 1995 numbers compared to teammate Ramon Martinez and you'll see how much run support can mean.

Pitcher	ERA	W-L
Ramon Martinez	3.66	17- 7
Tom Candiotti	3.50	7-14

They pitched in the same ballpark for the same team. The difference? While the Dodgers generated just 3.45 runs per nine innings for Candiotti, they produced 5.32 for Martinez. Here are a couple of other pitching pairings we analyzed.

Pitcher	ERA	W-L
Orel Hershiser	3.87	16- 6
Mark Gubicza	3.75	12-14

Pitcher	ERA	W-L
Pete Schourek	3.22	18-7
Joey Hamilton	3.11	6-9

The Indians got Hershiser 6.08 runs per nine innings, while the Royals gave Gubicza just 3.97. Schourek got 5.49 runs per nine innings in Cincinnati, compared to the 3.55 Hamilton got from his San Diego teammates. But nothing illustrates what the lack of run support can yield better than Nolan Ryan's 1987 season with Houston. That season, Ryan led the National League with 2.76 ERA. . . and finished 8-16. You know why.

Talk about run support and you can't help think of Storm Davis and his 1989 season. That year, Davis was a member of the World Series champion Oakland Athletics' staff along with Dave Stewart, Mike Moore and Bob Welch. Here's Davis' pitching line for 1989:

IP	H	HR	SO	TBB	ERA	W-L
169.1	187	19	91	68	4.36	19-7

By itself, those number aren't very significant. What gives this story its bite is what happened following the season. The Kansas City Royals, apparently impressed by the number 19 (the number of wins), shelled out several million dollars for Davis' services. That should go a long way toward explaining why the Royals haven't seen postseason play since 1985.

Look at those numbers and think for a second. It's pretty obvious that Davis received some massive run support in 1989. How else do you explain a pitcher with those numbers (particularly a 4.36 ERA) going 19-7? Remember the '89 Athletics? Carney Lansford, Rickey Henderson, Jose Canseco, Mark McGwire—those guys could put some runs on the scoreboard. In fact, they scored 122 runs in Davis' 169.1 innings on the mound, or 6.48 per nine innings—the second-highest figure in all of baseball that season. If a Kansas City fan can explain what the Royals were thinking, please share it with the rest of us. Heck, forget about the won-loss record for a second. A 4.36 ERA in the Oakland Coliseum? That's one of the best pitcher's parks in all of baseball—if not the *very* best. That should have told the Royals something right there. No, I won't leave you hanging. Davis went 7-10 with a 4.74 ERA for the Royals in 1990. Stunning.

To show you how much the run support helped Davis, let's figure what his record would have been with average run support by an average American League team. To start with, the average A.L. team scored 4.29 runs per game in 1989. Davis? Remember, his 4.36 ERA figure represents only the *earned* runs he allowed per game. The data shows that the average A.L. pitcher gave up about 0.45 *unearned* runs per nine innings in '89, meaning Davis' "runs allowed average" goes to 4.81 (4.36 + 0.45).

Those of you who have followed Bill James' work probably know where I'm going next with this. Bill's "Pythagorean method" allows us to approximate Davis' winning percentage using the new numbers, 4.29 (runs for) and 4.81 (runs allowed). That tells you right away that Davis didn't deserve a winning record. Here's what his winning percentage should have been:

Winning Pct = (4.29 squared)/(4.29 squared + 4.81 squared)

. . . or a winning percentage of .443.

Another effective approximation is to assume a pitcher gets one decision (a win or a loss) for every nine innings pitched. Davis threw 169.1 innings in 1989, meaning he should have had about 19 decisions (169 divided by nine is 18.8).

A .443 winning percentage on 19 decisions translates to a record of about 8-11. That's how well Davis pitched in 1989. Not 19-7, but 8-11. His run support made all the difference in the world. You could have filled the bleaches of the Oakland Coliseum with the number of pitchers capable of duplicating what Davis did that year. He was a pitcher at the right place at the right time—and little else.

— Scott McDevitt

May 17—TSN vs. BW

Lucky for you, I went through the *Baseball Weekly* a couple days ago at lunch and today I went through the *Sporting News*.

The best thing I found in the new *Baseball Weekly* is the Marge Schott ESPN talk transcribed in its entirety. It's good to read the whole thing and not just the "way they want it to sound" version that the media gives you. For example, I'm sure you've heard the story about Marge videotaping players exiting team flights to nail them for taking their girlfriends on flights. This, as I understood it, was for cost reasons. In the real interview, one finds out that Marge is really trying to catch married players taking their girlfriends on flights. In other words, her crime in this case is identical to her attackers'—forced morality. But my favorite portion is the infamous Hitler part, which I'd never seen altogether. Here's the whole thing: "Everything you read, when he came in he was good. They built tremendous highways and got all the factories going. . . but then he went nuts. He went berserk, I guess. I think even his own generals tried to kill him, didn't they? Everybody knows that he did good at the beginning but then he went too far." To tell you the truth, the *only* sentence I'd ever read before was the last one. Now, let's face it, with that "highways" sentence in there, the point is clear that she was trying to make. It's also clear that she doesn't have a very good understanding of history, but that's not the point either. The point is that it's nice to see the whole story and draw your own conclusions, rather than concentrating on only the "highlights" that the media wants you to see. It reminds me of the first red *Baseball Book—1990* that Bill James put together and the fascinating story in it on "The Dowd Report" about the Pete Rose gambling case. There's so much in there that I never saw anywhere else and I suggest you find it if you've never read it.

The *TSN* Fly reports that Fox Sports President David Hill says, about Fox baseball, "If anybody talks about dead guys during a broadcast, I'll sack'em. I'm sick of dead guys! Whenever I turn on baseball, all I hear about is dead guys. If I hear a name, I'm gonna ask, 'Is he dead?' And if he is, you're fired." Way cool! And I like dead guys, especially guys long-dead, lots more than the average baseball fan. But, wonder-of-wonders, I can read between the lines and grasp the meaning of what Hill's trying to say, I think. Now let's see if Fox practices what they preach. To tell you the truth, I think the problem is that the reason most of today's announcers talk about dead guys all the time is that they have one foot in the grave themselves. I challenge Fox to break the same-old-same-old mold. We'll see.

Surprise, surprise. *TSN's* book reviewer doesn't like Dennis Rodman's book and Sparky Anderson doesn't like the DH. Snore.

But, you know, I still think *TSN* kicks *Baseball Weekly's* butt. Even if it is outdated-as-hell sometimes. At least *TSN* has some color and flair and opinion. I don't care if the color's sometimes gray and the flair's sometimes dried-out and the opinion's sometimes as stupid as mine. *At least it's there* and that kicks the crap out of *BBW's* dry, boring, dead-as-a-door-nail style. I swear, you give me any topic and I could pretty much tell you all the major points *BBW* will make about it in their article. That's how predictable they are. At least The Fly is often interestingly informative and Bob Nightengale sometimes says something that really ticks (I'm not sure the "P" word is legal on AOL) me off. I can't remember the last time *BBW* made me think anything but blah.

And lastly for this week, *TSN* prints the boxscore of that Rochester/Pawtucket 33-inning longest game of all-time on the magazine's last page. The final pitcher for Rochester was a guy named Cliff Speck, hopefully no relation to Richard Speck, who's truly shocking video is going to be shown this weekend on A&E (I think on Saturday night).

— Steve Moyer

May 17—Milwaukee: The Bermuda Triangle for Athletes. . .

KRETSCHMANN: Did you see where Tony Phillips got into it with a County Stadium fan yesterday? What's up with athletes and Milwaukee?

I know in Chicago there's the "Painting of Sheridan's Horse's Balls" that teammates will tell the rookies that it's really not a crime, you'll just sign a book and you'll get to go. Do these bozos think they can act like a 12 year old in the playground in Milwaukee too? I can't remember all the crap that's happened, but these are the ones that stand out:

Charles Barkley—started brawl in Milwaukee bar while with 76ers

Reggie Jackson—took offense to a fan asking for an autograph, decided to break his hand instead

Tony Phillips—thumps a fan

Of course, I think all these guys got suspended sentences so why not break the law?

COOPERSON: For the record, Sir Charles was walking from a bar and was being hassled by a single person who would not leave him alone. Charles was provoked into slugging the guy to get him to go away.

May 21—Who You Callin' "Bush League?"

Did you catch the Tigers' highlights on SportsCenter the other night? They played their Triple-A team, the Toledo Mud Hens, and they lost, 14-1. I'd hate to be that Mud Hens pitcher who gave up the lone run, though. The Mud Hens will probably demote him to Detroit.

—Mat Olkin

May 24—Extra-Base Hits

Albert Belle is at it again. After becoming the first player in baseball history to hit 50 homers and 50 doubles in a single season in 1995 (not bad considering the short schedule), Belle finds himself atop the offensive leader boards again this season. With 17 home runs and 11 doubles in only 44 games, Belle may take another run at 50-50 in 1996—yet another tribute to the staggering offensive totals that are becoming so common in the major leagues.

Adding in his one triple this season (way to leg one out, Albert!), Belle has 29 extra-base hits out of 59 total, meaning that 49.1 percent of his hits have gone for extra bases. Take a look at how that compares to the major league average over the past few seasons and it's easy to see that Belle is on his way to another monster year.

Belle's 49.1 percent figure so far in '96 is still well behind what he did last season. Is Belle slipping? Hardly. His '95 campaign was the best *ever* in terms of XBH percentage.

Greatest Percentage of Extra-Base Hits

Player, Team	Year	2B	3B	HR	Hits	Pct
Albert Belle, Cle	1995	52	1	50	173	59.5
Babe Ruth, Yanks	1921	44	16	59	204	58.3
Willie Stargell, Pit	1973	43	3	44	156	57.7
Babe Ruth, Yanks	1920	36	9	54	172	57.6
Reggie Jackson, Oak	1969	36	3	47	151	57.0
Willie McCovey, SF	1970	39	2	39	143	55.9
Kevin Mitchell, SF	1989	34	6	47	158	55.1
Gorman Thomas, Mil	1979	29	0	45	136	54.4
Mike Schmidt, Phi	1979	25	4	45	137	54.0
Babe Ruth, Bos	1919	34	12	29	139	54.0

(minimum 100 base hits)

Of Belle's 173 hits in 1995, 103 went for extra bases. Take a look at the other names on the list—Ruth, Jackson, McCovey, Schmidt—and you can see that Belle is in truly historic company. Those four players are among the top 10 home-run hitters in baseball history. Belle may very well be considered in that class before he's through.

So what's the *lowest* percentage of extra-base hits in a single season? The list of trailers (not surprisingly) is saturated with players from the early part of the century, with Philadelphia's (N.L.) Roy Thomas earning "top honors" in 1900—four doubles, three triples and no home runs in 168 total hits. No player with at least 100 hits in a season has ever had a lower percentage of XBH than Thomas did that year—4.2 percent.

The five lowest totals during post-war seasons are as follows:

Player, Team	Year	2B	3B	HR	Hits	Pct
Horace Clark, Yanks	1968	6	1	2	133	6.8
Sandy Alomar Sr., Cal	1973	7	1	0	112	7.1
Dick Groat, Pit	1952	6	1	1	109	7.3
Don Kessinger, Cubs	1966	8	2	1	146	7.5
Sonny Jackson, Hou	1966	6	5	3	174	8.1

(minimum 100 base hits)

The name that immediately jumps out at you is Dick Groat, who rebounded from a tough rookie season in 1952 and eventually earned N.L. MVP honors while with the Pirates in 1960. After moving on to St. Louis, Groat nearly won a second MVP Award in 1963, finishing second in the balloting to Sandy Koufax. That, season, the once light-hitting Groat hit 43 doubles, 11 triples and six homers—60 XBH out of 201 total safeties (29.9 percent). That's pretty respectable for a shortstop of any era.

— Scott McDevitt

May 28—Wil Cordero

One last thing and I'll let it go. So far this year, I've used this space to harp on a number of my pet peeves. More than a few managers have been taken to task for abusing their pitchers' arms, the wisdom of Bob Boone's experimental lineup selection has been drawn into question, and by now, it's abundantly clear that not another word needs to be said about Ray Knight's Captain Queeg impersonation. But there's still one more thing that I need to get off my chest.

Wil Cordero. I love the guy's bat—always have—and I think it's a damn shame that he was dealt such a crummy hand this year. When the Red Sox got him, my first thought was, "God. What a steal for the Red Sox!" And my second thought was, "Cordero is going to put up *some* numbers in that park."

The kid is already a very good hitter, and at his age, there's every reason to expect that he'll grow into being a great one. If you just take his stats in Montreal over the last couple of years and park-adjust them for Fenway, you'll see that he's entirely capable of hitting .300 with 40 doubles and close to 20 homers. And this is without making any adjustment at all for the fact that he's still improving as a hitter.

So after the Montreal General Manager had flatly stated that Cordero lacked a shortstop's arm, and Felipe Alou had given up and moved him to left field, and the Red Sox had convinced Jose Canseco to play the field shortly before acquiring Cordero, I just assumed that the next logical step would be taken. It seemed obvious that Dan Duquette had cleared out the DH spot for Cordero, and that the former shortstop would have the chance to start making a good living with his bat.

And I thought that would have been a brilliant move. It's a move that teams are reluctant to make, but when they bite the bullet and commit to it, it almost always pays off. When you have a young player who can hit, it certainly is an added bonus if he's also able to play a key defensive position. But there are many players who aren't capable of doing both, and when the team throws them a glove that they can't use, it ends up affecting their batting as well.

Remember when Gary Sheffield came up? He was a shortstop, and wasn't happy at all when he was moved to third. But that's where he ended up doing his hitting. Gregg Jefferies pressed as a second baseman and third baseman, but blossomed when he was moved to first. Dale Murphy went from struggling catcher to MVP center fielder almost overnight. Carlos Delgado has finally emerged this year, without shinguards.

When the Red Sox got Wil Cordero, I thought that all they would ask from him was that he bat sixth and learn how to feed the Monster. But they wanted more. They wanted him to play second base as well.

All right then, that's a reasonable enough idea. He couldn't play shortstop in Montreal, but if he's able to play second, you could really have something—a Baerga-type player, possibly. On the other hand, you could end up impeding the development of a great young hitter by trying to crowbar another bat into the lineup. But I could see the rationale for trying to *find out* if he could play second base.

In hindsight, it's obvious that this is not what the Red Sox had decided to do. During spring training, before Cordero had even had the chance to try to turn a double play during a game, they released their real second baseman, Luis Alicea.

When they made that move, their plan was abundantly clear: they hadn't decided to *see* if Cordero could play second base; rather, they had decided that he *was going to play* second base.

He did, and you can see what happened. At this point, to even comment on his defense (or the rest of the team's) would be like piecing together the remains of a dead horse, just to beat it one more time.

But the injury was the crowning blow. Did you see it? In the late innings of a game against the Athletics last week, Cordero went to turn two. He took the feed from the shortstop, tagged the bag, stopped and threw to first base. After the throw, he stood at the bag with his weight on his right leg, knee locked, foot next to the bag. And the baserunner slid into him and broke his leg.

Now an injury like that doesn't happen all that often, for one simple reason: any second baseman who's played more than three weeks at the position will know to *get the hell out of the way of the baserunner*. You come across the bag and make the throw, or you jump over the runner, but you never, *ever* stand there and permit the baserunner do damage to your skeleton.

It was inexperience, pure and simple. Cordero is out for two months because the Red Sox asked him to do something that he wasn't qualified to do.

—Mat Olkin

May 31—Fibonacci Win Points

In a year in which even Kevin Elster has become a power threat, it's refreshing to know that there's still quality pitching left in the major leagues. No hurler has illustrated that point better than Atlanta's John Smoltz, who sits at 11-1 with a 2.24 ERA after 51 team games. That's right, 11 wins before June. Do the math and it's easy to see that Smoltz is currently on pace for a 30-win season—something no pitcher has accomplished since Denny McLain went 31-6 for the Tigers back in 1968.

It's not likely that Smoltz will catch McLain, but we can have a lot of fun speculating anyway. Not only is he on pace for one of the greatest single-season win totals of all time, but his winning percentage (.917) might end up pushing some historic barriers as well. Loyal readers of the Online Abstract might remember some references I made earlier in the season to the "Fibonacci Win Points"—another statistical gift from Bill James and a useful tool for putting a pitcher's won-lost record into a single dimension.

The formula for Fibonacci Win Points is as follows:

Win Points = (Wins x Winning Percentage) + Games over .500

That gives Smoltz a current total of 20.1 Win Points ((11 x .917) + 10), which is clearly the best in baseball to this point. If Smoltz can maintain his current won-lost pace (and again, it's not very likely), he would finish with a gaudy 35-3 mark in '96, good for 64.2 Fibonacci Win Points. How would that stack up against history?

Babe Ruth changed the face of baseball forever with his amazing offensive totals in the early 1920s, so let's use the Babe's first season in Yankee pinstripes (1920) as our lower parameter. Here are the top 10 seasons since 1920 in terms of Fibonacci Win Points:

Pitcher	Year	Team	W	L	Win Points
Lefty Grove	1931	Athletics	31	4	54.5
Denny McLain	1968	Tigers	31	6	51.0
Dizzy Dean	1934	Cardinals	30	7	47.3
Lefty Grove	1930	Athletics	28	5	46.8
Dazzy Vance	1924	Dodgers	28	6	45.1
Ron Guidry	1978	Yankees	25	3	44.3
Robin Roberts	1952	Phillies	28	7	43.4
Bob Welch	1990	Athletics	27	6	43.1
Lefty Gomez	1934	Yankees	26	5	42.8
Whitey Ford	1961	Yankees	25	4	42.6

Smoltz' "potential" 64.2 Fibonacci Win Points would shatter the existing mark set by Lefty Grove in 1931. I wouldn't put my money on it, but you never know in this crazy baseball season. If Dan Wilson can hit three homers in a game, I suppose anything's possible.

The fact that Grove has two of the top four seasons in history should tell you a lot. In fact, you could make a very strong case that Grove was the best pitcher in baseball history—better than Walter Johnson, better than Sandy Koufax. . . better than anyone. Grove led the American League in ERA nine times in his career (1925-1941), racking up a 300-141 lifetime mark with Philadelphia and Boston. He was a truly dominant pitcher during an era dominated by sluggers. McLain's 31-6 season was incredible, but it occurred in 1968—the best season for pitchers in modern baseball history. Given the quality of Grove's performance, the context in which he performed and the length of his career, you'd have a tough time arguing against him. My top five: Lefty Grove, Walter Johnson, Sandy Koufax, Greg Maddux and Tom Seaver. . . but that's another article for another day.

Not surprisingly, the three most recent seasons on the list have all come from pennant-winning teams: Whitey Ford in 1961, Ron Guidry in 1978 and Bob Welch in 1990. To show you how amazing Smoltz' start has been, consider that Welch had just a 7-2 mark through the end of May in his magical season. But the summer months were where Welch really kicked into high gear. He won six games in June, three in July and six more in August, sitting at 22-5 heading into September. If Smoltz can keep up his current pace, he'll clear that milestone with a month to spare—but don't count on it.

— Scott McDevitt

May 17-28—More Disorderly Baseball Blather

SICKELS: Strange Name. . .

While trolling for prospects, I discovered this guy in the Pirates system:

"Wikleman Gonzalez"

He's a Venezuelan catcher and not much of a prospect, but ya gotta love that name. Sounds like a Venezuelan game show host.

PALACIOS: How times change. . .

If the pitchers of record remain the same for the Colorado game tonight, it means that the Benes brothers will have lost their last nine games straight, allowing 55 earned runs in 47 innings pitched (0-9, 10.53 ERA).

Meanwhile, Tim Wakefield has a 3.79 ERA in his last three starts.

Ryne Sandberg has been getting much heat for his low batting average, but here are the numbers:

AVG	R	H	2B	3B	HR	RBI	OBP	SLG
.212	22	29	6	1	9	19	.322	.474

Last year, Rey Sanchez, hitting number two, through the same number of games:

AVG	R	H	2B	3B	HR	RBI	OBP	SLG
.306	25	48	9	1	0	10	.314	.376

However, this year Sanchez and Dunston combined have:

17 R, 11 RBI and 15 errors (to Sandberg's one). Who would you take?

Greg Maddux looks human and Randy Johnson's back is a large pain. David Cone is hurt. Weird year.

Well, at least David Justice is on the DL, so everything is not different.

JAMES: If Albert Belle continued to hit home runs and drive in runs at the same rate per game as he had before this season, he would break the major league record for career RBI in his 2,877th major league game, and the record for home runs in his 2,942nd game.

That's a lot of games and a long ways away, but Henry Aaron (who holds both records) played 3,298 games. While it may be true that Belle's ratios will fall later in his career, for the moment these ratios are not going down, but going *up*.

FAUST: Belle's last 162 games. . .

AVG	G	AB	R	H	2B	3B	HR	RBI	TBB	IBB	SO	SB	CS	ERR
.330	162	609	138	201	52	2	62	152	88	8	87	4	2	9

PINTO: Gooden is currently at 16 consecutive hitless innings, and the record is 23 by Cy Young. Does anyone know of a list of the longest consecutive hitless inning streaks?

PINTO: I think I have a top three list:

Cy Young: 23 or 24, depending how you count one particular inning

Eckersley: 22.1

Vander Meer: 21

SPEAR: Expos new pitcher Derek Aucoin

According to the Montreal media guide, Quebec native Aucoin "wears the number 66 in honor of his hockey idol Mario Lemieux." Has anyone ever heard of a baseball player choosing his uniform number because of an athlete in a different sport?

Aucoin also lists as his hobbies "golf, hockey and writing restaurant reviews."

MILLER: Didn't Deion Sanders wear #21 for the Cincinnati Reds because his favorite football player also wore #21?

May 27—Johnny Berardino Dies

ZMINDA: Johnny Berardino, former A.L. second baseman who starred for years as a doctor on the soap opera "General Hospital," died on Sunday. According to the obit in the Lifeline section of *USA Today*, he was "a second baseman who led the Cleveland Indians to a World Series victory." Hmm. . . Berardino played for only one pennant winner, the 1948 Indians. He batted .190 during the regular season and did not play at all in the Series against the Braves.

I can't wait until Chuck Connors dies. He'll probably be described as "the heart and soul of the great Brooklyn Dodger teams of the early 1950s."

DEWAN: Chuck Connors died in 1992.

ZMINDA: Guess I'll report this one, also, then:

Chuck Connors Dies, Too!

Chuck Connors, the heart and soul of the great Brooklyn Dodger teams of the early 1950s, has passed away.

Actually, it happened in 1992 (thanks, John), but news travels slowly here. Gee, and I coulda sworn I just saw him on an episode of "The Rifleman". . .

May 29—Fallout from the Lee Smith Trade

MOYER: Big Trade

The Reds just got the all-time (fattest) saves leader Lee Smith for Chuck McElroy. That sure was the Reds big problem, their closer. Do you think Lee can lead off?

ZMINDA: At least Big Lee is old enough to remember the careers of Vince Coleman and Spuds Sabo.

COOPERSON: How many teams has Smith pitched for? . . .

Courtesy of Mr. Pinto:

Chicago Cubs, Boston Red Sox, St. Louis Cardinals, New York Yankees (no one else remembered he was rented by them for two months), Baltimore Orioles, California Angels and Cincinnati Reds.

May 30—Red Sox Hi-Jinks and Other News. . .

MILLER: Two thoughts on Wednesday, June 12 BOS@CHA game:

It's a 1:05 p.m. start and billed on the White Sox' calendar as "Senior Citizens Run The Bases" day.

Are they going to be made to run the bases before the game around noon when the sun is its hottest? Just think what Mayor Daley will be accused of if the city isn't prepared to handle the heat related deaths!

However, maybe they'll be asked to run the bases following the game. The Sox don't play at home the following day, so they can finish at their leisure Wednesday or Thursday.

ZMINDA: "Senior Citizens Run the Bases Day."

Sounds like every Boston Red Sox game.

OLKIN: Not quite. The Red Sox make them play the field, too.

June 3—What's Wrong with Sandberg?

HENZLER: I don't know what the climate is there in Chicago regarding Ryne Sandberg, as he limps along with a .217 batting average. I do find it interesting, however, that his .377 secondary average actually leads *all* second basemen in baseball with a minimum of 160 plate appearances.

It doesn't appear that his year and a half away from the game has robbed him of all his offensive contribuations, anyway.

PINTO: I don't think the Cubs are getting what they expected or wanted. I believe they thought Ryne would have no power, but be on base a lot in the two slot. Just the opposite has happened. His power's been good, but his .303 OBP is not what you want at the top of the order. It seems to me if this keeps up he should be batting No. 6.

COOPERSON: For the 15th straight year, the Cubs would be better off with someone other then Sandberg hitting second.

OLKIN: Ryno seems to be taking a different approach at the plate this year, and that may be one reason that his production has been so different than in the past. He used to go after the first pitch as often as the next guy, and when he hit it, he was lethal (average around .400, slugging over .700 from '89 until his retirement, if I remember correctly).

This year, he simply refuses to swing at the first pitch. He's put the first pitch into play only four times all year, which must be among the lowest (if not *the* lowest) in baseball. As a result, he's working deeper counts, and his 4.18 pitches seen per PA surely places him in the N.L. top 10.

Why has he been taking the first pitch so much? My guess is that he has to in order to give Brian McRae more of an opportunity to steal second. This is the first time in a long while that Sandberg's been batting No. 2 behind a true basestealer (Jerome Walton was the leadoff man from '89 to '91, more often than not). I haven't read any quotes about it from Riggleman, but maybe this is the real reason he dropped him to No. 6. Maybe they're just trying to get Sandberg to concentrate on being aggressive again.

Oh yeah—I mentioned that he'd put the first pitch into play four times this year. The results? Two singles and a double.

If the move to the No. 6 spot gets him to come out hacking, I'll look for his average to pick up.

DEWAN: Taking the first pitch is not a new thing for him. He was doing this before he retired. It became more pronounced, however, in his last couple of seasons.

OLKIN: First pitches in play:

Year	%AB	Avg	Slg	Pit/PA
1989	10.1	.361	.705	3.39
1990	12.2	.427	.813	3.52
1991	3.2	.474	.842	3.97
1992	3.3	.400	.750	3.85
1993	2.9	.385	.462	3.90
1994	1.8	.250	.250	3.96
1996	2.3	.750	1.000	4.18

It looks like John is right: Sandberg stopped going after the first pitch in '91. But he's still seeing more pitches this year than he ever has. It still seems to me that he's looking at strike one—and strike two—more than he used to.

June 6—It's June, and That Means. . .

—It's June, and that means the annual baseball draft.

It certainly isn't the sexiest draft around. There are no ESPN or TNT cameras and microphones supplying the play-by-play coverage, largely because very few people know who the heck most of these players are. The NFL, NBA and to a lesser extent, the NHL all have drafts driven by name recognition and instant expectations at the professional level. Not so with Major League Baseball, which still drafts players first and worries about timetables later. Basically, the June draft is largely a crap shoot, and people are more riveted by "sure things." Still, it's always fun to look to the past to see what the future may hold for the newest group of "unknowns." To the surprise of no one, the Pirates used the first pick on Kris Benson, the Clemson pitcher who ate the ACC for lunch in '95. With past number-ones such as Griffey Jr., Strawberry, (Jeff) King, Baines, (Andy) Benes, Surhoff, (Chipper) Jones and (Alex) Rodriguez in mind, Benson's future looks pretty bright. But what about the number-two choice, Travis Lee (a first baseman), who was grabbed by Minnesota? Take a look at his predecessors from the last 20 years:

Year	#2 Pick	Year	#2 Pick
1975	Mike Lentz (SD)	1985	Will Clark (SF)
1976	Pat Underwood (Det)	1986	Greg Swindell (Cle)
1977	Bill Gullickson (Mon)	1987	Mark Merchant (Pit)
1978	Lloyd Moseby (Tor)	1988	Mark Lewis (Cle)
1979	Tim Leary (Mets)	1989	Tyler Houston (Atl)
1980	Gary Harris (Tor)	1990	Tony Clark (Det)
1981	Joe Carter (Cubs)	1991	Mike Kelly (Atl)
1982	Augie Schmidt (Tor)	1992	Paul Shuey (Cle)
1983	Kurt Stillwell (Cin)	1993	Darren Dreifort (LA)
1984	Billy Swift (Sea)	1994	Ben Grieve (Oak)

A couple of great ones, a few middle-of-the-roaders and plenty of no-namers. Best of luck, Mr. Lee, at filling the black hole that has been first base in Minnesota since Kent Hrbek's retirement.

—It's June, and the Independent League season is in full swing.

Was anyone else struck by the irony that on the day after Doc Gooden weaved his no-hit gem in Yankee Stadium, Darryl Strawberry reported to the St. Paul Saints of the Northern League? Talk about a complete juxtaposition of how far one had fallen and how far one had gotten up. So why did I feel so much better for Gooden than I felt bad for Darryl? Probably because Doc has shown a level of maturation and contrition that I have not seen from

Strawberry. Still, I was at Yankee Stadium the night that Darryl made his debut there, and he's still enough of a draw, and still creates enough electricity, to make it worth a big-league team's while to give him a shot. Through Tuesday, Strawberry was 7-for-15 with two homers and six RBI for St. Paul.

—It's June, and Albert Belle is once again facing suspension.

June and Albert Belle? You may as well be talking about fire and ice. The two don't seem to go together. Belle is facing his third June suspension since 1990—the year he was suspended from Triple-A Colorado Springs. He also added another in mid-May of 1991 (I guess he wasn't able to wait until June that year). But while the others were legit—charging the mound. . . hitting a fan with a baseball—this time his crime is knocking down another player who was in Belle's basepath. I have to agree with Cubs' first baseman Mark Grace on this one. "It was a perfectly legal play. You can fine (Belle) for throwing an elbow, but don't suspend him." It's only June, and Belle already has 23 homers. I'd hate to feel cheated if he fell five games short of 62.

— Tony Nistler

June 7—Teddy Ballgame

I saw the other day where the amazing Frank Thomas is now fifth among career leaders in slugging percentage. As of this writing, the Big Hurt's "big number" stands at .597—sixth all time behind Babe Ruth (.690), Ted Williams (.634), Lou Gehrig (.632), Jimmie Foxx (.609) and Hank Greenberg (.605). Pretty good company.

Of all the players above, I've always found Williams to be the most compelling from a statistical standpoint—not just because of what The Kid accomplished, but because of what he *might* have accomplished had it not been for two career interruptions.

Let's put Williams' .344 career batting average (sixth of all time), .483 on-base percentage (first) and .634 slugging percentage (first) aside for a moment and look at purely raw numbers. (Despite missing nearly five full seasons (1943, 1944, 1945, 1952, 1953) during his service in World War II and Korea, Williams finished with 2,654 hits, 521 home runs, 1,839 RBI and 2,019 walks—truly staggering totals by any standard. But they're even more staggering when you play around with the numbers and come up with some reasonable projections on what five more seasons of Ted Williams would have meant.

Let's start first by looking at the three seasons Williams missed due to his service in World War II—1943 through 1945. After hitting .406 in '41 and winning the Triple Crown in '42, it's safe to conclude that those three years showed a lot of promise. . . to say the least. To estimate what Williams might have accomplished during that period, let's average his "sandwich seasons"—1942 (the year before he left) and 1946 (the year after he came back). The composite season is shown in the Average line below:

Year	H	AB	AVG	HR	RBI	TB	BB
1942	186	522	.356	36	137	338	145
1946	176	514	.342	38	123	343	156
Avg	181	518	.349	37	130	341	151

Multiply that Average line by three and the numbers start to pile up in a hurry:

Years	H	AB	AVG	HR	RBI	TB	BB
1943-45	543	1554	.349	111	390	1023	453

Well, Williams just cleared the 3,000-hit and 600-home run barriers. . . and we've still got two seasons to go.

In fact, Williams played six games in 1952 and 37 in 1953, but he essentially lost both seasons to his Korea service. For the sake of our estimates here, let's scrap both of them and put together another "composite season," using 1951 and 1954. Here it is:

Year	H	AB	AVG	HR	RBI	TB	BB
1951	169	531	.318	30	126	295	144
1954	133	386	.345	29	89	245	136

The average of those two seasons times two is, of course, the sum of the two original seasons:

Years	H	AB	AVG	HR	RBI	TB	BB
1952-53	302	917	.329	59	215	540	280

Okay, now for the numbers you've been waiting for. Here is Williams' "new" career line, adding in the estimates for the five lost seasons, what I've called "War Years."

	H	AB	AVG	HR	RBI	TB	BB
War Years	845	2471	.342	170	605	1563	733
Other Years	2613	7605	.344	507	1802	4793	1998
TOTAL	3458	10076	.343	677	2407	6356	2731

Take a look at those final numbers. For those of you scoring at home, Williams' 3,458 projected hits would place him sixth all-time, just ahead of another Red Sox left fielder by the name of Carl Yastrzemski (3,419). The 677 home runs? Only two players have more, and you know who they are. The 2,407 RBI? That would have cleared Hank Aaron's current mark by more than 100. Total bases? That mark still belongs to Aaron (6,856), but Williams' 6,356 projected total bases would make him second of all time, ahead of Stan Musial (6,134). And the walks? Despite his five missed seasons, Williams nearly caught Ruth for the career walks record anyway (2,056 to 2,019). Five *more* seasons for Williams would have sent that mark into the statistical stratosphere.

Now, I'll confess something here. It's very easy to get caught up in this sort of analysis with any player who had a career interruption. Military service, the color barrier, suspensions, injuries. . . they all provide ample ground for looking at what Josh Gibson *might* have done.

. . or Fred Lynn *might* have done. . . or Sandy Koufax *might* have done. But the Williams case is a little different for a few reasons:

1. We're not looking at just a good player or a great player—but one that's arguably the most powerful raw offensive force the game has ever seen. No matter what Lyman Bostock's career might have held, it's safe to say he wasn't likely to put up Hall-of-Fame numbers.

2. The years Williams missed were in the absolute heart of his career, and he was more than capable of winning an MVP Award in any of the five. Williams wasn't "playing them out" at the time he went into service for World War II. He was getting ready for another Triple Crown. And his early-1950s seasons weren't too bad, either. Remember, this is a guy that hit .388 in 1957 at age 37.

3. There are no fluke seasons in Williams' career. Ted Williams was an amazing hitter the day he arrived in 1939 until the day he circled the bases at Fenway Park after homering in his final at-bat in 1960. It's very difficult to put together similar projections for players like Koufax—a pitcher who really didn't "kick into high gear" until his late 20's, having put together a relatively average career up to that point.

4. The data shows that Williams may have made an assault on baseball's marquee stat—career home runs. A career total of 677 would have left him just 37 short of Babe Ruth's mark. In short, if not for World War II and Korea, Hank Aaron may very well have been chasing Ted Williams' home-run mark, not Ruth's.

And one more thing. . . Williams played during the 154-game era. Think about that. Adjusting for *that* difference puts Williams at a gaudy 712 home runs (but remember Ruth had the short schedule as well). So who's the greatest hitter of all-time, Ruth or Williams? Bill James summed up that question pretty well in *The Historical Baseball Abstract*.

"The race for the distinction of being the greatest hitter of all time as measured by formal analysis is between Ruth and Williams, and it is so close that any revision of the method, however small, is likely to reverse the outcome."

The answer is. . . nobody really knows. And in a strange way, I think that's kind of a blessing.

— Scott McDevitt

June 6—Where Have You Gone, Don Zimmer?

On an almost daily basis, the Red Sox situation presents us with new developments to keep our minds and rosters churning. This week was especially eventful. In his marvelous weekly column in the *Boston Sunday Globe*, Peter Gammons spent a good chunk of last Sunday's essay detailing the transgressions of Red Sox manager Kevin Kennedy.

Gammons was uncharacteristically direct. His relentless indictment of Kennedy detailed: Kennedy's disrespectfulness of his own scouting department, and even his own General Manager; his inability to run a bullpen; his lack of control over the team; his inflammatory comments directed at other teams; and his penchant for finding a scapegoat for each of his failures. Gammons noted the ill will this has generated around the league, and cited it as the reason that "this will be Kennedy's last major league job."

Hot damn! We've seen a lot of crazy stuff going on over there, but I don't think any of us had realized just how bad the situation had become. Even without Gammons' revelations, however, the warning signs are becoming more alarming by the day.

The latest head-slapper was Kennedy's stubborn refusal to go to his bullpen on Monday night. Aaron Sele had been scheduled to start against the White Sox that night, but he came down with the stomach flu, so Tim Wakefield was pressed into service with only two days' rest.

Now, starting Wakefield on two days' rest isn't necessarily nuts. After all, he'd done it one time last year, and ended up pitching a gem, suffering no ill effects afterward. Another knuckleballer, Tom Candiotti, was able to get away with it one time a couple of years ago. A knuckleballer's arm can probably handle a start or two on only a couple of days' rest, as long as the pitch counts are kept within reasonable limits.

Which brings us to Monday night. Wakefield didn't have much, and the White Sox hit him early and often. When his floater moved, it dove well out of the strike zone, and when it didn't move, it just hung up there and waited for the wood. After six innings, Wakefield was behind by four runs, and he'd already thrown upwards of 100 pitches. It was time for a reliever.

Kennedy didn't think so. He sent Wakefield back out there for the seventh. He gave up another run and threw another 20 or 30 pitches. Trailing by five runs in the bottom of the eighth, Kennedy again chose to save his bullpen and waste Wakefield. By the time the game was finished, the White Sox had wrung another run out of Wakefield, who finally completed the game on his 162nd pitch.

That's 162 pitches. On two days' rest. Just to appreciate how excessive that is, consider that no other pitcher this year has even broken the 145-pitch mark. And if you're inclined to think that Wakefield should be able to "take it" just because he's a knuckleballer, don't be so sure. When he gets behind in the count, he also throws a low-80s fastball. With his compact, slide-step delivery, he's forced to generate velocity almost entirely with his arm. And remember, he throws it when he's *behind* in the count. He was behind a *lot* Monday night.

The last time someone did this to Wakefield, you might say that he didn't respond very well. As I'm sure you remember, he came up with Pittsburgh in the middle of '92 and enjoyed a great stretch run. When he began the '93 season, he struggled with his control, and after his first four starts, his numbers were 2-2, 5.28. Then, on April 17, he started a game in Atlanta.

In that start, he put a million Braves on base with walks, but he kept landing on his feet, and even took a 2-1 lead into the bottom of the ninth. Then Ryan Klesko tied it up with a solo shot off the tiring Wakefield, and Jim Leyland had to decide whether to lift him. He left him in. The Pirates eventually broke through for the extra-inning victory, but only after the knuckleballer had thrown an astounding 172 pitches. In the past five years, no pitcher has topped that mark.

Leyland got the victory, but it cost him Wakefield. Over the next three months, he went 1-6 with a 7.71 ERA. Then he was sent down. He didn't pitch effectively again for two years.

It's hard to know what Leyland was thinking, but it's clear what was on Kennedy's mind. Frustrated by an inconsistent bullpen, he simply buried his head in the sand and waited for the game to end. The sad irony is that his relievers are capable of doing the job, but like the rest of the staff, they can't possibly succeed under Kennedy's increasingly erratic leadership.

—Mat Olkin

June 12—Random News

OLKIN: The Steve Moyer Stupid Quote Of The Week

From Today's *USA Today*:

Manager Davey Johnson on when he will remove SS Cal Ripken from the lineup: "God will let me know when it's time."

Although meddling in managerial decision is usually to be avoided at all costs, the Almighty is considering making an announcement sometime next week. It seems that apart from ending world hunger and preventing the melting of the polar ice caps, the Good Lord's main aim right now is to find a way to get Manny Alexander into the lineup.

MOYER: God is the only justification for getting Manny Alexander into the lineup.

SPEAR: I have a question. . .

Jim Riggleman almost never lets Luis Gonzalez bat against lefties. In the game on Wednesday, Luis was 3-for-3 with a double and two RBI against Astacio, a righty. As soon as the Dodgers bring in a lefty, Gonzalez is taken out.

This year, Luis is hitting just .080 (2-for-25) against lefties. However, last year he hit .268 (with a .500 SLG) in 112 at bats vs. southpaws, and over the last three years (1993-95), he has a .283 average in 385 at bats.

I understand the manager wanting to get bench guys some at bats, but this seems silly. The guy has proven he can hit lefties. . . why all of a sudden just totally bench him against lefthanders?

Is there something here I'm missing? Can a guy all of a sudden just lose the ability to hit lefties?

MILLER: It's obvious, you don't want to keep a talent like Doug Glanville in the minors or on the bench because of Luis Gonzalez! Come on, didn't you see Glanville's diving catch in his debut, or look at his minor league power numbers? If you can put a Greg Gross-type player in left over a player with more power, wouldn't you?

June 13—Tiger Town

Will the Tigers lose more games than the '62 Mets? I was talking to Bill James about this at the SABR convention last week, and he thought the Tigers would do a lot better after the All-Star break. They'll still be terrible. . . we're talking about 106 losses or something like that. But I think that Randy Smith and Buddy Bell are on the right track. Lest we forget, it wasn't that long ago that the Braves and Indians were about this bad. The Braves were 54-106 in 1988; they made it to the World Series three years later. The Tribe, 57-105 in 1991, went 100-44 four seasons later. The Tigers probably have less to start with than either of those clubs, but a dramatic turnaround *can* take place. . . and in a shorter period of time than most people think.

— Don Zminda

June 18—So Far, So Good

Joe Torre has never been—and it's safe to say that he never will be—my favorite manager. As a man who likes to make decisions by the seat of his pants, his style is often perplexing and quite frequently infuriating.

It's not that the decisions he makes are *indefensible*—it's just that a lot of his moves run directly counter to other moves he made just a short time ago. If he were a chess player, his favorite move might be to castle—over and over again, until he was checkmated. In making a decision, he seems to have no interest whatsoever in being consistent, or adhering to any sort of long-range plan. The decision depends entirely upon whichever way the seat of his pants goes.

His tenure as manager of the St. Louis Cardinals provides a perfect illustration (or indictment) of his managerial style. Torre took over a Cardinals team with a good amount of talent and zero definition. Before the team could contend, a number of things had to be settled, for example: whether Ray Lankford would be a table-setter or an RBI man; whether or not Bernard Gilkey would hit enough to be the regular left fielder; whether Brian Jordan deserved a shot in right field; and who the regular second baseman should be. In addition to all of that, the pitching needed to be straightened out.

When he left the team several years later, not one of those problems had been resolved. Lankford was still bouncing up and down in the lineup, Gilkey was still being shuttled in and out of left field, and Brian Jordan had never gotten a full shot. The pitching staff was still comprised of 11 starters-slash-relievers, and the second base situation was the most damning failure of them all. The competition between Luis Alicea and Geronimo Pena turned into a virtual Vietnam from which neither player could escape. Torre allowed the battle to rage on for years without declaring a winner.

On the other hand, he did make two particularly courageous decisions, moving Todd Zeile from catcher to third base and Gregg Jefferies from third base to first base. Each move opened up Torre to criticism, but each of them ended up working out fairly well. So it can't be said that Torre's decisions were all that bad. It's just that he didn't make nearly enough of them. It sure must have been frustrating to watch him manage that team—sort of like watching a potter sitting in front of a wet lump of clay, staring blankly at it until it hardens into a useless, shapeless mass.

Which is why I was so skeptical of Torre's chances of bringing order to this year's Yankees. Buck Showalter had been successful there because he had been able to find roles that maximized the talents of each of his players. It didn't seem very likely that Torre—whose evaluation of a player seems to depend on his last two weeks' batting average—would be able to organize the roster so well.

But look at what he's done. It's been a masterful job. I don't know how anyone could possibly think otherwise.

The Yankees have had to contend with more injuries and uncertainties than just about any team in the league. Through it all, Torre has been there to provide solutions and steady the ship.

First of all, he's quietly defused sensitive situations involving the young players. Derek Jeter's ascension to starting shortstop was met with enormous expectations, but Torre has eased the pressure and allowed the youngster to grow comfortable. Camouflaged in the number-nine spot in the order, Jeter has enjoyed a slump-free rookie season so far.

Ruben Rivera's trial was another potentially touchy situation. Prematurely billed as the next Mantle, the youngster was promoted to cover an injury. He hadn't been hitting at Triple-A, and his stay was intended to be brief. But he started out hot, and the press trumpeted the emergence of this "great young slugger." Torre knew better, and he resisted the temptation to join in the chorus. He just kept sending the kid out there until he cooled down, which he inevitably did. Then, when it had become clear to all that the kid needed more seasoning, Rivera was finally sent back down.

But Torre's greatest triumph has been his adept handling of a pitching staff that has been in a constant state of flux. Cone was lost after only four starts, and Gooden and Pettitte have been the only reliable starters. Torre's shown remarkable patience with the recovering Jimmy Key, who has regained his velocity but not his old movement. Torre knows what Key needs to win, and his patience may yet be rewarded. Kenny Rogers has been in and out, but Torre's stuck by him, too.

Even more remarkable has been Torre's refusal to raid his bullpen to patch the holes in the rotation. Mariano Rivera has been brilliant in middle relief, and everyone had expected Torre to move him back into the rotation, but Joe seems to have learned from his experiences in St. Louis. Rivera had failed once before as a starter, and came into his own with his phenomenal relief work during the '95 postseason. Torre decided that the kid belonged in middle relief, and that's where he kept him.

He also chose to keep Bob Wickman in the bullpen, and the Rivera/Wickman tandem has done great setup work for closer John Wetteland. If Jeff Nelson and Steve Howe had been setting up instead, the team would not be where it is now.

And exactly where is this team? Even with all the pitching problems, they're *third* in the league in ERA. The fact that they've stayed ahead of the more talented Orioles is the best testament to the amazing job Joe Torre has done.

—Mat Olkin

June 20—Molly

Anyone who follows baseball will inevitably have a favorite player. I mentioned in an article I wrote a few weeks ago that mine is Paul Molitor, which seems like an odd choice; after all, I live in the Chicago area and have been a White Sox fan all my life. But here's how much I like Paul Molitor. Every morning, the first thing I do when I open the paper is to look for the Twins box score to see how Molitor did, and in particular, how many hits he got. He's closing in on 3,000 for his career, and after looking at that box score, I can tell you exactly how many more hits he needs; the current total of "hits needed" is 115. He's also having another great year, adding to a list of accomplishments that I can recite from memory: a .306 lifetime average, career totals of more than 200 homers and 450 stolen bases, a World Series Most Valuable Player Award (1993), a lifetime postseason batting average of .368—including a .418 mark in 13 World Series games. I could go on for about 100 more pages, but you get the point: I know all about Paul Molitor, and I've shared all his triumphs and sorrows. When Molitor hit safely in 39 consecutive games back in 1987, toward the end of the streak I never went to bed until I knew that he'd gotten his hit. I think I also vicariously shared every one of his numerous injuries.

But why do I like him so much—especially since he's always played for teams that were bitter rivals of my own favorite club? Well I don't want to get too corny here, but does the term "role model" mean anything to you? It does to me, and my admiration for Paul Molitor has to do with more than just his being such a great player. . . it has a lot to do with the way he comes across as a person. He brings an attitude of total professionalism to the game; he's one of those guys who plays clean but hard, always hustles, always sets the right example for younger players. I only talked to him once, on the field at the Metrodome back in the late 1980s, and that was what really sealed the deal. He just seemed like a genuinely nice man, and not at all like a millionaire who was also one of the biggest stars in baseball. He was totally friendly, cooperative and unpretentious with me and my colleague Bill Young, even though we were a couple of media nobodies doing an interview for Bill's cable-access baseball show. That interview, and the kindness Paul Molitor showed to us, will always be one of my favorite baseball memories.

— Don Zminda

June 21—RBI to Hits

While looking through some Similarity Scores for Jay Buhner the other day, I couldn't help but think back to his unique statistical season of one year ago. For those of you who may not remember, Buhner finished with nearly as many RBI (121) as hits (123)—for an average of 0.98 RBI per safety. As it turns out, that was the highest ratio in baseball history.

Highest Ratio of RBI to Hits

Player	Team	Year	RBI	H	RBI/H
Jay Buhner	Mariners	1995	121	123	0.984
Jim Gentile	Orioles	1961	141	147	0.959
Oyster Burns	Brooklyn (N.L.)	1890	128	134	0.955
Harmon Killebrew	Twins	1962	126	134	0.940
Harmon Killebrew	Twins	1971	119	127	0.937
Rudy York	Tigers	1938	127	138	0.920
Harmon Killebrew	Twins	1969	140	153	0.915
Hank Greenberg	Tigers	1937	183	200	0.915
Hack Wilson	Cubs	1930	190	208	0.914
Dave Kingman	Mets	1982	99	109	0.908

(Minimum 400 at-bats)

The fact that Buhner hit 40 home runs (nearly one-third of his total hits) had a lot to do with the numbers you see above. He seems to take a "feast or famine" approach to the plate, striking out 120 times last year alone. That's not quite in Dave Kingman's territory, but it's still a hefty total. When Buhner made contact last season, he certainly made it count, but—like Kingman did for years—Buhner often found big gaps between those occasions on which he *made* contact... sort of like a 30 percent field-goal shooter in basketball who shoots nothing but three-pointers. There was very little "middle ground" with Buhner offensively.

Whatever the case, this stuff got my head spinning and I decided to play around with some more RBI numbers, looking at, among other things, RBI-to-home run ratios.

Lowest Ratio of RBI to HR

Player	Team	Year	HR	RBI	RBI/HR
Harmon Killebrew	Twins	1963	45	96	2.13
Felix Mantilla	Red Sox	1964	30	64	2.13
Willie Mays	Giants	1965	52	112	2.15
Rick Monday	Cubs	1973	26	56	2.15
Brook Jacoby	Indians	1987	32	69	2.16
Tony Conigliaro	Red Sox	1964	24	52	2.17
Rickey Henderson	Athletics	1990	28	61	2.18
Frank Robinson	Reds	1956	38	83	2.18
Hank Aaron	Braves	1969	44	97	2.20
Matt Williams	Giants	1994	43	96	2.23

(Minimum 400 at-bats)

Harmon Killebrew, who showed up three times in our first list, makes another appearance here. It's not a total surprise to see him either place, since the Killer was one of the game's all-time big swingers—573 career home runs and 1,699 career strikeouts. Like Buhner last year, Killebrew had an all-or-nothing season in 1963, with more than one-third of his hits going for home runs.

Another interesting thing to note about the list are the years in which these seasons occurred. Six of the top 10 are from the 1950s and 60s—an era in which stolen bases and "station to station" baseball were primitive by today's standards. The '63 Twins stole just 32 bases on the season, the '64 Red Sox stole just 18 and the '65 Giants swiped just 47. It was a very conservative era on the bases, and the home run was often the *only* thing—literally—that could get a runner home. Fortunately for the '63 Twins, they had Killebrew to do the dirty work.

Another factor to consider when analyzing a list like this is position in the batting order. Rickey Henderson has a very low RBI/HR ratio during his 1990 season for the most obvious of reasons—Rickey hit leadoff, batting with the bases empty more often than any other player in the Oakland lineup. Mantilla and Monday also hit leadoff during their seasons above.

— Scott McDevitt

June 21—Baseball Babble-On

I don't know if any of you folks who read me are Howard Stern fans, but I am. The reason I bring this up is that one of his cohorts, Fred Norris, recently changed his name to Eric. It reminded me of years ago when Cardinal/Padre Harry Rasmussen also changed his name to Eric. I guess if you name your baby boy Eric, there's a good chance he'll be happy with his first name.

One thing you won't get here (but I'll bet you'll get in every other baseball column from here to kingdom come) is my All-Star picks, why the fans picks are wrong, why the whole thing is a big, unfair travesty, etc. I really never figured out who made up the unwritten, media-fueled rule that the All-Star game is a reward for the players having the best first halves of the current season. I think it should be a game played between the "stars," as decided by the fans. Do I want to see Jose Vizcaino out there on the field because a few too many of his batted balls fell in between April and now? You bet I don't. Give me Barry and Albert and Rickey and Jose and Junior and Matt. (I've seen enough of god-of-gods Cal, although you can gladly out-vote me like you will.) Now that's an All-*Star* game.

Bob Nightengale fills this week's *TSN* (Friday lunch reading time) with all kinds of old goat, things-that-only-us-insiders-know nonsense. His biggie is telling us the Dodgers are disappointing because they have no "team chemistry." They lose because they have so many players of so many different origins. Well, I don't buy it. I see a team that's dead last in both on-base percentage *and* slugging percentage *in all of baseball*. I don't think Hideo Nomo can do much about that. I see a cleanup hitter named Eric Karros with a batting average of .240 and an OBP of .301. Ain't much Ismael Valdes can do about that. I see supposedly one of the most talented players in baseball, Raul Mondesi, batting .260, with an even worse-than-Karros .292 OBP. Help us, Ramon Martinez. And, finally, there's their solid 1996 leadoff man, Brett Butler, with a career OBP of .379, at home with throat cancer. Chan Ho? What were you doing about this? Were you out buying a Mosh Schott Booick when you should've been generating team chemistry? But you know what? If Lasorda's patient with Roger Cedeno (.344 OBP) or they deal for another Butler and a few guys come around (which they will) and provide some support for Mike Piazza and LA's excellent pitching, the Dodgers are going to win that division, and fairly easily at that. And then the team chemistry will all of a sudden be just peachy.

— Steve Moyer

June 27—All-Star Debates

1996 STATS, Inc. All-Star Voting

(First-Place votes in parentheses)

NATIONAL LEAGUE		AMERICAN LEAGUE	
CATCHER			
Mike Piazza	(11) 58	Ivan Rodriguez	(10) 59
Todd Hundley	(2) 39	Dan Wilson	(2) 36
Javy Lopez	9	Mike Stanley	(1) 8
Charles Johnson	6	Terry Steinbach	8
Benito Santiago	2	Sandy Alomar Jr.	3
Jason Kendall	1	Chris Hoiles	1
Scott Servais	1	Don Slaught	1
FIRST BASE			
Jeff Bagwell	(13) 65	Frank Thomas	(8) 53
Fred McGriff	36	Mo Vaughn	(3) 40
A. Galarraga	6	Mark McGwire	(1) 9
Jeff King	4	Edgar Martinez	(1) 5
Mark Grace	2	Julio Franco	3
John Mabry	2	John Jaha	1
H.Rodriguez	1	Rafael Palmeiro	1

SECOND BASE

Craig Biggio	(6) 46	Roberto Alomar	(12) 60
Mike Lansing	(3) 28	Chuck Knoblauch	39
Eric Young	(2) 26	Mark Lewis	(1) 8
Carlos Garcia	(1) 5	Ray Durham	4
Mickey Morandini	(1) 5	Carlos Baerga	3
Jose Vizcaino	3	Fernando Vina	1
Mark Lemke	1	Mark McLemore	1
Delino DeShields	1		
Jeff King	1		
Mark Lemke	1		

THIRD BASE

Matt Williams	(12) 63	Edgar Martinez	(8) 40
Chipper Jones	(1) 39	Jim Thome	(4) 28
Ken Caminiti	7	Wade Boggs	(1) 19
Vinny Castilla	2	Robin Ventura	10
Leo Gomez	1	Kevin Seitzer	6
Sean Berry	1	Dean Palmer	6
		Travis Fryman	3
		Tim Naehring	3
		Jason Giambi	1

SHORTSTOP

M.Grudzielanek	(9) 57	Alex Rodriguez	(12) 63
Barry Larkin	(4) 44	Cal Ripken	(1) 34
Walt Weiss	8	John Valentin	9
Jeff Blauser	3	Omar Vizquel	8
Rey Ordonez	2	Derek Jeter	2
Jay Bell	1	Kevin Elster	1
Shawon Dunston	1		

OUTFIELD

Barry Bonds	(11) 58	Albert Belle	(12) 61
Gary Sheffield	(7) 45	Brady Anderson	(9) 53
Ellis Burks	(5) 39	Ken Griffey	(8) 52
Henry Rodriguez	(4) 34	Jay Buhner	(5) 41
Ryan Klesko	(3) 26	Kenny Lofton	(1) 27
Sammy Sosa	(2) 26	Bernie Williams	(2) 23
Dante Bichette	21	Tony Phillips	23
Ray Lankford	(2) 18	Paul O'Neill	(1) 16
Tony Gwynn	(2) 16	Joe Carter	14
Lance Johnson	13	Jose Canseco	(1) 12
Eric Davis	(1) 8	Manny Ramirez	11
Marquis Grissom	(1) 8	Greg Vaughn	11
Derek Bell	7	Geronimo Berroa	3
Larry Walker	6	Juan Gonzalez	1
Rickey Hendrson	(1) 5	Marty Cordova	1
Bernard Gilkey	5	Jim Edmonds	1
Brian McRae	3	Ernie Young	1
Steve Finley	3		
Lenny Dykstra	1		
Pete Incaviglia	1		
Reggie Sanders	1		
Jim Eisenreich	1		

ZMINDA: Mark Lewis? Eric Davis? And we complain about how the fans vote!

MOYER: I don't complain about how fans vote (except for the fact that we have to watch that half-grey, half-bald old goat at SS for the A.L. every year). It's all about voting for who you like. Hooray!!! (I voted for Mark Lewis, too, and I also vote for him every time I go to the park, so there.) Throw off your media shackles, fans, vote for who you like, not who you're supposed to vote for. (As if I'm telling them something.)

PINTO: What's wrong with voting for Eric Davis? It's not like the N.L. is bursting with strong center fielders. They are more like a lot of fast guys that can't get on base. Grissom, McRae, Devo, Lance Johnson. . .

July 2—The Next Juan Nieves

Bucky Dent's home run made me a Brewers fan. I grew up in New England, and my dad has been a lifelong Red Sox fan. The year baseball found me was also the season that my dad thought he'd been waiting for all his life: 1978. At first, I must have been a Red Sox fan too, although I'm sure I never gave it much thought to that point.

Then came the home run. As I watched my dad experience it, one thing became strikingly obvious: being a Red Sox fan didn't seem to be a heck of a lot of fun. So, I did the only logical thing a nine-year old could do. . . I picked another team. Dad had always lamented the fact that the Red Sox had traded Cecil Cooper to Milwaukee for George Scott, so I decided to root for Cecil and his Milwaukee Brewers.

For a while, it was a lot of fun. The Brewers got into the postseason in '81, sort of. The next year was even more thrilling, although they ultimately ended up losing Game 7 of the World Series to Whitey's Cardinals. Then the wheels came off. Everybody on the team got old, got hurt or got traded, all in the space of about, say, 17 seconds.

But there was hope. There was always hope, because down in the minors, a tidal wave of prospects was gathering momentum. I'd sit in study hall and happily construct a future lineup (projected: 1987) featuring Billy Joe Robidoux at first base, Glenn Braggs in left field, Randy Ready at third, Ernie Riles at short, and B.J. Surhoff behind the plate, among others.

The pitching was going to be even better. They had a young strikeout pitcher named Chris Bosio; looking at his stats, I figured he must have thrown pretty hard. They also had a kid named Juan Nieves who a lot of people were talking about. They had Ramser Correa (Remember him? He's still down in the minors pitching for someone). Teddy Higuera soon established himself as a legitimate staff ace. Throw in an ace lefty reliever named Dan Plesac and young starter Bill Wegman, and you were looking at an exciting young team. The only thing that got me through the lean years was the hope that by '87, they'd be ready to start marching to the top of the American League.

It almost happened. The Brewers began the '87 season with a record 13-straight victories, and all the prospects seemed to arrive at once, exactly as planned.

Then something went wrong. At first, it was little things. A minor injury to Riles; Nieves complaining of a sore arm. But not to worry; more help was on the way. The farm system produced more jewels like Gary Sheffield, Billy Spiers and Don August, and we still had a good, young team.

Soon we had a good, young, *disabled* team. A rash of injuries swept over the club, annihilating the talented crop of youngsters that had been so carefully cultivated. By the end of '90, just about every single member of the starting rotation had suffered a career-threatening injury. Don August was an exception; he didn't need an arm injury in order to lose his effectiveness overnight.

Dan Plesac went downhill. Glenn Braggs and Rob Deer didn't develop. Dale Sveum broke his leg. B.J. Surhoff stopped hitting. Gary Sheffield developed the wrong kind of reputation. Out of about a dozen can't-miss prospects, *every single one of them* missed.

So you'll pardon me if I remain skeptical about Jeff D'Amico's chances for overnight stardom.

—Mat Olkin

July 2—Is Anderson Worthy Enough to Break Maris' Record?

HENZLER: I know it's only the first week of July, and he's not even halfway there, *but. . .*

If I'd have told you before the season that someone would break Maris' record this year, and then given you 50 chances to guess the player's identity, do you think you would have guessed Brady Anderson?

There's quite a drop-off from Ruth to Maris, at least in terms of historical stature. I'm not sure Anderson would qualify in most fans' estimations as a worthy successor to possibly the greatest record in sports, either.

MOYER: If I'm not mistaken, Bill was sticking up for Brady Anderson back when he was struggling to get 250 at-bats per season. He must've known. (Now if only they'd have let Ken Phelps play every day.)

COOPERSON: Is Anderson worthy?

Yes, but I don't really believe fans are "worthy" of determining who is a worthy successor to whom. . . Anderson plays zero games a year in Denver. . .

PINTO: Is he worthy? . . .

He dates Mary Pierce, so he's worthy of something. . .

COOPERSON: That's because, unlike Cal Ripken, Brady's not losing his hair.

July 4—Inter-League Play

I wanted to comment on reader response to my column asking people how they felt about inter-league play. The interesting thing was that there was *no* consensus on the subject—none whatsoever. There seems to be just as many people who hate the idea of inter-league play as there are people who like it. And among those who *do* like it, there's no consensus about how it should be set up. Some people think every team should play every other team each year, the way they do in the NBA and NHL. Others think inter-league play should focus on geographical rivalries, with East playing East, etc. Some people want a lot of inter-league games, others a bare minimum. And some people would like to see the entire current league structure abolished and have new leagues set up on a geographical basis, so that those rivalries like Yankees vs. Mets can take place *without* inter-league play.

So what does the Zee-man think? I'm very lukewarm on the whole subject. One thing I really don't like about baseball these days is that the number of games between the clubs in a particular division keeps on decreasing. In the American League West, for instance, teams play fewer than 40 games against other A.L. West clubs. . . less than a fourth of their schedule. So how is that really a "divisional race"? I'm afraid inter-league play would only make this situation even worse, until the divisions basically mean nothing at all, as is the case with the

NBA and NHL. I could accept inter-league play in a limited way, but only if it didn't further dilute the divisional races, which ought to be a key element in any season. On the contrary, I'd like to see a schedule with *more* focus on divisional play.

This could be done fairly easily. Let's begin by delaying inter-league play until 1998, when the two new expansion teams enter major league baseball. If you put one team in each league, we'll have two 15-team leagues, each of which would have three five-team divisions. . . and inter-league play would be a necessity, since without it one team in each league would be left without an opponent each night. This is what the major leagues will probably do in 1998, anyway, so there's nothing revolutionary here.

Now, the scheduling. If you played 18 games against each of the four teams in your division, that's 72 games. If you played each of the other 10 teams in your league six times apiece (two three-game series, one home and one road), that's another 60 games. Then you could play six games apiece against the clubs in one of the divisions in the other league—30 more games, for a total of 162. A.L. East teams would play the N.L. East one year, the Central in Year 2, the West in Year 3. If you wanted to increase the amount of seasons in which the Yankees would play the Mets, etc., you could do a four-year cycle, with East vs. East in Year 1, East vs. Central in Year 2, East vs. East again in Year 3, and East vs. West in Year 4. Under this plan, every team would have a chance to play every other team within three or four years, so the fans in Boston would finally get their chance to see Barry Bonds and (ahem!) Jeff Bagwell. . . but they'd also have more games each year against the Yankees and Orioles, their *real* rivals.

All this is very logical, but I don't think it has a snowball's chance in hell of being adopted. To begin with, can't you see all the screaming from the Seattle people who would suddenly have three fewer home games against the Yankees? And while the Red Sox would get more games against the Yankees under the plan I've sketched out, they'd also get more against the Tigers and Blue Jays. . . and fewer games against the Indians, who have become a big draw on the road in recent years. That's how we ended up with the "balanced schedule" to begin with. Which is why I think that adding inter-league games will mean fewer divisional games, not more. And I hate that.

But it doesn't really matter whether I hate it or not. Inter-league play is coming because major league baseball thinks the fans want it, and they're *sure* the television networks want it. Logic will have nothing to do with it, either, when they draw up the schedule. Ready or not, here it comes.

— Don Zminda

July 9—The Half That Was

Well, how was *that* for a first half? Looking back, it's still difficult to fully comprehend all the lunacy that we've witnessed. In one 87-game stretch, things that used to seem impossible became less and less improbable, and ultimately grew to be almost commonplace.

Brady Anderson proved that in order to chase Roger Maris, you don't have to be a rude, self-centered misanthrope. Albert Belle proved that it doesn't hurt.

The Rangers established that they can contend without bankrupting their health care provider. The Mariners, however, showed that you don't necessarily need the Big Unit or Junior just to keep up with Texas.

The Red Sox proved that defense counts. The Tigers proved that pitching counts. The Rockies proved that sometimes the only thing that counts is to get the last at-bat.

Jose Mesa pitched great, and then he pitched horribly. Hershiser did the opposite. Meanwhile, the White Sox kept creeping closer to "the team that couldn't be beat."

Two of the most durable pitchers in baseball, Randy Johnson and David Cone, got hurt. Dwight Gooden, who'd pitched in seven games over the past two years, threw a no-hitter.

Kevin Elster, who hadn't played regularly in five years, set a pace for 25 homers and 100 RBI. Paul Molitor, who'd played regularly for 18 years, and needed 211 hits for 3,000, set a pace for 217 hits.

Roger Pavlik proved that you don't need an ERA under 5.00 to make the All-Star team. Ozzie Smith proved that to make the team, you don't need to be any better than Royce Clayton, either.

Mo Vaughn showed us that you don't need a healthy hand to stay on a 40-homer pace. Greg Vaughn showed us that you don't have to be Mo Vaughn to do it, either.

Edgar Martinez reminded us that we should all take a minute to remember Earl Webb before he's erased from the record books. Alex Rodriguez reminded us that a 20 year old *can too* be that good.

John Smoltz taught us that you don't have to be Greg Maddux to start out 14-1. Greg Maddux taught us that you don't have to be John Smoltz to have tough luck.

Darryl Strawberry proved that no matter how long you've been gone, you can still make it back to the majors, as long as you can hit the longball. Kurt Stillwell proved that the hitting part is optional.

Jim Abbott showed that being left-handed sometimes isn't enough. Rick Honeycutt showed that sometimes it is.

—Mat Olkin

July 10—Bob Costas & Other Sports Broadcasters

ZMINDA: I actually like Bob Costas, who's one of the few announcers with a real knowledge of the history of the game. He made several good points during the All-Star game broadcast, including the comment that Maris' record has now lasted longer than Ruth's, and that no one has seriously challenged it despite all the HRs being hit.

But I thought he was really off base on a lot of stuff. I agree with David that his projections were wrong. . . but what was *really* bad was that he was just using them for shock effect. The old *Baseball Weekly* "Stop the Madness!" stuff.

The worst thing, though, was all the pontificating about how awful all this slugging is because it's out of context with the rest of baseball history and how terrible that guys who aren't really great sluggers are putting up big numbers. What the hell does he think the 1920s and '30s were like? And how about the deadball era. . . isn't winning 35 games with a 1.20 ERA "out of context" too?

Relax, Bob, and enjoy 1996. It's one of the most fun seasons I can ever remember.

HENZLER: I agree with Don. I was talking with a researcher at ESPN yesterday after yet another report lamenting the deplorable state of major league pitching, and I said that we should be celebrating the current surge in offense. As we all know, these things run in cycles, and yes, the quality of pitching has been affected by a number of factors, but the era we're living through is a special one. Let's appreciate it.

SICKELS: Speaking of the All-Star game announcers. . .

Joe Morgan was a great player. Joe Morgan seems to be a bright man. Joe Morgan seems to be a nice man.

Joe Morgan leaves a lot to be desired as an announcer. I actually turned the channel off of the game a few times, flipped to CNN, checked out the hurricane on the Weather Channel, just to get away from him. . . and what, exactly, is Bob Costas' attitude problem? I wanted to throw a brick through the set when he brought up the strike at the end of the game.

Did these things irritate anyone as much as they irritated me? Or am I just irritable?

FAUST: I can't stand Joe Morgan either. He falls into every trap we try to expose, and poor Jon Miller (who's one of my favorites) is stuck with him.

A month or two back, during a Rockies game, they threw a stat on the screen that showed the home/road home-run splits from 1995 for Bichette, Walker, Castilla, et al, and Morgan is sitting there arguing that these guys can hit anywhere. Huh?

Then he got to talking about how plenty of hitters play in small parks, like that Albert Belle. . . The Jake isn't a pitchers haven, but it doesn't help Albert hit home runs one bit.

It's almost comical, really.

SICKELS: Exactly. I remember that Rockie thing, and the Albert Belle thing. In the game yesterday, did anybody catch how when the A.L. couldn't get a runner home from second base, according to Morgan this showed how the American League plays a more selfish style of baseball, hoping for the home run instead of moving runners over. Gee, I just thought it meant that in this particular game, at that particular inning, they didn't get the runner home. I see the Cubs do that all the time. . .

QUINN: John, next time, consider radio. I enjoyed Jerry Coleman and Jeff Torborg.

MILLER: I prefer watching it on Sports Trax. That way I can make up my own play-by-play!

JAMES: Jerry Coleman is every bit as bad as Joe Morgan. I *did* listen to the radio for a good bit of the game. When Dante Bichette came up, they spent several minutes wondering how the Angels and Brewers could have given up on a *great* hitter like this, and then speculating about what could have caused his amazing transition. Coleman summed it up, eventually, something like this, only he went on for about 12 times as long:

Sometimes when a young hitter gets into a park, like Coors Field, where good things happen when he just makes contact with the ball, that will help him to relax, and let his confidence start to grow, and then when he gets his confidence up, he can hit in any ballpark.

This was all that he *said*, but he used the word "confidence" at least 40 times in getting it said.

I've known Bob Costas since 1978, and I consider him a friend, but frankly we both seem to be turning into cranky old bastards. He's turning into a cranky old bastard who bitches about how the game isn't what it used to be. I'm turning into a cranky old bastard who just can't *stand* to listen to announcers running down the modern game.

ZMINDA: I'd still like to see McGwire, Belle or Thomas playing 81 games at Coors. I'm sure it would do wonders for their "confidence."

I talk regularly with a Milwaukee radio guy who saw Bichette throughout his career with the Brewers, and he insists this is still the same old Dante. Maybe Jerry Coleman and Joe Morgan can set him straight. . .

PINTO: I agree about Uecker. I was happy to see that Costas tried to stop acting as his straight man. I really disliked that last year.

COOPERSON: The work of Jerry Coleman is a huge insult to every announcer who works hard at knowing the teams and the players whose games they are announcing.

July 11—Attendance

Attendance this year, on a per-game basis, is about five percent higher than in 1995. However, it's more than 15 percent *lower* than in 1993, the last full season before the strike.

Does this indicate a serious erosion in interest since the strike—that a lot of fans have lost interest in the game and are never coming back? Many people are saying that, but I'm not sure I agree with them. Let's look at the average attendance per game over the last 10 years. I prefer studying attendance on a per-game basis, rather than per date, because until the last 20 years or so, doubleheaders were an intentional gimmick designed to pull in more fans than would show up for two single games. That's important when studying attendance over the course of baseball history. These days doubleheaders are almost always makeups of games that have been postponed, but there are so few of them that it doesn't make much difference to the study. Anyway, here are the figures:

Major Lg Attendance, Last 10 Years

Year	Per Game	Year	Per Game
1987	24,709	1992	26,530
1988	25,238	1993	30,964
1989	26,198	1994	31,256
1990	26,045	1995	25,022
1991	27,003	1996	*26,078

* Through All-Star Break

As you can see, the "troubling" 1996 attendance level is pretty much the same as that of most seasons in the recent past. What makes it *look* bad are the two years in which the major leagues averaged more than 30,000 fans a game, 1993 and 1994. However, those years were undoubtedly aberrations, and attendance almost certainly would have dropped even *without* the strike. There are several reasons for this, starting with the National League expansion of 1993. One of the two new teams, the Colorado Rockies, spent 1993-94 playing in Mile High Stadium, which had a seating capacity of more than 70,000. The combination of big park, new team and entertaining, high-scoring games led to attendance levels that were unprecedented in baseball history—nearly 4.5 million fans in 1993 alone. In 1995, however, the Rockies moved to the much smaller Coors Field (capacity 50,200). Interest among Denver fans remains high, but 1993-94 attendance levels are simply impossible; Rockies attendance at Coors is about 10,000 fans a game lower than in the Mile High years. As for the other new team, the Florida Marlins, they followed the typical pattern of a new club with a bad record: high attendance in Year 1, then a dropoff. The Marlins averaged nearly 38,000 fans a game in 1993, 33,000 in 1994, then 24,000 in '95.

The 1994 attendance numbers were boosted by the addition of new parks in Cleveland and Texas. Jacobs Field in Cleveland turned out to be a big success, and *that* combination—great new park and great young team—has kept Jacobs filled to capacity. The Ballpark in Arlington, though, didn't seem to provide quite the same kind of lasting impression, and when the Rangers had a bad year in 1995, attendance dropped by nearly 12,000 fans a game. The strike was a factor, sure, but as far the case with the Marlins, attendance would have dropped off significantly anyway.

With all those factors at work, it's no surprise that baseball attendance hasn't approached the artificially high levels of 1993-94. This is not to say that there aren't real problems; we all know there are, and baseball *should* be concerned with them. But the extent of the problems are being exaggerated. Averaging 25,000-plus people a game over a six-month, 162-game season is no mean feat. Know what the average attendance was in 1927, the year Babe Ruth hit 60 homers? A little over 8,000 fans a game. Baseball didn't average 10,000 spectators a game until 1946, and the highest average attendance in the 1950s—"The Golden

Age," by many accounts—was 15,464 per game in 1959. Some Golden Age. The major leagues finally cracked the 20,000-per game barrier for the first time in 1979, and attendance first averaged 25,000 a game in 1988—exactly eight seasons ago. The last 10 years have been the most well-attended in baseball history. . . by far.

So tell me baseball's been having problems; I'll agree with you. But don't tell me baseball's dying. It just ain't so.

— Don Zminda

July 15—Live from the All-Star Game!

DARRRYYYLLLLL!!!!! DARRRYYYLLLLL!!!!!!

Let me begin with some random observations from my first in-person All-Star game, before they get too stale:

1) The neatest thing, I found, about being at the game in person was watching the groups of players that formed who weren't on the same team. For example, Mo Vaughn and Frank Thomas spent the pre-game walking around the field together. Then they'd run into another group, shake hands, talk, etc. It was like observing a cocktail party of major league players. I also noticed that Albert Belle seemed to be as friendly with his fellow players as anyone else, which struck me as a little unusual, considering the ogre the media creates.

2) I've never seen Vet Stadium with nary an empty seat before.

3) The organist played Billy Idol's "Rebel Yell" (you know, "Mo, mo, mo") every time Vaughn batted. Pretty clever, I have to admit.

4) When Ripken batted, the organist played this music like they'd play when the president enters the room or something and some people would give standing ovations. For heaven sakes, enough already, people. Why don't the Orioles have a "Kiss Cal's Old Grey-Haired Butt Night" where fans can line up and plant a big wet one on his stinky buns? Then maybe we could be done with this "We're Not Worthy" crap once and for all.

5) Most of the crowd booed loudly when Belle batted, proving that they've thoroughly digested the sheep feed the media's been giving them since poor Hannah got yelled at. I cheered, and of course was mad when Belle whiffed like every time up. I have to give creativity credit to the two guys who carried the "Two Cracked Belles in Philly (Liberty and Albert)" banner, however.

6) Some guy carried around a banner that had "Clinton Sucks" on one side and something good about Dole on the other. Don't bore me with politics at a baseball game, man. I think some security guys made him put it away. I'm not sure if I like that or not.

7) They probably didn't show this on TV, but another guy in a Flyers shirt jumped out of the seats behind first base, dove into second, then got up and almost made it back into the stands around third base before the stormtroopers tackled him. Ozzie Smith was at shortstop

and just stood there. I think everyone in the park thought the guy wanted to: a) tackle, b) shake hands with, or c) kill Ozzie because the guy headed straight for him. It was really a little tense, but the guy was just interested in diving into second and Ozzie didn't seem to care at all.

8) Just so you know, I yelled something nasty about hitting ability and Coors Field each time Bichette batted, even though no one but the people around me could hear it. I felt it was my duty as a baseball fan.

9) I think it's time to give up on "gress-UHL-lawn-neck," the way the Expo media guide tells me to pronounce it, after the All-Star game PA guy repeatedly said, "grud-zuh-LAN-ik." Do I have the only copy of their media guide? Did Mark decide to change the pronunciation of his name since he's become a star? Is the Expo pronunciation just a cruel joke intended to create mental anguish for "get-a-life's" like me?

There was a real gripe session going on via E-mail last week about the sad job both the radio and TV announcers did for the All-Star game. Wrong numbers, Morgan saying that Bichette can hit anywhere, etc. I, fortunately, didn't have to listen to anyone but the fans booing Belle. And it'll stay that way until people other than ex-jocks automatically get those jobs. Who decided that the best people to analyze and comment on a complex game are the same guys who are the best at running fast and jumping high and hitting the bejeezuz out of a baseball? Would the most skilled sewing machine operator in the plant be the person most qualified to explain how the textile industry works?

— Steve Moyer

July 16—The Meek Have Started Inheriting

Well, it finally happened.

When Earl Weaver moved Cal Ripken from third base to shortstop back in 1982, people said, "That's nuts. He's too big to play short. He'll be going back to third as soon as the Orioles come to their senses."

After Ripken had settled in at short, the '82 Orioles made up seven games in the last month and a half and tied the Brewers for first place on the next-to-last day of the season. The next day, the Brewers defeated them for the A.L. East title, but for the time being at least, Ripken was allowed to remain at shortstop.

The next year the Orioles won the Series, and Cal won the MVP award. People talked about how big he was for a shortstop, and everyone seemed to agree that he'd have to move to third base eventually.

That kind of talk went on for 14 years, more or less. During that time, Cal set the A.L. record for most assists in a season by a shortstop (1984) and set the major league record for highest fielding percentage by a shortstop (1990). He also won another MVP award in 1991.

It's a bit absurd to have to point this out, but over the last 14 years, Cal has proved that he can play the position. So why is it that the third base talk has never completely died out? Maybe Cal should have concentrated less on becoming a better shortstop and more on simply becoming *smaller*.

When he came to the park last night, he found that his position had been given to Manny Alexander. Alexander, who is six inches shorter and 70 pounds lighter than Cal, has been called the "shortstop of the future," either for Baltimore or for someone else.

Now, I don't have a problem with this, at least from Cal's standpoint. Ripken has had a wonderful career in the middle infield, but I certainly don't think he's earned the right to play there until he keels over. If Davey Johnson believes that he can put a better team on the field with Alexander at short and Ripken at third, then he's obviously doing the right thing. However unpopular the move may be with Ripken or the fans, Johnson is just doing his job—he's trying to win.

But that's where I've got a problem. When people look at Alexander, they see a guy who physically resembles Ozzie Guillen. He simply *looks* like a shortstop, so people are perfectly willing to leap to the conclusion that he can actually play baseball. The impression holds until you actually watch him play.

Can Manny Alexander help a team win? Sure. He does it all the time. The problem is that it's the Orioles' *opponents* that he helps.

Alexander was tagged as a "prospect" several years ago, and despite doing what simply comes naturally to him, he's been unable to shake the label. In his first season in Double-A, he hit .259 with no power. The next season, he played in Triple-A and hit .244 with no power. He remained there the following year, hitting .249 with no power. Last year, he finally made it to Baltimore. He hit only .236, and you know what? He showed absolutely zero power. Funny; he was supposed to be such a good prospect and all.

Now, with his average at .150, Johnson apparently feels that the team would be much improved with Alexander in the lineup. He's been trying to get him in there all year, for some reason. I remember one time earlier in the year when Davey sent him in to pinch-run for Cal in the late innings of a tight game. Alexander promptly got himself picked off. The game ended up going well into extra innings while Cal sat fuming on the bench.

But still, Davey's just got to get Manny in there. Well, my suggestion is that someone should measure the ceiling height in the Baltimore dugout. Davey seems to have been banging his head on something.

Of course, everyone knows that the real reason they're playing Alexander is to showcase him for trades. But how good of an idea is that? It seems that his reputation would bring in a lot more in trade than his actual performance would. If people want to believe that he can play, the *last* thing I'd ever do is to let him step out of the dugout and destroy that illusion.

—Mat Olkin

July 18—Baseball Movies

What are your favorite baseball movies? It's probably fair to say that there have been more good films made about baseball than about any other sport, and there have also been more than a few clunkers. I thought I'd use this week's column to list my own favorites, along with brief comments on a number of other baseball films. Then I'd like to hear from you. Let's get right into it.

The Zee-Man's 10 Favorite Baseball Movies

1. "Bull Durham." I like everything about this movie. . . except maybe for the fact that Tim Robbins isn't *quite* convincing as a pitcher who throws 100 MPH. Kevin Costner *does* look a real athlete, however, and Robbins is great in all the other scenes. The other performances are all excellent, the script is really funny, and the portrayal of life in the minor leagues is excellent. Throw in the fact that I was once desperately in love with a woman who looked a lot like Susan Sarandon (I was the player she chose for the "1984 season"), and you have an obvious number one.

2. "The Natural." I was at a SABR convention a few months after "The Natural" came out, and Bill James asked me what I thought of it. Before I could answer, he said, "I thought it stunk." So I guess this is a controversial choice, particularly among people who love Bernard Malamud's novel. Well, I liked the novel *and* the movie, though the film is obviously very Hollywood with the happy ending and all—completely different from the book. I'll admit that a lot of it is pretty sappy, but the game sequences really work for me; in particular, the buildup to the pennant-winning homer really captures the tension of a big game. And there are some nice, subtle touches that make it seem real—the photographers with the cameras and flashbulbs standing near home plate, for instance, or the fact (never mentioned, you just have to notice it) that Roy Hobbs has trouble with low, inside pitches. Like Kevin Costner, Robert Redford really *looks* like an athlete, and that helps, too. But what really seals the deal for me is Randy Newman's music—one of the best scores ever for *any* kind of movie, baseball or not.

3. "Field of Dreams." Also sappy, also corny. . . but like "The Natural," it works. Kevin Costner is great again, though not as a ballplayer this time. The story is so good that I'll forgive things like having Shoeless Joe Jackson bat right and throw left (it was the other way around). Anyway, how can you not like a movie that has both Burt Lancaster *and* James Earl Jones in it?

4. "Bang the Drum Slowly." A terrific movie, based on a terrific book by Mark Harris. One thing that hurts it is that neither one of the male leads, Robert DeNiro and Michael Moriarty, is very convincing in the baseball scenes. But they're such great actors that I got past that. And the story is great, also. If you haven't seen this one, check it out.

5. "It Happens Every Spring." Pretty lightweight, but I love it. It's the story of a college professor played by Ray Milland who accidentally invents this chemical that repels wood. . . meaning that if you rub the stuff on a baseball and then throw it at a guy swinging a bat,

the ball will jump *over* the bat. So naturally the professor becomes the greatest pitcher in baseball and hurls the St. Louis Browns (I think it's the Browns. . . it's *some* St. Louis club) to the pennant.

6. "Eight Men Out." Great John Sayles movie about the Black Sox scandal. Unlike Sayles, I don't hold much sympathy toward the guys who sold out—I mean, does the fact that Shoeless Joe was illiterate mean that he couldn't distinguish right from wrong? Despite that, Sayles is such a good filmmaker that this movie really works.

7. "Long Gone." Not a very well-known film, this was an HBO made-for-TV movie about a minor league team called the Tampico Stogies. Very entertaining, with great performances by William Peterson and Virginia Madsen.

8. "Major League." Another lightweight movie, but extremely funny with an all-star cast including Wesley Snipes, Charlie Sheen, Corbin Benson, Tom Berenger and Bob Uecker, whose "*Just* a bit outside. . ." call is one of the all-time classics in baseball filmdom.

9. "Soul of the Game." A recent HBO movie about Jackie Robinson, Josh Gibson and Satchel Paige, all vying to become the first black player to break the color line. There are a number of historical inaccuracies in this movie, but the story and the performances are so great that I was able to get past that.

10. "Pride of the Yankees." I'm sure a lot of people would have ranked this one higher, but it's about 100 times as corny as "The Natural," and the ballfield sequences don't work at all due to Gary Cooper's extreme awkwardness. Also, it's dumb: in the movie they take Gehrig out of a game already in progress, and the announcer starts moaning, "The streak is over!" No, it isn't, you knucklehead; he's already *played* in this game! (Let's hope they don't make this mistake in "Pride of the Orioles.") But the scenes at the end are powerful enough to make up (mostly) for the other stuff. And there's a big bonus in the movie: Babe Ruth, playing himself. He's fabulous, of course.

So that's the top 10. Now for some random comments on other baseball movies I've seen, in no particular order:

"The Bad News Bears." Very funny flick, nearly made the top 10. I wish they hadn't made all those sequels, though.

"Major League II." Ditto; this sequel was so lame it was embarrassing.

"Fear Strikes Out." Tony Perkins is so stiff and awkward as Jimmy Piersall that he makes Gary Cooper look athletic. Otherwise a winner, though.

"The Jackie Robinson Story." Not bad, with Jackie playing himself. He's the best actor in the movie.

"The Stratton Story." Jimmy Stewart as Monty Stratton, the 1930s White Sox pitcher who shot off his leg in a hunting accident. Stewart's great in everything, and when you toss in one of the ultimate 1940s babes, June Allyson, you've got a winner.

"The Pride of St. Louis." Dan Dailey as Dizzy Dean. Another movie with unathletic-actor problems. Sort of fun, but this movie would have been *much* better with Dizzy playing himself.

"The Winning Team." Ronald Reagan as Grover Cleveland Alexander, with Doris Day as his wife. Didn't buy it. Reagan was a much better president than he was a pitcher. . . and as for Doris, I would have much preferred a movie about her real-life affair with Maury Wills. (Now *there's* a story!)

"Mr. Baseball." This one got panned by the critics, but I kind of liked it. Like Kevin Costner and Robert Redford, Tom Sellick really *looks* like a ballplayer, and that helps a lot.

"Tiger Town." Roy Scheider as a washed-up Detroit Tiger whose career gets revived because of a kid's wish. Not the worst baseball movie I've ever seen, but it doesn't have enough redeeming features to make up for all the corn.

"Rookie of the Year." This 12-year-old kid breaks his arm, and when it heals he can throw 95 MPH fastballs. So naturally he pitches the Cubs to a pennant. Yeah, sure.

"Little Big League." In this one, a different 12-year-old kid—actually, it might have been the same one—inherits the Minnesota Twins. So he makes himself the manager and leads them to victory. Kid, you're no Tom Kelly. But I did like this film better than "Rookie of the Year."

"The Scout." The only unfunny movie Albert Brooks ever made. Actually, this film does have a few funny scenes, but most of it is just plain awful. . . like the big climax in Game 1 of the World Series, where the kid phee-nom discovered by Albert throws the ultimate perfect game: 81 pitches, 27 three-pitch strikeouts. Surrrrre. Heck, Ray Milland threw pitches that could dodge the bat, and even *he* never did anything like this.

"Angels in the Outfield." There are two versions of this; I've only seen the more recent one with Danny Glover. I hope the first one was better.

"Talent for the Game." Another HBO movie (I think) about a scout played by Edwin James Olmos who signs a phee-nom for the Angels. In the big climactic scene, Edwin James secretly inserts himself into the game as the catcher to calm his young phee-nom down. Wonder if Joe Torre has thought of this?

"Cooperstown." TNT movie about two old-time ballplayers; one, Alan Alda, makes the Hall of Fame; the other, played by one of those Indian guys in "Dances with Wolves" (another Kevin Costner connection!), doesn't like it 'cause Alan Alda killed him (I think). It's better than it sounds, particularly among those of you who remembered it better than I do.

"The Sandlot." A kid's movie about the angst of being a young sandlotter. My colleague Tony Nistler calls it "The Wonder Years" of baseball. Lots of good scenes.

"Stealing Home." Mark Harmon comes to grips with the death of his former babysitter, played by Jodie Foster. This movie was written by Will Aldis, a former member of Second

City, and (this is really true!) I knew both Will Aldis and his babysitter! All I can say is, she was no Jodie Foster.

"The Babe Ruth Story." Not the worst baseball movie I've ever seen, and only the second-worst movie ever made about Babe Ruth. As Bob Costas has pointed out, this film's so bad at times that it's good, with stuff like a choir of kids humming "Take Me Out to the Ballgame" from out on the street while the Babe's dying in his hospital room.

"The Babe." This truly *is* the worst baseball movie I've ever seen. I like John Goodman, but when it comes to playing the Babe, even William Bendix was better. Which is saying something. Every frame is awful.

— Don Zminda

July 19—Rickey

Despite just a .227 batting average this season, Rickey Henderson has already drawn 82 walks and has an on-base percentage over .400. Although Rickey's league may have switched, his hitting philosophy certainly hasn't. He's taken the first pitch more than 90 percent of the time this season with San Diego, something he's done throughout his career. If there's ever been a .227 threat from the leadoff spot, it's Rickey. Note also that Rickey is the only N.L. player in the top 10. That's not surprising considering the diminished quality (even after you adjust for league differences) among A.L. pitchers.

Since Henderson will easily surpass 100 walks in '96, I thought it might be interesting to see which players have had at least that many walks and compiled a very low batting average. Here are the 10 worst single-season batting averages in baseball history for players with at least 100 walks:

Player, Team	Year	Walks	Avg
Eddie Joost, Athletics	1947	114	.206
Jimmy Wynn, Braves	1976	127	.207
Yank Robinson, St. Louis (AA)	1889	118	.208
Gene Tenace, Athletics	1974	110	.211
Eddie Lake, Tigers	1947	120	.211
Jack Crooks, St. Louis (N.L.)	1892	136	.213
Wes Westrum, Giants	1951	104	.219
Mickey Tettleton, Orioles	1990	106	.223
Roy Cullenbine, Tigers	1947	137	.224
Gene Tenace, Padres	1978	101	.224

Notice that three of the seasons come from 1947, part of an era (extending into the early 1950s) that saw an incredible number of walks in the major leagues. You'll also find some free-swinging power hitters on the list, particularly Jimmy Wynn (who struck out 111 times in 1976) and Gene Tenace (105 in '74 and 98 in '78). It's a strange combination, since you'd figure that any batter with enough plate discipline to draw 100 walks could get his batting average up to a respectable level. But it doesn't always work that way.

— Scott McDevitt

July 20—Does Jack Lang Know Anything About Baseball?

ZMINDA: Things I learned from the Sportsticker. . .

Did you see that quote from Jack Lang about Lance Johnson—"an ideal leadoff man even though he rarely walks?"

According to Lang, Johnson was the top free-agent signing of the season. I guess Tony Phillips doesn't qualify because he doesn't swing the bat enough.

MOYER: I see Lance Johnson is nowhere in the vicinity of the OBP leaders at his almost-acceptable .340 mark. He is a whopping tie for 8th in the N.L. runs scored leaders, though. Rickey Henderson, whom I'm sure *Jack Lang* would tell you is having a crappy year has 74 runs scored in 323 at-bats. Johnson has 72 runs scored in 433 at-bats. But, as all *Jack Langs* know, the important stats for a leadoff man are batting average and stolen bases (and maybe hits). But, let's not overlook the fact that he's a *fine influence in the clubhouse*. How do these cardboard same-old same-old columnists get or keep their jobs? Such groundbreaking stuff—rag on TV controlling baseball, rag on Strawberry, ho hum.

JAMES: Little Lancie Johnson

Actually, I was impressed that Lang actually *noticed* that Johnson doesn't walk. I took that to be a sign of progress.

July 22—Is the Ball *Really* Juiced This Season?

JAMES: Funny Stats of the Jumping Baseball

Kansas City Royals second basemen this year have hit 38 doubles, no more than 16 by any one players. At the rate they're going, their second basemen will wind up the season with 62 doubles.

PINTO: Does anyone believe that the ball is different? I have always found that theory hard to believe. Bill, what do you think is the reason for the offensive increase?

One insightful producer at ESPN notes that pitching has been diluted as much by expanding staffs to 11 pitchers as by expansion. Why, if pitching is so bad, do teams carry more of it?

SPEAR: I heard an interview with someone (Tony Gwynn, maybe?) who thought the increase in offense was due to the better bats. Better wood is being used and many players are going to lighter bats with ultra-thin handles so they can generate more bat speed.

Personally, I like this theory. It also (the thin handles part) explains why there are eight broken bats every game (or so it seems).

COOPERSON: Teams have to carry more pitchers because pitchers today have no durability.

JAMES: Pitching staffs have in fact expanded very rapidly in recent years, for no obvious reason, and I agree (and in fact mentioned in my last book) that this is contributing to the perceived shortage of pitching.

Yes, I think the ball itself is probably more lively than it was ten years ago. The nature of the baseball is that it is almost impossible *not* to alter it's construction over time, either by accident or design. There is, further, no standard of resiliency built into major league baseball's purchasing of baseballs. Look at it this way, why would there *not* be fluctuations in the resiliency of the balls over time?

I mean, suppose that, in purchasing shoes, you failed to control for the softness of the soles. Given the complexity of manufacturing shoes, the way in which shoes were manufactured would inevitably change over time, which would impact on any uncontrolled factor, such as the softness of the soles. You'd have hard-sole eras, and soft-sole eras.

Of course, that doesn't happen, because, in purchasing shoes, we do check out the soles, and if the soles are too hard, we don't buy the shoes. Baseball doesn't perform any resiliency test on baseballs. Inevitably, I think, you're going to have periodic fluctuations in the resliency of the balls.

An interesting study, I think, would be to identify the *parks* which are exactly the same now as they were ten years ago (pre-1987), and figure out how much runs per game have increased in the games played in those parks. Then, at least, we'd be able to divide the increases in offense accurately into two categories:

   a) that resulting from new ballparks,

   b) that *not* resulting from new ballparks.

PINTO: Baseball may not test the balls, but the manufacturer certainly does. I've talked to Rawlings, and they claim that they have very tight testing, and the balls they produce are the same and very consistent. I would love ESPN to do a story on the manufacture of baseballs and put the lively ball theory to rest, but they've never found the idea interesting enough (I guess they would rather depend on the subjective opinion of their analysts).

July 23—Kennedy's Crimes

Through the years, Red Sox fans have learned to expect that when crunch time came, the Sox would somehow end up a pitcher short. Whether it was Denny Galehouse, Jim Lonborg on two days' rest, or Mike Torrez, this has been the history of the Boston Red Sox.

Roger Clemens fills that void. Not only can he give the team two starts during a five-game playoff, but he can actually instill confidence that the series itself can be won. This is no mean feat in New England. Without Roger Clemens, there can be no hope, and thus, no pennant.

Kevin Kennedy gives little thought to such concerns. His main aim right now is to extend his day-to-day existence in uniform. By forcing Roger Clemens to throw a staggering 162 pitches on Sunday night, Kennedy has told Red Sox fans all too clearly: "Screw your tomorrows. I want another *today*."

Sunday night's game got that message across loud and clear. Fifteen games out of first, Kennedy managed like it was the seventh game of the World Series. Clemens battled Mussina deep into the night, and the Sox finally scratched out a couple of runs to take a 5-3 lead going into the ninth. Clemens had thrown a ton of pitches, and three outs away from victory, he began to falter. He put the tying runs on base with two out, bringing B.J. Surhoff to the plate.

The situation demanded a reliever. Clemens' pitch count was already into the 150s, one of the highest of the entire year—for anyone. Surhoff had always hit Clemens well, and lefty Mike Stanton was awaiting the call in the bullpen.

Kennedy simply refused to lift Clemens. He was determined that Roger was going to get this hitter, and the consequences be damned.

Damned, indeed. On Clemens' 162nd pitch of the game, Surhoff lined a triple into the triangle to tie the game. The Sox eventually lost the game (with Stanton working later), but that isn't what's important.

One hundred sixty-two pitches, *that* is what's important. How excessive is that? Well, there have been three individual pitch counts over 144 this year: Roger Clemens, 162; Tim Wakefield, 162; and Roger Clemens, 157.

Clemens himself has topped that number only once in the last nine years. He did throw 165 pitches in a game once, in August of 1990, but four weeks later, he went on the disabled list for several weeks with tendinitis. Of course, he was 27 years old back then; today he's 33.

And the worst part is that Sunday night was not just an isolated event. Kennedy has been working Clemens' shoulder to the bone for months now. Over his last 10 starts, he's thrown an average of 135.2 pitches, which is the shortest route to an arm injury this side of Philadelphia. During the decade of the '90s, *no* pitcher has thrown that many pitches over a 10-start span, save for one. Randy Johnson, at age 28, once threw 14 more total pitches over a 10-start stretch in late '92, but that's it. Aside from that, Clemens now holds the title of "Most Brutally Overworked Pitcher Of The Decade."

—Mat Olkin

July 1-30—Baseball Chatter

OLKIN: Bonds vs. Reynoso

Barry Bonds will be facing Armando Reynoso for the first time today in about three seconds. The Bonds-Reynoso match-up is one of the most lopsided in baseball. Going into this year, Bonds had a .778 OBP against him (third highest in baseball, min. 15 AB. Oops—make that 2nd highest). His SLG was 1.636 (third highest). That's 11 AB, 7 H, 2 HR and 7 BB. If the building starts to shake, you'll know why.

OLKIN: Bonds Update

First at-bat: two-run single.

Second at-bat vs. Reynoso: single.

PINTO: Odd coincidence

In St. Louis, in 1903 and 1904, Dave Brain played for the Cardinals, and Pinky Swander played for the Browns.

They did not succeed in taking over the world.

SPEAR: Darryl Strawberry. . .

Now that the Yankees have the best record in the majors, why on earth would they sign Mr. Distraction?

ZMINDA: The more HRs he hits, the less of a distraction he'll be. I don't recall any problems last year, do you?

PINTO: Edgar Martinez. . .

While I'm sure you're all aware that Edgar Martinez is on pace to break the doubles record, were you aware that he's also on pace to break the record for extra-base hits in a season? (119 by Babe Ruth in 1921). Ruth had 59 HR, 44 2B, 16 3B. Edgar's current pace would put him at 126!

HENZLER: Offensive Winning Percentage

Here are the leaders in offensive winning percentage, among players with at least 250 plate appearances....

Player	OW%
Mike Piazza	.820
Mark McGwire	.785
Gary Sheffield	.772
Edgar Martinez	.736
Chuck Knoblauch	.717

And the trailers....

Player	OW%
Mike Matheny	.115
Gary DiSarcina	.144
Mike Bordick	.181
Ron Karkovice	.224
Jody Reed	.241

The "great" Dante Bichette has an offensive winning percentage of .545, which ranks no better than 10th among all right fielders with at least 250 plate appearances. Bichette has created 6.63 runs per 27 outs, while teams are averaging 6.06 runs in all Rockie games.

How about that Knoblauch?

SICKELS: Over the last two weeks, the Twins have been playing mega-prospect Todd Walker at second base, despite the fact that he was playing quite nicely defensively at third. Is a trade of Knoblauch in the offing? Stay tuned. . .

PINTO: Game Streaks

With Thomas going down, here's the new active consecutive-game leaders: (Through the All-Star break)

Player	Games
Cal Ripken	2,239
Barry Bonds	316
Edgar Martinez	283
Sammy Sosa	267
Fred McGriff	253

Bonds last game missed was 5/6/94, Martinez 6/11/94, Sosa 7/2/94, and McGriff 7/20/94.

SICKELS: Kent Mercker

Kent Mercker has now walked 31 men in 53 innings. At what point do people start talking about Steve Blass Disease?

PINTO: Cal Ripken. . .

Will start at third base tonight.

COOPERSON: 101 days and counting

Dick Schofield has now now been on the DL since April 20, due to "personal reasons." Must've been a pretty bad problem.

OLKIN: I heard that he happened to take a peek at the *Baseball Encyclopedia*, and when he saw how closely his lifetime totals matched those of his father, he lapsed into a severe identity crisis.

August 2—Todd Van Poppel

SICKELS: Todd Van Poppel was designated for reassignment yesterday. This means that the Athletics will probably lose him on waivers. Does anybody think that he has any chance to develop at all now? I think his best bet would be to end up with somebody like the Dodgers or Braves, and to go back to Double-A and rebuild his career. Opinions?

WOELFLEIN: He's 24 years old. If he had gone to college and then the minors, he might be just making his debut now. I have no doubt that he still can, and will, develop into a quality pitcher. You can probably name numbers of pitchers who didn't *really* develop until almost 30.

MOYER: I always hoped Van Poppel would succeed, mostly because everyone else seemed to be hoping for him to fail I guess. Van Poppel never has shown much of anything either in the minors or the majors. He walks way too many guys. He seemed to maybe be getting the hang of things last season, especially in relief, but he was horrible in either role this season and even his impressive strikeout totals have fallen. I think I totally agree with John that Van Poppel's only hope is to be babied for a year or two or three. He's only 24, could screw around in the minors for three or four years and still have a major league career. Wouldn't it be funny if he ended up succeeding for the Braves? Remember how the mighty A's "pulled one over" on the hapless Braves and lured Van Poppel into signing while the poor Braves had to settle for Chipper Jones? How things change in a few short years.

In addition—I'll bet the media and the average fan will perceive Van Poppel as "washed up" and if he does have success later on it will be a big shock to everyone. This seems to happen time and time again. The Red Sox just picked up the same kind of "washed up" 24 year old in Roberto Mejia. You can't be washed up when you're talented and 24.

SICKELS: The main problem I see is that he no longer has the velocity he did in high school. In high school he threw 93-95 MPH. Now he throws 89 MPH on a good day, at least when I've seen him. He has good movement on his curve, but can't throw it for strikes. The only hope for him as I see it is to 1) get with an organization that *doesn't* need pitching and won't rush him; 2) go to Double-A; and 3) stay there for a long time and learn to pitch.

If the Tigers, Twins or Giants claim him, he'll continue to struggle. If he ends up with the Braves or the Dodgers, he *might* turn it around. It is too early to say he's washed up... Steve is right, he's just 24, and many pitchers develop late. But I think in his case he needs a certain set of circumstances to maximize his chances.

ZMINDA: I agree that it's way too early to give up on him. I'm kind of surprised that the A's are releasing him. . . you'd think they could get *something* for him. Sometimes a guy just needs a new team.

Steve's comment on the A's "putting one over" on the Braves in drafting Van Poppel reminded me of another guy: Josh Booty. Everybody thought the Marlins put one over on the other teams by picking Booty, who was supposedly certain to go to LSU to play football. Now Booty better hope someone gives him a chance to toss the pigskin, because he sure can't play baseball.

SICKELS: Booty is a complete disaster. It is interesting that the Marlins seem to have learned something about tools vs. performance. This year they drafted Mark Kotsay, an outfielder from Cal State Fullerton and the Olympic Team, in the first round. Kotsay doesn't have tools. All he does is hit and play baseball.

OLKIN: Van Poppel seemed to be doing very well in middle relief last year, with marked improvement in all phases of his game, especially his control. After they moved him back into the rotation, he did well for his first six or seven starts. The only problem was that he was throwing too many pitches to go deep into games. At that point, I think La Russa and Dave Duncan may have pressured him to throw more strikes. Over his last six or seven starts, his pitches per batter dropped tremendously, but he got completely hammered.

I think he can still have a good career, but there are only two scenarios where I can see him succeeding. The first one is the "Eric Plunk scenario." Considering his dramatic turnaround when he was moved to middle relief early last season, I think he can thrive there. His control would be less of a liability in that role, and pitchers with equally poor control (Plunk) have made it work.

His other chance for success is to fall into the hands of a manager who can accept the fact that he's going to be a six-inning pitcher if he's put in the rotation. I think Felipe Alou is very sensitive to a pitcher's limits, and Van Poppel would do quite well for him. He just throws too many pitches to go nine, but he showed last year that he can pitch well in the rotation if you can live with the fact that he'll work deep counts and tire before the seventh inning.

SICKELS: Todd Van Poppel? In Tiger Stadium? Like Charlton Heston said at the end of "Planet of the Apes"—oh my God. . .

OLKIN: Hey, this is good news for those who want to see Maris' record broken.

MOYER: By the way—any opinions on the Red Sox snagging Greg Pirkl? I never could figure out why he never got any kind of a real chance in Seattle. It seems like Piniella sometimes just has a mindset that he hates a guy and won't play him no matter what.

ZMINDA: I like Pirkl, too, and never could understand why Seattle didn't give him a chance. I think this is a really good move by the Red Sox.

OLKIN: Pirkl's a 30-homer guy, but doesn't do much else. I guess he'll fill the Sox' glaring need for another DH.

August 6—Trade Winds

I love the Greg Vaughn deal—from both ends. Each team got exactly what it needed. The Padres finally addressed a lack of power that has lingered since the offseason, and I'm picking them to win the West.

After finishing 11th in the league in home runs last year, it was clear that the Padres lacked power. With the left field spot open, they had the perfect opportunity to go get a run producer over the offseason. . . and they blew it. With a lineup already top-heavy with on-base men like Finley, Gwynn and Joyner, they went out and got Rickey Henderson. Not only did that signing add something they already had, but it clogged up the one spot where they could have added a power hitter. This has become increasingly obvious as this season has worn on.

But rather than be bullheaded about it, the Padres simply admitted their mistake and moved to correct it. Hey, after spending millions on Rickey, it would have been very easy for them to be stubborn about it. GMs don't like to admit they're wrong any more than you or I do. You see it all the time. For instance, right now you've got the Dodgers maintaining that all their offense needs is a Chad Curtis or two. Earlier, the Red Sox kept insisting that Wil Cordero was going to be their second baseman, come hell or high spikes.

The Padres didn't do that. They had a problem, and even though it was of their own creation, they faced up to it. They paid a steep price, but they fixed the problem.

One cost of the trade is that they'll need to find a taker for Henderson, who does not envision himself (we may safely assume) as a fourth outfielder. And then there's the price they paid in talent.

When I saw who the Brewers got for Vaughn, I was floored. And based on the messages I've been getting, I wasn't the only one who was impressed with Sal Bando's horse trading. For Vaughn, who's 30 years old, earning a ton of money, and due to become a free agent at the end of the year, the Brewers got:

1. Marc Newfield. One of the youngest players in the league at age 23, Newfield is capable of hitting .280 with a ton of doubles right now. He's shown a remarkable ability to put good wood on the ball in the minors, and he projects to mature into a middle-of-the-order hitter.

2. Ron Villone. An absolutely dominant left-handed short reliever who's struck out a man an inning wherever he's gone. At age 26, he should be just coming into his prime.

3. Bryce Florie. Also 26, he throws a heavy fastball that produces whiffs and ground balls. He's a good set-up man, and could eventually go beyond that role.

Does that strike you as a substantial return? Consider this: last year at this time, Andy Benes was traded for Newfield and Villone alone. Based on that, the Brewers should have been happy just to get those two guys. But they got a *lot* more: first, they got Florie, and second they got a Marc Newfield and a Ron Villone who were one year more experienced. Each of them have developed over the last year, and the Brewers are expecting each of them to contribute in the second half.

How did Sal Bando wring so much out of the Padres? Well, he took advantage of two things. First, the Padres *needed* to make this deal. They had been dealing off their players for years, and the fans had long since tired of it. Now that they were finally in a pennant race, they absolutely *had* to make a pennant race-type of deal. If they hadn't, the fans would have said, "See? They're throwing in the towel again," and they would have abandoned the bleachers for the beach.

Second, the Padres could afford to part with some of their middle relievers. They were one of the few (only?) organizations in baseball with a glut of pitching talent. Look what they did—after tossing away Villone and Florie, they simply called up Dustin Hermanson and Dario Veras, and suddenly, their bullpen was back to its dominant self.

So the Padres have become my pick for the N.L. West title because they still have the deepest pitching staff in the league, and they've now filled their single-most glaring need. The Murph has always been a good park for a right-handed power hitter (Sheffield used to go nuts there), and Vaughn's eyes will light up when he sees Finley, Gwynn and Joyner on base ahead of him. He may not continue to put up A.L. playground stats, but he'll do the job. And he'll do a heck of a lot more for the Padres than Chad Curtis will for the Dodgers.

—Mat Olkin

August 6—Johnny Mac Returns

SICKELS: Marcel Lachemann has resigned as manager of the Angels. Three members of his coaching staff have been fired. John McNamara has been appointed manager.

COOPERSON: Maybe McNamara will bring Dave Henderson or Donnie Moore to the Angels.

MILLER: I think Donnie Moore would be a tough sell. I think he likes his closer role in heaven!

SICKELS: Who, exactly, does John McNamara have pictures of? How'd he get the Angels job? I think they would have been better off hiring Snake Plissken.

MOYER: McNamara has postseason experience. What more could you want from a manager? (He's probably great in the clubhouse and knows when to hit the ball to the right side too.) A proven loser is better than taking a chance.

PINTO: My understanding is that Mac is there to finish out the string. He isn't the Angels long-term solution, and won't be there next year.

OLKIN: Ten games out, we give up!!! Too bad for the Angels that the Mariners didn't hire John McNamara last year.

SICKELS: Yeah, I know he's just temporary. . . but still. I guess I just don't like the whole idea of interim managers anyway.

ZMINDA: If Johnny Mac doesn't work out, I guess they'll turn to Gene Mauch or Bill Rigney.

August 6—Odds and Ends

MILLER: The Reds started Kevin Mitchell at first base today! He makes a good target!

MOYER: Did any of you happen to notice the Giants' lineup today? You know I don't believe in that protection crap any more than the next good sabermetrician, but it's like Barry and the Bums out there today.

KRETSCHMANN: Todd Zeile. . .

His four errors at first is the most since Glenn Davis turned the trick on 4/18/91. Nobody else since '87 has had that many errors at first in a single game.

COOPERSON: Better yet—Zeile struck out three times and had four errors. Has anyone else had the sum total of their strikeouts and errors in a game equal or surpass seven?

MUNDO (August 15) Question: Should Pittsburgh's John Ericks be a starter or reliever?

Daily pitching log for John Ericks

From Opening Day to 4/20/96 (before being sent to Triple-A):

ERA	G	W	L	Sv	SvOp	GS	CG	ShO	GF	IP	H	R	ER	HR	TBB	SO
10.20	4	0	3	0	0	4	0	0	0	15.0	27	19	17	5	5	15

From 7/24/96 to Today (after a stint in the minors):

ERA	G	W	L	Sv	SvOp	GS	CG	ShO	GF	IP	H	R	ER	HR	TBB	SO
1.38	9	3	0	2	3	0	0	0	4	13.0	9	2	2	0	8	8

Or maybe a better question: What the heck did they do to him in Calgary?

SICKELS: Ericks' mechanics were all messed up. The pitching coach at Calgary had worked with him in the past, so they sent him there to get his mechanics worked out. I think he would be better off in relief. . . he has a good arm, but a terrible injury history and he has no stamina.

SPEAR (August 20): Highlights from today's Marlins/Cubs game

Florida starter Mark Hutton was taken out of the game with a no-hitter going. Cubs starter Kevin Foster lost his perfect game when he walked a relief pitcher. Foster had a triple and a double by the third inning and ended up with more total bases (five) then the Marlins (two). Sammy Sosa got his 100th RBI of the year on a bases-loaded HBP. The Cubs scored eight runs in the first without a homer. The Marlins' two hits were from guys whose average size is 5-9, 153 lbs.

August 8—Best Baseball Books

A few weeks ago, I wrote a column about my favorite baseball movies. It generated quite a bit of reader response, so I thought it might be fun to get into a kindred subject: favorite baseball books. I'll list my own top 10, using these guidelines:

1. Nonfiction books only. Baseball novels are a whole different category, and I'll cover them in another column.

2. No encyclopedias, annuals or books containing statistics only. That leaves out *Total Baseball*, the *Elias Analyst*, the *Bill James Abstracts*, the *Baseball Register*, etc. Again, I would consider such books a separate category.

That said, here's my personal top 10.

1. *A False Spring* by Pat Jordan. One of my favorite books in *any* category, sports or no. Before becoming a writer, Jordan was a bonus baby who pitched for several years in the Milwaukee Braves' farm system. The book is the story of Jordan's baseball career. . . and a lot more. The writing is incredibly vivid; he puts you right there as he struggles to become both a pitcher and a man.

2. *The Glory of Their Times* by Lawrence Ritter. This book makes virtually every top 10 list, and with good reason. If you're not familiar with it, it's a book of interviews with former players, most of them stars from the early years of the 20th century. There have been a million books of "interviews with ex-players" since Ritter invented the genre, but nobody ever did it better than he did. These players—guys like Davy Jones, Smokey Joe Wood, Al Bridwell and Rube Marquard—had some amazing stories to tell, and Ritter had a rare gift for getting them to open up.

3. *The Pitch That Killed* by Mike Sowell. Another book that makes the past come alive. It's the story of Ray Chapman, the only player ever killed in a major league game, and Carl Mays, the man who threw the pitch. The story itself is incredible, and so is Sowell's writing. I would feel very comfortable putting this book first on the list.

4. *Babe* by Robert Creamer. Creamer's bio of Babe Ruth is generally considered the best baseball biography ever, and I agree with that assessment. It's the Babe, warts and all, but somehow knowing the whole story does nothing to diminish his status.

5. The *Bill James Historical Baseball Abstract*. There are a lot of statistics in this book, but it isn't really a stat book. Bill goes through baseball history decade by decade, with extensive

commentary on all the top players. It's Bill at his best; you can turn to any page of the book, start reading, and find something of interest. Bill is apparently going to do an updated version of this book in the near future, and I can't wait.

6. *The Unforgettable Season* by G.H. Fleming. One of the more unique baseball books ever published. Fleming's book tells the story of the incredible 1908 National League pennant race—the one in which Fred Merkle missed second base—through the newspaper accounts of the period. If you think that "tabloid journalism" is something that began with Geraldo Rivera, check out this book.

7. *The Long Season* by Jim Brosnan. The first of the baseball diaries, and still the best of the genre by far, in my opinion. It's a wonderfully funny account of Brosnan's experiences pitching for the Cardinals and Reds in 1959, from the day his contract arrives to the end of the season. I read it again this spring, and it seemed as great as ever to me. Brosnan's sequel, *Pennant Race*, which covers the Reds' 1961 season, is just as good.

8. *Veeck as in Wreck* by Bill Veeck with Ed Linn. Veeck's autobiography through the early 1960s, and an extremely funny and insightful book. The ghost writer, Ed Linn, was one of the best baseball writers ever; along with this book, he did *Nice Guys Finish Last* with Leo Durocher (a particular favorite of Bill James), *Koufax* with Sandy Koufax and several excellent books on his own, with my personal favorite being *Steinbrenner's Yankees*.

9. *The Hidden Game of Baseball* by John Thorn and Pete Palmer. This is much more of a stat book than the *Historical Baseball Abstract*, but it mostly consists of writing *about* statistics, so I think it qualifies. One of the most useful things Thorn and Palmer do is to review the entire statistical history of baseball, with space devoted to all the important analysts and statisticians. I can't say I agree with all the formulas presented here, but I sure learned a lot from this book.

10. *The Summer Game* by Roger Angell. Angell's still probably the best essayist around, and he's published a number of books which are mostly compilations of his *New Yorker* articles. This is the first of them.

Honorable mention (in alphabetical order):

Eight Men Out by Eliot Asinof

Ball Four by Jim Bouton

The Baseball Chronology by James Charlton

The Fireside Book of Baseball by Charles Einstein

Willie's Time by Charles Einstein

The Boys of Summer by Roger Kahn

The Ultimate Baseball Book by Harris Lewine, David Nemec and Daniel Okrent

Pitching in a Pinch by Christy Mathewson

Baseball: The Golden Era by Harold Seymour

Baseball's Great Experiment: Jackie Robinson and His Legacy by Jules Tygiel

— Don Zminda

August 12—Alex the Great

Last week I got a trade offer in one of my fantasy leagues of (his) Barry Bonds for (my) Alex Rodriguez. It's funny how ridiculous that trade offer would've looked last year, but, as I told the guy, he's one year too late now. It got me thinking about that article Bill James wrote in the 1986 *Baseball Abstract* with the All-Star teams for each position and age. So Mat Olkin and I dug it up and looked at the 20-year-old shortstops. Bill's selection was a little-known guy named Rogers Hornsby from 1916. Let me show you how he stacks up against Alex this year:

Player	Year	AVG	AB	H	2B	3B	HR	R	RBI	BB	SB
Hornsby	1916	.313	495	155	17	15	6	63	65	40	17
Rodriguez	1996	.359	415	149	40	0	26	100	91	39	9

I think it's safe to say that if Bill were to update his lists now, there would be a new choice for greatest 20-year-old shortstop season of all-time. As a matter of fact, there're only a few 20-year-old seasons from Bill's list that stack up to Rodriguez' '96, period:

Player	Year	AVG	AB	H	2B	3B	HR	R	RBI	BB	SB
Ott	1929	.328	545	179	37	2	42	138	151	113	6
Williams	1939	.327	585	185	44	11	31	131	145	107	2
Cepeda	1958	.312	603	188	38	4	25	88	96	29	15
Pinson	1959	.316	648	205	47	9	20	131	84	55	21
Rodriguez	1996	.359	415	149	40	0	26	100	91	39	9

That's Ted Williams, by the way, not Billy Dee. I think it's clear that Ott's (Mel, not Ed) and Williams' rookie years were better than Rodriguez', but Cepeda's and Pinson's are definitely debatable. And remember, Alex' season isn't over either. And how about stacked up to Barry Bonds:

Player	Year	AVG	AB	H	2B	3B	HR	R	RBI	BB	SB
Bonds	1996	.307	411	126	23	3	32	92	97	98	23
Rodriguez	1996	.359	415	149	40	0	26	100	91	39	9

That's pretty crazy, isn't it? Of course, Barry would tell you that since all his teammates stink (besides Matt Williams—not Billy Dee) he never gets anything to hit and that's why he loses this battle. But of course, we know that most of Barry's best years are behind him and chances are most of Alex' are still to come. It's kind of ironic that Felix Fermin, who totally wasted 200 of what should have been Rodriguez' at-bats last year, got released by the Cubs over the weekend.

— Steve Moyer

August 13—Playing First Base for the Taiyo Whales. . .

Hey, did you hear that the Royals might sell Bob Hamelin to Japan? If they're smart, they'll sell him by the pound.

Sorry about that. I didn't mean to make light of such a weighty issue.

—Mat Olkin

August 13—This Didn't Have to Happen

In a sense, putting Todd Van Poppel in a Tigers uniform is strangely appropriate—he's finally amongst his peers. Maybe the Detroit hurlers will form some sort of support group, and sit around telling each other that "it's OK to have an ERA over 5.00. It doesn't make you a bad person."

How do we begin to make sense of his career, which has been so compellingly tragic? We all remember the hype that accompanied Oakland's' selection of Van Poppel in the first round of the 1990 draft. Widely acclaimed as the best amateur player in the country, Van Poppel received a three-year, guaranteed $1.2 million deal—the most lucrative one in history to that point. In an odd sidelight, the A's inserted a clause in his contract prohibiting him from doing yardwork. It wouldn't be the last time that he would be taken out of the yard.

But at the time, his potential was unlimited. To get a sense of the high regard in which he was held, all you need to do is take a look at the other players who were selected in the first round that year. Van Poppel was deemed comparable to other first-round pitchers such as Mike Mussina, Alex Fernandez, Scott Sanders and Donovan Osborne. Some pretty decent hitters went in that round, too: Dan Wilson, Tony Clark, Rondell White and Chipper Jones.

Van Poppel put up somewhat disappointing numbers in the minors, but with all that had gone on, it was difficult for people to have realistic expectations. Todd was very young, very raw and very wild. His performance didn't call for a promotion to the major leagues, but unfortunately, his contract did.

As per the agreement, the A's inserted him into their rotation at the 1993 All-Star break. Over the next year and a half, he went 13-19 with a 5.65 ERA. By the end of '94, defending him in baseball circles became downright un-hip. Trashing him was just too easy: he was supposed to be great, and instead, he was, well, Todd Van Poppel. End of story. Going into '95, carrying Van Poppel on your fantasy team was regarded as a badge of idiocy.

Funny how a few minors details can be so easily overlooked. . . little things, like the fact that he was only 22 years old, or that he still threw hard, or that he was trying to learn how to pitch at the major league level in spite of all the adversity.

Then the strangest thing happened: *he turned it around*. La Russa moved him to the bullpen, and it was as if Van Poppel suddenly figured out why he and his right arm had been put on this earth. His formerly nonexistent command finally materialized. From late May of '95 until the All-Star break, Todd put up a strikeout-to-walk ratio of better than 3-to-1—this after not even breaking even during the previous two seasons. His hits-per-inning plunged, and his ERA dropped into the low threes. He'd found his niche.

But La Russa had other ideas. After turning his career around by moving him to the bullpen, La Russa reversed field and dropped him back into the rotation. For a short while, it worked.

At first, Todd was less overpowering than he had been in the pen, but he was still miles ahead of where he'd been a year before. In his first seven starts, the numbers were respectable: 2-2 with a 4.26 ERA and a 2-to-1 K:BB ratio.

But still, La Russa wanted more. Van Poppel was encountering a common problem for a youngster: inefficiency. He was throwing about 4.5 pitches to each batter, which is very high. Even though he was throwing a ton of pitches per start—121—he was only averaging 6.1 innings per game.

I've always suspected that at that point, Dave Duncan and Tony La Russa sat him down and ordered him to change his approach. *Something* forced him to change, because after that point, he was a completely different pitcher. Over his next seven starts, he suddenly started throwing strikes. As a result, he grew much more efficient: his pitches per batter dropped below the league average, and his walks fell.

Oh, and one more thing: he got absolutely hammered.

Over his last seven starts, he went 1-4 with a 6.90 ERA, losing his spot in the rotation at season's end. Beginning with those last seven starts, he has never pitched effectively again. In fact, his late-season work was so awful that hardly anyone noticed the fact that earlier in the year, he'd finally come around.

What happened? Did he injure himself during a string of high-pitch outings when he first returned to the rotation? Or did La Russa simply ask him to do something he wasn't capable of doing? If Van Poppel was convinced to simply lay the ball over the plate, instead of relying on his ball's natural movement, I think the results of that philosophy have been obvious. Van Poppel just isn't the type of guy who can throw strike one and work into the seventh inning.

But he also showed what he *can* do. He can be very effective if he's allowed to work off the corners of the plate. This may limit him to bullpen work or six-inning starts, but he's shown he can succeed with that approach. That's enough for me. I don't need to see any more.

You won't catch me condemning Van Poppel because he's failed to live up to expectations. I refuse to write this guy off. His failures have been the result of a number of unfortunate circumstances, but a lack of talent has not been one of them. If guys like Doug Jones, Rob Dibble and David West are able to keep getting tryouts, then Van Poppel surely must have a few more chances coming. I'm not optimistic that Detroit will be the place where he finally breaks through, but like Al Leiter, sooner or later, he's going to make it.

—Mat Olkin

August 13—Mickey Mouse, Indeed

Okay, time for me to vent.

JOHN MCNAMARA???!!!

Whew. Much better.

—Mat Olkin

August 16—Free-Swingers

In the 1996 edition of the STATS *Baseball Scoreboard*, Jim Henzler penned an interesting article entitled "He Can Slug, So Why Can't He Walk?" Jim pointed out that the two skills in question, hitting home runs and drawing walks, would seem to be complementary. Good plate discipline often results in seeing "fat" pitches (translating into home runs), and "home-run prowess" often results in a pitcher working around the hitter (translating into walks). In short, one should feed off the other.

But it doesn't *always* work that way, especially for many of today's sluggers—Sammy Sosa immediately comes to mind—who seem content to hack away. We seem to be in an era of free-swinging power hitters, and the data below backs up that conclusion. Here are the worst single-season BB/HR ratios in baseball history for players with at least 20 home runs. Note that four of the top 10 have come since 1994.

Lowest BB/HR Ratio—Single Season

Player, Team	Year	BB	HR	Ratio
Dante Bichette, Rockies	1995	22	40	0.55
Andres Galarraga, Rockies	1994	19	31	0.61
Fred Whitfield, Indians	1965	16	26	0.62
Juan Gonzalez, Rangers	1995	17	27	0.63
Abner Dalrymple, Chi (N.L.)	1884	14	22	0.64
Andre Dawson, Cubs	1987	32	49	0.65
Bob Horner, Braves	1979	22	33	0.67
Cory Snyder, Indians	1986	16	24	0.67
Walker Cooper, Giants	1947	24	35	0.69
Dante Bichette, Rockies	1994	19	27	0.70

(Minimum 20 home runs)

You know, some day I'm going to make it through one of these articles without talking about Dante Bichette. It'll happen eventually.

Bichette, clearly one of the greatest offensive forces of the modern era (is my cyber-sarcasm getting through?), owns two of the seasons in question, with teammate Andres Galarraga having another one. Both have displayed this pattern throughout their pre-Colorado careers—Bichette in California and Milwaukee and Galarraga in Montreal and St. Louis—but their BB/HR ratios have plummeted in Colorado, simply because of the inflated home-run totals for both players.

The other name that jumped out at me was Cory Snyder (.272-24-69), who spent his rookie season of 1986 with a high-scoring Cleveland club that included Julio Franco (.306-10-74), Joe Carter (.302-29-121), Tony Bernazard (.301-17-73), Mel Hall (.296-18-77), Brook Jacoby (.288-17-80), and Brett Butler (32 stolen bases). The Indians led the league in runs scored and finished 84-78 in '86 (after going 60-102 the year before), and were the "trendy pick" to take the A.L. East in 1987. I'll never forget heading into my high school library that April in search of the latest *Sports Illustrated*. My beloved Indiana Hoosiers had just edged Syracuse for the NCAA basketball championship, and I anticipated seeing Steve Alford or Keith Smart on the cover. Two smiling Cleveland Indians (I think Snyder and Carter) got the cover instead and proceeded to finish dead last—61-101—in 1987. Thanks, *SI*.

— Scott McDevitt

August 18—Is Baseball Dying?

My column on best baseball books last week proved one thing—there's a lot of good baseball books out there! Thanks to all of you who sent in your own submissions, most of which were very worthy of consideration. It demonstrates once more that there are more good books about baseball than there are about any other sport. Movies too. Always have been, probably always will be.

So who says interest in baseball is dying? Well, lots of people. I hate to even get started on this subject, but don't you just get tired after a while with all the baseball-bashing that fills the papers and the airwaves? The Orioles were in Chicago last weekend, and I had a long talk with Jon Miller, the O's radio announcer and the voice of ESPN Sunday Night Baseball. I was the stat man for Sunday Night Baseball during most of the first year that ESPN did games, so Jon and I know each other pretty well. Anyway, Jon was all upset about the NBC broadcast of the All-Star game, in which Bob Costas seemed to spend about half the telecast deriding the big hitting numbers of 1996. Jon just couldn't believe it. "This is the first game NBC's doing all year," he kept saying, "and they go out of their way to run down the players they're supposed to be promoting! Unbelievable."

He's exactly right, of course, but that's just the tip of the iceberg. To hear some people tell it, you'd think that baseball is this hopeless old fossil, and that nobody under the age of 60 follows it any more. That's ridiculous. I go to a lot of games at both Comiskey Park and Wrigley Field, and every time I look around the stands, about half the people in the crowd—maybe more—appear to be under the age of 30. These people may not watch much baseball on television, but they sure show up at the park, and for a good reason: attending a major league game is fun.

Look at it another way. Whatever problems it has on and off the field, baseball has two things going for it that none of the other major sports can offer:

1. For the most part, the games are played outdoors in the summertime.

2. You can get into the park virtually any time you want, and at a fairly reasonable price compared to most other forms of entertainment.

These are *huge* advantages, and unless the players and owners hopelessly screw things up (which is possible), they pretty much guarantee the survival of the sport. I live in Chicago, one of the ultimate multi-sport towns, and I'm very much a fan of both the Bulls and the Bears. . . and also of the Blackhawks, though to a lesser extent. Know how many regular-season Bears games I've been to in my life? Exactly one. And it wasn't very much fun, either—it was a huge hassle getting tickets, they were way overpriced to boot, and the seat itself was lousy. Frankly, I was sorry I hadn't stayed home and watched the game on television. I haven't been to a Bulls game since the Reggie Theus era, which was before Jordan joined the team. You basically can't get a Bulls ticket unless you want to spend 50 bucks or so, and when you do go to a game, the experience, as with football, isn't as good as watching the game on TV. . . the players seem distant, remote and a lot smaller than they do on the tube. As for hockey, I've been to maybe a half-dozen Hawks games. It's a little easier getting tickets to hockey than for basketball, but not *that* much easier, and again the prices are pretty outrageous.

Baseball, of course, is completely different. Sure, people complain about the ticket prices, but they're a bargain compared to the NBA, NFL or NHL. With so many games on the schedule, it's usually not much of a problem getting tickets to a game, except maybe in Cleveland and a couple of other places. The weather is generally good except in April and September, which tends to make it a pleasant experience even for people who aren't die-hard fans. (My wife, for example.) And unlike the NFL or NBA, watching baseball is *better* at the park than it is on TV.

And that's why all those young people show up at Wrigley. Maybe they're not the fans their fathers were, but—as I noted in my column a few weeks ago—there are a lot more of them in the seats these days than there were in 1976 or 1956. (Yes, there are fewer people in the seats than in 1993 or 1994, but as I pointed out in the same column, those years were unusual and unlikely to be repeated. Attendance in 1996 is back to the same level it was in the late 1980s-early 1990s, and rising.) They'll probably keep coming out, as well, because they know a good time when they see it.

So here's my advice: if you think baseball's dying, think about the sports book market, which is a field I know a little about. At STATS we produce 11 sports books a year, and seven of them are about baseball. The reason? It's simple: our baseball books are the ones that sell the best, by far. And those sales are rising, not dropping.

If you think baseball's dying, think about fantasy leagues, where baseball's still the dominant sport. Or think about all the tabletop and computer-baseball leagues there are in the country. I'm currently in three different historically-based computer leagues. One league uses the players from 1927, one the players from 1947, the third the players from 1959. All three leagues are going on simultaneously—we'll go on to 1928-1948-1960 next year—and if you want to get into any of them, you have to get on a waiting list and hope your turn comes up in a year or two. (It's kind of like trying to get a Bulls ticket.) Gee, I wonder how many people play in a computer league where they use the NFL players of 1927. . .

And if you think baseball is dying, just go to a game at Wrigley Field. Walk around the neighborhood. Talk to the fans. Enjoy the ivy and the "friendly confines." Sing along with Harry. *Then* tell me baseball's dying.

I dare you.

— Don Zminda

August 20—A New Position: Pitcher/DH

I keep resolving to lay off the Red Sox, but man, it just keeps getting weirder. The Red Sox' strange defensive alignments this year have been well-chronicled. We've seen Wil Cordero impersonating a second baseman; Jeff Manto at both second base and shortstop; Jeff Frye at each of the outfield spots; 12 different left fielders; and yes, it's true, the vast pastures of center field have actually been entrusted to Mike Greenwell on one occasion. And I haven't even said the word "Canseco." But like Nixon's final days, just when you thought it couldn't get any more bizarre. . .

Greg Pirkl. Minor league first baseman/DH, picked up on waivers from Seattle a few weeks ago. Good hitter. Probably a 30-homer man if given a chance. The Red Sox want to move him to another position. Which one? Take a guess. What's the most ridiculous spot you could move a power-hitting DH to? Center field? Try again. Shortstop? Even weirder.

Try *pitcher*. Yes, apparently one of their coaches clocked him throwing 94 MPH ("You got that gun right-side-up, Bill?") and they got the bright idea to make a pitcher out of him. Hey, what better way to simultaneously address the team's backlog of DHs and shortage of pitchers? Yeah, fine, but the only problem is that *He Isn't A Pitcher*, and he doesn't seem too keen on trying to become one. He's pitched in one professional game in his life.

Oh well. Cordero wasn't a second baseman, either, and that didn't stop them.

—Mat Olkin

August 23—Power vs. Finesse

Are power pitchers more successful than finesse pitchers, or is it the other way around? With a little help from our STATS database, I searched for every pitching season from 1980 to 1995, breaking down each season performance by strikeouts per nine innings—a reasonable gauge for measuring power pitchers. For each group, I calculated the total won-lost records for all pitchers who fell into each particular range. Consequently, there are very few seasons at each end of the "spectrum" (as you would expect) and a ton of seasons centered around 5.58—the average strikeout-per-nine-inning figure for the 16 seasons. Most of the results aren't too surprising.

1980-95—Strikeouts per Nine Innings

K/9 IP	W-L	Pct
10.00+	490-441	.526
9.00–9.99	726-697	.510
8.00–8.99	1887-1561	.547
7.00–7.99	3146-2921	.519
6.00–6.99	5771-5463	.514
5.00–5.99	7978-7914	.502
4.00–4.99	7531-7766	.492
3.00–3.99	3764-4325	.465
2.00–2.99	909-1042	.466
1.00–1.99	59-92	.391
0.00–0.99	2-16	.111

Starting at the bottom of the list and working your way up, it's easy to see that strikeout ability correlates very well with winning, which isn't anything you probably didn't already know. Bill James' research over the years has shown that, for pitchers, durability and strikeout ability go hand in hand. Want to know which young pitchers will still be in the major leagues in 10 years? Look at their strikeout totals.

Now, let's move on to walks and see if we can gain any more insight into the "power versus finesse" debate. I performed an exercise similar to the one above, this time looking at walks per nine innings.

1980-95—Walks per Nine Innings

BB/9 IP	W-L	Pct
0.00–0.99	147-80	.648
1.00–1.99	2843-2297	.553
2.00–2.99	11895-10497	.531
3.00–3.99	11261-11616	.492
4.00–4.99	4390-5223	.457
5.00–5.99	1178-1618	.421
6.00–6.99	321-495	.393
7.00–7.99	102-171	.374
8.00+	72-187	.278

Nothing new here, either. As the scouts say, "If you ain't got control, you ain't got nothing." But what if we *combine* the two elements and see if a low-strikeout/low-walk pitcher fares better than a high-strikeout/high-walk pitcher? Do the strikeouts help more than the walks hurt? Do the walks hurt more than the strikeouts help?

Let's separate all the pitchers from 1980-95 into into four categories. We'll define a "good power pitcher" as any pitcher who strikes out at least 5.58 batters per nine innings during a season, and a "poor power pitcher" as any hurler with a figure below that. And let's do the same thing for a "good control pitcher" (less than 3.29 BB/9) and a "poor control pitcher." Drum roll, please.

	Pct	20-game winners
Good power, Good control	.550	32
Poor power, Good control	.514	20
Good power, Poor control	.485	2
Poor power, Poor control	.440	3

Well, I'm sold. The pitchers in group #2, the poor power, good control pitchers, fared *much* better than the group #3 pitchers (let's name this group after Mitch Williams). And look at the number of 20-game winners! It's clear for pitchers at the *top* of the scale, control's worth a lot more than power.

So who are the three 20-game winners in group #4 who defied the odds? Steve Stone for the Orioles in 1980 (25-7, 3.23 ERA), Rich Dotson for the White Sox in 1983 (22-7, 3.23) and Tom Glavine for the Braves in 1993 (22-6, 3.20). Talk about some eerily similar ERAs!

So why did those pitchers manage to win 20 (and Stone win a Cy Young Award) with less-than-stellar stuff? They won, in great part, because their teams won; every one of their teams won at least 99 games that year. They all stayed healthy and they all got a little lucky. Indeed, all three pitchers set their career high in victories during the three seasons. In addition, all three pitched with another 20-game winner on the staff: Scott McGregor (20-8) for the Orioles, LaMarr Hoyt (24-10) for the White Sox and Greg Maddux (20-10) for the Braves. For both Stone and Dotson, it was the *only* 20-victory season of their entire career—the exception rather than the rule.

— Scott McDevitt

August 26—Dallas Bites the Dust

PINTO: In case you haven't heard, Dallas Green has been fired and replaced with Bobby Valentine.

COOPERSON: Dallas never should've left the Phillies.

SPEAR: Replacing Dallas Green with Bobby Valentine may be, in my opinion, the worst managerial change ever.

OLKIN: Actually, Valentine's very well-qualified for the job. His previous job in Texas gave him vast experience in handling young broken-down pitching phenoms.

August 26—Why is This List Interesting?

PINTO: Why is this list interesting, and what does it have to do with this year's potential winners in the A.L., Rodriguez and Jeter?

Year	MVP	Rookie of Year
1952	Bobby Shantz	Harry Byrd
1954	Willie Mays	Wally Moon
1957	Hank Aaron	Jack Sanford
1970	Johnny Bench	Carl Morton
1971	Vida Blue	Chris Chambliss
1974	Jeff Burroughs	Mike Hargrove
1983	Cal Ripken	Ron Kittle
1988	Jose Canseco	Walt Weiss
1994	Frank Thomas	Bob Hamelin

ZMINDA: My guess is that in each case cited by David, the MVP was younger than the Rookie of the Year. Am I right?

PINTO: Mr. Zminda hit the nail on the head. The list was generated starting in 1949, the first year the Rookie award was given out in each league. This will also be the first year this decade that the A.L. Rookie winner is younger than Ken Griffey Jr.

August 27—Maybe He'll Be Nicer This Time

And I thought the return of John McNamara was the height of insanity! Even after having spent three years there, I'm still learning that anything you can do, New York can do bigger. Yesterday the Mets fired Dallas Green for his inability to bring along the Mets' young arms. In his place, they hired. . . *Bobby Valentine.*

How can I say this. . . hiring Bobby Valentine is like hiring George Wendt to teach your aerobics class. It's like hiring Roseanne to sing the National Anthem. . . again.

I say "again," because like the Roseanne fiasco, it's already happened once before. In a parallel so eerie that it sends chills down the rotator cuffs of pitchers everywhere, Bobby Valentine was once hired to oversee the development of a brilliant young pitching staff. The team was Texas, and the results were horrifying.

You think Pulsipher, Isringhausen and Wilson are talented? Take a look back at the young Ed Correa. At age 20, Bill Pulsipher was in Double-A, and Isringhausen was in Single-A. When Paul Wilson was 20 years old, he was in college, pitching between keg parties. In 1986, Ed Correa, age 20, fanned 189 batters, eighth in the American League.

Or perhaps you would have preferred Bobby Witt. He pitched for Valentine for four years before finally harnessing his vast talent. In 1990, over his last 19 starts, he went 14-2 with a 2.40 ERA, fanning over a man an inning.

Some people would have taken Jose Guzman over Correa or Witt. He broke in under Valentine as a 22-year old, and by the time he was 25, he'd cut his ERA to 3.70 and boosted his strikeouts to 157.

Now if you didn't already know how all of this turned out, you'd naturally assume that all three of those pitchers would have had many good years ahead of them, even if they never progressed another inch. And if their skipper was truly a genius at handling young hurlers, who knows? They could have set the world on fire.

Somehow, despite Bobby Valentine's "better" efforts, all three of them missed stardom. In fact, they missed it like Columbus missed Asia. For the rest of their careers, they were about as successful as the kids from "Diff'rent Strokes."

After approaching 200 Ks in his first full season, Ed Correa put up a 7.59 ERA over a half-season, hurt his arm, and quietly slipped under the waves.

Bobby Witt went 17-10 in 1990, but the next year, his ERA ballooned to 6.09 and he tore his rotator cuff. Since then, he's been a career number-four starter.

Guzman seemed to be coming into his own in 1988, but the next year, his shoulder went, and he missed the whole season. And the next. He returned to pitch well in 1991 and '92, but then the arm went again. He was down in Triple-A a few months ago when the Cubs cut him. The Cubs. Kevin Foster. Jim Bullinger. Cut him.

How could three pitchers with such overwhelming talent each fail to make it? You might want to ask Bobby Valentine. He was given seven years to develop them, and all he did was make the surgeons rich. What was it? Was it the 202 innings squeezed from Ed Correa's underage arm? Was it the string of 130-pitch outings during Witt's final big run? Was it Guzman averaging 114 pitches for his first 12 starts of 1988?

I ask you: was it Valentine's rough handling, or just an unfortunate string of bad luck? Well, I'll tell you what I think. It's a damn shame that for the foreseeable future, Bill Pulsipher, Jason Isringhausen and Paul Wilson will be living with Bobby Valentine.

Go Fine Yourself

Hey—this Yankees-Brewers trade sure creates an interesting scenario, doesn't it? For years, I've maintained that Bud Selig's concurrent tenure as the Brewers' owner and baseball's "Commissioner" has been a blatant conflict of interest. Now Selig's Brewers have traded the broken-footed Pat Listach to New York, and the Yankees are in a position where they have to go to Selig and say, "Bud, you screwed us. Punish yourself."

—Mat Olkin

114

August 29—My Achin' Back

I'm off from work for a little while after undergoing surgery for a herniated disk in my back. But it ain't all bad. One way I can make myself useful during my recovery period is by offering a little personal perspective on the Mariners' Randy Johnson, who decided earlier this week to undergo surgery on *his* herniated disk. While the M's organization supported the decision, one Seattle writer caused a stir when he suggested that Johnson was being selfish, and that he should have attempted to keep pitching despite the injury.

Did the writer have a point? Not if my experiences mean anything. A herniated disk, in case you're not familiar with the injury, occurs when the cushiony area between the back vertebrae bulges out unnaturally, pressing against the sciatic nerve which runs down your leg. The result is numbness and pain which often goes all the down to your toes. In many cases, including my own, there's very little back pain involved; almost all of the pain is in the leg and foot. And if the injury's bad enough, the pain never really goes away.

Can you perform athletically with a herniated disk? Yes. . . but only up to a point. I'm hardly a professional athlete, but I am pretty active—I've completed four Chicago Marathons, and I work out at a health club four or five times a week. When I suffered my own herniated disk, I could still work out to a limited degree, but running became all but impossible. And if I exercised too vigorously, the pain in my leg and foot would really flare up.

Like Johnson, I attempted to treat the injury without undergoing surgery. Rest didn't help much, so I was given a couple of epidural steroid injections, a treatment that often solves the problem if the injury is minor. That didn't work either, and so surgery became the only viable option if I wanted to avoid hobbling around for the rest of my life. The doctors—and I saw a bunch of 'em—were very clear that the longer I continued to delay the operation, the more I would lower my chances for a quick and complete recovery. The reason is that the constant pressure of disk against nerve often causes nerve inflammation which can remain even after the pressure is removed.

I'm pretty sure this is the situation Johnson found himself in. He tried to come back and pitch with the injury, and at first he was very effective; I don't know if he had some steroid injections, but chances are that he did, and they *do* offer temporary relief, as does complete rest. But then the pain returned and Johnson started getting cuffed around. He could have tried pitching once a week or something like that, but what would be the point? The odds are that he would be unable to pitch effectively, and the longer he waited, the more he was compromising his chances for complete recovery. So he finally gave in and agreed to the surgery. From where I sit, that seems like the right decision. Johnson wasn't doing his team much good trying to pitch with the injury; with surgery now, the odds greatly increase that he'll be pitching like Randy Johnson again next April. Without the surgery, that would have been a lot less likely. The reward for continuing to pitch at partial effectiveness simply wasn't worth the risk.

— Don Zminda

August 30—Slamming

COOPERSON: Mark Whiten's grand slam tonight—a little turnaround of the May 17 Seattle/Baltimore game, won on a Hoiles slam in the bottom of the ninth? I love coincidences like that—or maybe they're not coincidences.

Further Seattle irony—Whiten hit that grand slam in his first game with Dave Hollins as his new teammate. In 1995 Hollins and Whiten were traded for each other.

PINTO: Big day in grand slam land yesterday. Garret Anderson's set the record for most in MLB in a season, and Whiten's gave Seattle 10, tying an ML record they also tied last year. At the current pace, we could end up with 150 slams this year.

September 3—Somewhere, George Bell is Cackling

With a month to play in the regular season, and four divisional races left to be decided, I thought it was too early for this. Silly me.

As Mel Antonen's column in Tuesday's *USA Today* reminds us, it's never too early to become sidetracked with arguments over the MVP voting. However premature Antonen's serve may be, this is one volley I must return.

Mel asks: should Alex Rodriguez's production translate into A.L. MVP votes if the Mariners don't win the West or qualify as the wild card?

As we ponder this vexing question, Antonen rescues us from our philosophical quagmire, instructing us, "The answer is no." Alex shall not be MVP. "Not when there are credentials from players on first-place teams."

Fascinating. According to Antonen, Rodriguez—despite his historic season —ought not to win the MVP, through what amounts to a quirk of bad timing. If he wanted to win, he should have picked a year when none of the first-place teams had any MVP candidates. Granted, a year like that doesn't come around all that often, but still, at the rate he's going, Alex ought to be able to snag an MVP trophy or two before he hangs up his spikes—even under those rules.

It sounds like Mel is trying to drag out the old argument that the MVP necessarily must come from a winning team. This is a tired, oversimplified, intellectually repulsive argument, which reasons that if the team didn't win, none of the players could have been any good. It's the kind of reasoning that made George Steinbrenner famous.

In effect, Antonen would deny Rodriguez MVP honors simply because the Mariners (presumably) will not make the postseason. If Alex were really an MVP, he would have propelled them into the A.L. West lead, he seems to say. In other words, Alex can't be the MVP because Randy Johnson got hurt and the Mariners' pitching went to hell.

Now, I may be way off-base here. I may be wrongheaded and overly-literal, but I've always been under the impression that the Most Valuable Player Award was supposed to go to the *the player who was the most valuable*. The way I understood it, having a good supporting cast was not a prerequisite. If a disc bulges in Randy Johnson's back, how does that nullify Alex Rodriguez's obvious value on the diamond?

Besides being flatly unfair, disqualifying the players from the 11 A.L. teams who will miss the postseason would be inconsistent with recent voting. Where was Antonen in 1991, when the ever-so-selfish Cal Ripken callously padded his MVP numbers in the midst of the Orioles' 95-loss season? How could Robin Yount have had any value when his '89 Brewers finished at .500? And how about Andre Dawson in 1987? The Cubs could have finished last without him.

But let's give Mr. Antonen a chance to defend himself. He endorses a number of candidates over Rodriguez, the first being last year's Mr. No-Soup-For-You, Albert Belle. Now, there's no denying that Belle deserves consideration, but the timing's a little strange, don't you think? Last year, his numbers dwarfed Mo Vaughn's, but they punished his bad behavior by sending him to bed with no MVP. This year, he's been the same old Albert, except his stats don't stand out the way they did last year. *Now* you want to give him the award? Perhaps we've started to worry about how last year's vote will look in the record books?

But Antonen presses on: "Belle's offense is more consistent. Last season, he had 19 home runs after July when the Indians had all but won."

Am I standing in a pasture? This is the same argument they used to *deny* Belle the award last year. "Sure, he hit all those home runs," they said, "but he hit most of them after the Indians had already wrapped it up." Since when did these "meaningless" home runs become a badge of "consistency"? And why is the 1995 season even being discussed in the first place?

Antonen goes on to plug Jim Thome, Ivan Rodriguez and Juan Gonzalez, which is all well and good, except for one thing: *Alex Rodriguez is the best player in the league this year.* Period.

—Mat Olkin

September 5—205 Pitches

I've read a number of good baseball books this year, and one of the best was an oldie: Sandy Koufax's autobiography, *Koufax*. The book was written after the 1965 season, so it doesn't cover either Koufax's great final season, 1966, or his retirement after that campaign. But it's terrific for several reasons. One is that Koufax himself was intelligent and insightful. Another is that he was working with one of the best ghostwriters ever, Ed Linn, the man who co-wrote two other classics, *Veeck as in Wreck* and Leo Durocher's *Nice Guys Finish Last*. But the book offers another big bonus: a game-by-game compilation of Koufax's career through 1965, complete with footnotes. The stat section, which is worth the price of the book all by itself, was compiled by the great Allan Roth, one of the founding fathers of modern statistical research.

It was one of the footnotes in the stat section of the Koufax book that prompted me to write this column. On September 20, 1961, Koufax worked overtime to beat the Cubs. This is what the footnote says:

• Made 205 pitches in 13 innings.

Wow. Two hundred and five pitches! We at STATS have been keeping pitch counts since the late 1980s, and it's unusual these days for a pitcher to throw even 150 pitches in a game. Two hundred and five? That's off the map.

Let's put that Koufax game in a little more perspective:

1. It came at the end of a season in which he would work more 250 innings, face over 1,000 batters, and toss 15 complete games. That was a pretty heavy workload, even by 1961 standards. Only two National League pitchers faced more batters that year, only three worked more innings, and only Warren Spahn had more complete games.

2. Koufax was working for the third time in six days. He had thrown a complete-game five-hitter on the 15th of September, then had worked two innings in relief, facing 10 batters, two days later, before his 205-pitch stint on the 20th.

3. He was also only 25 years old (he'd turn 26 in late December) and, by any standards, the most valuable young pitcher in the game.

One thing is obvious from this: they sure didn't baby their pitchers back then.

To our knowledge, Koufax didn't work any more 200-pitch outings after 1961. But he was hardly taking it easy; in fact, his workload *increased*, dramatically in the following years. In three of the next five seasons, Koufax pitched more than 300 innings. In 1965, the year he was worked the hardest, Koufax pitched 336 innings, faced 1,297 batters, and threw 27 complete games. A year later, his workload lessened only slightly. But he paid a heavy price for it: when the 1996 season was over, Koufax retired with arthritis in his left elbow.

The subject of pitchers, and how much they're asked to do, fascinates me. In Koufax's prime, a 300-inning season wasn't unusual at all, and neither was a year in which a pitcher threw 20 or more complete games. And not all of them broke down like Koufax did, either. Nolan Ryan, for instance, worked 326 innings with 26 complete games in 1973, and 332.2 innings with another 26 complete games in 1974. He lasted 19 more seasons after that, finally retiring at the age of 46. Steve Carlton worked 346.1 innings with 30 complete games in 1972, and subsequently had four more years with 290-plus innings. Carlton pitched until 1988, when he was 43. From 1968 to 1971, Fergie Jenkins had four straight seasons with both 300-plus innings and 20-plus complete games every year. Jenkins lasted until the age of 39, in 1993. There are other cases we could cite: Gaylord Perry, Robin Roberts, Mickey Lolich, to name three.

Use a pitcher like that these days, and they'd arrest the manager.

Back to Koufax. We at STATS have only been recording pitch counts since the late 1980s, so it's not possible to figure out exactly how many pitches Koufax threw in 1965. But we can make a pretty good estimate. At the top of his game, Koufax struck out a ton of batters, didn't walk very many, and was very tough to hit. That sounds a lot like the young Roger Clemens, and we *do* know how many pitches Clemens threw in, say, 1988. In 1965, Koufax faced 31.5 batters per start; in 1988, Clemens averaged 30.4 batters per start, just a little less. Strikeouts and walks both consume a lot of pitches, and the two hurlers are very comparable in that way as well: Koufax averaged a combined total of 12.1 K+BB per nine innings in 1965, Clemens 12.0 K+BB in 1988.

Now to the math. In 1988, Clemens averaged just under 120 pitches per start, and threw a total of 4,186 pitches for the year. That's a lot of pitches; since 1989, when we first started keeping a leaders list in this category, only Cal Eldred (4,250 pitches in 1993), Randy Johnson (4,240 in '93) and Clemens himself (4,243 in 1989), have thrown more in a single season. Koufax, though, almost certainly had to throw close to *5,000* pitches in 1965, when he started 41 games. And maybe more. If we figure Koufax for 119.6 pitches per start— Clemens' 1988 average—you get 4,904 pitches. But remember that Koufax faced an extra batter per game compared with Clemens, and that he also worked a couple of short stints in relief that year. So 5,000 pitches doesn't seem like an unreasonable estimate at all. You also have to remember that a lot of those pitches came in the eighth and ninth innings, when Koufax was most tired. In '65, Koufax averaged 8.15 innings per start, and threw 27 complete games. In '88, Clemens averaged 7.54 innings per start and tossed only 14 complete games.

One more thing: Koufax wasn't done when he threw all those pitches in the 1965 regular season. The Dodgers won the pennant in '65, and Koufax made three more starts, working a total of 24 innings, in the World Series. He finished the Series by throwing a three-hit shutout—his second consecutive shutout—in Game 7. Koufax made that start on two days' rest. It boggles the mind.

So is the point of this that Sandy Koufax was a Real Man, while Rogers Clemens is a wimp?

Not really. . . . I, for one, am not about to challenge Roger Clemens' manhood. Or Greg Maddux's or Randy Johnson's, for that matter. But the game has changed so much, and in such a short time, that it begs for an explanation. One possible explanation is that pitchers paced themselves more in years past—they were expected to go nine innings, so they didn't go all-out from the first pitch like a modern pitcher is expected to. I would say that explains a good part of it, but not everything. I have several tapes of Koufax in action, and he sure doesn't *seem* to be pacing himself very much.

There's also the physiological argument. It goes like this: the arm is a muscle, and the more you use it, the stronger it'll get. Twenty or 30 years ago, pitchers worked in a four-man rotation much more than they do now (not everyone had a four-man rotation in the '60s and '70s, of course, but a good number of the teams did, and a good percentage of the best pitchers worked on three days rest). By most accounts, pitchers also threw in between starts more than they do now; they even threw batting practice. Did that help them strengthen their arms? It's sure possible. The Atlanta Braves, among today's teams, are known for having their pitchers throw between starts, and the Braves have also kept their outstanding staff relatively healthy. But even the Braves haven't been tempted to try a four-man rotation. And that modern workhorse, Greg Maddux, has never worked more than 268 innings in a season, or thrown more than 10 complete games in any year.

So will we ever see the likes of Koufax again? Or Carlton or Jenkins—the pitchers who work every fourth day and usually complete what they start? It begins to seem that we won't. As Bill James has pointed out, one consistency in baseball history has been that pitchers have been asked to do less and less with each passing generation. Bill thinks that before long, we'll have a season in which *nobody* pitches a complete game. That would be a pity.

I keep hoping that, one of these years, some team will break out of the mold and make a real commitment to a four-man rotation—not for just a few months, but for a whole season. Or maybe they need to make an organizational commitment, from the minor leagues on up, to try some of the old theories about developing arm strength. Would it work, or would we end up with a staff of cripples? Who knows, but I'd love to seem someone try it.

— Don Zminda

September 5—Cy...

SPEAR: Before handing the Cy Young Award to Andy Pettitte, has anyone in the media looked at Pat Hentgen's numbers recently? Pettitte just won his 20th, Hentgen has 17 wins now. Except for that, Hentgen has *far* superior numbers across the board.

I will boo loudly if Pettitte wins the Cy.

WENZ: Pettitte's numbers are largely a function of two starts. He gave up 10 runs one game without making it through the third, and nine runs in another without making it through the second. Discount those two games, and their numbers are a lot closer.

WOELFLEIN: You could do that for anyone. Those starts still count. If Frank Thomas didn't miss the month of July he would have better numbers. If Roger Clemens got even some run support the first half of the season, he could be the choice for a Cy. Pat Hentgen is just about at the top of all the major pitching categories and on a far inferior team.

ZMINDA: Pettitte would have the highest ERA by far for a Cy Young winner if he does win the award. Knowing the voters, though, he'll be the favorite if he has 23-24 wins and no one else has more than 20. I agree Hentgen is a much stronger choice.

MOYER: Before handing the Cy Young Award to Andy Pettitte, make sure you get a good grip on it and *don't drop it*. It's really valuable.

MUNDO: . . . And in the N.L., how many more wins will it take for Kevin Brown to convince the dunderheads that he's the most dominating pitcher in baseball this year? Even the *Baseball Weekly* "experts" are toting Smoltz as a Cy lock.

JAMES: The A.L. Cy Young is obvious. Roberto Hernandez.

MILLER: Wimpy and the Hawkaroo would agree with you wholeheartedly regarding Roberto!

FAUST: But, can you "Put it on the board. . . Yes!"?

September 5—205 Pitches (Cont'd)

ZMINDA: I wrote my AOL column about this today, so hopefully you can read the whole thing. But in case you can't, according to the stat section of the book *Koufax* by Sandy Koufax and Ed Linn, with stats by Allan Roth, Koufax threw 205 pitches in a 13-inning win over the Cubs on September 20, 1961!

Blows me away.

P.S. I highly recommend the book, also.

JAMES: 1) I strongly recommend *all* Ed Linn books, including the one about Koufax. Ed Linn is the best writer of baseball books ever, period.

2) The 200 pitches. . . I'd bet that that wasn't all that uncommon at that time. Remember the famous game Milwaukee/San Francisco in 1963, Spahn against Marichal, which was decided 1-0 in 16 innings. Spahn and Marichal both pitched the entire game. Unless their pitches/inning were just phenomenally low, they had to throw 200+ pitches apiece.

Jack McKeon in 1975 ruined Steve Busby's career by allowing him to pitch 12 innings on a day when his arm was right. I've never seen an actual pitch count, but I'd be shocked if he didn't throw 200 pitches that day.

ZMINDA: The more I think about it, the more I think Bill is probably right that a 200-pitch game wasn't all that uncommon 20+ years ago. As in the famous Spahn-Marichal game, they'd often leave a pitcher in an extra-inning game indefinitely, as long as he wasn't giving up runs.

September 6—Opposite-Field Homers

KRETSCHMANN: In an interview with Greg Maddux recently he was talking about why now you have Frank Thomas and other sluggers who now can lead the league in home runs in addition to having a good batting average, unlike the past.

He said the reason was that everybody's diving into the ball so that the power hitters who used to be dead pull hitters are now getting more of their homers between the alleys. Well, I decided to run the numbers and see if it actually works out that way.

| | Pull | | | Opp Field | | Pull | | | Opp Field | |
Year	Strt	Ally	CF	Ally	Strt	Strt	Ally	CF	Ally	Strt
1988	1647	958	215	183	156	52.1	30.3	6.8	5.8	4.9
1989	1531	973	254	180	142	49.7	31.6	8.2	5.8	4.6
1990	1626	1096	270	193	132	49.0	33.0	8.1	5.8	4.0
1991	1673	1089	235	226	160	49.5	32.2	6.9	6.7	4.7
1992	1668	963	147	160	100	54.9	31.7	4.8	5.3	3.3
1993	1876	1334	324	268	228	46.6	33.1	8.0	6.7	5.7
1994	1421	1051	308	297	229	43.0	31.8	9.3	9.0	6.9
1995	1800	1303	430	317	231	44.1	31.9	10.5	7.8	5.7
1996	1886	1334	425	431	312	43.0	30.4	9.7	9.8	7.1

I guess Greg knows what he's talking about.

September 8—It's Great to Be a Computer Baseball Nerd

PINTO: It's great to be a baseball computer nerd.

I'm sitting here in my basement, working on ESPN game notes. I have the Braves game on TV, the Indians game simulation on Instant Sports, and the Yankee game on my beeper. Isn't life wonderful?

September 10—Hey Beavis, Is 24 More Than 17?

I'm increasingly annoyed by the discussion of the N.L. Cy Young race, where there seems to be a very real possibility that the award-bestowers will give the trophy to the wrong guy. As always, I'll start with a disclaimer. I have nothing against John Smoltz. He's a fine pitcher, and he deserves all the credit in the world for overcoming the "unfulfilled potential" tag that haunted him for so long. To the best of my recollection, he has never berated me in public or run over my children with a van.

Smoltz burst from the gate with such a flourish this year that people began to consider him to be on par with—and perhaps even superior to—Greg Maddux. Barely four months had passed since Maddux had been hailed as the dominant pitcher of our era, compared to the likes of Christy Mathewson.

The naysayers, myself included, waited for the inevitable slump that would signal Smoltz's return to earth. It never came. On a pace to win 24 games, the media—myself excluded—has largely conceded the Cy Young Award to him.

He's been outstanding; there's no arguing that. If you want to go ahead and give him the Cy Young, that's fine, except for one thing: someone else has pitched better ball. Now, if you don't know who I'm talking about, then our newspapermen have truly failed us. This guy has an ERA almost three-quarters of a run lower than anyone else in baseball. He pitches for the Florida Marlins, and his name is Kevin Brown.

Brown has simply pitched better. If there were some universal mechanism which ensured that justice was doled out daily in equal amounts, one of the consequences would be that Brown would have a better record than Smoltz. Brown's earned the glory, but unless everyone suddenly wakes up and acknowedges it, his award will go to Smoltz. I'm here to sound the alarm.

Ironically, while John Smoltz seems to have shed his bad luck and poor run support, both curses have come to reside in the house of Kevin Brown. Brown's started 29 games, and in 25 of them, he's held his opponent to three earned runs or less. That's right—this year, he's been "roughed up" a total of exactly four times, twice surrendering four runs, and twice allowing five. (Smoltz, on the other hand, has been touched up for four or more earned runs seven times, almost twice as often as Brown.) Given five runs a game to work with, Brown could easily be something like 25-2. But he isn't; he's "only" 15-11. Why?

It's because his run support has been inexcusably poor, particularly in the close games. I ask you: if you have a pitcher who permits exactly one or two earned runs in every single start—never more—what should his record be? Smoltz has had 13 such games (an admittedly impressive total) and his record in those games is 10-1. Brown, on the other hand, has allowed one or two runs in 15 of his 29 starts (and remember, we're not even counting the seven starts where he was unscored upon), posting a 1.64 ERA over 109.2 innings. His record in those games? 8-6.

How is it possible to put up a one-something ERA and still just barely manage to crack .500? Well, it's pretty darned difficult. To even come close, you need to have the worst run support in baseball, as Brown does. In fact, the entire difference in Brown and Smoltz's won-loss records can be traced to the varying amounts of support their lineups have given them. McGriff, Jones and Company have provided Smoltz with 5.36 runs per nine innings, which makes him one of the 15 best-supported pitchers in the N.L. Meanwhile, Brown has had to eke out a meager existence on just over three-and-a-half runs per game. It's almost criminal. Here we have the best pitcher in the game this year, and he can't get the recognition he deserves because through some cruel coincidence, his teammates have conspired to ruin his record. The man should sue for non-support.

Should his teammates' ineptitude be held against Brown when voting time comes? That's what this is about. The Braves are a better team than the Marlins, which creates the illusion that Smoltz is better than Brown. But an illusion is all it is. The bottom line is that Brown has been more effective than Smoltz at retiring hitters and preventing the scoring of runs. That's the central issue here, and we can't lose sight of that. It isn't about who "wins" the most games; it's about who's the *best*. This isn't the "LaMarr Hoyt Award." May the best pitcher win.

—Mat Olkin

September 11—Lance, Roger and My Wife

Today I went to my pregnant wife's gyno appointment. There are four doctors who work at the place she's going now and since we just got to Pennsylvania they want her to meet with a different one every time because any of them may deliver the baby. We met doc number three today and he asked me what I did. I told him I do sports statistical work and he asked me if it had anything to do with "that guy who used to write those books." I told him I now know Bill personally. Isn't it cool to have something in common with the guy who's checking out your wife's private parts?

It sure looks like no one is going to break Roger Maris' record after all, or even come real close. It makes me think that all that put the end of last season together with the beginning of this season and see what numbers we get is pretty much hooey. It doesn't take into account the fatigue that a player goes through in a 162-game season and maybe that's more important than at least I've thought about before.

Rod Beaton's "next to the stats" column woke me up this morning with: "It's good for a chuckle to recall how the signing was criticized because (Lance) Johnson always had an unexceptional on-base percentage for a leadoff hitter. His batting average is .329. Why quibble with quality?" Yes, yes, Rodney, his batting average is .329. And that makes his on-base percentage a whopping .362, actually adequate for a leadoff hitter. And he actually ranks a whopping seventh in N.L. leadoff OBP. And do you know who three of the top four are? John Cangelosi at .410, who isn't good enough to play every day, Rickey Henderson at .408, who's having a "bad" year, and Quilvio Veras at .383, who lost his friggin' job. And their runs scored to at-bat ratios you ask, RB? Well, Cangy's is 46/236, Rickey's is 105/438, Veras' is 40/253, and Mr. 200 Hits and five walks is 104/609. How many runs do you think those other three would score using up 609 outs? Sure, Lance is a pretty OK hitter at .329. But I'll not only chuckle, I'll laugh my head off the year (and it could be next year) when he's hitting .280 and his OBP's .300.

— Steve Moyer

September 11—Thoughts from Bill

JAMES: 1) Where does Cal Ripken rank among the all-time shortstops? He has to rank second, doesn't he? We've still got Wagner number one, but the other guys that we grew up thinking of as the all-time great shortstops—Joe Cronin, Luke Appling, Aparicio—don't seem to me to match Ripken as a total package. What do you think?

2) Kevin Appier is winding up his seventh consecutive winning season, during all of which he has pitched enough innings to qualify for the league ERA title, and had a better-than-league ERA. This brings up several questions? How many guys in baseball history have had seven consecutive winning seasons, period? I'd bet the number is in the area of 100 or so.

Of those, how many pitched enough innings to qualify for the league ERA title every year? Less than half of them, obviously, so let's say 40.

Of those, how many actually had good ERAs every year?

It can't be very many. Whitey Ford did, Spahn I suppose, Don Sutton maybe. I'm sure there are others, but I'd bet it's not 20.

PINTO: I think Alex Rodriguez is going to bury Ripken before he's through.

Actually, I did some research for ESPN recently, and I've convinced myself that Rodriguez's 1996 season is the best by a shortstop this century. He'll be in the top five of every major category, and no other SS season is in more than two (that's among SS seasons). I can't wait to see what his stats look like in 10 years.

KRETSCHMANN: Number of pitchers with 7+ consecutive winning seasons and qualifying for the ERA title: 58 (30 in Hall of Fame).

With ERAs of less than or equal to the League Average: 38 (26 in Hall). Here's the list:

Seasons	Hall of Fame?	Player
11	Yes	Carl Hubbell
	Yes	Warren Spahn
10	Yes	Pete Alexander
	Yes	Bob Gibson
	Yes	Walter Johnson
	Yes	Bob Gibson
	Yes	Kid Nichols
	Yes	Cy Young
9	Yes	Steve Carlton
	Yes	John Clarkson
	Yes	Juan Marichal
	Yes	Red Ruffing
	No	Sam Leever
8	Yes	Three Finger Brown
	Yes	Whitey Ford
	Yes	Clark Griffith
	Yes	Addie Joss
	Yes	Tim Keefe
	Yes	Joe McGinnity
	Yes	Eppa Rixey
	Yes	Mickey Welch
	Yes	Early Wynn
	No	Jack Morris
	No	Don Sutton

Seasons	Hall of Fame?	Player
7	Yes	Don Drysdale
	Yes	Lefty Grove
	Yes	Christy Mathewson
	Yes	Eddie Plank
	Yes	Tom Seaver
	No	Bob Caruthers
	No	Roger Clemens
	No	Wilbur Cooper
	No	Mike Cuellar
	No	Ron Guidry
	No	Jim Kaat
	No	Dennis Leonard
	No	Steve Rogers
	No	Hooks Wiltse

I'm sort of shocked how many guys from the '70s/'80s showed up. Steve Rogers, Dennis Leonard, Jim Kaat, Ron Guidry, etc.

September 12—What's Up with That?

SPEAR: Mickey Morandini batted third for the Phillies last night.

Reason #142 why Philadelphia will not make the playoffs this year.

September 13—Jim Abbott

If you're like me, you couldn't help but crack a small smile Sunday after hearing that California's Jim Abbott had *finally* picked up his second victory of 1996 after 11 consecutive losses (he beat the Twins, 4-2). It's been a truly miserable season for Abbott (his ERA remains a hefty 7.56), one in which *nothing* has gone right. A stint to the bullpen. . . a new manager. . . a trip down to Triple-A—none of it has worked. Out in Anaheim, the Disney Company has built its empire on telling happy stories, but not even *they* could spin Abbott's 2-15 mark into anything positive, assuming they wanted to try. It's simply a season to forget.

How does Abbott stack up against history? Thirteen games under .500 is a bunch, but Abbott can breathe a sigh of relief that he's not even *close* to some of the worst pitching seasons in major league history.

The table below lists all pitchers since 1921 who finished at least 16 games below .500—well away from where Abbott currently stands (there are a ton of pitchers at –13, –14 and –15). Take a look and you'll see that it's one heck of an interesting list. With Abbott's future in mind, I also decided to include each pitcher's future won-loss mark to see which of the hurlers were able to rebound and which went in the tank following their disaster.

Most Games Below .500—1921-1996

Pitcher, Team	Year	W	L	Diff	Future Record
Ben Cantwell, Braves	1935	4	25	–21	9-10
Paul Derringer, StL/Cin	1933	7	27	–20	187-163
Don Larsen, Orioles	1954	3	21	–18	71-58
Roger Craig, Mets	1963	5	22	–17	10-14
Jose DeLeon, Pirates	1985	2	19	–17	70-84
Roy Wilkinson, White Sox	1921	4	20	–16	0-1
George Smith, Phillies	1921	4	20	–16	8-20
Jack Fisher, Mets	1965	8	24	–16	32-49

Before we get started, please know about the paradox of generating a horrible won-loss record. In a way, it's an art form. Each pitcher has to pitch just well enough to keep on losing. Pitch *too well* and the losses start turning into wins. Pitch *too poorly* and you're either yanked from the rotation, banished to the minors or given your walking papers.

The single-season mark for futility belongs to Ben Cantwell, who suffered through his 4-25 mark just two years after going 20-10 with a 2.61 ERA in 1933. He turned 33 at the start of the 1935 season and was essentially finished after the disaster. But he wasn't alone. In 1935, the Braves finished 38-115, a whopping 61.5 games behind the pennant-winning Cubs. The pitching staff posted a 4.93 ERA—astronomical for Braves Field. Want to hear something remarkable? Cantwell struck out only 348 batters in 1533 lifetime innings, or just 2.04 per nine. And no, that wasn't terribly unique for the era. My, how the game has changed. . .

Some details on the other pitchers. . .

Paul Derringer—Derringer rebounded from his 7-27 season at age 26 to put together a sparkling career and finish with 223 lifetime victories. He won 20 games four times (all for the Reds), finishing third in the N.L. MVP race in 1939 (25-7, 2.93) and fourth in 1940 (20-12, 3.06). The Reds won the pennant in both of those seasons and downed the Tigers in the '40 World Series, four games to three. Derringer started three times in that Series, winning Game 7, 2-1. He also turned in one of the best pitching performances by a rookie in baseball history, going 18-8 with a 3.36 ERA for the pennant-winning Cardinals in 1931 (he lost both of his World Series starts against the Athletics, although St. Louis still won in seven games).

Don Larsen—Most people forget that Larsen went from also-ran to World Series legend in just two years, tossing the only perfect game (or no-hitter) in World Series history in '56 with the Yankees against Brooklyn after going 3-21 in '54. Following his October glory, Larsen spent most of the rest of his career in the bullpen, finally calling it quits in 1967. (I love to point out that Larsen's perfecto was the genesis for the most ridiculous question in the history of sports journalism: "Casey, is that the best game Larsen's ever pitched?")

Roger Craig—An original member of the '62 Mets (when he went 10-24), Craig actually went *further* in the hole in '63 despite a much better ERA (3.78 from 4.52). What happened? Don Zminda informed me that Craig lost a record-tying *five* 1-0 games in 1963, which certainly explains a lot of it. He's probably best known for managing the Giants to the N.L. West title in 1987 and the pennant in 1989, as well as helping develop the split-fingered fastball—a pitch that first started to flourish in the late 70s and early 80s.

Jose DeLeon—DeLeon was just 24 in 1985 and bounced back to have a couple of solid seasons with the Cardinals in 1988 and 1989. I'll best remember him for his performance on the night of August 30, 1989 (I listened to the game on radio in my college dorm room) against the Cincinnati Reds: 11 innings, one hit allowed, no runs, no walks, eight strikeouts. . . and a no-decision. The Cardinals couldn't come up with a run, either and lost 1-0.

Roy Wilkinson—An infamous member of the 1919 Chicago White Sox, Wilkinson appeared in just four more major league games after going 4-20 in 1921. In 36 games that season, Wilkinson allowed 259 hits in 198 innings (ouch!).

George Smith—"Columbia George" finished 41 games under .500 (41-81) in his major league career, which is something very few pitchers today can do if you think about it. Opponents batted .308 against the Phillie staff in 1921.

Jack Fisher—Like Roger Craig, Fisher was able to rack up some ugly pitching numbers in the early days of the New York Mets, finishing 38-73 in four years with the team. His claim to fame is probably being a part of the 1967 Mets staff that included Tom Seaver, Jerry Koosman. . . but *not* Nolan Ryan. Fisher missed out on the glory in 1969, spending his final season with the Reds.

Let's not stop here. It's probably easier to compare Abbott to pitchers from the recent era, so I decided to come up with a second list of pitchers since 1969 (the year of divisional alignment) exclusively. Abbott will be happy to know that it includes one Cy Young Award winner.

Pitcher, Team	Year	W	L	Diff	Future Record
Matt Keough, Athletics	1979	2	17	−15	47-49
Mike Parrott, Mariners	1980	1	16	−15	3-6
Anthony Young, Mets	1993	1	16	−15	10-13
Randy Jones, Padres	1974	8	22	−14	85-95
Clay Kirby, Padres	1969	7	20	−13	68-84
Ken Reynolds, Phillies	1972	2	15	−13	0-5
Terry Felton, Twins	1982	0	13	−13	0-16
Rick Honeycutt, LA/Oak	1987	3	16	−13	19-22
Kyle Abbott, Phillies	1992	1	14	−13	2-1
Jim Abbott, Angels	1996	2	15	−13	—

Matt Keough—He became the poster-child for a truly terrible Oakland team (54-108) that finished 34 games behind California. But what a difference two years can make. In 1980, Billy Martin came aboard as manager and Rickey Henderson began to blossom into a superstar. The following year the A's made the playoffs with many of the same pitchers who had endured the disaster of '79—Keough (10-6), Rick Langford (12-10), Mike Norris (12-9) and Brian Kingman (3-6). After falling back to 11-18 in '82, Keough never consistently started again in the majors until departing in 1986.

Mike Parrott—He shined for the Mariners in 1979 as a 24 year old, going 14-12 on a team that finished 67-95. The following year his ERA jumped to 7.28 and he never pitched again in the majors following the strike year of 1981.

Anthony Young—As I mentioned earlier, some pitchers pitch *just* well enough to keep on losing. That personified Young from May 6, 1992 until July 24, 1993, when he went 0-27 with a 4.36 ERA. That's about as unlucky as you can get. Heck, post a 4.36 ERA in the American League this year and you can have your spot in *any* rotation. He's spent nearly all of the last two seasons in the bullpen with the Cubs and Astros.

Randy Jones—After losing 22 games in 1974, Jones turned around and *won* 20 in 1975 before winning the National League Cy Young Award in 1976 (22-14, 2.74). But he never had another winning season in the majors and finished 100-123 lifetime. I had forgotten that Jones finished his career with the Mets in 1981 and 1982, so I thought it would be interesting to see the combined won-loss records of the teams he was associated with (his San Diego stint lasted from 1973 to 1980). The total. . . 664-896, for a .426 winning percentage—which equates to 69-93 for a 162-game slate.

Clay Kirby—Most fans remember Kirby as a member of the World Champion Reds in 1975, but he actually spent only *two* of his eight major league seasons in Cincinnati. An original member of the expansion San Diego Padres in 1969, Kirby teamed with a rookie named Randy Jones in 1973 before heading off to the Big Red Machine. And yes, it's considerably easier to win games with Joe Morgan, Pete Rose, George Foster, Johnny Bench and Tony Perez giving you plenty of runs to work with.

Ken Reynolds—The lefthander's days as a starter ended after going 2-15 for the 1972 Phillies—the same year teammate Steve Carlton (a better-known Lefty) won the Cy Young Award by going 27-10 with a 1.98 ERA (remember that the *team* won only 59). Reynolds' final major league won-loss record: 7-29

Terry Felton—Yes folks, Felton went 0-13 with the '82 Twins. . . spending most of the season as a reliever! I haven't done any research on Felton, but I'd love to see his game logs from that year to see how such a thing could come about. To add insult to injury, Felton had gone 0-3 with the Twins in 1980, meaning his career record will live forever in the baseball record books at 0-16. The man pitched in 55 major league games in his career and couldn't find a way to win one of them. That's truly remarkable. The 1982 Twins yielded a league-high 208 homers in the first season of the Metrodome, inspiring the tag "Homer-dome," which will probably live forever.

Rick Honeycutt—Still going. . . Honeycutt went a combined 3-16 with the Dodgers and Athletics in 1987 before going to the bullpen and becoming another yet miracle product of the Tony La Russa/Dave Duncan magic. He was brilliant when the A's finally captured the World Series in 1989, saving 12 games with a 2.35 ERA on a staff that included a handful of relcamation projects—Dennis Eckersley, Mike Moore, Bob Welch, Dave Stewart and Storm Davis. He's back with La Russa in St. Louis this year at age 44—the oldest player in the majors.

Kyle Abbott—Now in the Angels organization with Jim Abbott, Kyle Abbott has always fought injuries and showed little sign of turning around his career in 1996, allowing nine runs in his only four innings of major league work and spending the rest of the season starting at Double-A.

So what does the future hold for Jim Abbott? Stories of Paul Derringer and Randy Jones certainly provide hope, but the odds are clearly against him. Word is that his velocity is down considerably this year, and his control has been almost nonexistent (72 walks in 122.2 innings). With a new manager on the way, the Angels might very well do some house-cleaning prior to 1997 and sweep Abbott right out the door. Perhaps a stop somewhere in the National League (in St. Louis with La Russa, perhaps?) would do him some good.

— Scott McDevitt

September 17—HBPs

OLKIN: It seems to me that a lot more hitters are hanging over the plate in recent years. When guys like Jim Thome, Jaff Bagwell and Jose Canseco go into their stance, it looks like parts of their body are actually in the strike zone. Watch Mo Vaughn at the height of his follow-through: his head and upper body are directly over the plate. I may be wrong, but it seems like the crowd-and-dive school of hitting has grown by leaps and bounds.

WENZ: I wonder if HBPs go up when ejections/fines for charging the mound go up. It seems to me they decided to crack down on brawls about eight years ago. Part of the scoreboard article maybe?

FAUST: Is the "crowd-and-drive" school also responsible for the jump in opposite-field homers? Thome obviously has a bunch of opposite field power, and I can't say I think of Bagwell, Mo, or Canseco as dead pull hitters.

JAMES: I had noticed this really rather amazing jump in HBP totals.

My thinking at the time was that HBP totals shot up when the league acted to crack down sharply on batters charging the mound. I still believe that is essentially true, but the Maddux comments on batters going to the opposite field, and the subsequent discovery that this was in fact true, have made me reconsider. I think now that what happened was an interaction between these two events—the effective crackdown on batters charging the mound, combined with an escalation in hitters crowding the plate, has led to this explosion in HBP—and explosion which, by the way, far outpaces the much-noticed explosion in home runs (now) or in stolen bases during the 1970s/'80s.

Solution? Move the batter's box backward about four inches. It makes a better game anyway, unless you are addicted to these five-homer extravaganzas. Make the hitters back off the plate, and certainly don't give them first base if they lean over the plate and get hit with a strike (which is what the rules call for even now, although it is unevenly enforced.)

PINTO: Maybe if teams found players that could actually throw the ball over the plate there wouldn't be as many hit batters. The numbers for the leaders aren't all that high compared to the last 20 years, which means there's a lot more at lower levels. Maybe the right solution is to limit teams to 10 pitchers. That would eliminate 56 pitchers from the game who can't pitch anyway.

COOPERSON: If that happens teams will pay more in medical bills than they'd pay in salary to the 11th pitcher on the team.

WENZ: I'm not sure how shrinking pitching staffs would make for better pitching. If it did, then teams would be doing it already.

PINTO: Why do teams carry 12 pitchers? Because they have 12 great pitchers and they want to use them all? This year proves that isn't true. Is it because they get hurt so often? Well it's pretty easy to run pitchers up and down from the minors, so that can't be the reason.

It's because they feel pitching is so bad, they feel they need more pitchers so they can make more changes. But the pitchers they add can't be any better than the pitchers they have, so pitching just gets worse. I guess I'm saying I'd rather see a bad relief pitcher pitch three innings than four bad relief pitchers pitch three innings.

JAMES: Regarding Pinto comment on pitchers missing the plate:

1) I question whether it is true that the best pitchers now don't hit more batters than they did 20 years ago. Since there are so many zeroes in this column, it would be extremely difficult to show that such a thing was true, whether or not it was.

2) Whether or not it is true (that the best pitchers now don't hit more batters than they used to), anything that happens in baseball can always be explained as a failure by one party or the other. If more runs are scored, the pitchers fail. If fewer runs are scored, you can say that the hitters aren't as good as they want to be. This is a fine logical solution, if you want to wind up as Tony Kubek, bitching about how baseball isn't what it used to be.

But the fact is, this change *isn't* created by the pitchers doing something different. It's created by the *hitters* doing something different. So regulating the pitchers because the hitters are doing something different just doesn't make any sense.

If we don't do something about it, there is every likelihood that someone will be killed or very seriously wounded by a pitch within the next five years.

In my opinion, that's a problem. Just me, maybe.

PINTO: We could get into a real chicken-egg argument here. I know for a few years now that Peter Gammons believes that pitchers can't pitch inside anymore because they've been raised pitching to hitters with aluminum bats. If pitchers no longer can pitch inside, then as a batter, I'm going to crowd the plate.

Now if enough Bagwells and Vaughns and Griffeys break hands or heads because of this, then batters will start backing off again. This will also happen if they regularly face pitchers who can actually pitch, which cutting rosters to 10 pitchers would help create.

By the way, how many batters crowd the plate on Randy Johnson? (Remember John Kruk?)

So what is so different about any other time in the history of baseball? Would your suggestion have helped Conigliaro or Blair or Slaught? We've had one player killed by a pitch in the majors this century, and most of that time they weren't using helmets. Even with an increase in hit batters, I have to think the probability of a death is very low compared to the first half of the century.

My feeling is I'm not communicating my points very well. I need to sit down when I'm not under deadline pressure and put my points down more logically. However, I still feel I have a valid point to make, that lots of bad pitching is more responsible for the rise than simply hitters crowding the plate.

OLKIN: David, I'm curious as to why you feel the pitchers are responsible for what's been going on. Is it really possible that the quality of pitching has dropped off that much since 1992?

September 18—Nomo's No-No

MCDEVITT: Mat Olkin and I just did some rough approximations on what the odds of this happening are in Coors Field *this year*. The Rockies hit .345 as a team in Coors, meaning the odds of Colorado *not* getting a hit in a particular at-bat are .655 (1.000-.345). You need 27 outs for the no-hitter, so .655 to the 27th power comes out to .0000109, or about 1 in 91,513. There are 81 home games per year in Coors Field, meaning we'll see the next no-no in that park—assuming the Rockies keep hitting the way they are there—in about 1,130 years. Despite the presence of a quality pitcher (Nomo), doesn't this have to be the most unlikely no-hitter in baseball history? Perhaps our guys at ESPN are already at work on this.

FAUST: Scott's message got me crunching through a few numbers. Let's assume an average team hits .260. Then, following Scott's logic above, the odds of a typical no-hitter are 1 in 3,394. A "season" of games is 2,100-2,300 games with 26 to 28 teams playing a 162-game season. It seems to me that we see two or three no-hitters a year, not one every year and a half.

To me, the math doesn't quite work out, but I won't argue with the conclusion that this may be the most unlikely no-hitter ever.

CARLSON: I think it just goes to show that the pitchers who do get the no-hitters are usually good pitchers who break through the "odds" that a no-hitter should only be thrown every season and a half, which actually makes sense. If the league hits .210 against you, you definitely should have a better chance of a no-hitter than if the league hits .280 against you.

WENZ: But every game has two teams with the potential to get no-hit, so there are effectively double the games, or 4,600. That means we should expect slightly more than one a year.

KRETSCHMANN: The problem with saying a team doesn't get a hit in .655 ABs and the sending it to the 27th power is that the assumption is then that a hit is a random event. I think a few batters and pitchers would disagree with that notion.

MOYER: Argh. I'm starting to hate baseball stats. Give me opinion & nonsense!

PINTO: I got home last night and was able to watch the last half-inning of the no-hitter on ESPN. I especially wanted to see how Nomo reacted. The team mobbed him, everyone taking a turn rubbing his head. At one point, they tried to carry him off the field, but it looked like Nomo didn't want them to. He was happy, but I don't think he cared for all the affection he was getting from his teammates, although he did embrace Wallace, who I assume is the pitching coach.

COOPERSON: If they had cut up his suit would he have flung mushrooms at them and stormed out of the clubhouse?

PINTO: I had been Nomo, I would have shown up with a samurai sword and scared the bleep out of someone on that team.

OLKIN: Are there any high-altitude parks in Japan? Maybe Hideo's a seasoned thin-air pitcher. That would explain why he didn't seem all that impressed with himself.

ELMAN: Taking the giant assumption that you believe him, I would have to put the no-hitter thrown by Doc Ellis in nomination for most improbable. Standing 60'6" away and having to pick which catcher you throw to is pretty impressive.

DEWAN: Drew, your additional calculation verifies Scott's conclusion. The method calculates the odds assuming average opposing pitchers. No-hit pitchers, by definition, are better than average in one or both of two ways: 1) they're above average in general and 2) they have above-average stuff that day.

Therefore, the odds are better than either of you calculated because no-hitters are thrown by above-average pitchers.

JAMES: For that matter, do they even pay any attention to no-hitters in Japan? It isn't inevitable, you know. American sportswriters didn't invent the concept of the no-hitter until about 1911—35 years after major league baseball began.

FAUST: I just realized that this team chock full of pure hitters has now been no-hit twice this season. Is that rare?

PINTO: If you look at their road numbers, you might start doubting that they are pure hitters.

FAUST: I was being sarcastic. . .

JAMES: Regarding McDevitt and Olkin's computations:

Your estimate of the chance of a no-hitter against a team like the Rockies in Coors field is wrong by a factor of at least several hundred. First of all, no-hitters on average involve getting out 26 hitters and one baserunner (either Caught Stealing or GIDP), rather than 27, which significantly effects the calculation.

With that exception, your calculation would be reasonably near the chance of no-hitter by an average pitcher on an average day. Well, not exactly, for this reason. The chance of getting out a .400 hitter, then a .300 hitter, is different from the chance of getting out two straight .350 hitters. Applied to a long string of hitters, the fact that not all hitters are at the average significantly alters the chance of getting them all out. This effect, however, would make the no-hitter even *less* likely than you estimated.

However, just as all hitters are not the same, all pitchers are not the same, either. The chance of a no-hitter in any one game is somewhere around one in a thousand. However, if a given pitcher decreases the team batting average just from .345 to .335, this increases the chance of 26 straight outs by about 60 percent. It is relatively common for a given pitcher to decrease the likelihood of a hit by such a margin that he makes the no-hitter 10 times more likely than it otherwise would be.

And this, again, does *not* even out as the averages do. If the chance of a no-hitter is 10 times greater one day and 10 times less the next, the sum is five times greater than in two random days.

Now take Hideo Nomo. The National League batting average is .263. Against Nomo, it's .213. So the Rockies batting average against Nomo is something like (.345 times (.213/.263)), or .279.

The chance of a pitcher with an opposition batting average of .279 pitching a no-hitter is about .000199, or one in 5,000. In other words, if Nomo pitches in Coors Field just twice a year, *he alone* would account for about one-half of the no-hitters that you anticipated.

Even this, however, dramatically under-states the real chance of a no-hitter, for this reason: that batting averages rise and fall with the weather. I don't know if you have noticed this, but a huge percentage of no-hitters occur in the last half of September. Batting averages drop in late September by about 10 to 15 points (from June).

Again, it doesn't even out. The no-hitter is maybe three times more likely in cool weather, and about one-third as likely in hot weather. It doesn't even out; the random fluctuations in hit probability tend, in sum, to make no-hitters more common.

As to whether this would be the unlikeliest no-hitter in baseball history, I don't know, but:

a) it would depend on what conditions you considered in the "likelihood" computation, and
b) even so, I doubt it.

There have been no-hitters pitched by pitchers who allowed like 11 hits per nine innings. *That's* unlikely. There were teams in the 1890s that hit .340 for the season, which no doubt means that some of them hit .380 in their home games. I suspect if you studied it hard enough, you'd find a more unlikely situation in which a no-hitter has been thrown.

September 19—Nomo's No-No (Cont'd)

On Tuesday night, Hideo Nomo pitched a no-hitter. . . at Coors Field, yet. And last night Roger Clemens tied his own record for most strikeouts by a pitcher in one game. Both these feats happened in what is clearly a "Year of the Hitter." What's going on here? Bill James, responding to some e-mail messages from various STATS people about Nomo's no-hitter, had this to say (one of the fun things about working for STATS is that you get e-mail comments from Bill on a regular basis):

I don't know if you have noticed this, but a huge percentage of no-hitters occur in the last half of September. Batting averages drop in late September by about ten to fifteen points (from June). Again, it doesn't even out. The no-hitter is maybe three times more likely in cool weather, and about one-third as likely in hot weather.

To underscore that point, the temperature at the start of Nomo's no-hitter was 46 degrees, with rain coming down and the wind blowing in. It must have gotten much cooler during the game, so if you were ever going to pitch a no-hitter in Denver, this was the night.

Clemens' game wasn't a no-hitter, of course, but it *was* one of the dominant pitching performances of recent years. However, he wasn't helped much by the weather: it was 72 degrees and clear at game time. It was just an awesome pitching performance. . . but then, so was Nomo's, weather or no weather.

— Don Zminda

September 23—Baseball Babble-On

What kind of odds do you think I could've gotten in April of Willie Greene having a better season than Butch Huskey? (He did.)

So who's season was worse, Mike Moore's 1995 or Greg Keagle's 1996? It's a toughie. Isn't it also amazing that by this time, someone hasn't signed Moore and put him on the major league roster? After all he is an innings-eater who takes that ball every fifth day and he has all kinds of postseason experience.

Here's a name I'll bet you haven't thought of for a while: Jose Rijo. All the fantasy drafters who took a gamble on Rijo lost and all those who took a gamble on Mark McGwire won—big time. That's the way the cookie crumbles in fantasy baseball. It sure ain't all skill.

It always floors me the way the public is forced to perceive things through the media. Take for example the case of the Dodgers' two late-season centerfield acquisitions—Wayne Kirby and Chad Curtis. The media would have you believe that Kirby came over from the Indians and has been a fine contributor to the Dodger division chase, especially since Brett Butler's unbelievable comeback was cut short. They'd also have you believe that the acquisition of Chad Curtis was a major waste of time and Curtis has been a huge flop. (And Bill Russell seems to believe this too, evidenced by the fact that he platoons the duo. This gives most of the ABs to the left-handed Kirby, even though the guy with the most star potential surely is Curtis, who has hit OK if not spectacularly against righties in the past.) Well, here are the facts: Kirby's numbers: .277-.333-.358, Curtis' numbers: .229-.339-.344. Yep, the old best friend of the sixth-grade baseball fan, batting average, strikes again. I'm not saying Curtis has been great and Kirby's been awful, but I certainly don't see any evidence of the vice-versa either. And that's what the media's got everybody believing.

Speaking of on-base percentage, definitely a favorite topic of mine, looking at the Brewer lineup today shows me a team with some good offensive potential screaming for a good leadoff hitter. They have the sluggers: Dave Nilsson's always been the real thing when he's not getting bit by mosquitos, John Jaha's finally making the American League look like the Texas League, Marc Newfield might finally get a chance to show what a talent he is, Jeff Cirillo is a talent already, and Jeromy Burnitz has decent potential. But then at the top of the order, you've got Fernando Vina having his career year with a whopping .341 OBP. The guy Garner'd probably really like to see there is Chuck E. Carr and his .310. Or maybe Gerald Williams and his .292. Granted, Jeff Cirillo would be fine at .391, but he can't steal bases (you know how important manufacturing runs is) and he has "too much" power for a leadoff hitter. And, boy, I see a perfect fit here. A forgotten star of 1995 that probably even the Brewers could afford. A guy who got sent to the minors in early August even though his OBP was in the .380's. A guy who put up .327-407-.471 in exile at Triple-A yet didn't even rejoin the team in September. A guy who plays second base. A guy named Quilvio Veras. I can dream.

It pains and mystifies me to see what happened to Veras. So much so that I questioned our Florida reporter for Tuesday night's game about the situation. Maybe I'll have an answer Wednesday.

I have a brand new baby and I'm worried about Quilvio Veras. I bet he's not worried about me, my wife, or our baby.

— Steve Moyer

September 26—Very Quietly. . .

CANTER: Barry Bonds needs one SB to be 40-40. He's also got 149 walks. . .

Jim Henzler points out that's the N.L. record for BB (149).

Bonds' OBP before Williams went out for the year: .434. After: .536.

DEWAN: Bonds has stolen 10 bases in the last 10 games!

ZMINDA: And he's thinking only of the team as always, not himself.

September 30—Bill James Trivia

JAMES: A couple of trivia questions about the late baseball season.

1) Kevin Brown of Florida and Kevin Ritz of Colorado both wound up the season 17-11. Which one wound up with a better ERA in road games?

2) Which major league manager used the most relievers this year?

3) Which one used the fewest?

SPEAR: My guess for most relievers is Terry Bevington.

PINTO: I know Brown had an excellent ERA on the Road, in the low twos. It seems the ballpark did not make that much of a difference to him, although it did bring his ERA under 2.00.

JAMES: Answers to trivia questions

1) Kevin Brown had an ERA on the road of 2.19. Kevin Ritz was at 4.65.

2) Don Baylor, for at least the fourth consecutive season, led the majors in relievers used, this time with 447. He did not match his major league record of 456, set in 1995, nor even his previous major league record of 453, set in 1993.

3) Cito Gaston used the fewest relievers, 303. I believe this is also the fourth consecutive year (at least) that Gaston has used the fewest relievers.

FAUST: Continuing the "trivia theme," I just figured out expected wins and losses for each team based on Bill's Pythagorean Theorem. Who was the "luckiest" team in 1996? Who was "unluckiest" (hint: it's a three-way tie)?

Which is the only playoff team to finish with fewer wins than the formula predicts?

Team	Runs	R All	W/L%	Wins	Losses	E W/L%	Exp W	Exp L	Diff
Bal	949	903	.543	88	74	.525	85	77	3
Bos	928	921	.525	85	77	.504	82	80	3
Cal	762	943	.435	70	91	.395	64	97	6
WSox	898	794	.525	85	77	.561	91	71	−6
Cle	952	769	.615	99	62	.605	97	64	2
Det	783	1103	.327	53	109	.335	54	108	−1
KC	746	786	.466	75	86	.474	76	85	−1
Mil	894	899	.494	80	82	.497	81	81	−1
Min	877	900	.481	78	84	.487	79	83	−1
Yanks	871	787	.568	92	70	.551	89	73	3
Oak	861	900	.481	78	84	.478	77	85	1
Sea	993	895	.528	85	76	.552	89	72	−4
Tex	928	799	.556	90	72	.574	93	69	−3
Tor	766	809	.457	74	88	.473	77	85	−3

Team	Runs	R All	W/L%	Wins	Losses	E W/L%	Exp W	Exp L	Diff
Atl	773	648	.593	96	66	.587	95	67	1
Cubs	772	771	.466	76	87	.501	82	81	−6
Cin	778	773	.500	81	81	.503	82	80	−1
Hou	753	792	.506	82	80	.475	77	85	5
LA	703	652	.556	90	72	.538	87	75	3
Mon	741	668	.543	88	74	.552	89	73	−1
Mets	746	779	.438	71	91	.478	77	85	−6
Phi	650	790	.414	67	95	.404	65	97	2
Pit	776	833	.451	73	89	.465	75	87	−2
StL	759	706	.543	88	74	.536	87	75	1
SD	771	682	.562	91	71	.561	91	71	0
SF	752	862	.420	68	94	.432	70	92	−2
Col	961	964	.512	83	79	.498	81	81	2
Fla	688	703	.494	80	82	.489	79	83	1

September 30—The Alomar Incident

PINTO: Does anyone have any recollection of a player being suspended for the post season for transgressions during the regular season?

SPEAR: I don't recall anything. But the last I heard (from SportsCenter, I think) was that Alomar's suspension would *not* be factored into the postseason. . . Is that not the case?

OLKIN: Otis Nixon.

ZMINDA: Maybe before Game 1, they could just let all the umpires spit on Alomar.

JAMES: Remember 1965. . . well, of course you don't, but Don Zminda and I do. Juan Marichal cracked John Roseboro over the head with a bat in early September. They didn't have the "suspension appeal" process then, but the National League president suspended Marichal for something like 10 days and fined him what seemed at the time like a substantial amount of money.

The Giants got red-hot down the stretch, despite the absence of Marichal, and went into the last weekend of the season with a chance to catch the Dodgers. At this moment, the National League President chose to announce that *if* the Giants could beat the Dodgers, Marichal would not be allowed to pitch in the World Series, either. He had been under fire for not coming down hard enough on Marichal, who actually could have killed Roseboro, and hadn't anticipated the Giants making a run, so when they did, he just piled this little bonus onto the penalty. The Giants lost the race in the final series, and always blamed the N.L. Prez. . . I forget who it was. . . for announcing the additional suspension to Marichal just before that series started.

138

October 1—It's Just a Game

Was that last San Diego-Los Angeles game weird, or what? Here we've got this great race for the N.L. West title, and it just happens to come down to a head-to-head confrontation on the final day of the regular season. . . and neither team really cared if they won or lost! I guess I should just bite my tongue and write it off as one of the unfortunate side-effects of the wild-card format, but the whole thing just rubbed me the wrong way.

Not that either team was actively tanking it—far from it. Lifting Ramon Martinez after one inning was hard to overlook, but Pedro Astacio is hardly Greg Booker out there. In fact, the longer the game went, the more each team seemed to want to win. We were assured that both clubs would merely be going through the motions and trying not to get hurt, but when it was all said and done, each team had used its closer, and no one had set up any lawn chairs in the outfield. Perhaps the moral of the story is that once you cross those white lines, it's hard _not_ to want to win.

And by winning, the Padres have spared themselves from the Braves' wrath for at least another round. Last weekend, everyone debated whether it would be better to play the Braves now, or later. In the end, everyone seemed to throw up their hands and say, "It doesn't matter. No one's going to beat Atlanta anyway."

Well, if you assume that Atlanta's unbeatable, then no, it doesn't make much difference if they knock you out of the playoffs this week or next. But I look at it this way: What If? Yeah, what if the sun sets in the East, apples fall up, and the Cardinals somehow take out the Braves? You can debate the chances of that happening until next spring, but the fact is that in a short series, there are no guarantees. Take the League Championship Series for example.

Since the Series was created in 1969, the team with the better regular-season won-loss record has won only 60 percent of the time. Does that mean that the Cardinals could beat the Braves? Not necessarily. But it does tell me that an inferior team can string together enough upsets to beat a good team in a short series. It happens all the time.

I think it's realistic to say that at _worst_, the Cardinals stand a 20 percent chance of prevailing over Atlanta. So if you're San Diego, does that give you something to play for? I think it should. If you're Bruce Bochy, you say to yourself, "Hmm. . . now if I win, St. Louis plays Atlanta, so I face an 80 percent chance of facing Atlanta if I advance to the next round. And if I lose to the Dodgers here today, I face a _100_ percent chance of meeting the Braves." Hmm. Eighty, one-hundred. Eighty, one-hundred. The beer, the ball.

It don't take no slide rule, class. That's why both managers finally woke up and went with their closers with the game on the line. And that's why the playoff format turned out to be not nearly as flawed as everyone had said. In what everyone had expected to be a meaningless game, there turned out to be one very large reason to win: the dark and ominous silhouette of the Atlanta Braves in the rearview mirror.

—Mat Olkin

October 1-4—Managers

MOYER: My local paper mentioned that Kevin Kennedy supporters would blame Duquette for his "rotisserie approach to filling out a roster" and that he "filled the team with designated hitters and fielders playing out of position." Hmmm. Isn't that interesting? Wonder why no other team does that stuff? Now, what the Red Sox need, in my opinion, is a manager who's willing to play guys who can play baseball (Dwayne Hosey) over guys who look like athletes and have postseason experience (Mike Greenwell). I don't think Jim Leyland or Jim Fregosi is the answer. (The Red Sox will end up with Mark Johnson at first and Ruben Amaro batting cleanup.) I'm very much hoping that Duquette will continue to go against the grain and pick an unknown guy who thinks like us, or even a guy with experience who understands the concepts somewhat (maybe Torborg?), over a proven "baseball man."

ZMINDA: Well, not to sound like an old fart, but I thought the way Kennedy structured his roster this spring was completely idiotic. Duquette deserves to share a lot of the blame for that, but Kennedy deserved to get fired just for the way he abused his pitching staff, let alone all the other stuff.

I'll take my chances with Jim Leyland any day.

PINTO: The Red Sox are going to try for Leyland, but if that fails they will probably go with an unknown, although Tommy Lasorda wants the job.

OLKIN: Three years from now, Kennedy will still be managing Canseco. They'll both be starring for the St. Paul Saints.

MOYER: I'm so sick of hearing about "poor Jim Leyland" it makes me want to puke. If he's so great, he should've found talented minor leaguers to fill the holes around the good players he did have. Anymore, all he had to do was win five games and everyone friggin' screamed "Genius." He's a baby for walking out early on a challenge he couldn't handle if you ask me.

WENZ: I agree about the poor Jim Leyland mantra that's become so popular. Give anyone Barry Bonds in his prime, Bonilla in his prime, Drabek in his prime, and two good glove men up the middle and they damn well better contend. Then they had one more good year after they started to split up, and everyone hopped on his bandwagon.

COOPERSON: As an N.L. East follower, I think you guys are all wrong about Leyland. I "totally" agree that once the media thinks you're great, you can do very little wrong, and you're great forever in their eyes. But Leyland earned it. The Pirates in 1990 were not as talented or as deep as the Mets, yet they won the division. Can anyone tell me who their starting pitchers were, beyond Drabek? Or who was in their bullpen? That team platooned at four different positions, and one of the guys who *wasn't* in a platoon was Jose Lind, who's not exactly headed to Cooperstown. Other than the big three in the outfield and Drabek, there weren't exactly stars on that team. Rafael Belliard? Sid Bream? Gary Redus? The manager got a lot out of some less than stellar guys.

OLKIN: But how good were those guys before Leyland got them? Bonds was a .220-hitting center fielder. The Yanks weren't impressed with Drabek and traded him to the Pirates in the Rick Rhoden deal. The White Sox traded them Bobby Bonilla for Jose DeLeon, for God's sake. It was under Leyland that they became Barry Bonds, Doug Drabek and Bobby Bonilla.

ZMINDA: The Astros just named one of their radio announcers, Larry Dierker, as their new manager. He's never managed anywhere prior to this.

I've had a little personal contact with Dierker. When we first took over the Scouting Report book, we were going to use former players-turned-broadcasters to give comments like they did in the previous editions of the book. Dierker was one of the people I talked to; in fact, he agreed to do the work, but the deal fell through because I couldn't work out a satisfactory agreement with Jim Kaat, who was going to be the other commentator.

So I know Dierker from those negotiations. Seemed like a good, straightforward, no-nonsense guy. Whether that'll make him a good manager is another question, but I sure wish him well.

October 2—Postseason Babble-On

Wowee wow wow. The Indians are down two-zip. There can only be one reason for this and that's because the Orioles are the team I'd most like to see lose in the postseason. I can't remember the last year the teams I was hoping for in the postseason won. Believe it or not, research done by the Elias Sports Bureau shows that the last time a team that Steve Moyer was rooting for won the World Series was in 1989 when the A's beat the Giants.

I guess I never really noticed before last night, but isn't that David Weathers one ugly dude?

Speaking of ugly dudes, go check out the six baseball columnist's heads they show you on ESPN SportZone. Every one is fat or bald and most are both. Not that I couldn't afford to lose a few #'s (pretty clever there with the pound sign huh? pretty bleeding eXXxTReMe if I do say so myself). That's why no one's banging down my door to hire me for their mainstream publication or website, I guess. I'm just too pretty. (But honestly, old Mr. Turkey-Neck Gammons would look good next to these six.)

Speaking of fat, bald, ugly dudes, let's have a big crybaby party for the major league umpires. Waa waa waa. Boo hoo hoo. For God's sake, it was only spit. Big Deal. Get your fat butts out there on the field before they find a few of the million other umpires that could replace you in about five seconds. But of course, when that happens, ESPN will be quick to show the "Blown Call Of The Day" (as if there couldn't be one every day now) five million-billion times over to make all the sheep at home think there really are only a chosen handful of guys who can really ump in the bigs.

And I see they've already begun the second annual "Let's Totally Berate Manny Ramirez Because He's Only A Hitter And Not A Pitching-And-Defenser That We Love So Well." There's certainly no guarantee at all that Chris Hoiles was gonna be out at home. And, in addition, everyone seemed to forget that Ramirez had three hits including a homer and two runs scored. But, what's that old baseball adage? Anyone can hit. It's only Pitching and Defense that counts.

Oh, and I forgot the other thing that counts—Postseason Experience. Take David Cone versus John Burkett for example.

Finally, let me list who I'm rooting for, in order:

1. Yankees 2. Rangers 3. Padres (despite Ken Caminiti) 4. Dodgers 5. Indians 6. Braves 7. Cardinals 8. Orioles

And, finally finally, thinking about Ken Caminiti reminded me of a quote I read from him today about Todd Stottlemyre, "Nibble, nibble, nibble. He doesn't challenge anybody." That reminded me of the macho guys on my old fastpitch softball team who, after going hitless against a junkball pitcher would say, "He was too slow for me." Macho outs or wimpy outs all look the same in the scorebook.

— Steve Moyer

October 3—A Fun Year

You know the big records, but here are some statistical tidbits you might not be aware of from the amazing 1996 season:

1. Todd Van Poppel, working 99.1 innings for the A's and Tigers, posted an ERA of 9.06. That's the highest ERA for any pitcher this century who worked at least 90 innings in a season (Old record: 8.29 by Luther Roy in 92.1 innings for the Phillies and Dodgers in 1929).

2. Jim Abbott of the Angels went 2-18 for a winning percentage of .100. That's the fourth-lowest winning percentage in this century by a pitcher with at least 20 decisions in a season. The bottom three: Jack Nabors, 1916 A's (1-20, .048); Joe Harris, 1906 Red Sox (2-21, .087); and Jose DeLeon, 1985 Pirates (2-19, .095).

3. Rudy Pemberton of the Red Sox batted .512 in 41 at bats. That's the highest in this century for a player who batted at least 40 times in a season (Old record: .500, 21 for 42, by Gil Coan of the 1947 Senators).

4. The Mariners scored 993 runs, most for any major league team since the Red Sox scored 1,027 runs in 1950.

5. The Indians batted .293, the highest team average since that same 1950 Red Sox club batted .302.

6. The Mariners posted a team slugging average of .484, a figure topped by only two teams in the 20th century, the 1927 and 1930 New York Yankees (both .488). Two other teams have also slugged .484: the 1936 New York Yankees and the 1994 Cleveland Indians.

7. The Colorado Rockies scored 961 runs, the most scored by any National League club since 1930.

8. The Rockies also batted .287, the highest average for an N.L. club since the Cardinals hit .294 in 1939.

9. The Rockies, who tied the all-time National League record with 221 homers, became the first major league team in history to top both 200 homers and 200 stolen bases (they swiped 201) in the same season.

10. Toronto Blue Jay batters were hit by a total of 92 pitches, a 20th century team record.

11. Houston Astro hitters were hit by 84 pitches, the most for any N.L. club since the Giants were plunked by 84 pitches in 1903.

What a fun year.

— Don Zminda

October 7—Full of Spit

The entire Roberto Alomar-John Hirschbeck affair has been disgusting, embarrassing and distracting, at a time when baseball can least afford it. Still, there is a bright side to it all. The general public has come away from it having learned one very important lesson: it's not nice to spit on the umpire.

I think we owe all parties involved a hearty thank-you for this valuable contribution to our collective moral code. We all felt fairly certain that murder, for instance, was wrong. Running a red light, we all agreed, was to be frowned upon. But spitting on the ump? A timeless conundrum, certainly. We can all rest easier now, knowing that this little gray area has been cleared up.

This seems to be moral of the story here, doesn't it? Public opinion is virtually unanimous: spitting on ump is wrong; Alomar spit on ump; Alomar *bad*.

Is it really that simple? Does it have to be? Are we really to the point where we require life to be as simplistic as a Steve Seagal movie?

Alomar bad, ump good. It's easy to report, easy to digest and easy to understand. But it's not what happened. It's not true. It's wrong.

Now, let me start off by saying that I am not here to defend what Alomar did. He violated one of the most sacred laws of the game, the requirement that the umpire be safe from physical attack. But if you look at one unfortunate microsecond to the exclusion of all else, you miss a lot. Here's what I saw.

I saw one of the best players in baseball at the plate with a chance to help his team reach the playoffs. It was a crucial at-bat in an important game, and with two strikes on him, he was looking to fight off anything close. And let me say that from a personal standpoint, there are very few players I'd rather watch hit with the game on the line than Roberto Alomar. Robby is *into* it, in a way that the most hard-core fans best appreciate. He's unblinking, wide-eyed and focused. You know that his every thought is centered on achieving success. There are no dollar signs, tales of the tape or photo ops floating around in his head. All he sees is a chance for victory. He is, quite simply, the one player on the field who wants to win as badly as you do.

Like I said, he was ready to fight off any pitch that was remotely close to the strike zone. The pitch he got wasn't. It was at least five inches outside, as the overhead replay would clearly show. It was quite possibly low, too.

The umpire, John Hirschbeck, called it strike three. Alomar, having been cheated of his chance to deliver, turned to protest. Hirschbeck jawed right back. Later, Alomar claimed that Hirschbeck told him, "Swing at it, you %$#@." Robby said that the ump called him a "name," but he refused to repeat the epithet.

Whatever it was, it only made things worse. Alomar flew into a rage, and as they were being separated, Alomar lost control and committed an act that he will probably regret for the rest of his life. His insensitive comments afterward didn't help.

"Alomar's fault," was the immediate judgment. But was it? What about the blatantly erroneous call? What about the (alleged) provocation immediately afterward? What if Hirschbeck purposefully, knowingly and intentionally called out Alomar on a pitch well outside the strike zone, and then proceeded to provoke Alomar—at a time when Alomar, on the eve of the playoffs, was especially powerless to respond? There's no excuse for Alomar's reaction, but I ask you: *was he provoked?*

Has anyone even *asked* this question yet?

If there's even the *possibility* that one of the game's "impartial" arbiters has taken the rules into his own hands, and violated them in an attempt to settle some personal score with one of the players, doesn't that deserve some attention? And when the situation escalates to the point where one of the game's biggest stars might have to be yanked off the stage before millions of people, while the umpires refuse to work until they are satisfied with the level of discipline imposed by the league offices, isn't it fair to ask: Who started this?

The umpire is the absolute authority on the baseball field; he has to be. Without an impartial umpire, there can be no level playing field, and the sport cannot maintain its integrity. You cannot have the umpire provoking a confrontation in which the player might be suspended and the pennant race might be affected. And most of all, you cannot have all of this going on when it might result in the removal of a star player from a postseason team. It is the umpire's duty to *avoid* disturbing the natural outcome of the games on the field.

What could possibly be more disruptive to the championship race's progression than to force the Orioles to play without Roberto Alomar?

Did Alomar screw up? He sure did. Does he deserve to be disciplined? Of course he does. But if there is even a possibility that an umpire has abused his authority here, with such far-reaching implications, that issue must deserve just as much attention. Rule-breakers must be dealt with, but giving the enforcers absolute authority is not the answer. Stamping out anarchy is a poor excuse for implementing a dictatorship.

—Mat Olkin

October 8—Sportswriters

FAUST: Here's Derek Jeter according to Paul Sullivan in today's *Chicago Tribune*:

"Jeter is the hands-down favorite for A.L. Rookie of the Year because of his .314 average and 78 RBI (sic)—not bad for a player considered to be a slick-fielding, no-hit shortstop."

What?

PINTO: He obviously confused him with Rey Ordonez.

ZMINDA: I'll bet Paul Sullivan thought Alex Rodriguez was a "slick-fielding, no-hit shortstop" also. . .

MOYER: The original quote that Drew threw out was not that shocking to me in that I'm pretty sure I had read the same assessment of Jeter's preseason. The reasons? Probably because, as we all know, minor league batting averages don't mean anything combined with the fact that Jeter hit .250 in 48 at-bats last year. (Willie Greene can't hit for power against major league pitchers, either.)

October 14—More Postseason Babble-On

Oh dear, oh my. The Braves and Luis Polonia should've bunted and didn't. Oh woe is baseball. They just don't know the fundamentals like they used to anymore now do they? These young kids, all they want to do is hit solo homers and make millions of dollars. And especially in these times when the game of baseball can least afford a missed sacrifice bunt opportunity. Oh woe is baseball. Oh dear, oh my.

It just didn't mean a darn thing earlier this year when Darryl Strawberry was hitting .800 with 20 homers in 50 at-bats in the Northern League, just like everyone said, now did it?

I have to hand it to Joe Torre, a manager whom I was very much less than fond of coming into this year. While Buck Showalter, a manager I was quite fond of (I have a big picture of his head pasted on my bedroom ceiling) coming into this season, let Darryl smolder on the bench last playoffs, Torre had the guts and good sense to use him. More than anything else, I loved his bases-loaded walk early in the series, which pretty much got things rolling for him. I swear last year he would've done the same thing last year in that David Cone/Andy Benes struggle, in the inning in which Benes just couldn't find the plate while Don Mattingly, Mike Stanley and Paul O'Neill flailed away. I think Showalter would've brought in Mariano

Duncan (what a horrible, horrible player) if he'd have had him. I'm just really happy for the Straw.

Postseason experience is everything. Ask Fred McGriff.

Postseason experience is everything. Ask Dmitri Young. A rookie never would've had the presence to deliver in the clutch like that. Must've been Willie McGee's clubhouse influence.

I'll finish with a Joe Torre quote, "The reason we out-homered them is we pitched a little bit better." That's right, Joe, even good hitting is a result of pitching. Because, as I'm sure you know, pitching's 75 percent of the game, and defense is 14 percent. (And manufacturing runs is the other one percent.)

— Steve Moyer

October 15—Championship Series

I sure have been enjoying the NLCS. Game 4 was definitely the turning point. Now when I say that, you must think I'm referring to the Cardinals' late comeback that gave them the victory and a 3-to-1 advantage in the Series. Actually, I'm not talking about that at all. To me, the real turning point came before the game had even begun.

Each manager faced the same options in choosing a starting pitcher for Game 4: bring back the opening-game starter on short rest, setting him up for a possible Game Seven in the process, or go with the fourth starter instead. Tony La Russa selected option "A," Bobby Cox chose "B," and the results of their choices have played a huge role in the Series from that point forward.

Each manager proceeded exactly as we might have expected, given their past histories. In his first trip to the postseason, Bobby Cox pitched Jimmy Key, Doyle Alexander and Dave Stieb on short rest in the 1985 ALCS. Alexander was shelled in the sixth game, and Stieb—starting for the third time in nine days—was hit hard and took the loss in the seventh and deciding game. Stieb came up with a sore elbow the following spring and was never the same pitcher again.

In his next trip to the playoffs, Cox used four starters to get past the Pirates in '91. He didn't start using them on short rest until the last three games of the World Series. The Twins won two of those three games to take the championship, although the Braves' pitchers didn't seem to suffer from the heavier use at the end.

In 1992, though it was different. In the NLCS, Cox dropped Charlie Leibrandt and went with a three-man rotation, and it almost cost him dearly. On three days' rest, John Smoltz barely survived Game 4, but hung on as the Braves went up 3-1 on Pittsburgh. Then it got scary. Steve Avery retired exactly *one* batter in his Game 5 start, and the Braves fell, 7-1. In the sixth game, Tom Glavine didn't fare much better, as the Pirates pasted him for eight runs in a single inning to tie the series. Smoltz pitched six solid innings the next day, and before he had a chance to blow up too, Cox yanked him and prayed for his bullpen. They did the job, and the Braves were in the World Series. But Cox didn't relent: he stuck with a three-man rotation against Toronto, and the Braves fell in six games.

That was the last time he tried *that* strategy. Since then, he's always used all four starters in the postseason, giving them normal rest in-between starts. While it's true that the addition of Greg Maddux has helped him to do that, it hasn't always been that simple. In last year's postseason, Cox was *twice* confronted with the choice of bringing back Maddux on short rest, or going with Steve Avery instead. Despite the criticism he brought upon himself, Cox chose Avery both times. Both times, it worked. When he chose Denny Neagle to start Game 4 Monday night, it was just a continuation of that pattern.

La Russa, on the other hand, has always taken the opposite tack. During the days of Oakland's mini-dynasty, he never hesitated to use Dave Stewart every fourth day. Except for '92, when Stewart's days as a workhorse were over, that's always been the way La Russa's done it—pick a horse and ride him. This year, Andy Benes was his man.

At first, it worked out for St. Louis. They survived Benes' shaky work in Game 4. The St. Louis bats finally broke through against the Braves' relievers, after Denny Neagle had been removed. Benes remained on target for the seventh game, if necessary. The Braves, however, would only be able to use John Smoltz for Game 5, and after that, he'd be out of the Cardinals' hair for good.

But in the bigger picture, have the Cardinals won the gamble? After all, Todd Stottlemyre—who was starting on three days' rest for the first time all year—got absolutely shelled last night. Sure they're still up 3-2, but I'd hate to be standing next to them on the ice. As the Series shifts to Atlanta, they now have to send Donovan Osborne to the mound on three days' rest for the first time this year, while the Braves will counter with a fully-rested Greg Maddux. And who do you like for Game 7? A worn-down Andy Benes, or a relaxed and rested Tom Glavine? Anyway you look at it, it's going to be an uphill battle for St. Louis.

—Mat Olkin

October 16—Postseason Babble-On Continues

I have to admit, I'm starting to like La Russa's Cardinals, whom I didn't like at all just a couple of weeks ago. Three reasons the Cards are growing on me:

1) Feisty Tony La Russa basically telling the Braves to stick it in reference to their dislike of the Cards' displaying of emotions. The Braves have basically become the stuffed shirts of the league, so well-respected and well-behaved. Tony La Russa says, "Screw the Braves."

2) Dennis Eckersley saying, "So what? I could care less what Schuerholz says." And "[Schuerholz should] quit looking at me. What are you looking at me for? Get the [bleep] outta here." And "Who the [bleep] is Schuerholz?"

3) That well-respected, stuffed-shirt, "good pitching beats good hitting every time," "pitching, defense, and timely hitting," announcer's dream horse manure that the Braves are all about. Steve Moyer says, "Screw the Braves."

— Steve Moyer

October 17—Postseason Ponderings

Have you ever seen a worse call in a big game than Bob Davidson calling Mark Lemke out for tagging up at third too soon last night? This is a call that probably gets made no more than five times a year, and it shows a lot of guts to call out the home team's runner in the late innings of a 2-1 game. Only trouble was, Davidson got the call wrong; Lemke *hadn't* left too soon, as the replays clearly showed. It was an absolutely horrible call to make at a crucial point of a playoff game. Simply brutal. You just can't call a runner out like that unless it's obvious the runner left too soon, and in this case it was obvious that the runner *didn't*. What amazed me even more, though, is that Bobby Cox didn't make a fuss about it. Has the Alomar incident made players and managers afraid to challenge the umps, even when they're right? I sure hope not. Fortunately for Davidson, the Braves got him off the hook by winning the game anyway.

The Braves-Cardinals match has been a fun series and I'm glad it's going seven games, but a lot of the stuff between the teams is a little silly. There's the Braves, complaining that Dennis Eckersley shows his excitement when he gets the last out of a game. Well, isn't *that* a crime? Maybe instead of worrying about junior high-school stuff like this, the Tomahawk Choppers could concentrate on beating the Eck so that he's got nothing to celebrate. The Redbirds are just as bad, whining about how the Braves don't "respect" them. Who cares if they respect you or not? Just win, baby. The Cardinals are starting to act like it doesn't matter if they blow the Series, just as long as the Braves say nice things about them. And if they lose, they'll probably get their wish.

Whoever wins the NLCS will get to play a Yankee team that will have been out of action from Sunday to Saturday. That's a long layoff, and it would be no surprise if the Yankees showed the effects of it. Back in the olden days, a league would sometimes try to keep its champion fresh by staging an all-star game during the layoff, with the pennant winner facing a team composed of players from its own league. They don't do fun stuff like that any more. . . not that I think it would help.

As for the Series, I personally am not looking forward to another week of Joe Buck, Tim McCarver and Bob Brenly. McCarver used to be good, but he fell in love with his own voice at some point along the way, and now all he does is talk, talk, talk. Even when says something insightful, he just keeps saying it over and over again. I like Brenly well enough, but McCarver hardly ever lets him get a word in, and when he does, Brenly often says something dumb. Like last night, when the Cardinals brought Todd Stottlemyre. Brenly kept going on about how good Stottlemyre was looking, how good his fastball was, etc. He kept at it even when Stottlemyre hit a batter and then gave up two hits—including a scorching line-drive single to noted batsman, Rafael Belliard—to give the Braves the run that put the game away.

More about the tube. Both LCS were highly entertaining, but the TV ratings have been pretty bad. . . especially by NBC standards. So get ready for a lot more of that "baseball is dead" talk. I maintain that this is a ridiculous overreaction. In point of fact, baseball postseason ratings compare very favorably with those of a sport that "everybody" supposedly loves, the NBA. While it's true that the NBA finals are played in June, when TV ratings are generally lower than they are in October, it's also true that the NBA finals were moved to June a few years ago because the networks didn't *want* them on during their crucial May ratings period. . . and because the NBA didn't want to start its season in October, when so many people were focused on postseason baseball. Another thing: all three rounds of the baseball playoffs are shown on the networks in prime time, with a game on either Fox or NBC virtually every night. Compare that with the NBA playoffs, where only the finals and a portion of the semi-finals are broadcast by a single network. So why is it that baseball is supposedly dying, while the NBA is considered red-hot?

I ain't done yet. Why is that if a guy has a few good games, like Mark Lemke this year, the announcers always tell us that "this guy has always been a great pressure player"? Not to confuse anybody with the facts, but prior to 1996, Lemke had played in 46 postseason games and batted a mighty .257 with no home runs and 15 RBI. Does that seem like a great pressure player to you? Lemke's a good ballplayer, but to hear the Fox guys talk, he's Mr. October.

So maybe I should just turn the sound down. Whatever. . . I'm looking forward to this Series. It says here the Yanks are gonna win it all.

— Don Zminda

October 22—David Cone

What is it with David Cone?

He's an ace in every sense of the word. Few people can carve up a hitter so many different ways, every five days, for eight innings at a time. Over the course of his career, he's led the league in a number of categories, including innings, strikeouts and winning percentage. He's won the Cy Young award. He has the fourth-best winning percentage among active pitchers, better than Randy Johnson, Kevin Appier, or his mound opponent tonight, Tom Glavine. . . and yes, better than Greg Maddux. There's no two ways about it: he's an ace.

But in the postseason, more often than not, he isn't. After losing to Texas in the Division Series and struggling to find the plate against Baltimore in the League Championship Series, Cone's lifetime postseason record over 11 starts now stands at 3-3, with a 4.35 ERA. Even Maddux—for all his memorable disappointments, from Will Clark to Gary Gaetti—owns a postseason record of 7-4, 3.50, in 13 starts.

What is it with David Cone?

Perhaps it all started before his first postseason appearance back in 1988. The Mets were leading the Dodgers in the NLCS, one game to none. Before he took the mound for Game 2, Cone, who had won his last eight starts, wrote a column for the New York Daily News where he disparaged several of the Dodgers. He called Jay Howell a "high school pitcher" and said that Orel Hershiser was "lucky" to have pitched so well in the first game of the series. You can imagine how well Tommy Lasorda used that to fire up his team. When Cone took the mound that night, the Dodgers knocked him out by the third inning. "We wanted to make sure he had plenty of time to meet his deadlines," quipped an uncharacteristically witty Steve Sax. The Dodgers beat the Mets in seven games when Hershiser proved to be too darned "lucky" to lose.

His unimpressive work in the '92 playoffs and World Series was his last postseason experience until last year's historic Division Series against Seattle. Cone pitched and won the opening game, despite allowing six walks over eight innings. But it was his heart-rending performance in the fifth and final game for which he will always be remembered. In the bottom of the eighth, Cone held a 4-2 lead and needed to get only six outs to send the Yankees to the American League Championship Series. He got the first two outs of the inning, but lost control of his breaking ball as he grew increasingly tired. The Mariners just sat back and watched as he loaded the bases, and finally walked in the tying run before trudging off the mound.

So far, this year has been no better. He absorbed the Yankees' only loss to Texas in the first round of the playoffs, and needed 132 pitches just to get through six innings against Baltimore. In that game, he departed after six with game tied 2-2, but the bullpen blew it as soon as he hit the showers.

So now, tonight, having pushed him back in the rotation as far as they could, and traveling to Atlanta carrying a crippling 0-2 deficit, the Yanks have no other choice. For all practical purposes, they must place a season's worth of hopes—not to mention a potentially unemployment rate-boosting stack of pink slips from above—squarely on the narrow, sloping shoulders of David Cone.

Can he do it?

Of course he can—that's the most frustrating part. As everyone knows, Cone's stuff is among the most dominant in the game. But for Cone, having five quality pitches is often a double-edged sword. He gets himself into trouble when he tries to get too cute and use all of his pitches in a single at-bat. When he isn't overanalyzing his pitch selection, he just cruises along on pure talent. The ironic truth is that Cone—an intelligent and articulate man—pitches better when he uses more of his arm and less of his head. Unfortunately, the bigger the game, the more he thinks, and pretty soon, he's throwing an impressive variety of breaking pitches, and bouncing them all over the place.

Keep a close watch on him tonight. If he skids a pitch to the backstop in the first inning, then you can start bracing yourself for Brian Boehringer. But if you see him strike out someone on nothing but fastballs, you just might want to stay tuned and see if the Yanks can pull this thing out.

—Mat Olkin

October 23—Andruw Jones

SPEAR: A guy on my SABR e-mail list pointed out that on the day Andruw Jones was born (April 23, 1977), the Braves began a 17-game losing streak that saw:

a. Ted Turner begin and end his managerial career
b. Ted Turner get suspended for a year for tampering with Gary Matthews
c. the Braves go from 1.5 games behind the first-place Dodgers to 15.5 games out d. Phil Niekro start on his way to a 20-loss season.

October 24—The Series

Thoughts on the World Series:

My old buddy Rob Neyer had a story on ESPNet SportZone yesterday on the greatest pitching staffs of all time. I believe he picked the 1906 Cubs, 1931 A's, 1954 Indians, 1971 Orioles and 1996 Braves. I would have substituted the 1966 Dodgers for the '31 A's, but it's a good list nonetheless. The strange thing about it, though, is that all the teams prior to 1996, including both the '31 A's and '66 Dodgers, *lost* the World Series. Now there's a good chance this may happen to the '96 Braves as well. Like I always say, pitching is five percent of baseball. . .

Of course, it's possible we've all been overrating this Atlanta staff, because while they may have one of the best starting rotations of all time, the Braves have real problems in the bullpen—and the Yankees have exposed those problems the last two nights. It's pretty apparent that the Yankees not only have a better bullpen than the Braves, but *much* better bullpen. In an era when most starting pitchers only go six or seven innings, that's a crucial difference. Maybe just enough to give the Yankees the Series.

Now on to last night's game. I have to confess that I didn't see the end of it. My wife and I are pulling hard for the Yankees, and when it was 6-0 and it looked like the Yanks were going to die like dogs, we switched to "Dr. Katz" and "Dream On"—the episode where Martin's girlfriend is one of life's Ultimate Women, Katherine Harrold—on Comedy Central. Two very funny shows. I switched back when they were over, and by that point it was 6-3 in the sixth and the Yankees were back in the game; in fact they had two men on with nobody out. But Mike Bielecki pitched the Braves out of the jam (Mike Bielecki?), and when the Yanks went out meekly in the seventh as well, I gave up and went to sleep. And missed some incredible stuff. Fortunately I caught all the highlights on SportsCenter this morning.

Of course, I wouldn't have turned off the game if the pace had been a little faster. By the middle of the seventh, the game was already three hours old, so I opted to go to sleep. I'm sure I wasn't the only one. And that ain't good for baseball.

I have to say that I blame the umpires for a lot of this. Last night's game started with Denny Neagle going 3-2 on every hitter in the top of the first, and that set the tone for the whole game. Atlanta pitchers wound up throwing 193 pitches in 10 innings, and the Yanks weren't much better with 182. Kenny Rogers went a little over two innings and wound up tossing 52 pitches. Neagle threw 93 pitches in five-plus frames. This will put the most dedicated fan, even someone like yours truly, to bed eventually.

I am absolutely certain that this sort of thing wouldn't happen if the umps started calling some high strikes. Instead, the strike zone just gets lower and lower. Two nights ago, David Cone threw a 3-and-2 pitch waist-high, right over the plate, and Tim Welke called it ball four to force in a run. The Yankees were screaming about it, especially Don Zimmer, but what could they do? In the modern ump's strike zone, Cone's pitch was "too high."

Of course, if you watched the rest of that game, you quickly realized that Welke has a way of compensating for not calling the waist-high strike: he calls strikes on pitches that are two, three and sometimes six pitches outside. That was great for Tom Glavine, who lives on the outside corner. It wasn't so great for Andruw Jones, who got called out on strikes in a crucial situation late in the game on a pitch that was several inches outside.

I'm all for helping the pitcher, but this is ludicrous. How can you call a pitch a strike when it's basically unhittable? (Jones couldn't have hit that called strike three with a paddle.) How can you call another pitch a ball when it's right down the middle? No wonder hitters get confused, pitchers have problems throwing strikes, everybody gets angry and the games take forever.

It is one of the strengths of baseball that it overcome all its problems and produce a finish as wild and as thrilling as last night's. Too bad that I—and a whole lot of other people—weren't around to see it.

— Don Zminda

October 25—Still More Postseason Babble-On

Postseason experience is everything. Ask Andy Pettitte.

So can the Yankees beat the invincible Braves and end my team-I'm-hoping-for-in-the-World-Series losing streak at six? I don't know. I sure thought La Russa's Cards had them all but finished off too. I'd really like to see the Straw get another Series ring since I think he's come full circle and become a really good person. I believe he's sincerely thankful for the blessing of the chance he's gotten after screwing up so many times. I'd like to see Fielder get a ring too. And Boggs. And I'm glad to see Bernie Williams getting the recognition he's deserved for quite a while now. And I'm glad to see Derek Jeter showing who's the *real* rookie shortstop of New York. Go Yankees.

To close (I have to get to Crystal Cave's haunted house in Kutztown—yes, John Mobley Kutztown—tonight), doesn't it strike you as strange that it's always been "the thing to do," upon winning a male team sporting event, to wrap arms around each other, hug, jump on top of each other, etc.? Do macho sports guys act like this at any other time in their lives? Would they act that way for any other reason? (Well, probably some would, but we don't know which ones those are.) It just shows me how, when society considers something "the thing to do" people will automatically do it and not think twice, no matter how ridiculous.

— Steve Moyer

1996-97 Offseason

October 28—Screw the Braves

Separated at birth: Jay Buhner and the Dolphins' Steve Emtman.

What's Hal Bodley going to write about anymore if the players and owners really do agree on a deal?

How much money do you think Ross Perot wasted on all those commercials during World Series Game 6? Geez, I think there was one every commercial break. I wish he'd have just given the money from one of them to me. It would have done a lot more good for me and been about equally as effective toward his presidential hopes.

Also during Game 6, I got to thinking about who are the people who actually get to sit like right where the camera points at on TV while the batter's batting, during the World Series. You know, like right behind home plate. I generally get to sit in real good seats nowadays, as I do have a few connections, but I've still never had the good fortune of sitting that close, even at a regular-season game. So who is it that gets to sit there during the World Series? I'll bet half the people who get those seats are only moderate baseball fans. You can tell just by looking at them. And I'll bet there are some for whom it's their first attendance of a baseball game all season. Life's just not fair.

I haven't seen any pictures of that New Jersey kid who interfered the Yankees into an all-important LCS Game 2 win lately. I guess his 15 minutes have just about run out.

I forgot to mention that during the radio broadcast of Game 1 of the World Series, I heard Vin Scully refer to Cecil Fielder as "SEE-sil" Fielder. Oy vey.

Well, I'm glad to see the Yankees won. I'm sure no one is noticing, because baseball cliches never die, but I hope this series at least left some doubt about the "postseason experience is everything" cliche. For heaven's sake, if postseason experience was so important, the Yankees wouldn't have stood a chance. Goodbye Braves, dream team of the announcers. Your pitching couldn't get the job done. Your defense couldn't get the job done. Your timely hitting couldn't get the job done. Your postseason experience couldn't get the job done. Although no one associated with major league baseball or TV or radio would believe it, sometimes you actually have to hit the ball to win. Screw the Braves.

— Steve Moyer

October 31—Post-Series Thoughts

How did a team with the highest payroll in baseball turn into a bunch of lovable overachievers who beat the odds and won it all? You got me, but count me among the folks who were genuinely happy that the Yankees took the crown. Joe Torre *is* a really nice guy, and how could I not feel good for people like Joe Girardi and Paul O'Neill? I don't care what they're making; anyway, the Yanks have had a megabucks payroll for years, and it didn't do them much good before this. This Yankee team was different. They worked their tails off to win, and they finally succeeded.

I met Joe Torre once, back in the early 1980s when I was just starting to work in baseball. It was at an All-Star Game banquet the night prior to the game, and Torre, who I believe was divorced at the time, showed up with this drop-dead blonde who looked like a *Sports Illustrated* swimsuit model. Good a guy as he is, Torre's not exactly a handsome man, and back then he was a lot heavier and even homelier than he is now. He wasn't exactly a snappy dresser, either, so here's Torre in this extremely ugly suit and tie, looking all jowly and five-o'clock-shadowy, with one of the most gorgeous women I'd ever seen draped on his arm. All I could think was, "So *that's* what 'being in the big leagues' means!" Anyway, I talked to him a little, and left with the same impression most people have of him: this is a really decent, down-to-earth guy. He waited a long, long time for his first championship, and I'm really happy he got it.

That said, I thought Fox and the other networks overdid the whole Torre family saga just a little. My favorite scene was when they showed his brother Frank in the hospital, holding a 1965-style transistor radio next to his ear, listenin' to the game and pullin' for the Yanks and his little brother Joe. Hey Frank! Dump that radio! The World Series is on TV now! Since 1947!

Speaking of television, most of the stories about the World Series TV ratings focused, typically, on how "bad" they were—the third-lowest rated Series *of all time!*—which provided more ammunition for the "baseball is dying" crowd. . . not that they ever need any. Not to confuse anybody with the facts, but:

1. The top four-rated programs on television last week were World Series Games 3 through 6.

2. The only other Series game broadcast last week, Game 2, finished ninth in the ratings—this despite the fact that it was a makeup game which was broadcast at an early hour, and despite the fact that the final innings of the game were in direct competition with Monday Night Football, a show that "everybody watches." And in case you're wondering, Game 2 cleaned Monday Night Football's clock in the ratings, knocking MNF out of the top 10 for the first time this year.

3. Sure, World Series ratings aren't what they used to be, but *no* network show gets the ratings that shows did in the days before cable came on the scene. How come we don't get any stories that "TV comedy is dying" because "Seinfeld" doesn't get the ratings that "M*A*S*H" did?

So tell me World Series ratings aren't as high as they used to be, and I'll agree with you. Tell me that the networks are paying too much money to broadcast them, and I'll say maybe that's true, also. . . though Fox seemed pretty happy that they won the weekly ratings for the first time in their history, thanks to the Series. But only an idiot could look at last week's ratings and conclude that "baseball's dying" and that "nobody was watching." But that's what you hear all the time. Drives me crazy.

— Don Zminda

November 1—Baseball Babble-On

I am excited. There's an auction place up the street from my house and this morning I saw they were auctioning off a whole bunch of sports memorabilia Saturday morning. The preview of the stuff is tonight. I just got back and, holey-moley, there's tons of good stuff there. I can't wait until tomorrow morning. It's like I'm 10 years old and it's friggin' Christmas Eve. There's an 1895 scorecard, a Mickey Mantle rookie and second-year card, a bunch of old baseball and football magazines and all kinds of other great stuff. I just hope a lot of people don't show up tomorrow who know what they're doing. Hopefully, there'll be enough bozos there who are looking for Ken Griffey Jr. cards and the Fleer Extra Ultra Extreme Metal Flake 1996 Prospects set that I'll get some good things for good prices. I'll let you know how I made out next week if I remember.

I see Butch Hobson gave up on his lame alibi. His friend who mailed him the coke package said he mailed him the package, but not with coke in it. I guess those naughty postmen were playing games again, huh Don Zminda? It shows how deep the old-boy network runs when Hobson can get a professional managerial job. They certainly wouldn't dare hire someone without major league playing experience though. That might be detrimental to the team.

An inside source that I spoke to this past week told me some really good stuff about Albert Belle. Surely you've seen many a major leaguer interviewed about some immortal's record he's breaking only to say, "Gee, is that true? I don't even know who that guy is." Well, this source told me Belle is totally the opposite. He's 110 percent baseball. He knows all the history, he keeps track of everything that might give him an advantage and he's a real student of the game. He's internally competitive with Bonds and Griffey to the point that if you tell Belle that Bonds hit two homers while he's in the dugout during an Indians game, he'll know Bonds' updated slugging percentage in his head. He very much understands park factors too. And he says before he's through he's going to hit 70 homers in a season. Ask him why and he'll tell you, "Because the pitchers f'ing stink." Now that's a competitor, in my mind. Keep that stuff in mind the next time you hear the media or the fans ragging him, as usual. This source told me don't get my hopes up for many major leaguers in the same regard, but Belle knows the game inside and out, past and present.

Don't you just love the intelligent questions they come up with for the World Series victors in the clubhouse after the clinching win? I just love 'em. I'm sure any of us could give the answers the players will give before they give them, because the questions are so dumb. Let me give you two actual mind-boggling questions from the just-completed World Series with answers I'd like to hear:

To Joe Torre: "Joe, everyone gave up on the Yankees at one time or another. Did you think you could win this all along?"

Joe Torre: "God no, Steve. I never thought we had a chance. I'm more surprised than anyone that we won. I gave up on us long ago like everyone else."

To Wade Boggs: "Wade, this Yankee team had a lot of heart. You've played on a lot of teams with heart. Where would you rank the 1996 Yankees on the list?"

Wade Boggs: "You know, Steve, it's tough, but I'd probably rank the 1996 Yankees about fourth, behind the 1986 and 1990 Red Sox teams and my 1980 Pawtucket club."

— Steve Moyer

November 5—Give Peace a Chance

Tomorrow, we'll found out if we're going to war. Again.

No, I'm not referring to the "War on Drugs," the "War on Crime," or Bob Dole's war on government spending. I'm talking about the owners' ratification vote on the labor deal with the players—the deal that's already been hammered out and agreed upon by both sides' negotiators, awaiting only the ratification of the owners.

If the hawks vote it down, we're all going back to '94 in a handbasket. Do we really have to replay the labor strife of the last two years? The mere thought of it is even more depressing than having to listen to four years' worth of Dole's staccato monotone. We *need* the labor war to finally take a back seat to the games on the field. You know it, I know it, and the American people know it.

But if the hard-line minority of owners get enough votes to veto the labor deal, then it's all been for nothing. The owners' unilateral implementation of their own plan in '94, the strike, the canceled World Series, the ridiculous farce of replacement players, the injunction that saved the '95 season, and the months' worth of haggling that finally produced an agreement —it all could go for naught. Back to square one. Do not pass "Go," do not collect 200 billion dollars.

The most difficult thing to stomach is the fact that *they already had a deal.* They appointed a negotiator, Randy Levine, and gave him the authority to negotiate an agreement with the union. He did just that. What happens now, if they decide that they prefer not to be bound by that agreement?

It will mean that the owners will have no credibility at the bargaining table. If they repudiate the deal that their own negotiator got them, how could they send someone to the table next time and expect him to have even a shred of credibility? When Donald Fehr sits down with the new guy, he'll ask him, "Do you have the authority to accept a binding agreement on behalf of the owners?" And the poor hack will be forced to say, "Yes, unless Jerry Reinsdorf and seven of his cronies decide they don't like it, in which case we'll have to negotiate the whole thing all over again, and I'll want to get even more out of you." I wonder if that exchange will lead to a successful resolution.

It also will mean that the baseball industry will have been taken hostage by a narrow, self-interested minority. These are the hawks, and they all want to trash the agreement for their own selfish reasons. Some small-market teams, like Seattle and Kansas City, believe that the deal doesn't provide enough revenue-sharing income for the poorer franchises (like. . . themselves). Some large-market teams, like the White Sox and Marlins, have owners who are thirsty to squeeze even more concessions out of the union. Some teams may be voting "no" largely because the deal would grant service time for the strike, making some of their players free agents. The teams that figure to lose the most in that respect are the White Sox, who would lose Alex Fernandez, and the Expos, who would lose Mel Rojas and Moises Alou. Both teams are anti-agreement, even through the Expos sure could use the extra revenue-sharing dollars.

And that's a damn shame, isn't it? Jerry Reinsdorf doesn't want to pay a little extra to keep Alex Fernandez, and so he shuts down the whole industry. Go Sox!

There's a strong sense that if the Commissioner's Office had any leadership ability at all, this agreement would be pushed through. Bud Selig, however, has steadfastly refused to use his influence to rally support for the agreement. Through his inaction, he's all but killed it, since the anti-agreement forces have been rallying while he's been dallying.

All of this serves to bring the true essence of the problem into greater focus. The players certainly are not the obstructionists here. The luxury tax that they've agreed to amounts to the single greatest *restriction* on free agents' bargaining power since the Messersmith decision created free agency in 1976. It's what Marvin Miller would have derisively labeled a "giveback"—a surrendering of rights the players have already won. But the Players Association has taken a longer view, judging that labor peace and gains in other areas are more important.

The owners tried to screw the players and failed, and now they're trying to screw each other. Jerry Reinsdorf wants to get his players more cheaply than the other owners. David Glass wants George Steinbrenner to subsidize his unprofitable organization even more heavily.

Who can make these guys get with the program and do what's best for the industry as a whole? Not Selig; he's just an owner himself. In order for the owners to fall into line, they need a higher authority to give them their marching orders. The problem is that every time they've had a Commissioner with the courage to do that, they've fired him over it. The last time it happened—with Fay Vincent—the hawks were so incensed that they ousted Vincent and replaced him with one of their own—Selig. The results are evident.

Did you ever read *Animal Farm*? In the end, the pigs fared no better. Which is fitting, because in baseball, all is not well. . . it's *Orwell*.

—Mat Olkin

November 5—Junior

FAUST: Did anyone else notice how well he did in the field this year? He was second among regular center fielders with a range of 2.95 (MLB Avg was 2.62), and posted a .829 Zone Rating (.816 was average).

Maybe he finally deserved a Gold Glove.

November 7-11—The Great Jose Offerman Debate

JAMES: American League first basemen in 1996, ranked according to runs created:

Player	Runs Created
Mo Vaughn	158
Frank Thomas	150
Mark McGwire	149
Rafael Palmeiro	137
John Jaha	119
Cecil Fatso	101
Tino Martinez	100
Jose Offerman	95
Paul Sorrento	89
Julio Franco	82
Will Clark	75
John Olerud	74
Scott Stahoviak	72
J.T. Snow	68
Tony Clark	56

Jose Offerman in 1996 created 6.09 runs per 27 outs. With making any park adjustments, he was more productive in terms of runs created per out than Tino Martinez (6.06), Cecil Fielder (5.84), Tony Clark (5.09) or J.T. Snow (4.04). If you *do* make park adjustments, he would also move ahead of Will Clark and Scott Stahoviak.

I believe that this clearly demonstrates that the attacks on Bob Boone for playing Offerman at first base are typical of the worst kind of old-school baseball knee-jerk thinking, or non-thinking as the case may be. People attacked Boone for playing Offerman at first not because Offerman cannot actually do the job fairly well, but simply because *he does not fit the traditional image of a first baseman*. The people who say that Offerman shouldn't play first are exactly like the people who don't want to let knuckleballers pitch, who think that all shortstops should weigh less than 160 pounds, and who think that anybody who can run is qualified to be a leadoff man. They're thinking in terms of images, rather than actually looking at what the player can do to help the team.

DEWAN: That's remarkable. I had no inkling that Offerman's season would compare that well against other A.L. first basemen. Nice work, Sherlock.

PINTO: The runs created you reported, are they for the full season or only at that position?

JAMES: The full season. I suspect Offerman may have hit a little better than that as a first baseman, because he was pretty awful early in the season when he was attempting to play shortstop. I'll check.

PINTO: Offensive Winning Percentage as first baseman only, 300 PA.

Player	PA	RC	RC/G	OW%	Outs
Mark McGwire	464	128.4	13.28	.857	261
Jeff Bagwell	719	150.5	9.74	.807	417
Frank Thomas	647	146.6	10.53	.802	376
John Jaha	360	86.2	10.82	.793	215
Mo Vaughn	688	146.4	9.76	.745	405
Fred McGriff	690	107.2	6.28	.672	461
Jeff King	346	60.3	7.12	.672	229
David Segui	476	70.6	6.17	.668	309
Mark Grace	614	97.0	6.71	.665	390
Rafael Palmeiro	720	134.4	8.01	.662	453
Hal Morris	588	89.8	6.26	.631	387
Wally Joyner	508	69.7	5.79	.625	325
Cecil Fielder	345	54.0	6.43	.612	227
Julio Franco	438	69.8	6.69	.610	282
John Olerud	384	54.7	6.05	.608	244
Andres Galarraga	689	125.0	7.37	.606	458
Jose Offerman	356	49.5	5.78	.596	231
Tino Martinez	654	95.0	5.88	.569	436
Eric Karros	670	85.9	4.78	.567	485
Paul Sorrento	526	83.8	6.60	.559	343
Will Clark	511	72.7	5.95	.555	330
John Mabry	564	70.3	4.82	.532	394
Mark Johnson	355	46.1	5.23	.526	238
Scott Stahoviak	416	58.7	5.70	.519	278
Greg Colbrunn	547	61.4	4.24	.494	391
Tony Clark	360	50.8	5.30	.453	259
Mark Carreon	431	47.6	4.20	.382	306
J.T. Snow	638	65.3	3.87	.348	456

JAMES: These figures are not park-adjusted, I assume?

PINTO: Offensive winning percentage is based on the players runs created per game and team average runs per game in his teams' games. So the OW% is park adjusted (I believe that's how you were doing it when you stopped writing the *Abstract*).

OLKIN: I was critical of the move, not because I felt Offerman wasn't productive enough, but because I felt he didn't give the team what they needed from that position.

JAMES: No, Mat. You were critical of the move because you indulged in precisely the same kind of know-it-all, knee-jerk, pre-logical conclusion-making for which we routinely criticize baseball men. And you have fallen back on the absurd argument below simply because you refuse to admit that you were wrong, exactly as baseball men often refuse to admit that minor league batting records *do* predict major league batting performance, even when we demonstrate that they do.

OLKIN: But it really didn't matter, because the lineup was so starved for power that they were using guys like Bip Roberts in the cleanup spot. Offerman's .290 average was nice, but it wasn't anything that Damon or Goodwin or Roberts wasn't already giving them.

You know as well as I do that they could have picked up a guy like Brent Cookson at zero cost. They could have given Vitiello more of a shot. Instead, they played Whiteyball without Jack Clark. It didn't work. I like Offerman at second, but not first.

PINTO: I don't know that I like the move. I defend keeping Olerud at first, and looking at the file I created, Offerman isn't that different, so I should be satisfied.

I guess what bothers me is that Offerman is capable of playing a middle infield position, and that level of offense is harder to come by there, so he should be (offensively at least) more valuable there. I guess the right move should have been to find a first baseman capable of Offerman's numbers and leave Jose in the middle. But's that's a GM's job, not the manager.

JAMES: In an ideal universe, yes. In the real situation in which Bob Boone found himself, he had many other second basemen comparable to Offerman, and no first baseman who was better. I went to a game last year in which the Royals had, with absolutely zero exaggeration, six second basemen in the lineup—Offerman at first, Lockhardt at third, Stynes in left field, Bip Roberts as the DH, David Howard at shortstop and Joe Randa at second base.

OLKIN: Bill, I'd be perfectly willing to admit I was wrong, if I really was wrong. So far, you have failed to convince me.

But since you feel so strongly about it, I'm going to break character and indulge in something other than know-it-all, knee-jerk, pre-logical conclusion-making.

JAMES: Correcting your enemies is easy. It's educating your friends that is hard work.

The tell-tale sign of knee-jerk thinking is the tendency to ridicule whatever is new, different, original or unexpected. Whenever you find yourself ridiculing someone for doing something *different* from the way it is usually done, I believe you really need to think hard about whether or not your assumptions are on solid ground.

OLKIN: I'm going to ask you this: what was wrong with the Royals last year?

JAMES: The problem with the Royals last year was the same as the problem with the Royals every year: they didn't get enough people on base. How many runs you score is *essentially* a function of how many people you get on base. The Royals were twelfth in the league in men reaching base, and played in a very poor home run park. Where do you think that combination is going to put you?

Jose Offerman, with a team-leading .384 on-base percentage (team-leading by far; I think the second guy was about .350) had nothing at all to do with this problem. He wasn't part of the problem. He was nearly the only guy who *wasn't* part of the problem. Which is why it is obscene to blame him, the one guy who *was* getting on base, for the team's failure to score runs.

OLKIN: To address that question—what was wrong with the Royals last year—the first things I look at are their offense and their pitching. Their offense scored fewer runs than any other team in the league. Their pitching staff finished third in the league in ERA.

JAMES: You don't suppose that having a first baseman with the range of a shortstop had anything at all to do with that, do you?

OLKIN: Now, I know they play in a pitcher's park, but I feel pretty safe in saying that the offense was the main culprit. I don't think they got Chili Davis because they though he could strengthen their rotation.

So it was the offense, are we agreed?

JAMES: What, are you taking rhetorical lessons from Ross Perot?

OLKIN: But which *part* of the offense was it?

I'll tell you what I think. I think it was the all-consuming, offense-sucking power void they had at the cleanup spot.

Their cleanup hitters batted .212, worst in the American League. They only drove in 87 runs, the worst figure in the league. They had a .354 slugging percentage. Do I need to say that no team was worse in this regard? That's .3-5-4. Twenty-two points lower than Willie Wilson's career slugging percentage, for those of you knee-jerking at home.

JAMES: Well, the problem with your argument is that it fails to recognize the difference between Joe Vitiello and Frank Thomas. If the Royals had had Frank Thomas and had put him on the bench so that Offerman could play first base, then I would agree with you that this was a mistake, because Frank Thomas is a far *better* hitter than Jose Offerman. But Boone's option wasn't to play Frank Thomas, it was to play Joe Vitiello. And this would have been a mistake, because Joe Vitiello is a far *worse* hitter than Jose Offerman.

See if you can follow the logic here. If you put in a *better* hitter, that will make the team score *more* runs. If you put in a *worse* hitter, that will make the team score *fewer* runs. Complicated, I know.

You're trying to analyze the team in terms of *types* of hitters, but that's nonsense, essentially because it assumes that Joe Vitiello and Frank Thomas are the same type of hitters, and the team needs one of those. The reality is that a lineup of eight leadoff hitters and one power hitter will work just fine, and will score lots and lots of runs—if the leadoff hitters get on base. A lineup of eight power hitters will work just fine—if the power hitters get on base. If they don't, it won't work.

OLKIN: Outside of Kansas City, it's common for teams to bat their first basemen in the cleanup spot. Royals first basemen hit 15 homers last year and drove in 69 runs. Both figures were last in the league. They slugged .405. Yep; last.

JAMES: Again, thinking in images, rather than thinking in terms of production. This is precisely the logic which has kept Mark Grace in the middle of the Cubs lineup for years, when any idiot should be able to see that his skills are those of a No. 1 or No. 2 hitter, rather than a middle-of-the-order guy.

OLKIN: So what I'm saying is: 1) the Royals didn't put a guy at first base who could hit for power and drive in runs.

JAMES: "A" guy who can hit for power. Frank Thomas, Joe Vitiello—any of those guys.

OLKIN: 2) because their offense lacked power and run production, they scored the fewest runs in the A.L.

3) because they scored the fewest runs in the A.L., they finished last in the A.L. Central, despite having the third-best team ERA in the league.

So do I still condemn Boone's choice to play Offerman at first? Well, after taking the aforementioned facts into full consideration, I have to say, I haven't changed my opinion one bit.

I don't doubt that Offerman put up better runs-created-per-game numbers than some of the other guys around. But what does the runs created method tells us? It says, basically, if you have this many men on base and this much power, you ought to score this many runs. But one thing it doesn't take into full account is the law of diminishing returns. You know what I'm talking about, Bill, but for the rest of you, it means that if you eat banana cream pie, three meals a day, for weeks on end, pretty soon you'll start to crave a nice plate of broccoli.

JAMES: The Ross Perot influence again, no doubt.

Ah. . . missed this the first time. I think we may have found the source of your confusion. *There is no law of diminishing returns as pertains to getting more runners on base.* It is simply mathematically wrong to say that there is.

Suppose that you take an offense of nine average hitters, all with on-base percentages of .350 and slugging percentages of .445 (the American League averages last year). They'll score an average number of runs.

If you take out one of those players and replace him with a low-average power hitter (let us say an on-base percentage of .340 but a slugging percentage of .465), you may well score more runs—let us say 10 more runs.

But if you make that substitution again, there will be a law of diminishing returns. The second substitution will be less effective than the first, the third less effective than the second, etc. It might well be that the second such substitution would gain you only eight runs, the third only five runs, the fourth only one run, and the fifth such substitution might actually cost the team runs.

But if you substitute in the other direction—increasing on-base percentage by diminishing power—the opposite happens. There will be a synergistic interaction among the players, and the second substitution will be *more* effective than the first, not less.

The on-base factor represents the opportunities for an offense; the power factor represents the ability to take advantage of those opportunities. When you substitute to increase power, you increase your ability to score, given an opportunity, but by so doing you decrease the number of opportunities remaining. This makes the second substitution less effective than the first.

But when you substitute to increase the opportunities and decrease the utilization, you are in effect increasing the opportunities in both directions—first, by creating more opportunities, and second, by leaving more opportunities unused. The result is a geometric expansion of opportunities, which gradually begins to off-set the lack of power.

Mat's argument might make some sense if the Royals were leaving tons of runners on base. In fact, they were next to last in the American league in runners left on base—hardly the sign of an offense with "too many" leadoff men. What's you're really doing is, you're blaming Offerman for the fact that the *other* leadoff men didn't get on base—while overlooking the fact that Offerman did.

OLKIN: "Synergistic interaction?" Geez, Bill, you sound like Bill Gates. Bob Boone just couldn't get enough pie, even though it was coming out of his ears and he was getting anemic from lack of broccoli. He wanted to get David Howard into the lineup. He wanted to play Joe Randa and Bip Roberts. He wanted to find room for Tom Goodwin, too. Now, that's hard to do. To do that, you've got to sit Joe Vitiello on the bench, and it makes it hard to find a spot for Mike Macfarlane. Craig Paquette's struggling for at-bats, and Jon Nunnally's down in Triple-A. But Boone wants more—he wants Offerman in there, too. So he puts him at first base, and in the process, he wrecks his whole offense, because there's no one left to hit. Offerman hits .303, and you still lose, because two singles plus three outs still equals inning over.

Now Bill, exactly what part of my argument do you disagree with? I wish you'd enlighten me, because I hate not knowing things. It makes me act like a know-it-all, rushing to knee-jerk pre-logical conclusions just to cover up the fact that I may be wrong.

P.S. Brent Cookson is a very good hitter. You should take a look at his minor league numbers—they really do mean something, if you know how to read them.

JAMES: Yes, and don't forget Patrick Lennon; they had him at season's start, and he's probably a better hitter than Cookson. They released him to sign Craig Paquette, and the sad part is, they *still* think they made a good move.

Bob Boone may perhaps be faulted because the Royals released a cleanup hitter and then didn't have one, but that has nothing at all to do with the issue of whether or not Jose Offerman is a good first baseman. Blaming Jose Offerman because the Royals don't have a cleanup hitter is like blaming Lance Ito because Fuhrman's a racist and O.J. is a murderer.

NEYER: Vitiello actually wasn't far off what you projected for him, Bill. In other words, he was bad. But I still wish he'd have batted more than 257 times so we could know for sure. Shoot, Kevin Young was killing the ball in Omaha, and he only got 132 at-bats for the Royals. Why didn't Boone agitate for Kevin Young early in the season? Because, apparently, he was happy with Offerman.

JAMES: He had every *reason* to be happy with Offerman. Offerman was playing *well*. This is what you still don't get.

Not thrilled with Offerman, perhaps, but if he as in an agitating mood, why wouldn't he agitate for a shortstop? Why pick on Offerman, probably the best player on the team?

NEYER: Also, I don't understand why Boone can't be faulted for not playing Cookson or Lennon. Didn't he have anything to do with them leaving?

JAMES: He can. Who said he couldn't?

PINTO: OBP is like compound interest rates. You get more than a 1% increase in principal when you raise your interest rate by 1%. The same is true of OBP; the difference between a .350 OBP and a .340 OBP is bigger than the difference between a .340 OBP and a .330 OBP, and so on up and down the ladder.

OLKIN: Maybe what's going on here is that people have been attacking Offerman for so long, while you've been defending him, that you interpret any attack on him as the work of the same ignorant mob.

I'm quite sure that there are a ton of people out there who look at Offerman and immediately write him off as a first baseman, simply because he doesn't hit for power. There certainly is a very strong prejudice against first baseman who don't hit for power. Offerman played well, and I'm sure you've done your share of arguing with those who are trapped in their own narrow way of thinking.

But I'm not one of them, Bill. If I were, I never would have read your books. "Enos Cabell isn't any good? What a load of crap! He hit .280!" No, I'm not like that, Bill.

JAMES: In other words, what you're saying is, "I'm not an idiot. I am merely a fellow traveller of these other idiots, who happens to be making an idiotic argument." I appreciate the distinction, and I am pleased to acknowledge that you are normally smarter than this.

OLKIN: "Idiotic argument?" Conclusory, your honor. Motion to strike.

In fact, I have a somewhat irrational fondness for the unconventional—even more so when such a strategy happens to make sense. When Davey Johnson used to put Hojo at short, I loved it. I figured that Johnson was so much better than Elster at the plate that he couldn't possibly give all those runs back in the field (especially when a flyballer like Sid Fernandez was pitching). When John McNamara used Tim Lollar as a pinch-hitter, I stood up and cheered. Lollar could hit, and besides, it was cool. But I absolutely resented the fact that the Red Sox refused to allow Greg Harris to pitch left-handed.

If a manager does something weird, I'm usually happy to see it, as long as it makes sense. But playing Offerman at first base didn't—and doesn't—add up. I'm not ridiculing Bob Boone because he did something different. I would never do that; I do so many things the "wrong" way that it sometimes seems as if I'm just doing it to prove a point. Maybe I am, sometimes. I'm different, and the world has to deal with that.

So trust me, I'm far from one of those Baseball McCarthyites who seem to get under your skin. I understand your point about Offerman's ability to get on base, and I agree that it was a huge asset for the Royals' offense.

JAMES: Well, that's *something*.

OLKIN: I agree that they needed to have him in the lineup. I think our main disagreement is about where it is that he should play.

The Royals had problems getting people on base, it's true. But their ability to put men on base was far from the worst in the league. Detroit and Toronto each put fewer men on.

JAMES: *Far* from the worst in the league? You're kidding, right? They were 12th in a 14-team league in on-base percentage, and they were one point ahead of Toronto. The reality is that if they *hadn't* found a way to put Offerman in the lineup every day, they would have finished last in the league in on-base percentage.

And the two teams which had worse OBPs than the Royals scored barely more runs than KC did, despite hitting about 50% more home runs.

OLKIN: But KC's power was the absolute worst. Their slugging percentage was .398; no one else was below .420. The way I see, it the lack of power was a more damaging problem than their failure to reach base more often.

And if you need a power hitter, what better spot to have open than first base? Now, I'm not condemning them for their inability to acquire a Frank Thomas, but it's fair to say that if they needed power, they had some options on their roster.

JAMES: The Royals play in a park which reduces their home runs by 30%, and they have no real power hitters anyway. Under those conditions, I really have to question whether it would be a wise strategy for them to force the best available power hitter into the lineup, merely because they need A power hitter. What they need is *good* hitters. It makes essentially no difference what *kind* of hitters those are, other than "good".

OLKIN: They could have used Mike Macfarlane. They had two other young catchers to look at, and Macfarlane's got as much pop as anyone on the team.

They could have used Jon Nunnally, who slugged .472 last year, but got sent down to Triple-A this year because the Royals wanted to play Tom Goodwin instead. Admittedly, Nunnally had never played first before, but then again, neither had Offerman. Nunnally had been a second baseman in the minors.

They could have used Brent Cookson, who can hit at least as well as Steve Balboni used to.

They could have given a better shot to Joe Vitiello. He hasn't hit well so far, but I think you'll agree that his MLEs say he can do better.

They could have used Patrick Lennon, who can flat-out hit.

JAMES: That's all true. But if that is what you are trying to say, then why pick on Offerman? Offerman is what Boone did *right*, not what he did wrong.

OLKIN: But this is my main point: they could have used any of these guys, *without taking Offerman out of the lineup*.

It's your old defensive spectrum, coming back to haunt you. Offerman was, at least in theory, a shortstop, the hardest position on the field. First base is the easiest position. In between, there are two spots in the infield and three in the outfield where you can find a place for Jose. If you do that, you can use any of the guys I've listed above. But if you put Jose at first, you eliminate all those options, because most of them can't play anywhere else.

Now I know, in real life, the Royals already had all those spots filled. To put Jose somewhere other than first base, you'd need to sit down one of Boone's exalted regulars. I've got an idea. How about Goodwin?

Are you willing to argue that Goodwin was helping the offense more than any of those other guys I've listed would have? Goodwin's .334 OBP was only two points higher than the team's mark, which you feel was poor. As for power, he had 19 extra-base hits and 35 RBI. Can we move Roberts to LF and play Jose at 2B? Please? I hope you're with me here, Bill, because the day you start defending a player like Tom Goodwin is the day I really start worrying about your health.

JAMES: So what you're saying is, Jose Offerman shouldn't be playing first base because Tom Goodwin isn't really that good? Just so I understand.

OLKIN: Bill, you ask me why I'm picking on Offerman. Maybe this is the root of our disagreement. What I need you to understand is: I am *not* picking on Jose Offerman.

When I walked out the door this morning, I discovered that a silver Mercedes was blocking my car in. It was a pretty nice car, even for a Mercedes. Looked brand-new; not a scratch on it. I'll bet it handled pretty well. My problem with it, though, was the same one I had with Offerman: *it just didn't belong there.* It was well-engineered and nice to look at, but it still impeded traffic flow—just like Offerman played well but still prevented the Royals from maximizing their offense.

As to your point that the Royals needed *good* hitters, rather than power hitters—you can have that one. You win. It's all yours, because I don't need it. My point remains the same: the Royals had quite a few "good" hitters capable of playing first base, but they threw all those options out the window when they put Offerman there instead. He was good too, but he could have been good at second, and it would have helped the team a lot more.

It would have helped, because it would have enabled them to put Tom Goodwin where he belongs: butt-to-wood with a major league bench. So am I saying, "Offerman shouldn't play first base because Goodwin isn't any good"?

Yes, that's exactly what I'm saying.

And a word of caution, Bill—try not to be so judgmental. It seems that you've branded all Offerman-attackers as "idiots," and you've lumped me in with them just because I reach the same conclusion that they do.

Their argument is wrong; mine reaches the same conclusion; ergo, I am wrong too. C'mon, Bill, you know better than that. All along, I've taken pains to distinguish my reasoning from the mob's. You'd do well to examine my reasoning on its own merits rather than to reject it out-of-hand.

But instead, what you're doing is going around classifying people as "idiots" or "non-idiots," according to their position on Offerman. And when you do that, do you know what you're really doing? You're dealing in *images*, rather than *reality*, that's what.

COOPERSON: I really like Jose Offerman.

I think he's one of my favorite players.

One time I saw a game and Jose was playing really good.

One time my friend saw him hit a home run.

I think you guys are really mean.

November 8—The Labor Deal

MOYER: Let's talk about the baseball labor deal. This conversation about Offerman is getting way too exciting.

DEWAN: Steve is right on!

I'll start. The owners' decision to not follow the advice of their negotiator was one of the poorest decisions that could possibly be made. The sharp decrease in baseball's popularity will be further fueled and any gains they might get in negotiation will be totally negated by additional loss of fans.

WENZ: Two years ago when the season started late, I made the prediction that in two years (1997), we'd open the season with replacement players. It was the first time in history I believed that the owners were united enough to not cave in, and they took the right steps (namely the three-fourths majority to ratify a deal) to make sure they wouldn't cave in. As for the players, Donald Fehr is a Marvin Miller disciple and an economist. He is and will always be of the opinion that it's not the union's fault the players make so much money. Free agents don't have such unbelievable leverage as to force an owner to pay a player more than his "marginal product." (Econ term—forgive me.) The economist in him will not allow him to give in on this issue.

Also now we have some issues the players would like to have addressed. For example, service time and the minimum salary. The status quo is no longer good enough, like it was before the 1996 season. The owners have an infrastructure in place to play scabs, something that was sorely lacking in '95. So the conditions are right for replacement ballplayers. Don't be surprised when it happens.

PINTO: John and I were talking last night about how when this whole thing started, we were both leaning toward the side of the owners, and how it's gone completely the other way now.

If I remember correctly, the original offer made back in 1994 was to guarantee the players a fixed percentage of the take. The owners expected baseball revenue to grow, and the player's percentage would grow with it. The percentage offered was lower than what the players were actually getting at the time, and some sources of revenue were not included in the percentage, but it was a reasonable starting point for negotiations.

It seemed to me at the time that the owners were trying to be reasonable, trying to control their costs, and were still going to pay the overall group of players a lot of money. What I didn't realize at the time was:

The owners were unwilling to negotiate the deal, because there were/are a large number of owners who wanted to break the union (the players also miscalculated this; they thought a strike in August would give them time to negotiate and save the postseason. In hindsight, they would have been better off playing the season out and striking during the postseason.)

As time went on, everything that helped me form an opinion went against the owners; the obvious exaggeration of how much financial trouble the small markets were in, the loss in court on the impasse, the lack of a real commissioner, and now finally the rejection of their own negotiator, after he had enlisted more concessions from the players than any time before.

On the players' side, we've had two good seasons of baseball, exciting races and postseasons, and a realization from the players that they had to give something back to the fans. With the exception of Albert Belle, players seem to be more involved with fans than in recent memory (Ripken staying after every home game last year to sign autographs, Buhner Buzz-cut night, players greeting the fans at the ballparks, etc.).

So now I'm dead-set against the owners. They aren't interested in helping the game or helping small market clubs or increasing their revenue through growth of the game. They are interested only in destroying the players' union, and that's a shame.

To take your point a step further, some sort of labor stoppage is likely. The owners are likely to seek an impasse again, and if they learned anything from the Mario Soto-Mayor decision it was how to get one. The only recourse for the players at that point would be to strike. I would hope, though that in addition to scabs, the players form their own league and compete against the replacements.

MOYER: Please, guys, I was only kidding, really. Soon Hal Bodley will be sending one-sentence paragraph messages:

"Baseball is doomed."

DEWAN: You may have been kidding, but this is pretty serious stuff.

PINTO: A point I wanted to make earlier:

During 1994 we heard how the small market teams couldn't survive under the current system. Well, we've played two more seasons, and I haven't seen any teams fold yet, and the old system is still in place.

ZMINDA: Sure, the small-market teams are suffering. Look at the poor Royals—they're so poor, they had to play Jose Offerman at first base!

I just wanted to be the first to make that connection.

OLKIN: At this point, it would be very tough for the owners to convince Judge Sotomayor that they had a real bargaining impasse. To get a court to recognize an impasse, you usually have to show that the two sides have broken off talks and are unwilling to make any further concessions. The fact that their negotiator actually reached an agreement with the players. . . well, you might say that it weighs against the idea of a bargaining impasse a little bit. If a court sees any hope at all that the two sides can reach an agreement without the court interfering (by declaring an impasse), the court will let things run their course. That's what's going to happen here. There's no way the owners will be allowed to implement. If a court allowed them to do that, it would be allowing them to choose between an agreement that they negotiated with the players or arbitrary rules that they made up themselves. No court would give them that choice—it would invalidate the entire collecting bargaining process. The current agreement will remain in force.

SICKELS: I agree with Mat. . . it will be *very* difficult for the owners to convince any judge with two marbles in his or her head that an impasse exists. By repudiating their own negotiator, it is now obvious where the fault lies: with the owners.

As for a labor stoppage: I doubt the owners could get the 3/4 vote needed for a lockout. And as long as the court injunction remains in place, the current system remains in effect, and the players have no reason to strike.

One thing that has been little noticed: the owners voted 30-0 to change the way an agreement can be ratified. Now, it just takes a vote of the executive counsel, not a vote of the entire ownership group.

MOYER: I read the *USA Today* at lunch. The debate on the editorial page today is "Baseball's Labor Tussle." The "Our View" initial article is entitled "Owners Drop Ball Again" and is written by an un-named *USA Today* writer. Let's see now, I count one. . . two. . . three one-sentence paragraphs. Wonder who that mystery-writer could be?

November 14—Trivia

ZMINDA: We just came up with a great trivia question: Who has caught the most Cy Young winners? Can anyone top Charlie O'Brien? The number of Cy Young winners Charlie O' has caught: Nine.

NYN: Viola, Gooden, Saberhagen, Cone
Atl: Maddux, Glavine, Smoltz, Bedrosian
Tor: Hentgen

OLKIN: I would assume that Rick Dempsey holds the record. He caught at least 11 Cy Young winners, and maybe as many as 13:

Steve Carlton	Sparky Lyle
Mike Cuellar	Jim Palmer
Mike Flanagan	Steve Stone
Ron Guidry	Rick Sutcliffe
Orel Hershiser	Fernando Valenzuela
Catfish Hunter	

And when he first came up with the Twins, he may have caught Dean Chance and Jim Perry.

KRETSCHMANN: Alex Trevino caught at least 10:

Steve Bedrosian	Mike Marshall
Vida Blue	Mike Scott
Mark Davis	Tom Seaver
Orel Hershiser	Fernando Valenzuela
Randy Jones	Bob Welch

. . . actually 11, he caught David Cone in 1990.

November 14—The A.L. MVP Vote

ZMINDA: Juan Gonzalez is the A.L. MVP by three points over Alex Rodriguez. Gonzalez had 290 points and 11 first-place votes, Alex 287 points and 10 first-place votes. Albert Belle was third.

I, for one, am very surprised by this.

WENZ: I, for two, am very surprised by this.

OLKIN: The Mariners didn't win, so Rodriguez must be a bad player.

WENZ: Or maybe. . . the Royals didn't win, so Jose Offerman must be a bad player.

Sorry, Mat. Had to.

PINTO: It's a travesty!

ZMINDA: Actually, what really hurt Alex was that Griffey got four first-place votes and finished fourth overall. In political terms, they split the Seattle vote and allowed the Texan to sneak in.

PINTO: I think the Mariners should have moved Rodriguez to first base, where power hitters belong.

WOELFLEIN: Jose Offerman didn't even get a single vote. How can that be?

COOPERSON: Put Offerman at short in Seattle's lineup, and he would've had a good year too! Put him at first base in that lineup, where power hitters belong, and he would have had a monster, MVP-type season with lots of homers!

SPEAR: John Olerud was tied with Offerman and Ron Karkovice for 22nd place.

COUVILLON: Offerman did have a higher OBP than Gonzalez!

SPEAR: Upon a closer examination of the voting. . . Alex Rodriguez got votes from every voter. But one voter ranked him seventh.

Seventh!!!!

174

Also, Ivan Rodriguez got a first place vote on his way to a 10th place finish. I just wonder if some voter got the two Rodriguez' confused and ranked Ivan first and Alex seventh.

That would totally suck.

ZMINDA: Not to mention all those votes for Alex Gonzalez. . .

MOYER: Reasons Alex Rodriguez should be seventh:

1) The Mariners didn't make the playoffs.
2) He is not a clubhouse leader.
3) He was rushed to the majors.
4) He doesn't have a lot of playoff experience.

MITTLEMAN: I argued for two hours with our BBWAA reps here in Toronto on this. The bottom line was they were fixated on Texas winning the division and Griffey's presence in the Mariner lineup helping Rodriguez.

OLKIN: When Griffey was on the DL from 6/20 to 7/13, Rodriguez played in 20 games, batting .310 with 10 doubles, seven home runs, 25 RBI and a .667 slugging percentage.

ZMINDA: Also, I'm sure the sportswriters considered Alex' woeful lack of "veteran leadership skills."

JAMES: I was real proud of the BBWAA voters for selecting Hentgen over Pettitte, when the New York media had rushed to the conclusion that Pettitte was going to win it. I guess you could say they got thrown out trying for a double. . .

November 15—Baseball Babble-On

Todd Van Poppel quietly moves to the Angels and David Nied quietly moves to the Reds. Three years ago either move would have been huge news.

How about those wacky American League MVP voters? Sure threw everyone at STATS into a frenzy, including me. Fellow STATS AOL'er Mike Mittleman apparently knows some Baseball Writers' Association guys and they told him the reasons Rodriguez didn't win were that the M's didn't make the playoffs and that he was helped too much by Griffey in the lineup. Reason One is stupid, but we've all come to accept that one, I guess. (Speaking of stupid, how about Ken Caminiti as unanimous N.L. MVP with Barry Bonds fifth and Gary Sheffield nowhere in sight.) Reason Two is unbelievable. Do you think for one second the writers would have had any trouble giving Griffey the award, despite the fact that he was helped too much by Rodriguez' presence? You know what it really all boils down to is the fact that Rodriguez was almost a rookie, hasn't paid his dues, etc., etc. and all that nonsense. I just hope Alex is as good as anyone who knows anything thinks he'll be and he gets an MVP somewhere along the way. Cause he was robbed. (By the way, we also found out he was seventh on some idiot's ballot. Now there's a guy that knows his baseball.)

Rod Beaton tells us today that the big Blue Jay deal yesterday moves the Jays "closer to the Yankees and Orioles." What about the Bosox, Bodney, who would've won the whole shebang if the regular season had been a couple of weeks longer?

My West Coast correspondent tells me he had a good laugh at a *USA Today* note Tuesday which said Cardinal GM Walt Jocketty said the Cards' first priority was signing Gary Gaetti, Tom Pagnozzi, and Willie McGee. Like he said, this is a team that almost went to the World Series last year. Like I say, it's amazing to me that they think what'll keep them at that level is a fading-fast has-been third baseman, an overrated catcher who can't hit, and an outfielder who should've been out of baseball three years ago.

I saw a note in Gammons' Baseball America column this week about how it was lucky Joe Torre had N.L. managerial experience so he didn't use up all his players in the extra-inning no-DH World Series games like Tom Kelly did a few years ago. Are you kidding me? Can you believe a major league manager can't keep that kind of decision-making straight in his head? A 13 year old playing Strat-O-Matic maybe I can see having trouble adjusting, but a major league manager? Either Gammons is really insulting the intelligence of Torre and Kelly (which is what I think) or these guys must really be dumb.

Run, regular readers of this column. Run for your lives, because I'm about to delve into something so boring, so typical, you'll certainly find it in every other baseball online column in existence. But here goes, it's Steve Moyer's "Offseason Baseball Trade Analysis." AAAAAAHHHH!! OOOOHHHHH!!!!! No, Steve, it's too boring. But, Steve, we can get this anywhere. No, please, God, no. Tough luck. Here goes. I don't think the Matt Williams trade was as bad as it seems. I've heard Williams may not be able to play third at all anymore, which would make him a lot less valuable. He almost always gets hurt. Yes, he may hit 60 homers. Getting out of Candlestick (I don't remember what it's really called these days) will help him. On the other hand, Jeff Kent isn't a bad player, apparently if you can put up with his personality. And Julian Tavarez was Mariano Rivera a year ago. Yeah, Jose Vizcaino is subtraction by addition (actually he's Rey Ordonez if Ordonez would ever have a prayer of hitting .290), but, oh well. It's not a good trade for the Giants, but it might not be as bad as everyone thinks. The Pirates trade, you don't ask? I don't know who those other three prospects will be (Shannon Stewart? Carlos Delgado? Pat Hentgen?) but it looks like the Jays really made out. You're gonna have to prove to me that Jose Silva and Jose Pett are anything at all and Brandon Cromer's high end is a lefty Jay Bell. Maybe their scouts know something I don't, but I doubt it. Luckily Jim Leyland's not around to cry about it.

— Steve Moyer

November 18—The Belle Signing

CANTER: From the wire—"Slugger Albert Belle, who has hit 98 home runs in the past two seasons, has reportedly agreed in principle to play for the Chicago White Sox."

HENZLER: I thought Jerry Reinsdorf was supposed to be one of the spear-carriers for "small-market" financial responsibility.

COOPERSON: All of the big-market owners want everything in the best interest of baseball—unless it means sacrificing their own individual interests.

ZMINDA: That's right. Reinsdorf's going broke, and it's all Donald Fehr's fault.

PINTO: I'm someone who really likes Albert Belle, and I'm glad he's making a big piece of change. It's a good thing the owners rejected the new deal, or the White Sox would have to pay taxes on all that money. Maybe that's why Jerry didn't want it, he wants to buy a winner this year.

Secondly, I don't think the White Sox are going to see too many left-handed starters this year. Thomas followed by Belle is a pretty scary combination.

ZMINDA: I'm waiting for the first sportswriter to say that Frank Thomas won't walk 100 times a year any more because Belle is hitting behind him.

JAMES: It's already happened. Somebody from the *Sun-Times* just called me, and asked me if I thought Thomas might hit 60 homers with Belle batting behind him.

COUVILLON: I'm waiting for Thomas to get ticked off because Belle is making more money.

PINTO: Of course the question now is who's going to protect Belle?

November 19—If You Can't Beat 'Em, Sign 'Em

Take *that*, Cleveland!

Maybe Jerry Reinsdorf really *does* want to beat the Indians. You'd be justified in assuming otherwise, after what happened in the second half the season. The White Sox were within striking distance of the Indians, but desperately needed another starter. Other teams shelled out extra bucks for a hired gun or two—Texas got John Burkett, Seattle got Jamie Moyer and Terry Mulholland—but the White Sox kept their wallets firmly in-pocket. Every five days, they threw another game into the toilet, and asked Joe Magrane to do the flushing. After Magrane, Ty-D-Bol men like Kirk McCaskill and Mike Bertotti kept sending games down the tubes, and the Indians gradually pulled away. The White Sox' fifth starter won exactly three games all year. They lost the division over it, and then they lost the wild-card over it—over money.

The White Sox fans seemed to pick up on it, too. The park was packed during the huge series with Cleveland just before the All-Star break, but by the end of August, the fans seemed to sense that Reinsdorf had thrown in the towel. The team was still very much in the wild-card race, but the ownership gave every indication that it could care less, and the fans followed suit.

So when Reinsdorf sabotaged the labor agreement, it seemed to confirm that he'd do just about anything, short of de-stabilizing the national money supply, to avoid upping his payroll. "Labor peace? Screw that! I ain't paying no free-agent money to Alex Fernandez! Billions of dollars in marketing income lost? That's all right, as long as I don't have to subsidize the Kansas City Royals' payroll!"

And then he signs Belle to a five-year contract with the highest yearly salary in the game. Why? Because it creates the *appearance* that the White Sox now can beat Cleveland.

The arithmetic is pretty simple, at first glance. If you subtract Belle from Cleveland and add him to Chicago, it goes a long way toward closing that 14-game gap.

How far? Probably not as far as you'd think. Belle will replace Danny Tartabull, who wasn't all that terrible. Bill James has estimated that this will enhance their run production by about 40 runs, which should translate into three or four additional victories. On Cleveland's side, they'll replace Belle with Brian Giles, or someone else who can hit, and the cost probably won't exceed 30 or 40 runs—about three games at most. So all the White Sox have done is to move seven games closer to Cleveland. They're still significantly behind.

But the appearance is what counts here. The White Sox are convinced that the real reason no one showed up at the park last year was that the fans were still mad about 1994. According to Reinsdorf, millions of disaffected White Sox fans felt cheated out of a long-awaited World Series berth in '94, and took out their frustration by dressing up as empty seats.

Now, the management can tell the fans, "C'mon back! We're number-one again!" People will believe it. Whether or not it's actually true is quite irrelevant.

Or perhaps it's mainly a ploy by Reinsdorf to rehabilitate his sagging public image. You know this game; Michael Jackson plays it all the time. You make bad news? Act weird? Look weird? Get sued for some unspeakable crime? That's okay. Just make some *good* news, and make it *bigger*. Marry somebody famous, out of the blue.

Think about it. In the past few weeks, Reinsdorf's become known as the guy whose behind-the-scenes maneuvering helped to trash the labor deal. But now, look what he's done: he's married somebody famous.

—Mat Olkin

November 19—Jimy Williams to Manage Red Sox

ZMINDA: There's a new Red Sox manager. It's Jimy Williams, former Toronto manager and Atlanta Brave coach.

PINTO: Someone else who's never won the World Series. All the Red Sox do is go out and get loser managers. Why can't they land someone like Alou or Davey Johnson?

Williams is going to be eaten alive in Boston. The players really liked Kennedy because he never was hard on them, he always took their side. He's going to need to be tougher to get that team to perform up to expectations, but the players aren't going to help him.

I really feel they needed someone like Whitey Herzog, who has a no-nonsense reputation to put them in line.

It's amazing to me that someone like Duquette, who makes great player moves, can't hire a decent manager.

MITTLEMAN: David—Williams was hired because Duquette lost confidence in Herzog after he originally turned down the deal. Besides, Williams is a better instructional guy and would be more dedicated.

PINTO: What's he going to do when Canseco is lounging around the clubhouse when he should be out on the field? What's he going to instruct him to do? There were a lot of bad examples set during the Kennedy era. Maybe he'll be a good manager for the rookies, but it's Valentin, Vaughn, Canseco and Clemens that will cause the problems, and I don't think Williams is up to putting them in their place.

MOYER: Never won the World Series?!? David, I'm surprised at you. Sounds like the ol' "postseason experience" nonsense to me. I was talking to Don briefly about Williams this morning and he seems like a guy who has a good chance at melding with Duquette. Especially when Don told me he was fried in Toronto because he wanted Domaso Garcia out of the leadoff spot.

JAMES: My impression of Jimy Williams in Toronto is that he did all of the right things and none of them worked. He put kids in the lineup who had talent, and they didn't play the way they should have. George Bell didn't really like him, and that team took a lot of their clues from George, plus I think Cito Gaston (who was the hitting coach) undercut him somewhat. I wish him well.

COOPERSON: Williams hasn't managed in seven years. Wouldn't it be foolish to condemn him for mistakes he made as a manager in the '80s? How many managers win the WS in their first stop as a manager? Not La Russa, not Leyland, not Cox.

PINTO: I think the fact that he hasn't managed for seven years says something about his perceived abilities as a manager. What's the reason he hasn't managed? Did clubs think there was always someone better? Or was he just happy coaching the Braves, another underachieving team? (The Braves are like the Royals of the '70s—a great team that just couldn't win in the postseason.)

The best the Red Sox are going to do under Williams is come close again.

MITTLEMAN: David—There's no question that the discipline on this club is awful. I watched them take BP and walked around their clubhouse about 20 times this year while in spring training, Boston and Toronto, and I was on the road with them in Texas and I saw exactly what you are talking about. Canseco hardly ever came out for stretching or for BP, only when he felt like it. I had a good friend there in Jamie Moyer who used to tell me how bad it was. Kevin Kennedy maintained a class system there which led to his firing.

Jimy Williams will only last if he can deal with this. I was only pointing out that between him and Herzog, Duquette had little choice. Herzog is too old for this and showed reluctance to even take the job. They might get some long-term gain out of Williams for improved defense as more of the youngsters come through. For next year, I agree that he won't be able to solve the rift that is present there right now. Not too many guys could.

HENZLER: The Braves in the 1990s are 7-4 in postseason series, quite a difference from the Royals of the 1970s, who were 0-3 before winning the pennant in 1980. Sure, the Braves are only 1-3 in the World Series, but to compare a .636 postseason series winning percentage to the Royals of the '70s is a bit of a reach, I think.

PINTO: I disagree. The Braves are so far in front of everyone in the 1990s they should have won five in a row. They should be the Yankees of the 1950s, but instead they are the Dodgers of the '50s.

JAMES: The Red Sox have had a class system since 1935, at least. It's endemic to the clubhouse. I know I wrote an article about how hard it was to get rid of the perpetual class system in the Boston clubhouse at least 15 years ago.

Go back and look, and you'll find that the only times the Red Sox have ever won was when about 70% of the team was new. They won in 1946, when nobody on the team had seen one another for three years. They won in 1967 with the youngest starting lineup ever to win a pennant; something like six of the eight regulars were 23 or under. They won in 1975 with Rice and Lynn as rookies. They won in 1986 when Clemens had his first full season and they had some eccentrics like Oil Can Boyd.

But without *new* managers, *new* superstars, and certified, gold-plated eccentrics, the holier-than-thou veterans will turn that clubhouse into the Ottoman Empire. They've done it for 60 years.

COOPERSON: They should've hired Lou Holtz.

OLKIN: Maybe they need Otto Velez.

November 19—News from Cleveland

WENZ: The Indians have traded for Matt Williams, and they're making a strong bid to sign John Smoltz. Would you trade Albert Belle for Williams and Smoltz?

JAMES: In a heartbeat. And I'd throw in Tonya Harding.

PINTO: That's a real good question. Williams isn't the hitter Belle is; he doesn't get on base enough. So from a hitting angle, the Belle for Williams isn't a good deal.

But if you get Smoltz in the mix, now it seems to be pretty good. It sure should be one exciting race in the Central this year.

QUINN: Yes, I would prefer Williams/Smoltz over Belle.

WENZ: If one of the two is a pitcher, I'd do it.

COOPERSON: But what about this:

Belle is a lock for a monster year. Williams has a chance at a monster year, but hasn't had one since 1994. Due to the likelihood of injury, he's a question mark. Likewise Smoltz and his fragile psyche. Both of those guys *could* have monster years; Belle is a definite. Would you give up a guaranteed MVP-type year in exchange for two *possible* MVP-type players?

November 22—Baseball Babble-On

From the very rare "Actually Something Useful In Baseball Babble-On" Department: you probably already know by now that Jose Rijo's probably not going to pitch in 1997 either. The new Teddy Higuera?

Remember that last paragraph for your spring Roto draft.

A couple of weird stats:

Andujar Cedeno walked nine times (two intentional) in 154 at-bats for the Padres last year. Then he walked four times in 179 at-bats for the Tigers. Finally, he walked two times in two at-bats for the Astros. Which one is not like the others? (This doesn't really translate well to prose. Look at your 1997 STATS *Major League Handbook* for full effect.)

Rockie prospect Derrick Gibson stole three bases and was caught 12 times last year at Triple-A. Holy 1994 Jose Vizcaino, Batman!

The Marlins signed Bobby Bonilla today, a far cry from Albert Belle. I think the Marlins had better go buy some more players, because they sure don't look to me like the team that's poised to make a big run that they seem to think they are. I'd love to see "poor genius Jim Leyland" flounder with a huge payroll in 1997. He coasted way too long on excuses in Pittsburgh if you ask me.

— Steve Moyer

November 22—Valentin Wants Out of Boston

ZMINDA: There's a news report that says John Valentin wants out of Boston.

PINTO: Here it comes, the player unhappiness. Clemens leaves, Valentin leaves and Jimy Williams loses.

OLKIN: I guess George Bell was right—Jimy Williams *is* a crummy manager.

PINTO: Well, you don't hear any players saying, "I want to stay and play for Jimy Williams."

MOYER: Screw Valentin and Clemens. Rudy Pemberton to the rescue!!!

PINTO: Oh, sorry, I didn't realize they had a .500 hitter on the team. I'm sure he'll make the Red Sox forget Ted Williams.

OLKIN: I heard Pemberton wants out of Boston, too. Says he wants Valentin to play shortstop.

JAMES: About Rudy Pemberton, thanks to Stefan Kretschmann—

Highest Single Season Averages (minimum 40 at-bats)

Avg	Player	Year	Hits	AB
.512	Rudy Pemberton	1996	21	41
.500	Gil Coan	1947	21	42
.463	Gary Ward	1980	19	41
.442	Monte Cross	1894	19	43
.440	Hugh Duffy	1894	237	539
.438	Babe Ganzel	1927	21	48
.435	Tip O'Neill	1887	225	517
.433	Walter Johnson	1925	42	97
.432	Dale Mitchell	1946	19	44
.429	Ross Barnes	1876	138	322
.427	Jack Bentley	1923	38	89
.426	Nap Lajoie	1901	232	544
.426	Stan Musial	1941	20	47
.424	Willie Keeler	1897	239	564
.424	Rogers Hornsby	1924	227	536
.422	Herb Goodall	1890	19	45
.420	Elmer Valo	1941	21	50
.420	George Sisler	1922	246	586
.420	Ty Cobb	1911	248	591
.419	Fred Lynn	1974	18	43
.416	Tuck Turner	1894	141	339
.415	Joe Judge	1915	17	41
.412	Fred Dunlap	1884	185	449
.411	Todd Haney	1995	30	73
.410	Ty Cobb	1912	227	553
.410	Ed Delahanty	1899	238	581
.410	Jesse Burkett	1896	240	586
.409	Jesse Burkett	1895	225	550
.408	Joe Jackson	1911	233	571

Avg	Player	Year	Hits	AB
.407	Phil Clark	1992	22	54
.407	Sam Thompson	1894	178	437
.407	George Sisler	1920	257	631
.407	Ed Delahanty	1894	199	489
.407	Ted Williams	1953	37	91
.406	Ted Williams	1941	185	456
.405	Jerry Coleman	1952	17	42
.404	Billy Hamilton	1894	220	544
.404	Ed Delahanty	1895	194	480
.404	Duke Farrell	1903	21	52
.403	Bob Hazle	1957	54	134
.403	Rogers Hornsby	1925	203	504
.403	Harry Heilmann	1923	211	524
.402	Maurice Archdeacon	1923	35	87
.402	Pete Browning	1887	220	547
.401	Rogers Hornsby	1922	250	623
.401	Bill Terry	1930	254	633
.401	Hughie Jennings	1896	209	521
.401	Ty Cobb	1922	211	526
.400	Frank LaPorte	1905	16	40
.400	Mike Davis	1982	30	75

If you read through this list, the interesting thing is that almost all of the late-season call-ups who hit .420 or more did in fact turn out to be outstanding hitters, as Pemberton in fact is. Edit the list down to the late-season callups who hit .415 or better, and in a list of ten or so players you've got Stan Musial, Fred Lynn, Joe Judge, Elmer Valo (who played 20 years in the majors, despite missing three years in World War II), Dale Mitchell, a lifetime .312 hitter . . .

November 26—Rumblings in the Distance

The $10.2 million signing bonus the Tampa Bay Devil Rays paid to former first-round pick Matt White may prove to be a significant event in the history of major league baseball. The sound of 10.2 million cash registers ringing simultaneously is far more than just a reminder of the staggering sum of money exchanged—it's a subtle foreshadowing of the second coming of Messersmith. Make no mistake: this is the contract that could bring down the entire Amateur Free Agent Draft.

Baseball is a monopoly, and it exploits its monopoly power whenever it's able to. In the past, abuse of this power has manifested itself in the form of the "reserve clause," a clause in each player's contract that denied him the right to sell his services to the highest bidder.

In the mid-'70s, the players were able to do away with the reserve clause, but it didn't just happen overnight. One of the events that sparked the revolution was the Catfish Hunter case. Hunter played for the Oakland A's, earning a $50,000 yearly salary. He was one of the best pitchers in baseball, but that was all the money he could command, since the reserve clause deprived him of all leverage in negotiations. When Oakland's owner, Charlie Finley, offered him a certain salary to sign, Hunter didn't have the option of shopping around for a better offer. He could accept it, he could hold out, or he could retire—that was it.

Then Finley screwed up. He failed to make a payment to Hunter as he was required to do by the terms of the contract. Hunter filed a grievance, and the arbitrator declared Hunter a free agent. For the first time in modern history, a superstar was freed from the restrictions of the reserve clause.

A bidding war broke out, and Hunter ended up signing with the Yankees for $3.5 million over five years. His annual salary went from $50,000 to $700,000.

Now, everyone had suspected that competitive bidding on the open market would yield a higher salary, but no one had imagined that the owners would be willing to pay such salaries as the one Hunter received. Although it would have been next-to-impossible for others to follow his route to free agency, Hunter's case provided a concrete example of the gains that were to be had if the reserve clause could be overturned.

It's no coincidence that one year later, the players achieved that exact result. The Messersmith case brought free agency to the players, but it never would have happened so soon if Hunter had not first provided a glimpse of the possible rewards.

In the 1996 Amateur Free Agent Draft, Kris Benson was the top pick in the country. The Pittsburgh Pirates paid him a signing bonus of $2 million.

Since then, four first-round picks have been declared free agents due to a technicality. Each of the four players have been signed by one of the expansion teams, and each of them received considerably more money than Benson did. Bobby Seay got $3 million; John Patterson got $6 million, Travis Lee got $10 million; and finally, Matt White got $10.2 million. Everyone had assumed that competitive bidding would yield higher bonuses, but no one had any *idea* that the difference between a free player and a drafted player would be in the neighborhood of $8 million.

This, my friend, is the rallying cry for a full-scale frontal assault on the Amateur Free Agent Draft. For the draft itself is nothing more than the reserve clause, dressed up in different language. When an amateur player is drafted by a particular team, he loses the right to sell his services to any other team, for the period of one full year. He can accept the bonus the team offers, he can hold out, or he can retire.

It's been pretty obvious that the draft has held down bonuses, but it's taken the recent quartet of free agents to truly illustrate the magnitude of the suppression. After Matt White landed a lifetime of financial security at age 18, every first-round pick—as well as their agents—will be looking to do the same. You can bet that the major league teams won't repeat the technical errors that resulted in the free agency of White and company, but there are other avenues available to the players.

The baseball owners occupy a unique position in the legal landscape, in that they have what's called an anti-trust exemption. This is said to mean that they are exempt from the nation's anti-trust laws. However, no one is quite sure exactly what this means, or which laws they ought to be exempt from, since no one else *has* an anti-trust exemption. The question of whether the owners should even have the exemption at all has been a long-standing source of contention.

In short, it's far from clear whether the draft would survive a legal challenge under anti-trust law. But one thing's clear: it's going to be tried, and soon. Owners beware: the second revolution is upon you.

—Mat Olkin

November 26—$$$

CANTER: A news report says high school pitching star Matt White is getting a $10.2 million bonus from the Devil Rays.

FAUST: I've never heard of the guy, but who would give $10.2 million to a high school pitcher? Nobody's that good, and young pitchers are far from a sure thing.

WENZ: It's times like these where it's really hard to see how the owners can blame the players for spiraling salaries.

ZMINDA: They say this kid is the best young pitching prospect since Todd Van Poppel. He could even be another Brien Taylor. . .

MOYER: Don't doubt the wisdom of MLB front office personnel, Drew, what's the matter with you? They know what they're doing. Almost all of them have major league playing experience and you have none. So there.

FAUST: Thanks, Steve, for setting me straight.

I rode a roller coaster once, so now I'm gonna go build one. Who wants to ride it first? Not all at once now. . .

QUINN: Drew, you *still* have it wrong. You need to ride the roller coaster 160+ times a year for twenty years. Then you should know how to build it.

FAUST: OH!!!

Well, I've driven my car about that much. I didn't think I knew enough to build one, but I must. I'll go build one tonight!

WENZ: If Drew builds a nicer car than I do, do I get to charge him a luxury tax on it?

FAUST: Absolutely not!

I plan to build my car way before a silly agreement like that can be made.

ELMAN: What are you going to name your car? Edsel and Yugo are already taken. Maybe Van Poppel or White can be used. You might even get more life out of the car then the people they're named for.

SICKELS: Guess who Matt White's agent is? Scott Boras. He strikes again.

White is a good prospect, but so what? The majority of high school pitchers burn out quick. It's stupid.

But hey, what do I know? I mean, just because I've studied the history of the draft doesn't mean I know anything about it. I mean, my best fastball topped out at 60 MPH when I was 18 years old. Obviously I know nothing.

MOYER: Kirby Puckett is Executive Vice President of Baseball for the Twins, probably collecting a six-figure salary from a team that can't afford anything. Now, they could hire a guy who has studied the history of the draft for years and make him very happy for, I'm guessing, mid-five figures. Or they can have good ole' roly-poly Kirby. Surely for the Twins, it's not even a decision.

OSLAND: Take it easy on Kirby now.

Now I'm not the brightest of guys on these baseball matters, so I probably shouldn't throw my two cents in. That said, I can't second-guess the Twins for bringing Kirby Puckett in and keeping him involved with the organization. He's loved by nearly everyone in Minnesota, he's a classy individual, and he has done a lot for the game. From what I heard he's going to be working with the minor leaguers primarily, which doesn't really seem like a stretch for him. Almost every player the Twins have brought up since the late '80s has told stories of how Kirby influenced them to respect the game and to play hard every day.

As far as his salary goes, are the Twins really one Chip Hale/Mike Trombley away from contention? That's about what a low six-figure salary could bring the Twins. So I may be a little defensive, and I may be wrong, but I don't think the Twins hiring Kirby really compares to a high school pitcher getting $10 million without proving that he will be a quality major leaguer.

MOYER: I agree, the Twins would get smoked by everyone alive if they didn't give Puckett some kind of position. My point is, however, that teams always seem to find money somewhere for this kind of stuff. Yet if John Sickels peddled his wares to the Twins tomorrow, do you think they'd give him the time of day? Of course not, they don't have money for stuff like that. Having an expert like John around can make a difference between Frank Thomas and Earl Cunningham. Do you think Kirby Puckett's ever studied the draft? I have a feeling his player-evaluation skills are more of the "he's really fast, maybe we can teach him to hit" variety, like seemingly everyone else involved in the majors. What I'm saying is a bunch of well-spent 50K people could really help a team. No one has money for that, though. They know better.

QUINN: Brent, I agree with you on Kirby.

I'll even go further to say it is easy and fashionable to be negative and the Kirby Puckett item is an easy target. I think we prove that the folks at STATS are just as prone to attack excessively as anyone else.

MOYER: So, Pat, you think Kirby Puckett's going to contribute a lot to the future success of the Minnesota Twins because he hit for a good average, hit a bunch of homers, won a World Series MVP, etc. and because he's generally a nice guy whose career ended suddenly and unfortunately. Maybe I can sell you a car.

FAUST: Perhaps the car I'm building, right?

QUINN: I am saying the Twins made a wise move, but not for your reasons.

1) Public relations *does* help a team become a winner because it brings in money—one of many things needed for success.

2) If almost every player brought up through the Twins organization gives some credit to Kirby for their success, this is also valuable.

3) Rewarding players for years of service and being a classy person helps a team in some intangible ways as well.

4) His salary is low by today's standards.

Steve, I agree with you the Twins need to hire John Sickels, but I also agree with Brent that the Twins were smart to hire Kirby.

DEWAN: Kirby Puckett is a class act who represents everything that is good about baseball. He deserves a high profile position that can been seen by the public. It's good for baseball and it's good for the Twins. He's been extremely helpful to his teammates for years. He'll continue to help the organization in many ways. And who knows? Maybe he'll develop into an excellent baseball executive. Despite our complaints, there are *many* former ballplayers doing excellent work in the front office of major league teams.

I congratulate the Twins on their excellent decision.

SICKELS: Well, as a Twins fan, I'm glad they are keeping Kirby around. He's a good influence on the younger players and farm system guys, plus having him continually associated with the team is good PR. Kirby is God in Minnesota. . . he's too valuable of a resource to let slip away. Any way they can keep him associated with the team is a plus for community relations.

COOPERSON: Kirby was never a World Series MVP.

MOYER: Leave it to Ethan to embarrass me.

November 26—Peace

HENZLER: Baseball owners have ratified the baseball agreement, by a vote of 26-4. Good News!!!!!

MOYER: I hope it's still too late for inter-league play.

OSLAND: Now there's something I definitely can agree with!!!

HENZLER: Sorry, Steve. . .

Bud has just said we still have inter-league play.

HENZLER: Selig says the Belle signing by the White Sox had absolutely no effect on today's vote.

Anybody buying?

QUINN: Jim, yes and no.

No, I don't buy the Albert Belle signing had *nothing* to do with the vote by the owners. It did make some contribution.

Yes, I do buy that the Albert Belle signing was *not* the most important reason the owners voted for the deal.

OK, experts, here's my theory: The owners tried one last bluff and it failed.

Here's my evidence:

1) Before the first vote, the rumors were the vote would be very close. If the deal was turned down, it would be only by a couple votes. Instead, 18 owners voted no! Approximately double the number of no votes predicted.

My theory for one last bluff says they wanted a strong no vote.

2) Days before the first vote, Randy Levine announced he would resign if the deal was voted down. After the vote he said he'd say on for a couple weeks. My theory says he was waiting for the *real* vote on the deal.

3) After Bud was totally turned down by Fehr, the owners did some thinking on the alternatives. After three weeks, they were ready for the *real* vote.

4) The *real* vote had four owners voting against it, a number much closer to the original number of owners against the deal than the 18 that happened with the first vote.

OLKIN: Selig also added that he has plenty of credibility and is proud of his hair, which is real.

PINTO: I for one, am happy it's done. It will be nice to concentrate on baseball alone for the next five years.

DEWAN: I congratulate Jerry Reinsdorf on bringing a great player to Chicago and getting the labor deal done. Ingenius!

PINTO: I still like the Indians' chances, especially if they sign a front-line pitcher.

I'm going to have a real hard time rooting for the White Sox now. I really like Belle and Thomas and Phillips and many players on the team. But Reinsdorf has replaced Steinbrenner in my mind as the symbol of what's wrong with baseball ownership. So go Indians! (It would be interesting if Jack McDowell leads the Indians over the White Sox.)

November 29—Baseball Babble-On

Hey, Catfish, can we call you Catfish Chapstick?

Hey, I've been seeing that "Surf" laundry detergent commercial a lot lately where the guy's trying to dry his pants by wedging them in the car window while he's driving around and they blow away. And every time I see it I think of Jose Lind.

Hey, I happened to mention to our little STATS baseball e-mail group about how I semi-questioned the Twins' Kirby Puckett position. Now, my point was not that the Twinkies shouldn't have given Puckett a job in the organization. That would be the worst PR move of all-time. My point was that teams, and especially ones like the Twins, never have money for anything like signing players or player development, etc., but they always seem to come up with surely six-figure salaries for things like making Kirby Puckett automatically "Executive Vice President of Baseball." Now signing players costs a lot of money, but I do know a whole bunch of people who'd be real happy to help a team with developmental issues and, honest to God, I've been in this business long enough to know a helluva lot more than the guys who are currently pulling the strings about how to build a winner. And they wouldn't demand six-figure salaries either. Of course, they can't say they've hit one major league home run between all of them, and, obviously, that's why no one would hire them for such a position. (But, like one guy on the STATS e-mail list said, "I've ridden the roller coaster a bunch of times, so now I'm going to build one. Who wants to ride first?") Well, a whole bunch of true-blue-tried-and-true you-must-be-a-gosh- darned-communist-to-say-anything-nega-tive-about-Kirby STATS baseball fans had things to say back to me. And the final note ended with something like, "no matter what you say, there are many former major leaguers doing excellent jobs in the front office." You know, I got to thinking about that. So if there are *many* former major leaguers doing *excellent* jobs in the front office, try to name five off the top of your head. And "Director of Peanut Sales" guys don't count.

Hey, so did you see, one of my main men, John Cangelosi, signed last week, with the Marlins? And here were the quotes: "He'll be one of our extra outfielders," Marlins general manager Dave Dombrowski said. "He'll get some playing time out there." "I'm a piece to the puzzle," Cangelosi said. "You don't need an everyday player all the time, but just to play where the team needs you." Poor, poor John. You know what it reminds me of? A few weeks ago, I saw the Disney version of "Hunchback of Notre Dame." John Cangelosi is Quasimodo. And I don't mean that in a bad way, John. (Remember, during the season when Cangelosi attacked 7-4, 490 pound Jeff Juden? He'd make mincemeat of me.) That mean guy (I forgot his name) told Quasi so many times that he was ugly and deformed that eventually Quasimodo lurched around saying, "But I can't go out in public; I'm ugly and deformed." (Maybe you know the story from the literary classic. I know it from the Disney cartoon.) Well, John Cangelosi, who could be a fine everyday major league leadoff hitter says, "I'm happy to be one of the extra outfielders; I'm not good enough to be a regular." Yes, Cangelosi's not as good as Sheffield. I could make a strong argument that he's better than Bonilla, but, I'll admit, it's not clear-cut. But Cangelosi's a ton better than Devon White, who had the best OBP of his career in 1991 at .342. That's 35 points lower than Cangy's career mark. But, never fear, if Leyland's the genius he's supposed to be, he'll figure it out. (Ha ha ho ho he he.) Kind of reminds me of a guy who was a great spare part for the Oakland A's, but was never quite good enough to play regularly. Then he was traded to the Tigers. Then, at just about 30, he finally was allowed to become Tony Phillips.

— Steve Moyer

November 30—Ruben Sierra

Well, I guess the biggest news in baseball this week was the stunning trade of Ruben Sierra to the Cincinnati Reds. After all that franchise has had to endure, it almost seems unfair that they'll now have to take on the most frustrating ballplayer this side of Van Poppel. Reds' G.M. Jim Bowden reportedly has said, "I love a good reclamation project." Hmm. Sounds a bit like General Custer declaring, "I love a good fight."

Once an MVP candidate, Sierra has now regressed to the point where the Tigers have agreed to pay almost all of his salary just to make sure he never ventures into their clubhouse again. It's hard to blame them; after coming over from the Yankees last year, Sierra surely must have been asked how he felt about going from a first-place team to a cellar-dweller. Over the remainder of the season, Sierra provided the answer to that question, nine innings at a time: he batted .222 with only one home run in 46 games. Just to make sure he drove his point home, he committed *five* errors in only 23 games in the outfield, and appeared each time to be genuinely annoyed that a fly ball would have the audacity to interrupt his brooding. Five errors in less than two dozen games—now, that's hard to do. It projects out to about *35* over a full season. Jose Offerman gets into that territory from time to time, but he has to handle three times as many chances just to get there. It must have taken a monumental amount of effort to work up that much indifference.

—Mat Olkin

December 1—Offense/Goodwin

HENZLER: News item from this week's *Sporting News*: "Outfielder Tom Goodwin is the Royals' player of the year, selected in a vote of Kansas City baseball writers. His qualifications included 80 runs scored, 66 stolen bases and a .282 average." A few more pertinent stats:

Major League Trailers, Isolated Power

Otis Nixon	.040
Rey Ordonez	.046
Tom Goodwin	.048
Jody Reed	.053
Mark Lemke	.064

(minimum 450 plate appearances)

Center Field Trailers, Runs Created Per 27 Outs

Marvin Benard	3.34
Chad Curtis	3.56
Tom Goodwin	3.56
Brian L. Hunter	3.68
Johnny Damon	3.83

(minimum 450 plate appearances)

Center Field Trailers, Secondary Average

Johnny Damon	.195
Tom Goodwin	.206
Marvin Benard	.232
Lance Johnson	.251
F.P. Santangelo	.262

(minimum 450 plate appearances)

Goodwin played 81 games in center field and 75 in left last season. If listed with the left fielders, he'd rank *last* in runs created per 27 outs, and second to last in secondary average (Garret Anderson—.161).

He also led the league in caught stealing, and was a good leader in the clubhouse, I'm sure. An offensive juggernaut, those Royals.

PINTO: Offerman not winning player of the year for the Royals is a bigger travesty than A-Rod not winning MVP!

December 2—Pink Floyd

SICKELS: For those Pink Floyd fans out there. . . don't the lyrics to the album "Animals" remind you of Jerry Reinsdorf?

December 3—Jerry Reinsdorf

According to all the papers, the man who set the stage for the ratification of baseball's labor agreement was the same hawk who'd been fueling the confrontation in the first place: Jerry Reinsdorf.

It's an easy story to swallow, admittedly. Reinsdorf, a large-market owner who opposed the labor agreement for various reasons, forged an anti-deal alliance with the small-market teams—a voting bloc powerful enough to defeat the agreement in the owners' initial vote. Then, he signed Albert Belle to a mega-deal that redefined the game's entire salary structure. The small-market teams felt betrayed by Reinsdorf, and abandoned him when the deal came up for another vote. The result was that the agreement was ratified —as a direct result of the actions of the man who most opposed it. It's a tale rich with irony, far too delicious for any storyteller to pass up.

But is it believable?

Now, it's true that Reinsdorf opposed the deal, and that he lined up support from the poorer teams. He convinced them that the deal did not provide enough revenue sharing for the smaller operators, and he may have been absolutely right. In any event, they believed him.

Now, it's one thing for the Pittsburgh Pirates to agree with Reinsdorf on that point, but it's quite another for the Pirates to think that Reinsdorf had become some sort of Santa Claus for the Pittsburghs of baseball. Reinsdorf's interests were completely different than those of the small market teams, except for one thing: they all opposed the labor deal. The Pirates and their underprivileged brethren didn't like it because it didn't contain enough revenue sharing. Reinsdorf opposed it because 1) he stood to lose his best pitcher if service time were granted, and 2) he wanted to extract even more concessions from the union.

Reinsdorf played up the revenue-sharing angle because he needed the votes to block the deal. Did the Royals really think that Reinsdorf was having trouble sleeping at night, agonizing over the plight of the small-market teams?

If we are to believe what we're being told, we must accept this premise: the small-market teams believed that Reinsdorf's commitment to their cause ran so deep that he would unilaterally abstain from signing expensive free agents—to his own detriment—purely for the benefit of the small-market teams.

To that, I say: horse-puckies.

It's much easier for me to accept the notion that the other seven owners switched their votes because they found it in their best interests to do so. OK then, you ask, what had changed between the first and second vote? Why would a team oppose the deal the first time and accept it the second time?

I'll tell you why: because they realized that it was all they were going to get. Perhaps Selig and Reinsdorf had convinced them that the players, when confronted with a "no" vote, would

192

assent to additional concessions. This possibility was quickly nixed during a two-minute telephone call between Don Fehr and Bud Selig. When that happened, it left the owners with two choices: ratify the agreement as it stood, or go without a deal.

The small-market owners had been convinced that the deal didn't have enough revenue sharing, and that they had to hold out for more. Now, it was clear that there was no more to be had. They had to choose between the moderate relief provided in the deal, or no revenue sharing at all. Easy choice.

In fact, the theory has been floated around the office by Pat Quinn—and I rather like it—that the first vote was a sham, designed to elicit more concessions from the players, while the owners secretly agreed to hold another vote to ratify the original deal if no more concessions were forthcoming. If that was the case, then the Belle signing provided a facile explanation for the owners' reversal.

The owners could say, with a straight face, that their first vote was not a sham, contrived for the purpose of squeezing another dollar out of the union. Their reversal was not an embarrassing surrender, or a bluff gone bad. It was the result of their collective sense of betrayal, their deeply wounded hearts, suffering in disillusionment at Reinsdorf's double-dealing. As I said, it's an easy story to swallow—as long as you don't chew on it too much.

—Mat Olkin

December 3—Pat Listach Signs with Astros

MOYER: Shucks. No wonder the Astros have no need for Cangelosi anymore! They've got panty-waste Pat, who's had one good season, yet everyone's still interested in. Love those MLB front offices!

ZMINDA: The correct term is actually "panty-WAIST Pat," not "panty-waste." Although the error is understandable in this case. . .

December 4—Fred McGriff Trade Rumors

ZMINDA: Word is that the Braves are ready to trade McGriff.

PINTO: I don't quite understand the McGriff deal from a baseball standpoint (I understand the money considerations). I assume the Braves believe that Andruw Jones will be able to replace McGriff's offense; I think he has potential, but he's really young and it might not be realized for a couple of years yet. In the meantime, the Braves may be moving closer to the Dodgers; a great pitching team with no offense. Now the Dodgers proved you can get to the first round of the playoffs with that type of team, but not much further. My feeling is (and it's just a feeling at this point) that the Braves need a power hitter like McGriff to keep making the World Series, let alone win it.

The Braves, after all, have become a boring team, with their fans not even showing up for the division series. (Let me say that I don't find them boring, but fan reaction seems to indicate that they are.) Depending more on their strength (pitching) by further weakening their offense can't make them more exciting in their fans eyes. They would have been much better served by signing Albert Belle, keeping McGriff and letting Smoltz go. Look how much the Braves offense on the road has slipped in the last two years compared to the rest of the National League:

Year	R/G Road
1991	3rd
1992	1st
1993	3rd
1994	2nd
1995	9th
1996	10th

This is the trend the Braves need to fight if they are going to keep winning, and keep fan interest alive. It seems to me they are putting all their eggs in the pitching basket, and that's a good place for them to crack.

MITTLEMAN: The other factor in the McGriff deal is that the Braves now realize they will be hard-pressed to get rid of Dave Justice and his $12 million. You are exactly right in that these moves all revolve around setting up a contingency fund to attempt to deal with Maddux and Glavine at the end of next season. Having said that, remember that if Justice comes back close to form, he will make up some of the shortfall they were missing last year when he was out. In an ideal world, it would be nice to keep both McGriff and Justice, but there's only so much dough to go around. It now looks like McGriff could be heading to Cincinnati for Bret Boone and others because Lemke appears to be going to the Yankees. This would cause the Reds to move Hal Morris and the Mets are interested in him.

PINTO: Getting someone like Boone would be fine, but from the way they were holding out for Hernandez from Florida, it seemed like they were trying to pick up more pitching.

I thought Justice was through with the Braves. What's his deal like?

OLKIN: If McGriff goes to Cincy, *duck*. Career numbers there: .320 avg, .680 Slg., with 16 HRs in 44 games.

COOPERSON: It comes down to four positions for six players: Klesko, Justice, Jones, Dye, Grissom and McGriff.

You've got three outfield spots and first base. Grissom is the only center fielder and is the leadoff man; he's not going anywhere. So you've got five spots for three guys. That's too many and one has to go. The reasoning (not that I agree) is that you've got to keep Dye & Jones because they're young with so much potential. Justice has no trade value, but he could come all the way back. Klesko can't hit lefties, but he may learn, and you don't want to give up a young 30-homer guy. So you dump McGriff, the oldest in the group who has trade value.

Personally, I might be inclined to trade Dye. What can he do that Jones can't?

PINTO: I agree with you. In a way, Dye may have more trade value than McGriff because he's young and therefore cheap, and upside is high. McGriff being old isn't going to get better than he already is but could also start declining (this may have already begun, his second half was poor). Now I believe that McGriff has a few good years left so I'd want him, but I can see the argument.

DEWAN: Good analysis, Ethan. I concur with you completely. McGriff is the oldest and should be the best candidate to trade. Dye should be considered, however.

JAMES: You all are missing the obvious on the thinking behind the Fred McGriff action. It's not Jermaine Dye or Andruw Jones or anything like that: It's Ryan Klesko. Klesko is probably a better hitter than McGriff right now, but he essentially disappeared during post-season play because:

1) his defense in the outfield makes him of marginal value overall, and 2) when you throw a lefty at them, that pushes him over the margin.

Klesko plays the outfield about as well as a monkey can drive a road grader. They're not giving up anything by moving him to first base.

PINTO: I'm not prepared to say Klesko is better than McGriff. McGriff hits lefties well, and Klesko doesn't, so McGriff plays everyday and Klesko doesn't. Klesko hits righties a lot better than McGriff does, but if they both played every day I think Klesko's numbers would be pulled down below McGriff's.

December 4—Rickey Henderson

ZMINDA: Latest trade rumor: John Valentin to the Padres for a package including Scott Sanders. The thing holding it up is that the Padres want to include Rickey Henderson in the package, and the Sox don't seem to want him. . .

PINTO: Oh, twist my arm! What kind of no-brainer is that? Scott Sanders and the greatest leadoff man of all time (who is still effective) for crybaby John Valentin? What does Duquette want, a pot of gold to fall on his head? Who in this group would not take that deal without thinking?

MOYER: What the [fill in your own word] are the Red Sox thinking and doing? The Red Sox better hope the Padres force Rickey on them or they won't come back with much from John Valentin. Eric Davis??? Chris Gomez?!?!?!?!

MITTLEMAN: They have Clemens' salary to deal with, Naehring's as well, and they want to add another pitcher. . . they also want to come in at $40 million in payroll next year. A 38-year-old Rickey Henderson and his $2 million-plus-incentives are not what they have in mind with all these other costly negotiations going on. The only thing I don't understand is what they are doing talking with Eric Davis. His demands were rumored to be ridiculous (near $6 million per year) and Nick Cafardo of the Boston Globe tells me that could be a done deal in 24 hours or so although I suspect for a lot less than $6 million. I can see why they want Scott Sanders and with Garciaparra at short next year they obviously would have different plans for Gomez. They must feel they are going to lose Naehring as well and are looking to cover themselves. I learned yesterday that Wil Cordero was asked to move to third base in winter league so something is up there as well.

December 5—Terry Steinbach Signs with Twins

MOYER: My first reaction was: "Just what the Twins need, an expensive old catcher." Then, I thought, maybe with all their promising young pitchers, it *is* just what they need. See, I am positive sometimes.

PINTO: It's also nice to see that everyone in baseball isn't greedy. It's interesting to watch the dynamics of free agency, the competitiveness of players vs. playing where they want. For a lot of players, the goal seems to be being the highest paid player. But as players get older, the goal seems to be 1) playing for a winner or 2) playing for the home team.

SICKELS: Well, even if he is getting old, he's better than Matt Walbeck. He should help the Twins.

December 5—Jim Leyritz Traded to Angels

PINTO: I also understand the Leyritz was one of the few 1996 Yankees who was not pleasant to be around.

CHERNOW: Hey now, guys. . . Leyritz always treated me okay at the good ol' University of Kentucky baseball camp many summers ago. Let's not be so hard on the man, eh?

ZMINDA: If I stood like that in the batter's box, I'd be crabby too.

December 6—Baseball Babble-On

I saw a *New York Post* note today that said: "Iraq defeated Iran 2-1 in soccer's Asian Cup at Dubai." Finally, a soccer game I might think about watching. (On second thought, I probably wouldn't watch that one either. I was just trying to be funny.)

Watch out for Jim Leyritz as the everyday Angel catcher. The man can hit and his defense is better than you've been led to believe. I'd rather have him than Joe Girardi any day.

Why has Moises Alou been christened "Prize Free-Agent Outfielder of 1996"? The man's 30 years old. He's never hit 25 homers, never scored 90 runs, and never driven in 100. What's the big deal?

Murray Chass of *The New York Times* printed a note on something Albert Belle's agent, Arn Tellem, told him about. It was a project that I coordinated and genius- new-boss-of-mine Mike Canter programmed projecting Albert Belle's last few seasons into the context of the major league parks Belle was considering other than Cleveland. In other words, what would Belle's '95 have looked like as a Marlin, White Sox, Rockie, etc. Of course, the Rockie numbers were the shockers (or not-shockers, to those of us blessed with baseball know-everythingness). We said Belle would've hit 85 homers in 1995 and 68 in 1996 as a Rockie. But wait. Chass says, "But the projection evidently did not consider the Rockie road factor." Yeah, I could make some silly ice cream joke here, but I'll leave those to zany Steve Rosenbloom. "Playing for Colorado, Belle might have hit more home runs at Coors Field than he did at Jacobs Field, but what would he have done on the road? This past season Belle hit 28 of his 48 home runs in other parks. The Rockies' home-run hitters, though, do not hit more home runs on the road than they do at Coors Field; in fact they hit half as many." Well, duh, duh, duh. Do you think that's because Coors is the best hitters' park possibly in baseball history or because of the mysterious "Rockie road factor"? "The team's top four hit 66 percent of their home runs at home. The Rockies, as a team, hit 67 percent of their home runs at home. At that consistent rate, even if Belle had played for Colorado, he would have hit 40 home runs at Coors but only 20 on the road, for a total of 60, one short of Maris' record." Did you ever see such convoluted logic? Rockie hitters are helped by Coors Field, but in addition, there's this mysterious factor that prevents them from hitting just as many homers on the road. Sure. I also love the "at that consistent rate" sentence, as if Albert Belle is just like Dante Bichette and Vinny Castilla. Someone should tell Murray that Dante and Vinny are sheep in wolves' clothing. Albert's the real deal.

Can someone please tell me why Tom Goodwin had a good year last year scoring 80 runs in 524 at-bats while Rickey Henderson stunk scoring 110 runs in 465? Sorry, I forgot about Goodwin's useless 66 stolen bases. (Sorry, they're useful for Rotisserie players. But, as any veteran scout will tell you, fantasy baseball and real baseball are two different games.)

Watch out for big fat Sid Fernandez in the Astrodome. He could put together at least a couple of good months before he goes out for the year.

Does it seem right to you that Mark Grace (1988) debuted only one year before Ken Griffey Jr. (1989)?

Can someone tell me why no one's ever given Chuck Ricci a real shot in the major leagues? His last two seasons at Triple-A, he's allowed less than a hit per inning, he's struck out a hitter per inning, he hasn't walked a whole lot of guys and his ERA's in the high twos. In 10 innings with the Phillies in 1995, he pitched excellent ball. No one can use this guy in middle relief? I'll bet he doesn't have a 90-MPH fastball, though. You don't have to necessarily be good to pitch in the majors if you've got one of those.

— Steve Moyer

December 6—Florida Marlin Signings

MOYER: I don't see what makes Alou/Conine better than Conine/Colbrunn unless the outfield defensive improvement is huge.

PINTO: I don't see where Fernandez should be getting John Smoltz money. Yes, he's a good pitcher, but his won-lost record over the last three years has as much to do with his good run support (5.64) as with his ERA 3.67. Now, I know 3.67 is good considering the offensive environment we are in, but given that Florida is a poor offensive team, I think it's a waste of money on their part. They would have been better off outbidding the White Sox for Belle.

ELMAN: Has anyone stopped to think that by signing Belle and not signing Fernandez (if that is in fact what happens), the White Sox took one step forward and two steps back? It is pitching that the Sox are in need of. Alex was one of the two, Tapani the other, that could actually get the game to the closer. Adding a big bat is always fun to watch, but how much fun will a four-hour, 12-10 loss be for Sox fans? SportsCenter should get a lot of offensive highlights to show.

PINTO: Thanks. One of the points I've been trying to make (especially about the Braves and the Marlins) is that teams seem to be trying to improve their strengths, not their weaknesses.

MOYER: The Sox were sixth in the league in hitting, fourth in pitching in 1996. Maybe I'm missing something.

December 9—Bordick Signs with O's/How Good Is Davey?

PINTO: Bordick vs. Naehring. I think I like the Orioles better with Naehring at third and Ripken at short than Ripken at third and Bordick at short. I like Bordick, but I don't think his defense makes up for the loss of offense at the position.

The Orioles seem to be a combination of the 1970s Red Sox, with power up and down the lineup but almost always finishing out of first, and the 1980s Yankees, trying to fix everything with free agents and trades for has-beens.

MOYER: They should call him bauk-bauk-bauk Bordick.

PINTO: Yes, that's another thing. Why would I want a player on my club that is afraid to take Ripken's spot? What sort of competitive person is this? I want the guy who tells me that he can play better than Ripken and wants to show the world and wants to win.

On a similar note, the Jose Canseco story is interesting. When he left Oakland, he was quoted as saying he didn't like it in Oakland because the only thing they thought about was winning.

JAMES: The Orioles have Baseball's best general manager, in Pat Gillick, and one of the best managers, in Dave Johnson. No other team except maybe Atlanta has the same combination of talent in those two positions.

These guys took over just one year ago, so to say that they are "almost always" doing *anything* seems to me premature. The fact that a strategy was used once and failed is really no indication that it will fail again. A sacrifice bunt may be used once and fail; this is no argument against the strategy.

Steinbrenner burned the '80s because he had no general manager (in essence; at that time he was using his general managers to do grunt work for him) and no real manager. I don't see any similarity to the current Orioles there. Jimmy Key is a good pitcher, probably better in his second season back than he was in his first season back (from the injury). Besides, he is what the Orioles *needed*—a starting pitcher. I think the Orioles will win that division next year, probably by 10 games.

PINTO: I don't know about that. Angelos is a lot like Steinbrenner; he sticks his nose into Gillick's business too much. There were moves that Gillick was not allowed to make last summer, and who knows, they might have been a better team if they had made the moves. I have much more respect for Pat Gillick's baseball knowledge than for Angelos'.

Davey Johnson went down a peg in my book last year. I thought the whole Ripken situation was poorly handled. Gillick and Johnson seem to be much more interested in moving Ripken to gain control of the team than because it actually makes sense from a baseball standpoint.

Ten games? We'll see. After all, they are going to lose Alomar for at least five of them. Brady's not going to hit 50 HR again. Everyone's a year older, and they weren't exactly young to begin with.

MOYER: Red Sox Uber Alles!!!

JAMES: I agree that Angelos is a lot like Steinbrenner. Steinbrenner won six divisional titles in his first 10 years owning the team.

I also agree that the Ripken situation was poorly handled, but mostly what you're talking about there is public relations. Johnson took over a 71-73 team and guided them to an 88-74 season. It's pretty rugged to mark him down for that, ain't it?

PINTO: Steinbrenner was suspended from baseball when the foundation for the Yankees was laid, so Gabe Paul was actually able to do what he wanted, much like Michael was able to build the present team.

Johnson took over the Mets in 1984 and with a lot less talent won 90 games I believe. I think the Orioles this year were a big disappointment.

COOPERSON: Davey Johnson, with all the talent he had in NY, won once in seven years. He won only two division titles in his tenure there. And he managed to overlook the fact that his players had alcohol and coke problems. He is *not* one of the best managers in baseball.

David has already decided that the talented Atlanta Braves have not won more in the 1990s because of the third base coach. Should we similarly blame Mike Cubbage for the fact that a team with Gooden, Strawberry, Carter, Darling, Ojeda, Aguilera, Dykstra, Orosco, Mitchell, & Fernandez was twice beaten out for division titles by a less-talented Cardinal squad? And Mike Cubbage certainly screwed up the 1988 NLCS, when the talent-laden Dodgers downed the Mets. Davey Johnson is vastly overrated.

Oh, Keith Hernandez should have been included in the above names.

PINTO: That's what happens when you shoot your mouth off, your words come back to haunt you.

And after all, what do I know. I wouldn't have sent Bream on Bonds' arm.

JAMES: The most interesting thing about Davey Johnson is that the man has the world's largest collection of disgusting personal mannerisms. Did you ever notice this? He spits, or more accurately "leaks," tobacco juice all around him from beginning to end, and he seems incapable of keeping his hands away from any of his bodily orifices for more than a few moments at a time.

All that talent he had in New York? The team went 68-94 the year before they hired him, and 72-90 the year after they fired him. "All that talent" included Howard Johnson, who Sparky Anderson thought was a loser, who never did anything anyway other than for Davey Johnson. All that talent in New York included Wally Backman, who had been proclaimed a defensive disaster are and sent back to the minor leagues before Johnson rescued him.

Johnson went 98-64 in New York with a team which included Rafael Santana as the starting shortstop, Mookie Wilson in center field, and a 36-year-old George Foster in left. Moving on to Cincinnati, he had the team in first place in his first full season there (1994) until the season was stopped by the strike. He won the division outright in 1995.

In Baltimore he improved the team by eight full games in his first season. I don't see how you can interpret that record as anything other than brilliant.

Cooperson says he "overlooked" the drug problems of Dwight Badboy and Darryl Cumquat, but another way to look at it is that he won *despite* these problems. Is Davey Johnson responsible for the drug problems of these guys? What, are you serious? Did he take them out and beat them over the head and force them to take drugs? If you take drugs, is John Dewan responsible for that, or are you responsible for that? Johnson's responsibility is to win. And he always has.

PINTO: Gee Bill, you had a different attitude when it came to Chuck Tanner. I remember you thought the way he let the clubhouse get out of control was horrible. Now granted, I don't think there were drug pushers in the Mets clubhouse, but Davey (and Mets management) did nothing even after they knew the problem existed.

You praised Whitely Herzog for getting rid of Hernandez because of his drug problem because it sent a message to the rest of the team.

Have you changed your opinion on this subject?

COOPERSON: Yeah, Bill, and the 1927 Yankees had a No. 2 hitter with a lifetime OBP of .316. Surely they won strictly on managerial brilliance.

JAMES: Well, Miller Huggins *is* in the Hall of Fame, largely because he managed this great team. It is normally assumed that the coach or manager is a part of the team and gets credit when they win, not that he is an obstacle which must be overcome as the team vaults from 68-94 to 98-64 in two seasons.

The New York Mets finished 64-98, 66-96, 63-99, 67-95, 41-62, 65-97 and 68-94 in the seven seasons before Johnson was hired. Under Johnson, they went 90-72, 98-64, 108-54, 92-70, and 100-60 in their first five seasons. On the surface of it, granted I am not as wise as Mr. Cooperson, I would take this to be a reasonably good record. But since Mr. Cooperson has such good and specific evidence for his argument, I concede that, had Johnson not been such a total failure as a manager, this magnificent collection of talent would surely have gone 140-22 or better every season.

COOPERSON: Of course the Mets were bad after Johnson was canned—they hired an even bigger flop of a manager in Bud Harrelson.

JAMES: Oh. Well, that explains that.

COOPERSON: Exactly how many managerial offers has he gotten since the Mets canned him?

You could pick any good team in baseball history, point out their weaker links, and say they won because of good managing. But can you name a better five-man rotation—or really, a deeper one, than Gooden, Darling, Fernandez, Ojeda and Aguilera?

JAMES: But that's not *all* that I was saying, was it? Johnson moved on to Cincinnati, and Cincinnati won. They fired him, because after all he is an arrogant and intolerable person to be around, and found themselves in fourth place before they could scrub the dugout floor.

Johnson moved on to Baltimore, and the Orioles, who had won as many as 88 games only once in the previous 13 seasons (89 wins in 1992) went 88-74.

Whether or not this is a good record is not a debatable proposition. It is a brilliant record. Your argument is that it *should* be an even more brilliant record. I think it's an argument worthy of the average call-in 3:00 talk show host.

December 9—Red Sox

PINTO: If they get Clemens back, I like their chances. Duquette is real good at picking up talent cheap (and you know why, Steve!).

JAMES: Good Expensive Talent will beat good cheap talent three times in four.

December 9—Danny Jackson

MILLER: Is Danny Jackson the left-handed equivalent of Steve Stone?

COOPERSON: He's a little too psycho to broadcast games alongside Harry.

December 10-11—Terry Mulholland Signs with Cubs

PINTO: Terry has given up 10 HR in 62 IP at Wrigley since 1987. We could be looking at Bert Blyleven in the Metrodome here.

MOYER: Yes, but David, he's an innings-eater who takes that ball every fifth day. I'm sure he's a great clubhouse influence, too. And, like any Chicago sports talk show will tell you, the Cubs *need pitching*. They have for the last twenty-billion years, yet they can never seem to find any. (Could it be related to the same reason the Rockies will always *need pitching*? Nah. That's nonsense.) Love those MLB GM's!!!

OLKIN: Steve, isn't it obvious? They needed to add another pitcher since Jose Guzman retired.

COOPERSON: To set the record straight: Mulholland is a loner who wasn't missed in the Phillie clubhouse when they dealt him away in February of '94.

MOYER: Leave it to Ethan to embarrass me. By the way, I will happily 100 percent knock the Cubs' acquisition of Mulholland.

PINTO: It seems to me the most successful Cubs pitchers have been the ones who tend to keep the ball on the ground. (And I believe the same is true of the Rockies.) Somehow I don't think Mulholland fits that bill.

COOPERSON: Brilliant—fly ball pitcher in Wrigley. Great idea.

FULLAM: If the Cubs were that desperate for pitching, they should've held on to Greg Maddux when they had him. I'm not knocking the pickup of Mulholland, but for $2 million?? As a pitcher with substandard strikeout rates, I don't suspect he'll last long in Wrigley.

COOPERSON: I'll bet anyone $2.3 million dollars that if Mulholland has any kind of a decent season, he'll be dealt to a contender late in the year.

PINTO: If the Cubs are contenders and they keep Mulholland, do you win your bet?

PINTO: Remembering a few years ago when I believe both Mike Morgan and Greg Maddux were pitching for the Cubs the staff had a really good year. I think we did an article about the wind blowing in that year, but I also remember looking at G/F and thinking it was pretty high for the team.

FULLAM: Bill, I'd agree with you that the groundball/flyball tendencies of a pitcher probably wouldn't matter in Wrigley or Coors, but I think that power pitchers would definitely tend to thrive better in those settings. More strikeouts means less balls put in play—which would help to reduce the park's influence. Since Mulholland is definitely *not* a power pitcher, I can't see him doing well with the Cubs at all.

DEWAN: Bill, we did study groundball pitchers at Wrigley (and all other ballparks) and found out that they *are* significantly more effective at Wrigley. It was about three years ago.

ZMINDA: That's right. It turned out that groundball pitchers' ERAs were about half a run better at Wrigley than flyball pitchers.

JAMES: Half a run better? Wow; that's huge. How could I have missed something that large, just looking at the data?

December 10—Tigers-Astros Trade

MITTLEMAN: Today's 10-player trade, including a player to be named later sent by Houston, between the Tigers and the Astros is significant from Detroit's point of view more so than Houston. The Tigers have improved their team in several ways without spending a great deal of money or mortgaging their future. Summarized below are the effects of the deal.

Detroit: They obtain two relatively young position players in Orlando Miller and Brian Hunter. Miller will play shortstop enabling the Tigers to move Travis Fryman back to third base. Miller also has surprising power. In Brian Hunter, Detroit has acquired one of the fastest players in the game who will bat in the leadoff spot and play center field. By trading Brad Ausmus, the Tigers make room for youngster Raul Casanova to play on a regular basis as well. The Tigers were woefully inept in the bullpen this year and with Todd Jones they have come up with a closer who has potential ahead of him. Doug Brocail can be an effective starter or middle reliever when he is healthy.

Houston: Brad Ausmus was the key for the Astros. He is a solid defensive catcher who also hit well when he played with San Diego. The rest of the deal is basically about the future. Jose Lima has been inconsistent, but is just 24 years old with major league experience. Trever Miller and C.J. Nitkowski are young hurlers who have had potential written all over them and need more seasoning but could have an impact in a couple of years. Class-A Lakeland infielder Daryle Ward is only 21 years old and is a prospect.

Detroit is helped out now and Houston is a question mark until their young acquisitions mature. The deal is not enough to bring the Tigers out of the cellar, but they are a better team today than they were yesterday.

PINTO: It will be interesting to see how far Nitkowski's and Lima's ERAs drop in the Astrodome. Still, you'd have to pay me a lot of money to take a pitcher from Detroit.

COOPERSON: Oh. That's considered a major trade?

PINTO: There's an Ivy Leaguer involved, so it must be major.

MITTLEMAN: There is another story here about this Tigers/Astros deal. Do you suppose people realize that while Randy Smith was GM in San Diego he makes a major deal with his father who is Tal Smith, President of the Houston Astros and now that he's in Detroit he does the same thing with his father again? Nepotism at work here or what.

WOELFLEIN: Can't Randy Smith trade with anyone other than his dad?

OLKIN: Or, to put if differently, can't Tal Smith rip off anyone other than his son? If we start to see the name "Bud Daley" being swapped back and forth, we'll know that we're *really* in trouble.

PINTO: So what if Brian Hunter is fast? How does that improve them at leadoff? Hunter had a .297 OBP last year, his first full season. Detroit leadoff men had a combined .370 OBP. Where's the improvement? I'd rather have Curtis Pride leading off.

MOYER: Geez, David, don't you learn anything working at ESPN? A good leadoff hitter hits for a high average and/or steals lots of bases. OBP and runs scored are not important. That's why Tom Goodwin is good and Rickey Henderson sucks.

December 10—Red Signings

MOYER: Can anyone give me any reason why MLB people seem to think Ricky Bones is anything? The only reason you can't use is "For some God-unknown reason, he had a decent year in 1994." Please, no one can tell me there aren't 200 minor league starting pitchers who don't have a better chance of succeeding in a rotation than Bones.

PINTO: Seems like Cincinnati is turning into a junk heap.

SCHINSKI: No way man, Bones rulz!

December 11—Reds (Cont'd)

COOPERSON: Yesterday it was a "major" news conference for C.J. Nitkowski being traded. Today a "major" news conference will announce some Cincinnati Reds wives charity or something. Next STATS, Inc. will have to have a "major" news conference to announce that Steve Moyer agrees with a GM on some player signing.

OLKIN: If Steve ever agrees with a GM on anything, it *will* be big news.

MITTLEMAN: It seems that the Cincinnati Reds were being truthful when asked earlier today what they had in store for this afternoon's press conference. Rather than announce progress on a trade involving Bret Boone and Fred McGriff, the news conference was to introduce the very first "Redsfest" which will take place in January at the Cincinnati Convention Center. Team chief executive John Allen said that it was the Reds way of enabling the community to feel closer to the team.

PINTO: It sounds like a good place to meet old communists.

MOYER: Redsfest? Who ever heard of such a thing? The MLB GMs should be spending their time studying the draft and looking at Ricky Bones' stats. (Wouldn't want to disappoint you.)

PINTO: There was a very funny skit on SNL about ten years ago where John Lithgow was being nasty to his family and his co-workers. He goes to the doctor who proceeds to remove a three-foot bug from Lithgow's behind. Steve, you may want to look into this surgery. . .

December 11—Kirt Manwaring Signs with Rockies

MOYER: The ultimate challenge to Coors Field has arrived. And his name is Kirt Manwaring.

December 12—Moises Alou Signs with Marlins

PINTO: I guess Eisenreich and Cangelosi will be the platoon DHs in the A.L. parks.

MOYER: Either Cangelosi or Eisenreich would wipe the floor with Overrated Alou if either played every day. If I hope for one thing this baseball season, it's that the Marlins crash and burn.

PINTO: I don't.

All in all, an outfield of Sheffield, White and Alou doesn't sound bad.

COOPERSON: I swear I'm not trying to embarrass Steve—Eisenreich takes medication for his Tourette's; the side effect of this medication is that it tires him out to some extent. Combine that with the fact that he's 36 years old, and I'm skeptical that he could play every day. Maybe 120-130 games, but doesn't the lefty hitter in a platoon start that many games anyway?

MOYER: Here's an equation:

$$\frac{\text{Coors Field}}{\text{Pitchers}} = \frac{\text{Ethan Cooperson}}{\text{Steve's Statements}}$$

December 12—Mike Bordick Signs with Orioles

PINTO: I guess Ripken is moving to third. He'll probably get injured his first game there and miss the rest of the season. Angry fans will want the heads of Johnson and Gillick on silver platters. . .

Actually. . .

For the first time in a number of years the Orioles offense at shortstop will be below average.

ZMINDA: Did you see that, before he signed with the Orioles, Bordick called Ripken to see if everything was cool about Cal moving to third?

MOYER: "I like to play with a chip on my shoulder." That's why baby Mikey had to call daddy Cal before signing the deal. I'll take Rickey Henderson's shoulder chips any day.

DEWAN: Geez, Louise—Moyer. Bordick's phone call to Ripken was a class act. You can't see a positive aspect to anything!

MOYER: If he wants to be a "class act" he shouldn't make tough-guy statements like, "I like to play with a chip on my shoulder."

PINTO: No, I agree with Moyer on this one. If you don't already think you are a better player than Ripken, you shouldn't be replacing him. This "Is this okay with you Cal?" business has to end. Cal's not the manager or the general manager. They shouldn't have to get his permission to do what they want with the team.

DEWAN: It's not a permission thing. It's a respect thing. Bordick wanted to show his respect for Ripken and his stature of being one of the greatest shortstops to ever play the game. Bordick gets huge credit in my book.

JAMES: If Mike Bordick *did* think he was a better ballplayer than Cal Ripken, what would you call that? Arrogance? Diagnosable? A Napoleonic Complex?

December 13—Roger Clemens' Possible Signing with Yankees

PINTO: It's a huge story in terms of Boston/NY history, but it's not nearly as big as Babe Ruth, or Steinbrenner's early free agent acquisitions (Hunter, Jackson). Clemens, as good as he's been in the past is not worth the money over four years now.

ZMINDA: I agree with David. I personally am amazed that a 34-year-old pitcher who hasn't won more than 11 games in a season since 1992 is being offered all this money. . . not to mention a long-term contract.

PINTO: The more I think about it, the more the comparison to Ruth bothers me. When the Yankees bought Ruth in 1920 (it wasn't a trade), they were getting a player in his prime that had already set batting and pitching records and was, even then, considered one of the all-time great players. Clemens is past his prime, and really hasn't adjusted to that fact that his fastball isn't what it used to be. The thing I worry about most is his control: he walked a lot of batters last year, and what made him amazing when he was young were his great K/BB numbers (in 1988, 291 K, 62 BB).

Still he probably helps the Yankees this year, but the team is going back to its ways of spending too much for free agents for immediate gratification, without looking at the long term implications.

COOPERSON: This is totally true. In Boston/NY terms this is *huge*. But as we well know, Boston media has no awareness that there are sports outside of Boston. From a *national* perspective, this pales in comparison to Albert Belle.

PINTO: I have to agree with Coop. Also, what's the story here? The media circus or the signing. We should be reporting the merits of the deal, not the fact that the whole city is buzzing.

MITTLEMAN: David, with all due respect, I think you and the guys are missing the point. Its not about what Clemens' numbers are today or his age. It's the symbolism of a legendary player being involved in a jump from the cursed Bosox to the hated Yankees. It's about the rivalry and the historical fabric between these two teams throughout history. Not whether Clemens is going to win "X" number of games or not. Right now, he *is* the Red Sox and to go to the dreaded Yankees is something the media will fawn over for weeks.

PINTO: I would pay him $8 million this year, and probably next, but I wouldn't want to commit to four years.

JAMES: What, are you guys asleep, or using Gabe Paul techniques to analyze players? Roger Clemens is still a great, great pitcher, one of the three or four best starting pitchers in baseball *right now*, arguably better than Maddux *now*. Look at him. He has had *consistently* awful offensive support for three or four years, but the man posted a 3.63 ERA last year (league average: 4.99) in a park that inflated runs scored by 13 percent. Since when is that mediocre? How do you figure that to be washed up? What is that. . . like, 1.6 runs better-than-context?

He made 34 starts (the league leader made 36) and led the league in strikeouts, while pitching in a park which reduces strikeouts by three percent. This is a *far* better indicator of what he has left than his year of birth.

Clemens was even more awesome in 1994, when he was probably the best starting pitcher in the American League, and was brilliant for much of 1995, although he did have a sinking spell and an injury. You guys are just off your rockers thinking he's over-paid. At $30 million in today's market, he's a tremendous bargain.

December 13—Pirates Fire Sale

MOYER: God help the Pittsburgh Pirates. If you have lots of money, you can make bad trades and still be competitive by buying all kinds of players and hoping some work out (ask the Marlins). If you don't have money and you make bad trades, you just might stink forever. Luckily the totally incompetent Pirates will get other teams' money soon. They can throw a big party and cry to each other about how much they stink, but it's not their fault. It is their fault. They deserve it.

And furthermore. . . The Pirates would be better off with Dale Sveum at third than Joe Randa.

December 16—Wells Signs with Yankees; Wetteland to Rangers

PINTO: Who will set up Rivera? Last year, Wetteland was out from 8/13 through 9/6, and here's what the bullpen did in that time:

Pitcher	W-L	Sv-Op	App	IP	ERA
Rivera	1-0	2-3	8	15.1	1.17
Others	1-6	1-3	49	66.0	6.41

A good closer can't do much if you can't get the game to him.

MOYER: What are the Yankees going to do with Melido Perez and Scott Kamieniecki if they're healthy? They have so many friggin' pitchers, they should be able to find someone to set-up.

PINTO: We have to get you your own radio show. I'd love to hear you heckle callers.

ZMINDA: I would guess Jeff Nelson would be the most likely set-up candidate. He wasn't great in '96, but he was a pretty good set-up guy for the M's in 1992-95.

PINTO: Of course, maybe the starters could pitch into the eighth inning once in a while.

OLKIN: If you're going to worry about Melido Perez's return, you might as well stockpile canned beans in case the Martians invade.

MOYER: Is Melido in Jose Rijo-land? He's still only 31. Do you know that he's not coming back anytime soon?

OLKIN: Do I *know* he's not coming back? Well, I guess it depends on how you define the difference between skepticism and certainty. All I know is that Melido and Pascual are the Thelma and Louise of the major leagues.

ELMAN: I'm pretty sure that Pascual has put in more driving time than Thelma and Louise.

December 17—It's Simple: Hit or Sit

We now have inter-league play, and along with it, a renewed debate about the use of the designated hitter. Of course, the game's self-described "purists" take this as their cue to step forward and issue their obligatory condemnations.

I'm not sure exactly what it is about these people that annoys me the most. Perhaps it's their nostalgia-clouded belief that the game was perfect when they were kids, so any changes since then must be for the worse. Or maybe it's the way that they knowingly wink at each other and nod their approval at each others' enlightenment. They carry on as if they belong to some sort of exclusive club—the sport's true intelligentsia, a select inner circle comprised only of the men who are wise enough to grasp the sinister implications of the DH rule. The rest of us? We're just hopeless primates who are too easily enchanted by high numbers, pitiable simpletons who lack the capacity to appreciate the game's subtler virtues.

Well, I must admit that it bothers me to be regarded as someone who ought to leave and come back when I'm done evolving. But the thing that bugs me the most is that when they blather on about the game's sacred "balance," I can't figure out what the hell they're talking about. Their argument just doesn't make any sense to me.

Their position, as best I can understand it, is that baseball is a sport where all players are required to play both offense and defense, and that the DH somehow destroys this uncluttered symmetry. While this argument might have held some water, say, about 100 years ago, the logic of it in 1997 escapes me.

You see, the role of the pitcher has changed so greatly since the game's inception, that the emergence of the DH has been all but inevitable. It's been a continuous process since before the Civil War, a trend that's about as likely to reverse itself as continental drift.

In the beginning, the pitcher's skill on the mound was irrelevant to the outcome of the game. He was forced to pitch the ball underhand, to the spot where the hitter requested. As such, a pitcher had to be a good hitter to stay in the lineup. In the field, his function was akin to that of the ball-return machine at the bowling alley.

Gradually, rule changes enabled the pitcher to *challenge* the batter, and as a result, pitchers relied more on their pitching skills and less on their batting. At some point, about 100 years ago, a pitcher's skill as a hitter became so irrelevant that a pitcher simply couldn't lose his job over an inability to hit. It was at that point that pitchers lost all incentive to work at their hitting.

As I said, this happened over 100 years ago. Since that time, pitchers' batting skills have steadily declined. And who can blame them? Can you think of a single pitcher who was capable on the mound, but lost his job because he couldn't *hit*? Of course not. It hasn't happened during this century, and it never will.

But it happens with catchers. It happens with shortstops and second baseman, all the time. We cut them a little more slack, but their hitting will never come close to being simply dismissed. They always will have to produce, and the introduction of the DH does nothing to threaten that circumstance.

But pitchers are different. When they're forced to bat, all they provide is a regular, predictable interruption to the game's series of confrontations between major league hitters and major league pitchers. It's like going to the symphony, only to find that once every nine minutes, the maestro interrupts the performance to give a one-minute demonstration of his juggling skills, or lack thereof.

I have been to several hundred major league games, and it seems to me that if someone claims to be looking forward to watching the pitcher hit, that person probably will fall into one of two classes. They're either waiting for the chance to get another beer, or they have to go to the bathroom.

Me, I can wait. The beer will be there after the game, and if Edgar Martinez is hitting, I'm perfectly willing to grit my teeth and hold it.

—Mat Olkin

December 17—Mike Greenwell Signs to Play in Japan

PINTO: I'd rather have Shane Mack anyway.

COOPERSON: Do you think anyone in Hanshin knows who Bill Buckner is?

December 18—Chad Curtis Signs with Indians

SCHINSKI: Cleveland just signed Chad Curtis.

PINTO: Well, now the Indians don't have to worry if they lose Kenny Lofton next year to free agency.

ZMINDA: Who needs Albert Belle?

December 18—John Olerud Trade/Release Rumors

OLKIN: It would be an ironic turn of events, considering that when the Blue Jays shipped McGriff to San Diego in 1990, a major consideration was their desire to make Olerud the full-time first baseman.

PINTO: As a member of the Olerud fan club, I'd love to see him land in Seattle. He's a hometown son, and I think Sweet Lou is the type of coach who could bring his hitting back to what it was. In fact, if I had Olerud on that team, I'd be tempted to lead him off.

OLKIN: If I had Olerud on that team, I'd be tempted to get Paul Sorrento, because *you just gotta have Paul Sorrento.*

SPEAR: Did that article from Mike Mittleman really contain the phrase "release John Olerud"? Ouch. . .

OLKIN: You see what you guys have done? A little loose talk, and now Allan's all worked up. Allan, it was just some baseless speculation.

PINTO: Unfortunately, it is baseless. The Mariners are probably too busy figuring out how to get more money out of Washington to notice a golden opportunity.

SPEAR: In the Spring of 1994, there was talk of a deal, Olerud for Randy Johnson straight up. I doubt that would go through now.

PINTO: Take your choice, bad back or soft head.

MOYER: You're getting out of line, Pinto. I'll make the tasteless jokes around here.

December 18—Pirates Infield

MOYER: Who do you guys think will play infield for the Pirates next year?

OLKIN: Volunteers.

SCHINSKI: The Pirates signed Kevin Elster.

MOYER: Well, at least the Pirates have an established, veteran, proven shortstop now. (Ha ha ho ho he he.) I swear, sometimes I wonder if this really stupid guy who's in my Rotisserie league doesn't secretly run the Pirates on the side.

QUINN: Steve, I really am not following you. I thought you write e-mails about how teams pay too much for over-the-hill veterans, when they could pay less and get the same quality from the minors or veterans nobody wants.

Aren't the Pirates doing exactly what you have advocated?

Sincerely confused, Pat

MOYER: Kevin Elster is 32, first of all. Second of all, he's a guy who, a year ago, couldn't hardly find a job, because, basically, he sucks. Then, last year, he stumbles into Benji Gil's job, has a decent first half of the year, and 99 RBI. That doesn't make up for the fact that he ended up batting .252, with a sorry-as-all-get-out .317 OBP, and that he still basically sucks. Even the other major league teams realized that he still basically sucks. So, who ends up signing him, surely for one million-plus? The Pirates, who need another sucky player like they need Joe Randa. (No, even he's not as bad as Elster.) I'm for *good* quality from the minors and *good* veterans nobody wants, not just any. The Pirates are like the sad-sack guy in my league. His team's full of bad players, but the sharks can always seem to sell him on one more.

And furthermore, the Pirates would've been much better off trying Lou Collier, or Brandon Cromer, or even Chad Hermansen, who's 19. Or maybe Collier and Cromer platooning. These guys aren't Alex Rodriguez (who is?), although Hermansen looks pretty darn good. Why waste time and money with Elster when you could let these guys cut their teeth? But then, why waste time with Mark Johnson when you have Ron Wright? I don't know, but I'm sure the guy in my league could explain it.

QUINN: Steve, I just learned Cleveland and Oakland also were trying to get him, thus the inflated price.

Also, can you state your position on the risk involved in "rushing" a player to the majors who is only 19?

OLKIN: Those Indians Viz-Quel me.

MOYER: I do think Hermansen can use another year in the minors, so Collier/Cromer would probably be the better option. As far as "rushing" goes, that's a fate worse than death among major league people. But for every guy you name that was "rushed" I'm sure I can name an Alex Rodriguez whose (see Don, I do learn) time was wasted behind Felix Fermin or a Roberto Alomar, who succeeded, albeit marginally at first, right from the start and his career was way better off for it. Lucky for Derek Jeter, Tony Fernandez went out for 1996 or he probably wouldn't have been "rushed" and the Yankees may have been watching the World Series on TV.

NEYER: Pat, are you suggesting that Steve thinks all GM's are stupid no matter what they do? Perish the thought.

December 20—Baseball Babble-On

I just simply cannot believe the moves the Pittsburgh Pirates have made over the last week. First Jeff King and Jay Bell for Joe Randa, and then signing big free-agent shortstop Kevin Elster for $1.65 million they supposedly don't have. Stinky Joe Randa and two no-big-deal minor league pitchers is all they could get for King and Bell? And Kevin Elster, 99-RBI pretender of last year, is where they do decide to finally spend some cash? Holy smokes. This team is going to be wretched. Right now, their infield looks like Mark Johnson at first, Tony Womack at second (that's what I've been told anyway), Elster at short and Randa at third. Egads. If it was my team, I'd play Ron Wright at first, Nelson Liriano at second, a platoon of Lou Collier and Brandon Cromer at short, and Dale Sveum at third. (Honest. I'm not joking about Sveum. It really looks like his bat's really picked up recently in the minors. I wouldn't start him on just any major league team, but he'd work for the Pirates.) From a fantasy perspective, an option might be to pick up Tony Womack now, pray that he flukes into a good April and sell him off as an everyday second baseman, because he can't really hit. How the heck to they expect anyone to come out to the ballpark? It's one thing to be poor; we've all heard the Pirate sob story over and over and over for the last few years. However, it's another thing to be poor and stupid. And that's what the Pirates are. They deserve to lose games, they deserve to lose any fans they have left, and they deserve to lose the team to anyone who has half a brain.

I wonder what it must feel like to be Kurt Stillwell? Every day he has to look at that list of available free agents that's in every paper every day and know people are all saying, "Kurt Stillwell? Hahahahaha."

How about Mike Bordick, calling to ask Cal Ripken's permission to play shortstop? If you ask me, Bordick's a baby and the "Ripken as God" thing has gotten out of hand. Then Bordick's quoted as saying, "I like playing with a chip on my shoulder." Yeah, right. Do you think Rickey Henderson would've asked Cal's permission? You bet not. He would've said, "Move your old white butt over. Let the man play." That's what a real man who doesn't mind playing with a chip on his shoulder says. I just can't picture Lou Gehrig ever being as arrogant as Ripken's become.

How about Indian first baseman Herbert Perry for the 1996 "Whatever Happened To Me?" Award? Oh, how those announcers loved him after he made that one postseason defensive play.

And Kelly Gruber signed a minor league contract with the Orioles yesterday. Here's all the jokes I can think of:

1) Maybe he didn't notice the players and owners had signed a contract and thought the Orioles were looking for replacement players.

2) How did the Orioles sneak him by the Pirates?

That's it—two. That's all I can think of.

And here's my first of something I'll do whenever I feel like it this winter. Take notes, expansion teams and Pirates:

Butt-Kicking Lineup That Could Be Had For Nothing

#1	LF	Warren Newson
#2	CF	Keith Mitchell
#3	1B	Roberto Petagine
#4	RF	Rudy Pemberton
#5	3B	Jimmy Tatum
#6	C	Tom Prince
#7	2B	Roberto Mejia
#8	SS	Webster Garrison

A full season of these guys would turn the Pirates into jelly.

— Steve Moyer

December 20—Kelly Gruber Signs with Orioles

MOYER: Did you guys see? The Orioles signed Kelly Gruber to a minor league contract yesterday. Wow. Don, is he in the *Scouting Notebook*? Maybe he forgot the owners and players signed a deal and thinks they're looking for replacement players. How did the Orioles get him by the Pirates? His last appearance in the *Major League Handbook* was 1994. He's 32 in there and at the end of February he'll turn 35. I guess it's possible that the Orioles signed him to be a player/coach or something, but it's still fun to make jokes.

PINTO: He's insurance against Cal Ripken finding out he doesn't like playing third. When he demands to be moved back to SS they'll have an experienced major league third baseman in the system.

It's hard to believe he could be a coach.

MOYER: As Roberto Petagine watches his career as a major league baseball player wither away.

December 20—Rickey Henderson on the Block?

PINTO: I've seen Greg Vaughn is going to be back with the Padres, leaving Rickey Henderson for whoever wants him, probably pretty cheaply. Where should Rickey go?

I think a good fit is Seattle. They've had problems finding a left fielder the last few years, and Joey Cora is an OK leadoff man at best (he had a .362 OBP in the No. 1 spot last year). Henderson, Rodriguez, Griffey, Buhner, Martinez is quite a frightening lineup.

The other place he might be useful is Toronto. They have a real good pitching staff now, but I think their offense is a little weak. If they end up landing McGriff, it would be nice for them to have someone in front of him to drive in.

COOPERSON: Who will lead off for the Pads?

PINTO: I assume Finley will lead off for the Padres. The Padres management clearly believes that power is superior to getting men on base.

I know we've discussed this before, but there were two instances in the playoffs where the ability to draw a walk paid off big for the Yankees. One was Darryl Strawberry against Benitez, where Straw couldn't catch up to Benitez to get a hit, but was patient enough to draw a walk; the other was I believe Boggs pinch hitting with the bases loaded and drawing a walk. Greg Vaughn is not going to do that for you.

ZMINDA: I would think that Veras would lead off for the Padres. That's a big reason they traded for him.

PINTO: Yes, I had forgotten about Veras, only the third player in major league history whose first name began with a Q.

I thought Veras did well as a leadoff man his first year, but the Marlins seem to have lost interest in him very quickly. Still, I'd much rather see:

Henderson, Veras, Gwynn, Caminiti, Finley than Veras, Finley, Gwynn, Caminiti, Vaughn

WENZ: The Cubs ought to get Rickey Henderson. They need a left fielder and they've needed a leadoff man for the last decade. Even if they only play him 100-120 games and let some youngsters play a little, he's a good option.

PINTO: With Dunston, Sandberg and Henderson they would certainly be an old team.

QUINN: Sorry to sound like Steve Moyer, but the Cubs would never sign a free agent with Rickey's attitude. That doesn't fit their image.

KRETSCHMANN: Yeah, Rickey's been on too many playoff teams.

ELMAN: What attitude? He's the greatest of all time. Just ask *him*!!!

PINTO: What attitude is that? Rickey gets a lot of criticism for not being a team leader, and he probably is a jerk, but has anyone actually watched him play the game? He concentrates on every pitch. He's constantly working the umpires to get better calls. When he's on base, I've never seen his attention wander from the pitcher. When he's in the outfield, he stretches between pitches to keep loose. I wish he were more of a media darling, but:

I've never heard of drug or alcohol problems with him. I've never heard he's assaulted anyone. I've never seen him abuse an umpire.

So what's the problem?

WENZ: I agree with David. The whole "Today I am the greatest" thing ruined Rickey in the press. It was a mistake, but I've never felt it was indicative of his personality. When it gets right down to it, the guy plays hard.

COOPERSON: Steve Moyer would like this: Henderson is more proud of his OBP than he is of his stolen base record.

PINTO: Yes, and he also once said the record he'd really like to break is the runs scored record.

Now think about this, who would you rather have on your team, someone who's trying to break the runs scored record, or someone who's trying to break the RBI record? Someone trying for the RBI record is only motivated when there are runners on base. Someone trying to break the run record is motivated at all times, because only by getting on base will he be able to score. I'd rather have the guy going for the runs scored record.

Top 10 all time runs scored:

1.	Ty Cobb	2245
2.	Hank Aaron	2174
	Babe Ruth	2174
4.	Pete Rose	2165
5.	Willie Mays	2062
6.	Stan Musial	1949
7.	Lou Gehrig	1888
8.	Tris Speaker	1882
9.	Mel Ott	1859
10.	Rickey Henderson*	1829
	Frank Robinson	1829

I really love this list. First of all, I think most people would put Rose on top. Many people are surprised that Ruth and Aaron are at the top, because they think of them as RBI men, but each of course had a great OBP as well. At this point, I don't think Rickey has a shot at the record, but I do think he'll become the sixth player to score 2000.

QUINN: David, I agree with you. As a Cub fan I'd like to see Rickey here. I am suggesting the Cubs avoid players with a bad public perception. Even if the facts are on Rickey's side, the perception is the problem. Being a jerk is the problem. Cub fans are known for going to Wrigley Field, *not* for watching the game. I believe the Cubs management bases its decision on this, no matter how false it might be.

ZMINDA: I'm not sure I agree. Henderson was born in Chicago, I believe his mother still lives here, and he's always had great rapport with the fans in the outfield stands. I bet the Bleacher Bums would love him.

QUINN: Does the Cubs management understand the Bleacher Bums might love him? David might be smart enough to understand Rickey is a great ballplayer and you might be smart enough to know the fans would love him. But the Cubs management must understand all of this. I don't think it does. That's why I started out by saying, "Sorry to sound like Steve Moyer."

MOYER: I'm surprised Ethan doesn't have a comment, especially with the preface: "Sorry to sound like Steve Moyer." Something like: "On June 24th, with the Padres in town to play the Cubs, in the bottom of the sixth inning, the Bleacher Bums threw two knives, five cups of beer, and an ironing board at Rickey Henderson. That proves that the Bleacher Bums, in fact, *do not* like Rickey Henderson."

December 23—Pavel Budsky

OLKIN: I just got the latest *Baseball America*, and read that the Expos signed Pavel Budsky, who's Czechoslovakian. And then I started to wonder what might happen if he turns out to be any good. Let's say he comes up in a few years, turns into a real star, and then starts to demand a big salary. If that happens. . .

. . . do you think Montreal will bounce the Czech?

December 27—Baseball Babble-On

Last week, I told you if I were the Pirates, I'd play Nelson Liriano at second. The only problem is that Liriano's been a Dodger since before Thanksgiving. Duh, Steve.

Reasons the Florida Marlins have become my least favorite team, in no particular order: 1) Everyone thinks they're automatic contenders now. I don't agree. 2) Moises Alou is way overrated. 3) Jim Leyland has been nothing but a bag of excuses ever since the Pirates stopped spending money. I'd like to see him fall flat with a huge payroll to work with. 4) No one's going to tell me that Fernandez/Brown/Leiter is Maddux/Smoltz/Glavine. 5) Bobby Bonilla's 34 and slugged under .500 last year. 6) Devon White is way overrated. 7) The team screwed one of my faves, Quilvio Veras, big time. Luis Castillo walks less and has less power. Of course he will waste time stealing lots more bases than Veras. 8) I'm not so sure that Edgar Renteria is really up to .309/.358/.399 again. He should be a great player, but his minor league numbers don't show him to be *that* good now.

Keep in mind going into last season, I thought the Cardinals and Orioles were way overrated too.

If any of you out there are waiting for huge things from Brooks Kieschnick, keep your pants on. Trade him now for a real prospect.

I was checking out preliminary stuff on John Sickels' *Minor League Scouting Notebook* today, and, once again, the book is really great. It's my favorite book STATS does.

Tomorrow a big critic-favorite movie, "The People Versus Larry Flynt" opens. Courtney Love, Kurt Cobain's former wife is a big star in it. Did you ever wonder how it is that singers (Love, that "Fresh Prince" guy), comedians (Tim Allen, Robin Williams) and even body-builders (Arnold) are some of our most popular and even most critically-acclaimed actors and actresses? I feel sorry for people who go through years of college and theater, etc. to watch people who really should be doing something else become big stars. You won't find this dad shelling out money for his daughter to take up formal acting. She can become a comedienne instead. She'll have a better shot. I also wonder why singers always seem to really want to be actors and actors always seem to want to be singers.

Kevin Mitchell could be the fantasy steal of 1997. Let's face it, if he comes to play, he *is* Albert Belle. And, from what I've been reading, he intends to come to play with the Indians. Of course, we've heard that before. However, if my Thanksgiving Rotisserie free agent draft was any indication, it won't take much to get him on your team. No one wanted any part of him and I snagged him real late.

You know, in this column the bad guys of baseball can finally find refuge. I thought about this last week. You know how in pro wrestling, most fans like all the good wrestlers and hate the bad guys, but there is a contingent of fans that hate the good guys and like the bad ones. Well, I'm starting that contingent for baseball. Go Albert, Rickey, Jose, and Barry. Boo Cal and Ryne. And don't laugh because I reference wrestling. The lamest, oldest joke in the book of sportswriting is to cut on pro wrestling. Yeah, I know it's fake, too. Big deal. So what?

Have you bought the *Baseball Weekly* in the last few weeks? It's about 12 pages long now and five of those are Minnesota Twins organizational stats—upside-down and sideways.

— Steve Moyer

December 27—Tony Phillips Trade Rumor

PINTO: Why is Chicago going to get rid of Tony Phillips? Don't they want someone on base in front of Thomas and Belle?

DEWAN: I hope that this time Mittleman's rumor is wrong. Getting rid of Phillips would be a *big* mistake.

PINTO: Maybe they are thinking of picking up Rickey cheap.

DEWAN: I'll take Rickey as a replacement but he wouldn't be near as good for the Sox. Phillips plays infield positions and with Mouton, Martinez/Lewis, Belle and Baines taking playing time as OF/DHs, Tony could spell Ventura, Durham and Thomas for about 25-30 games. Rickey doesn't bring that.

PINTO: I agree. I'd rather have Phillips than Rickey at this point.

ZMINDA: They want to get rid of Phillips because they're afraid of having a clubhouse with both Belle and Phillips in it. Personally, I'd take my chances.

DEWAN: Don, that makes sense. A clubhouse with both Belle and Phillips is just asking for upheaval. That's something to consider, which evidently the Sox are. Interesting.

COOPERSON: Je ne comprends pas about Phillips. Wasn't he considered great in the Angels clubhouse in '95?

DEWAN: Who considered him great in the Angels clubhouse?

COOPERSON: I read a quote from someone (Chili Davis maybe) last spring, talking about how much he missed Phillips, and how his absence had a lot to do with their drop-off in 1996.

DEWAN: I agree with Chili that Phillips' absence had a lot to do with their drop-off. His production on the field is excellent. But that doesn't mean his clubhouse presence is positive.

ZMINDA: Phillips had a few problems last year that I'm sure made the Sox think he might not mix very well with Albert Belle. There was the incident with the fan in Milwaukee, for one thing, and a clubhouse brouhaha over Phillips deliberately turning up his boom box all the way up so that writers and broadcasters wouldn't be able record interviews with players. His behavior may or may not have been justified, but I'm sure they're thinking that he and Belle together might be a very volatile mix.

December 31—It's Just Not That Easy

Well, I've been thinking and thinking and thinking about it, but I just can't figure out what makes the Toronto Blue Jays so special. Everyone's been lauding them for their recent makeover, but like most makeovers, this one only goes skin deep.

Admittedly, it isn't hard to see why people are so excited about them. First, they pulled off a deal with the Pirates that appeared to be, at least on the surface, completely one-sided. Then they signed Benito Santiago, who socked 30 round-trippers last season. And finally, they got The Rocket.

When you add all that talent to the existing lineup, the reasoning goes, you have to figure that the team will improve. Perhaps they will; it wouldn't surprise me a bit. But to expect them to close their 18-game deficit on the strength of these moves alone is just way, way out of line. Let's look at it transaction-by-transaction.

First we've got the Carlos Garcia deal, for which the Blue Jays were universally applauded. In exchange for a collection of prospects who weren't expected to make an impact in Toronto next year, the Jays received three serviceable major leaguers: Carlos Garcia, Orlando Merced and Dan Plesac.

People like Garcia because he can play second base and hit for a good average, but much of his value is illusory. Since he doesn't draw walks, he's ill-suited to hit at the top of the order. In that respect, his batting average actually may *hurt* the team, as Cito Gaston may be suckered into batting him second. At best, he'll fill out the bottom of the order. He will bring stability to a position that the Jays were never able to fill last year, but to expect him to improve much at age 29 is foolish—and quite a few people think he's actually much older than 29. If you missed Damaso Garcia, today's your day—he's back, under a slightly different name.

Orlando Merced essentially replaces John Olerud, as Joe Carter moves to first base. Forgive me for asking, but exactly how does this improve the team? I look at Merced and Olerud, and for each of them I see a left-handed hitter who bats around .280 with middling power. What's the difference? Merced's two years older, but that's supposed to be a negative, isn't it?

Then you've got Benito Santiago. Will he be more productive than Sandy Martinez? Of course he will—who wouldn't? But the more relevant question is: will he be as productive as everyone expects him to be? Let's see. . . this is a guy who had breakout years during the hitters' years of 1987 and 1996, and did very little during the eight intervening years. So that's two good years in 10. . . what does that give him, a 20 percent chance of having another good year next year? And as a rule, are 32-year-old catchers good investments?

And finally, you've got Clemens. This is the one that's generated the most talk. Let me be the first to say that over the last three years, Clemens has been as effective as any pitcher in the league. The only reason his win-loss record hasn't reflected it is because he's been the victim of uncommonly poor support. If he's able to perform as well for Toronto, he's a serious threat to win 20 games.

But the problem with the whole Clemens frenzy is the widespread, automatic assumption that he will continue to pitch just as well for Toronto. I don't think you can assume that. When I look at how he's been used over the past few years, I have grave concerns about his ability to continue this way for long.

I've hammered on this before, but it bears repeating: last season, Clemens was worked harder than any pitcher in baseball, by a mile. At age 33, he endured the heaviest workload of his entire career. He averaged 125 pitches per start, eight more than any other pitcher in baseball. Since we started keeping track of pitch counts eight years ago, that's the highest figure we've ever recorded.

Clemens may be able to give them exactly what they expect, and if he does, they'll have an extraordinarily valuable commodity, indeed. Dominant, bullpen-saving inning-eaters are the stuff contenders are made of, and there aren't many of them out there. Clemens is one. But at any moment, he could stop being one, and you have to acknowledge that possibility.

By my estimation, what you've got here is a collection of players who are almost all due for a major comedown. It may not happen to many of them; in fact, it many not happen to *any* of them. But that's my point: this team is perfectly capable of playing up to expectations and making the playoffs—but only if *every single player* continues to play over his head. If I'm running the team, that's not a bet I'd want to have to make.

—Mat Olkin

January 2—Pitch Counts

I've been looking at some our data on pitch counts, which we've been keeping since the late 1980s. A few highlights:

- If you want to know why the Red Sox bounced Kevin Kennedy, a good reason is this: he abuses pitchers' arms like crazy. There were only five games in 1996 in which a starter tossed more 150 pitches, and *all five* involved Red Sox pitchers: Tim Wakefield (162), Roger Clemens (162, 157 and 151) and Tom Gordon (151). You might excuse Wakefield, since he's a knuckleballer, but this really is asking for trouble.

- Our pitch count data goes back to 1988, and Wakefield has the record for most pitches in a game, with 172. Kennedy gets off the hook for this one, however; Wakefield did it while working for Jim Leyland and the Pirates in 1993. Knuckleballer or no, Wakefield didn't respond well at all to this heavy workload. He didn't pitch again for a week; then, after a couple of reasonably good outings, he fell apart completely and wound up back in the minor leagues. Mat Olkin of our staff thinks this was no coincidence, and I'd have to agree with him.

- Next to Wakefield, the pitcher who has thrown the most pitches in a game since '88 was Al Leiter, who threw 171 pitches for Dallas Green and the Yankees in April of 1989. A couple of weeks later, the Yankees traded Leiter to Toronto, and the Blue Jays immediately discovered they'd obtained a pitcher with a very sore arm. Leiter went on the DL after one start with the Jays and wound up missing the rest of the 1989 season. His arm didn't recover for several years. You can't blame all that on one start. . . but it sure didn't help him any.

- Dwight Gooden's arm problems began in 1989, the same year he was kept on the frigid Shea Stadium mound for 146 pitches in an April start. Again, one start didn't make Gooden break down, but what were the Mets thinking of, taking a risk with a talent like Gooden's? Judging by the recent breakdowns of Bill Pulsipher, Jason Isringhausen and Paul Wilson, they haven't learned a thing.

- Another 1989 horror story: Don Carman's career was never the same after a 167-pitch outing in May of that year. Carman, who had been one of the Phillies' more dependable starters in 1987 and 1988, went 5-15 with a 5.24 ERA in '89, went back to the bullpen in 1990, and then quickly faded out.

- Another fine pitcher, John Farrell of the Indians, threw 164 pitches in a game late in the '89 campaign. Farrell, who'd worked 200+ innings in both 1988 and 1989, broke down the next year and never recovered. We could have told the Indians this might happen.

- One last tale of woe. At the end of the (you guessed it) 1989 season, Tommy Lasorda kept his ace, Orel Hershiser, on the mound for 11 innings and 167 pitches in a totally meaningless game against the Braves. You could probably call that the straw that broke the camel's back. Hershiser, who had led the National League in innings pitched for three straight years from 1987 to 1989, came down with shoulder trouble the next spring and needed major reconstructive surgery. He pitched in only four games in '90, and didn't resume his career as a full-time starter until 1992.

Major league people learn from their experiences, and it's very clear to me that managers these days are a *lot* more reluctant to let their starters throw 140 or more pitches in a game. A good example is Phil Garner of the Brewers, who "got religion" after Cal Eldred broke down a few years ago. The sort of usage that Kennedy gave his pitchers last year is pretty much unheard of now.

This brings us back to Roger Clemens, the subject of my column two weeks ago. Will Kennedy's heavy usage of Clemens last year cause him problems in 1997? It's hard to say. In general, older arms handle heavy usage better than younger ones do. . . but I'm not sure that *anybody* escapes this kind of abuse unscathed. I'd argue that this was yet another reason why it was risky to give Clemens all that money. Am I wrong? We'll start finding out the answer in 1997.

— Don Zminda

January 6—Leadoff Hitters

FULLAM: During some research on baseball's most effective leadoff hitters, I came up with a few interesting tidbits:

Baltimore's leadoff combo of Alomar and Anderson combined for 45 HRs last season—more homers than any other team at any other batting slot except the third (where the figure would place second) and fourth positions. (A.L. only)

Speaking of production from the cleanup slot, Minnesota only got *nine* homers from its No. 4 hitters all season long to trail the league by a wide margin (next lowest was 19 by KC). Only Minnesota's seventh- and ninth-place hitters hit fewer homers. Pretty amazing—especially in a "juiced-ball" year.

PINTO: The Twins could have used Offerman in the cleanup spot. I know the Orioles as a team hit a lot of HRs last year, but it seems to make more sense to me to bat Anderson behind Alomar. I mean, the leadoff HRs are nice, but you would think they'd score a few more runs if Alomar were on once in a while.

January 6—Dodgers for Sale

PINTO: I think STATS should buy the Dodgers. Think what we could do with that team. They have all this overrated talent that we could probably trade for some good players. At $200 million, the team's a steal.

OLKIN: Then we could rebuild Ebbets Field and move them back to Brooklyn. Talk about tapping into the nostalgia market. . . the Mantle-worshipping generation would probably think it was the best thing to happen to baseball since the reserve clause was invented.

MOYER: The first thing I'd do is talk Tim Wallach out of retirement. Either that or inquire about Charlie Hayes. That would show all the GMs we're one of them.

SICKELS: Don't forget Mark Whiten. Have to have him.

MOYER: Yeah, but now that Whiten walks and had, arguably, his best season ever, no one wants him anymore.

HENZLER: I find it interesting that when Disney bought the Angels, head mousketeer Michael Eisner, or someone in the Disney family, said it's always wise to buy into a market that's fundamentally sound but is nevertheless perceived differently. Or something like that. Hence, Disney's interest in purchasing the Angels.

I wonder if O'Malley sees things the other way. Or if the competition from Disney concerns him. Anyway, the passing of the O'Malley family from baseball does cause me pause.

WENZ: I'm surprised to see the Dodgers up for sale also. As much as the owners whined and complained about their financial distress, and whether you believe them or not, the Dodgers were perhaps the one team that seemed to be a good business venture for the long haul, regardless of the economic conditions surrounding the rest of the league. $200 million doesn't seem like a very high price for that organization.

January 6—Niekro Makes the Hall of Fame

ZMINDA: Phil Niekro was elected to the Hall of Fame today with 380 votes, 25 more than needed. Don Sutton, with 346 votes, was nine votes short. Tony Perez (312), Ron Santo (186) and Jim Rice (178) were next.

PINTO: I was sorry to see Graig Nettles' name dropped from the Hall of Fame ballot after this year's election. I think his career compares very favorably with Brooks Robinson's. Offensively, he had a low batting average, but a higher OBP and slugging percentage than Robinson. He played in as many World Series as Robinson and won just as many. (Sorry, I forgot about SD; Nettles played in five series, Robinson four.) Nettles certainly was not a poor fielder; in fact, in his youth he might have been the equal of Robinson. Consider the single-season record for assists by a third baseman:

Player	Assists
Nettles '71	412
Nettles '73	410
Robinson '74	410
Harlond Clift '37	405
Robinson '67	405
Mike Schmidt '74	404

I'm not saying that Nettles belongs in the Hall. It's just that it seems strange to me that Robinson should be so automatic, while Nettles never got more than 38 votes.

FAUST: From the *Scoreboard*, we may have a program that will generate a list of the most-similar players to Nettles. I'd be interested to see it, and see if/where Robinson falls on the list.

MOYER: Batting average is god, David. Any sixth-grade baseball fan can tell you which stat is the most important. I doubt there are too many non-pitchers in the Hall of Fame with BAs under .250. OBP doesn't matter. It's way too advanced for those guys who cast the ballots.

January 7—Bichette vs. Klein

Coors Field is the best hitter's park of all time; of this there can be no doubt. In the two years that "baseball" has been played there, it has inflated scoring by 68 percent and home runs by 76 percent. No other park in the modern era has made such a dramatic impact on the statistics of the players who have played there.

Of course, in recent years Dante Bichette has become the poster boy for park-inflated stats. Some people point to his unremarkable performance before he came to Colorado and his mediocre road stats with the Rockies, and argue that his star status is the result of his home park rather than his ability as a hitter. Others contend that he's one of the most valuable players in the game, even after the park bias is taken into account. The latter position may not be the most popular one, but the fact remains that Bichette placed second in the National League MVP balloting in 1995, and has placed in the top 20 in each of the last three years.

But he wasn't a star before he came to Colorado, and—as many have noted—Bichette's road stats during his four years with the Rockies indicate that he's still the same old Bichette. In fact, if you double his road stats for those four years, you get numbers that are perfectly consistent with his early years:

Year	G	AB	R	H	2B	3B	HR	RBI	BB	SO	Avg	OBP	SLG
'90	109	349	40	89	15	1	15	53	16	79	.255	.292	.433
'91	134	445	53	106	18	3	15	59	22	107	.238	.272	.393
'92	112	387	37	111	27	2	5	41	16	74	.287	.318	.406
'93	144	556	70	140	28	0	20	76	30	124	.252	.291	.410
'94	118	486	68	124	34	2	24	80	16	84	.255	.281	.481
'95	136	554	76	166	38	2	18	90	22	118	.300	.329	.473
'96	156	594	76	150	34	0	18	84	34	110	.253	.296	.401

The truth is that in a neutral park, Dante Bichette is Devon White without the defense. Over the last four years, his road batting average is exactly one point over the league average, and his road slugging percentage is only 33 points over the league norm. That's hardly the kind of production you'd expect out of your right fielder and number-three hitter. But he's been able to snow the MVP voters by compiling ridiculous numbers in Colorado. These are his home stats in Mile High Stadium and Coors Field:

G	AB	R	H	2B	3B	HR	RBI	BB	SO	Avg	OBP	SLG
278	1139	238	419	86	10	79	288	63	152	.368	.401	.669

Project that out to 162 games, and you get:

G	AB	R	H	2B	3B	HR	RBI	BB	SO	Avg	OBP	SLG
162	664	139	244	50	6	46	168	37	89	.368	.401	.669

Now, in all fairness, Bichette should be given credit for being able to take advantage of what Coors gives him. Sure, the numbers are inflated, but those home runs are real, and they help the Rockies win real games. But the question is whether Bichette helps them win more games than Bonds helps the Giants win, or Maddux helps the Braves win. I trust we all know that answer to that one.

But as I said before, I'm not here to take my turn taking potshots at Bichette. No, I'm here to take potshots at the *original* Dante Bichette, Hall of Fame right fielder Chuck Klein.

Before there was Coors Field, there was the Baker Bowl, formerly the most hitter-friendly park since the dawn of the lively ball era. It inflated runs by 14 percent and home runs by 59 percent—figures that pale beside those of Coors Field, but still rank among the highest in history. And in the late 1920s and early '30s, when the offense reached its high-water mark and a .400 batting average didn't even guarantee you the batting title, there was the left-handed-hitting Klein, shooting for the Baker Bowl's 280-foot right field fence.

Klein played five full seasons for the Phillies from 1929 through 1933. During those five years, he put together five of the greatest back-to-back seasons of all time—at least in statistical terms.

How great were they, really? Hey, if you thought Bichette's home numbers were extreme, check this out. Here's Klein's home/road splits for the five years:

	G	AB	R	H	2B	3B	HR	RBI	BB	Avg	OBP	SLG
Home	371	1550	389	659	133	21	122	443	141	.425	.473	.774
Road	388	1564	269	459	99	25	58	250	142	.293	.352	.500

All in all, Klein and Bichette share some intriguing parallels. Each played (or play) in one of the most extreme hitters' parks of all time, in one of the most high-scoring eras of all time. Each achieved stardom by taking extreme advantage of their home field. Neither was able to excel for other teams, and neither played nearly as well on the road during their big years.

That being said, I think there's little chance that Bichette will be able to duplicate Klein's ruse by parlaying his puffed-up numbers into an invitation to Cooperstown. People have heard so much about Bichette's home/road splits that if he ever gets out of Colorado and puts up even slightly worse numbers, in people's minds, it will confirm their suspicions that he never really was that good in the first place. Klein, on the other hand, didn't have to deal with any such skepticism, and his post-Baker Bowl decline was largely excused as the result of injuries.

And besides, Klein was a better player. Although he may not have been a Hall-of-Famer, his road stats prove that he was quite a bit better than Bichette. Unless the next round of expansion awards a franchise to Mt. Everest, I don't think we need to be concerned that the gap-toothed grin of Dante Bichette will disrupt our future excursions to Cooperstown.

— Mat Olkin

January 9—Yankees Predestination

FAUST: *Wow*. It came true again! Check out the date on Pat's message!

From Quinn, 27-MAY-1996 Subj: Yankee hope. . . Did you realize that every time the Kentucky Wildcats have won the national championship, the Yankees won the World Series.

PINTO: Go Kentucky!

January 14—Iowa Farm Too Productive

I should have known something was awry in the Cubs' control room when they re-signed Luis Gonzalez before the '96 season. At the time, they had *three* young outfielders who were poised to make a run at the left field job. First, they had Ozzie Timmons, who had posted a .474 slugging percentage as a rookie the year before. Next, they had former number-one draft pick Brooks Kieschnick, who had batted .295 with 23 homers at Triple-A. Finally, they had Robin Jennings, who had hit .296 with 17 homers at Double-A. Kieschnick and Jennings are left-handed hitters, so several platoon arrangements were possible.

Instead, they re-signed Gonzalez, who's a decent hitter but not a bit better than any of the three youngsters. Gonzalez batted .271, the Cubs didn't win, and none of the three young outfielders came an inch closer to establishing themselves in the major leagues.

Now one year later, Gonzalez is gone, but the Cubs *still* haven't worked up the nerve to commit themselves to any of their farmhands. Reportedly, their next priority is to get a power-hitting left fielder.

Power? Hello? Timmons hit 24 home runs in 353 at-bats between Triple-A and the majors last year. Jennings hit 18 in a few more at-bats. Kieschnick hit 19. Even young Pedro Valdes has gotten into the picture: he hit .295 with 15 homers in less than 400 at-bats at Triple-A.

What do the Cubs want from these guys? I just can't believe that they're going to send all four of those guys back down and tell them, "We want power, we just don't want *your* power." And where will they send them? They'll have to create a Quadruple-A team just to hold them all. I swear, if the Cubs were running Kuwait, they'd be *importing* oil.

—Mat Olkin

January 14—Doug Drabek Signs with White Sox

SICKELS: This may not be a bad move. Drabek's strikeout data is still decent, and moving over to a new league could help him. Maybe.

PINTO: It's interesting you bring up his strikeout numbers. He's the same age as Clemens, and his K/9 was also one of the best ever by a 33 year old. Maybe the White Sox should have given him a long term contract.

January 15—Owners Meeting

COUVILLON: I guess Fay Vincent doesn't count. . .

"Colangelo, not yet a voting member, said he has told Selig and others they should write a job description and have definite qualities in mind before trying to fill the office left vacant by the death of A. Bartlett Giamatti."

ZMINDA: Actually, the office was left vacant by the death of Judge Landis. . .

January 16—Expansion

ZMINDA: The owners' latest hassle is over expansion. Where should they put the new teams?

PINTO: Put both new teams in the A.L. They we can have four four-team divisions.

Seattle, Anaheim, Oakland and Arizona; Texas, KC, Milwaukee and Minnesota; Chicago, Detroit, Cleveland and Toronto; Boston, NY, Baltimore and Tampa Bay

We can then get rid of the Wildcard and inter-league play.

The other nice thing about this realignment is that when the Texas, KC, Milwaukee and Minnesota division goes broke, they can be easily deleted and we can go back to a two, six-team division system where the Yankees and Red Sox play each other 18 times a year.

OLKIN: Put Detroit in the International League. That would solve everything.

ZMINDA: Actually, this is the A.L.'s dream—both teams in the A.L.—and a few owners are holding out for it. It won't fly because Jerry Colangelo has been assured for months that the Diamondbacks will be in the N.L. West.

I wouldn't be surprised if they just put the Devil Rays in the A.L. West, rather than move KC to the West. This is not as wacky as it sounds; with the teams almost certainly playing a balanced schedule, it's no costlier to put a Florida team in the West than anywhere else. Sure it looks dumb, but if the world accepts the Dallas Cowboys and Arizona Cardinals in the NFC East while the Carolina Panthers and Atlanta Falcons are in the West, what difference does it really make?

OLKIN: You know, I never could understand what a school named "Northwestern" was doing smack dab in the middle of the map.

COOPERSON: Like the NHL did when the Winnipeg Jets played in what amounted to the Pacific Division, the A.L. should just throw some cash at the KC Offermans, to help pay for the cost of their increased travel if KC gets moved to the West. What they should also do is, when KC plays on the coast, have the games start at 7 PM local time, or 9 PM KC time (rather than 7:30 locally). This would help the TV ratings in KC (not that the Offermans bring in that much in local TV revenue). . .

PINTO: MLB finally got things straight regionally when they made up the new divisions in 1994. Why should they screw it up again?

PINTO: Times change. When J.F. Cooper wrote the Leather Stocking Tales, the west was considered western NY.

COOPERSON: Another point: If the new teams go to different leagues, there will have to be either inter-league series all the time, or else teams will have to have weird days off, like Sundays and Saturdays. If each league has an odd number of teams, either there's an inter-league series, or else at least one team in each league is off, each day of the season.

MOYER: The most interesting thing about this from my point of view is Dave Pinto replying to his own message. I've never seen that before. (Ethan will surely recall a previous instance, however.)

HENZLER: Those of you in Chicago may have already heard the latest scuttlebutt, but a recent hot rumor has the owners possibly discussing a radical realignment. The scenario would involve the Astros moving to the A.L. West, and the Royals moving to the N.L. Central. The Astros would then be in the same division as the Texas Rangers, a natural rival, and the Royals would be in the same division as the cross-state rival Cardinals. The

Diamondbacks could then easily slip into the N.L. West, and the Devil Rays could move into the A.L. Central, or into the A.L. East with the Tigers going to the Central division.

Of course, the owners could also do something they're quite practiced at—postpone a decision for another time.

COOPERSON: So, when the Phillies and Astros meet in 1998 World Series, it will evoke all the memories of the 1980 NLCS. . .

It's radical, but giving the Astros and Royals the inter-state rivalries could only help two franchises that need help. Maybe MLB should go to an Eastern and Western Conference.

SCHINSKI: Yeah, and then there could be more inter-league play!

OLKIN: I'm having a real hard time getting comfortable with the concept of the Astros being an American League team. The Royals looked like a real N.L.-type team, but then they traded for some hitters and messed it all up.

PINTO: That would be great. I can think of a number of reasons:

Olbermann would really have a cow.

Offerman would be back in the N.L.

Jeff Bagwell could show Red Sox fans up-close-and-personal how good he is.

It would give the A.L. a super-majority in domed stadiums.

Bob Hamelin would be out of a job.

And I thought the change to Anaheim would be tough on our datasets.

January 20—Baseball Versus Other Sports

PINTO: Hockey doesn't go on strike every four years. If they start doing that, the fans will be just as alienated as they are in baseball. Remember, baseball fans always came back until the World Series was wiped out.

Also, I think some fan support is fickle. First football was the new big growth sport, then basketball, now hockey. Each one in turn will claim to supplant baseball as America's sport. The truth is they never can. For all the speed and excitement the NBA, NFL and NHL claim to offer, the truth is that most NHL games are alike; most NBA games are alike; and most NFL games are alike. There is little room for intellectual arguments in the NBA and NHL; have you ever heard people discuss the ability of a coach to call the proper line changes in the NHL? Strategy discussions in the NBA revolve around double-teaming and resting players.

There is a lot of strategy in the NFL, but frankly I think it's over most fans' heads. Broadcasters and writers seem to concentrate on the skill positions, whereas most of the strategy seems to come in blocking and defensive assignments. Some broadcasters do this well, but most of the time it's a pass to Michael Irvin, as if Aikman and Irvin are the only two players on the field.

But precisely because baseball is so slow, you can argue for two minutes about the bunt strategy, or the changing of a pitcher before the event actually happens, trying to cover most of the reasons why a manager should or shouldn't employ a particular strategy. Baseball gives you time to think and anticipate, rather than just react, which is why I feel in the long run, baseball will remain the Coca-Cola of American sports, while all the others will just be Pepsi.

COOPERSON: Hey, I like Pepsi much better. . .

David, I think your Harvard colors are showing through. Fans aren't that interested in intellectual discussions of strategy. They want quick action, they want sports that are conducive to TV. For all the discussions of secondary batting average and offensive winning percentage, fans get more excited about quick impact stats—like Hakeem outscoring Jordan 10-0 at one point in the third quarter. In an Internet, fast-information world, baseball simply moves too slowly. For all the money Fox poured into baseball last year, the network has done much more to advance hockey. There just isn't much you can do to enhance a baseball broadcast, because most of it has been tried already. But there is so much that can be done with the other sports on TV. That is not a criticism of baseball, just a reality about the game.

But there is a deeper problem with baseball. We all love the new, throwback ballparks, right? Well, a friend of mine who did an undergraduate thesis on baseball stadiums pointed this out to me: As nice as these stadiums are, they indicate that baseball must cling to its past, rather than moving forward to the present. Every time MLB expands, there have to be fights over realignment. For a team to switch leagues is a very tricky proposition, but let's face it—two separate leagues, with different rules—this setup is completely antedated, and does nothing but hold the game back. Unfortunately, it's so hardwired into the fabric of the game that it can't change.

Rob Neyer once complained how gaudy and cheesy (I'm sure he used a better word) an NBA arena is, with laser light shows and dancing girls, etc. And, he's right—but that's what sports are. Sports aren't about the "smell of green grass" or "the beautiful sound of the ball hitting the catcher's mitt," they're about a bunch of rich, often greedy entertainers who perform in a spectacle atmosphere. The NBA thrives on it, the NHL is starting to do the same. I don't know if baseball ever could.

FULLAM: Baseball hasn't jazzed up the production of its games *because* it moves much slower than the other sports. I don't think that sports are necessarily conducted in a "spectacle" atmosphere—it's just that lasers and cheerleaders would look ludicrous at a ballpark where it's tough to get the fans charged up for an extended period of time.

I think the real problem with baseball is mass free agency (which is starting to hit the other sports as well). It's a lot tougher for the average fan to stay on top of his or her *team*, let alone the leagues, and the lack of familiarity breeds lack of interest.

PINTO: No, lack of winning breeds lack of interest. Baseball's great attendance growth came from the late-'70s to the mid-'90s when no team but the Blue Jays repeated as World Champs. Most teams had some sort of winning season during that stretch (for a great example of this see the Twins pre/post 1987).

I think the poor attendance during the '50s had as much to do with the Yankees' domination of the leagues as it did with the style of play of that era.

HENZLER: I would like to point out, however, that when baseball did, in fact, gravitate to "futuristic" stadiums such as the Astrodome and other multipurpose stadiums, they were widely and roundly criticized. Not immediately, however. When they opened, the new stadiums of the '60s and '70s were actually applauded for not only their utility, but for their appearance, as well. Over time, those same parks eventually came to be known for their "cookie-cutter" sameness, abundance of concrete, and lack of identity.

I'm not sure if the recent trend to "traditional" ballparks means baseball is "clinging to its past." Growing up in St. Louis, the only park I attended through my youth was the new Busch Stadium, so I really have no memory of a stadium-past to cling to.

It's just nicer to attend a baseball game in a park with real grass and some character. I don't think that necessarily means the game is ultimately doomed.

MOYER: My stadium-past *is* the Vet (although I did attend a few Connie Mack games, I was too small to really remember or appreciate them) and I'm fine with that. My memories of those yellow upper-deck seats are really OK. I don't feel cheated in any way, really. Cheesy '70s stuff is in now anyway. (Check out "fashionable" clothes these days.) As for these new-fangled parks, as far as I'm concerned, fake, man-made, contrived historic-ness is just as cheesy as any cookie-cutter stadium. (Honest to God, I have fond memories of entering the Vet for my once-or-twice yearly visit as a kid and being overwhelmed at how green and pretty that carpet was every time.)

COOPERSON: This is overrated, because sports are so national now. Shaq would be popular if he played for a Skokie team.

FULLAM: Yeah, but that's because the NBA is marketed so much better than baseball is, and also because Shaq is arguably the biggest sports celebrity in the nation (behind Jordan). I mean, Jeff Bagwell is definitely as good a baseball player as Shaq is a basketball player, but who knows about him? And if he moved to Pittsburgh or Milwaukee, would anybody notice?

January 22—Piazza Signs Two-Year Contract with Dodgers

PINTO: I was hoping he'd be in Coors in 1998.

MOYER: Not after Kirt Manwaring adapts a new hitting style and attitude, gets along with the hitting coach great, finally feels like he's contributing to a team with a winning attitude, and hit 17 homers. Sixteen of which will come at home, of course, but that's not the point.

MILLER: How could Manwaring hit 17 homers? We only project him to hit three!

January 23—The Good Ol' Days

MOYER: In the new *GQ* magazine (Dennis Rodman and a topless blonde model on the cover—now I've got your attention), in an article entitled "The Illustrated History of Flipping the Bird," on page 170, there's a Boston Beaneaters team picture from 1886, showing Charles "Old Hoss" Radbourn with his middle finger solely extended. Cool. It's good to know some things in sports never change.

HENZLER: Wasn't "Old Hoss" ultimately confined to an asylum, where he died at age 42? It doesn't require a large leap in logic for many to recommend the same for Rodman. The committing I mean. Not necessarily the dying.

OLKIN: Epitaph: "Dead as I wanna be."

PINTO: Olbermann keeps that picture of Radbourn above his desk.

WENZ: I got kicked out of Riverfront stadium back in my wild and reckless college days for flipping Erig Gregg the bird. If I'd have had that picture, maybe I could have convinced them that my actions were just in keeping with the great traditions of the game of baseball. Probably not.

MOYER: I hope Eric Gregg didn't try chasing you down.

MILLER: Maybe Gregg thought the "bird" was a chicken and was going to eat it, that's why you were thrown out of Riverfront. It may have been for your own safety!

ELMAN: He didn't get put into an asylum, he surfaced years later on TV in "Bonanza". He was the *first* athlete-turned-actor.

January 30—Deion Sanders Back in Cincinnati

OLKIN: Does Marge know he's black?

MILLER: Does Ray Knight know his career on-base is .320?

JAMES: And does Deion know that Ray Knight's career on-base percentage was .325?

January 31—Baseball Babble-On

Get a load of this: Rod Beaton begins his article on page 11 of *USA Today* today with: "The Cincinnati Reds have gained a solid center fielder and leadoff hitter." Ho ho. Hee hee. What a hoot, Rod. I hope they made you say it that way, because no one who knows anything about baseball, or leadoff hitters in particular, would be stupid enough to actually believe that. But then the Reds' GM Jim Bowden follows up with, "If Deion played baseball every day, full time, he'd be one of the top leadoff hitters in the game. I expect he will hit .270, steal 60 bases." Ooh. Aah. Let's see, in 1995, he hit .268 and that bought him an OBP of .327, with 48 runs scored in 343 at-bats. So if you up him to 500 at-bats at the same ratio, that translates to about 70 runs scored. That's a nice big drainclog at the top of the lineup. But, gosh golly, those 60 steals sure will look good on your standard-rules Rotisserie team.

Hey, sorry. I lied about a couple of things last column. First of all, Greg Vaughn actually walked 82 times last season. And looking over his past career, it really hasn't been his walk totals that have made him a crappy player, but his .245 lifetime batting average. Oh well, he's still an overpaid load, just for different reasons. And I saw that Dennis Rodman *GQ* cover in the bookstore and the model isn't topless, she has on a full bikini. I don't know if only subscribers got the topless version or if there's two totally random separate covers, or maybe I just got lucky. But there really is one. Honest. Come over sometime and I'll show it to you.

There's this married woman in her late 40's who keeps sending me provocative e-mail messages. What do you think? Maybe some flowers?

Why do the White Sox seem so intent on getting rid of Tony Phillips? Honestly, they'd be better off trading Ray Durham and letting Phillips play second if they have no room in the outfield. Not that Durham's a bad player, but Phillips is primo. I guess the thought of Phillips-Ventura-Thomas-Belle all smashed in at the top of that order was too good to be true. Maybe they've decided Darren Lewis can hit .270 and steal 60 bases.

Does anyone know that Randy Velarde hit .285 with a .372 on-base percentage and scored 82 runs last season? I didn't.

This past week I traded Jeff Bagwell, Rod Beck, Jay Buhner, Greg Colbrunn, Chili Davis, Ramon Martinez, and John Valentin for Mark Johnson (yeah, I know he stinks, I just need a body at first), Alex Rodriguez, and a number-one and -two pick in next Thanksgiving's draft. Do you think I like Alex just a bit? Honest to God, if there's one thing you should try to do before the season begins (and you're in a keeper league) it's to get Rodriguez, if there's any way possible. And, believe me, I could see Rodriguez "slumping" to like .270 with 25 homers next season. Watch the media vultures circle then. There will be personal problems, and pitchers getting adjusted to him, and sophomore jinxes, and attitude flare-ups, and anything else they can come up with. But it won't mean a thing. Rodriguez is the real deal. Don't be fooled if he comes to earth a bit next season. If Pokey Reese (who's more than two years older than Rodriguez, by the way) would come up and hit .270 with 25 homers, the media would be damn excited.

My wife likes to watch "Home Improvement" like four times a day. A thought occurred to me the other day while I happened to be watching, not only about "Home Improvement," but about any sitcom: If these people are supposed to be a real family, how come you never see any of them in the same clothes from episode to episode?

Jimy Williams is taking a lot of media rap, highlighted especially by the Canseco trade, for being nothing more than Dan Duquette's puppet. What I'd like to know is, what's so bad about that? Maybe if all these players would just shut their stupid mouths, do what they're paid way too much to do, and go along with Duquette's ideas, the Red Sox might actually see that World Series Championship they've been waiting a trillion years for. Let me put it this way, do you remember what the Red Sox looked like in 1994, before Duquette got there? Here's a refresher:

C	Damon Berryhill
1B	Mo Vaughn
2B	Scott Fletcher
3B	Scott Cooper
SS	John Valentin
LF	Mike Greenwell
CF	Otis Nixon
RF	Billy Hatcher
DH	Andre Dawson
MGR	Butch Hobson

Now there was a team to be reckoned with. And, on top of that, they had a mighty bright future to boot.

So, I'm down to one column, once per week now. Don't worry, Steve Case, those high-traffic problems are sure to alleviate now.

— Steve Moyer

February 5—Jose Tolentino

MOYER: I was just going to use this for my Friday column, but I can't hold it in that long. Haven't there been some great signings lately? Kevin Bass with the Angels was great. But my favorite was Jose Tolentino by the Orioles. I haven't heard or read that name in years. Please tell me I'm not the only one who remembers him. If I'm not mistaken he had a big year in the Mexican league or in winter ball or something a few years ago and he was semi-known (maybe only by me and my friends) as the Mexican Jose Canseco, since he looked kind of like Canseco. He was in the minors for a couple of years, but he just disappeared lately. I'd love to see him miraculously earn a pinch-hitter role in the spring with the Orioles.

But how can you top Butch Hobson as "Special Assignment Scout"? I have to ask around about that one.

SICKELS: Yeah, I remember Jose Tolentino. Lefty-hitting first baseman, right? Had some power, never got a chance. I thought he had retired.

February 5—Baseball America

SICKELS: Look everybody, I *like Baseball America*. It is a good publication. But please, don't take the Top 10 Prospect lists in the most recent issue too seriously. Robin Jennings and Pedro Valdes, both fine prospects, were completely left off the Cubs list, while TJ Staton was left off the Pirate list. All these guys are fine prospects. Staton in particular. The failure to include them, especially in favor of some of these recently drafted guys that haven't played a full season yet is just incredible.

February 9—John Olerud

MOYER: The *New York Post* writes this today about your idol, Allan: "A personality like the soaked, rolled-up newspaper he has been taking to the plate the last three seasons. Decent man, seems strangely unconcerned with what's gone wrong." Just thought I'd ruin your day.

SPEAR: Ummm. . . thanks.

February 10—Howard Johnson Tries Comeback with Mets

SPEAR: HoJo looked *so* bad with the Cubs two years ago, I don't possibly see how he could come back this season.

CANTER: It'll be nice to hear Harry call him "HoJo Johnson" again, though. . .

PINTO: Harvey, Van Slyke, Johnson. It looks like it's old-home week in MLB. The scary thing is they are all younger than I am.

February 11—Greg Vaughn Re-Signs with Padres

MOYER: My local newspaper's AP account of the Vaughn signing includes this sentence: "But he struggled to adjust to N.L. pitching after joining the Padres, mainly because he had to share playing time in left field with Rickey Henderson." Since when is it the AP's job to decide for us why a guy did what he did? This is offensive to me.

PINTO: Vaughn is a great example of a player whose abilities have been misinterpreted. Greg's career averages are: .245 BA, .333 OBP, .459 slugging percentage. Nothing special. But with Milwaukee last year he hit .280, with a .378 OBP and a .571 slugging percentage, obviously good numbers. So what happens when he goes to SD? He hits .206, but with a .329 OBP and a .454 slugging percentage. In other words, he pretty much met his career averages , but with a lower BA. He didn't struggle against anything, he did exactly what the Padres should have expected.

Vaughn is a run-of-the-mill player at best. He had a lucky half season, and has parlayed that into a big contract (this may be the worst signing since Steinbrenner gave Dave Collins a lot of money because he was fast). Greg Vaughn shouldn't have been sharing time with Rickey Henderson, Rickey should have gotten it all.

ZMINDA: Steve's right. Everybody knows the real reason Vaughn struggled was that he didn't have enough "protection" behind him in the SD lineup.

KRETSCHMANN: What happened to Greg was just his typical August swoon; he always finds some reason for "why" it happened (once it was because he had to carry his own luggage at a hotel and that triggered back spasms. . . I never realized bellhops were such athletes).

Sal knew what he was doing, hanging on to Greg until he started hitting the skids in late July (he hit .128 in his last 10 games as a Brewer).

These are his numbers for his career, they don't make it as drastic as it was last year, but Vaughn's always been a head case—he thinks he's Bonds.

Month	Avg	OBP	SLG
April	.274	.374	.540
May	.235	.333	.449
June	.251	.335	.509
July	.242	.304	.427
August	.224	.331	.413
September	.253	.345	.461
Pre-All Star	.252	.342	.481
Post-All Star	.236	.322	.434

OLKIN: Based on the money they paid him, the Padres must think he's Bonds, too.

February 11—Phillies

MOYER: I can't figure out why the Phils don't just take Ricky Ledee from the Yanks for Curt Schilling, whom they seem determined to get rid of anyway. They seem stuck on Ruben Rivera. Why? Ledee is Rivera, plus some power, minus some defense, minus worthless stolen bases. Ledee is eight days younger than Rivera. Ledee is a lefty, Rivera a righty. I've not heard anything bad about Ledee's attitude. Why not make the move to get a right fielder for 10 years? The Phils need to spend money on Danny Tartabull like the Pirates needed to spend on Kevin Elster. Neither team is going anywhere in 1997.

OLKIN: Steve, get real. These are the Phillies. They can't tell the difference between a prospect and a chicken pot pie. Our cars will run on cold fusion before they figure out how to spot talent.

MOYER: That's true, Mat.

FULLAM: Come on! The Phils lineup was bursting with young talent last season. With guys like J.R. Phillips, Manny Martinez, and Rafael Quirco in the system, it's only a matter of time until Philly rises to the top of the N.L.

OLKIN: Ah, the "sh** rises to the top" theory. That must explain how Jon Zuber and Wendell Magee reached the majors in the first place.

COOPERSON: Somehow I think Jim Fregosi isn't too upset that he won't be managing the Phillies next year.

FULLAM: Will the Phillies. . .

Have a 20 HR hitter on the roster next season?
Have a regular with a .300 average?
Have a starter win more than 10 games (besides Schilling)?
Score more than 600 runs next season?

Unless Rolen turns into Babe Ruth, this team ain't going anywhere until the start of the next millennium.

JAMES: I don't know what the Phillies will do next year and don't think any of you do, either, but losing Fregosi has got to help. Last year Jefferies got hurt the first week of the season. They've got this guy Gene Schall who is:

a) certainly not great, but

b) not J.R. Phillips, either.

They gave Schall nine games to prove what he could do. He hit .192, so they started a first-baseman-of-the-week program.

One of the people they tried was J.R. Phillips, to whom they gave, as I recall, about 35 games. What I can't understand for the life of me is, if you give up on Gene Schall after nine games because he hits .192, why do you play J.R. Phillips, who has like 180 games in the major leagues and is a proven, bona fide .192 hitter?

Plus, if you draw up a list of the top 100 pitch counts in the majors over the last four years, I think about 30 of the games are going to be Curt Schilling. Here's a guy who bounces on and off the DL like a trampoline, but as long as he's not on the DL at the moment, his manager thinks he is indestructible.

COOPERSON: Bite your tongue, Bill. I agree Fregosi hung with the starters too long, but the personnel moves are the fault of Thomas. Thomas forced Fregosi to play Phillips ("How can I play the bleepin' guy when he can't even make contact?"). Moves like that were what caused the Thomas/Fregosi rift. Also, it was Thomas who succumbed to fan pressure and signed Dykstra and Daulton to long-term deals. Fregosi was opposed to the long-term deals. I think Thomas deserves much of the blame. What other GM can take over a god-awful team, and, in nine years return them to god-awful status with the mirage of one winning year in the middle, and still retain his job?

PINTO: From 1993-1996, there were 103 games where the starter threw 141 pitches or more. Schilling was not one of those starters. However, Randy Johnson did it 17 times.

COOPERSON: Interesting comparison—there were Johnson for Schilling trade rumors in 1993.

ZMINDA: I still think Fregosi was foolish in his handling of Schilling. I was at a Sunday night game in mid-September at Wrigley, and Schilling finished the eighth over the 120-pitch mark. The Phils had a big lead, and everybody in the press box was sure he was through for the night. But Fregosi sent him out there to finish the game. He wound up with 132 pitches, which isn't extreme, but why in the world would you risk it with a guy who'd had two years full of arm problems? That's just stupid.

MITTLEMAN: Just so you'll know not to look for him next year, Gene Schall was traded this winter to the White Sox for first baseman Mike Robertson.

February 13—Miscelleneous Facts

ZMINDA: Bob Davids, founder of SABR, reports these facts from the 1996 season:

1. Mark McGwire has gone 987 games and 3,222 at-bats since his last triple, which came on 6/20/88. This is the longest tripleless streak in major league history.

2. On the other hand, Lance Johnson's 21 triples were the most by an N.L. player since 1930 (Adam Comorosky, 23).

3. Alex Rodriguez and Edgar Martinez were the first teammates with 50+ doubles since Charlie Gehringer and Gee Walker of the 1936 Tigers.

4. Fernando Valenzuela is the only pitcher in major league history to win games in three different countries (Canada, Mexico and the U.S.).

5. Brady Anderson is the first player in major league history to have seasons of both 50 HR and 50 SB (not in the same year). Davids believes that no *minor* league player has ever done this, either.

HENZLER: Speaking of triples, if Mark Parent plays enough for the Phillies this season, he might set a rather dubious record. I doubt he'll ever catch McGwire, though.

Most At-Bats With No Career Triples
Craig Worthington	1,234
Mark Parent	1,077
Gaylord Perry	1,076

February 14—Ballparks

COOPERSON: There are a couple of mentions in *Scoreboard* essays of "new, smaller" parks. From looking at ballpark dimensions, it seems that the new parks are not any smaller than the old ones. Colorado (like Mile High before it) is pretty deep to dead center field, 423 feet. Baltimore's 410 to dead center. I know the popular belief is that the new parks are smaller (this is the reference in the essays), but I think that's a misperception. What do you guys think?

OLKIN: I think they should be talking about the "new, smaller" strike zone instead.

QUINN: I read just the opposite in an article written by someone not associated with STATS. He said a player was moving to the "A.L. and its larger parks." That sounded wrong, but I'd like to hear it from the experts.

FAUST: I wrote the main essay in question, and I do refer to the new parks as "smaller." Now that you mention it, that doesn't infer what I want it to. The essay shows that the new parks are more offensive; that doesn't necessarily mean they're smaller.

I think some of the new parks seem smaller because they put fans closer to the game, meaning they have less foul territory. That may be the main influence on the increase in offense. That would be a curious study. . .

ZMINDA: It's a misperception overall, but some of the new parks are indeed smaller down at least one of the foul lines. Most of the new parks of the 1970s were at least 330 feet down the foul lines; Camden is 318 down the RF line, Jacobs 325, The Ballpark 325. In that sense they are smaller, but often the same parks have deeper LF and CF.

What most people mean by this is that it's easier to hit home runs in the new parks. Our data indicates that overall this is true, but it's *not* true of many of the parks, including Comiskey and Jacobs.

February 14—Cory Snyder Signed by Cardinals

WOELFLEIN: Cory Snyder was signed to a minor league contract by the Cardinals and invited to spring training today. It's a world gone mad.

SCHINSKI: I think they should rename MLB to GLB (Geriatric League Baseball).

SICKELS: How many days before Jose Lind gets an invitation to spring camp? Heck, try Julio Cruz. Tony Bernazard. Jack Brohamer.

MOYER: It will be a while before Lind gets an invitation, because you have to wear pants to play major league baseball.

ZMINDA: First, Dale Sveum, then Cory Snyder. All the fluke heroes of 1987 are suddenly back in fashion. I'll bet Larry Sheets is sitting by the phone.

COOPERSON: Isn't HoJo a proud member of the fluke Class of '87?

FULLAM: You'd think so, but HoJo actually averaged 31 HRs a year between '87 and '91.

COOPERSON: Fine, but what about Steve Bedrosian?

FULLAM: If hitting was out of control in '87, wouldn't that make Bedrock's season that much *more* effective?

JAMES: The tragedies of life. . . Larry Sheets is waiting by the phone, and Andy MacPhail can't find his phone number.

February 18—Dan Duquette

COOPERSON: From Dan Shaughnessy in today's *Boston Globe*:

"General manager Dan Duquette has molded this new team in the image of himself. Boring."

PINTO: Shaughnessy is just complaining because there's no dirt to write about. It's impossible for a Globe beat reporter to write a positive story.

MOYER: As I said in my column recently, maybe all these Duquette-haters would like to go back to the pre-Duquette days when the lineup was:

1B	Mo Vaughn
2B	Scott Fletcher
SS	John Valentin
3B	Scott Cooper
LF	Mike Greenwell
CF	Otis Nixon
RF	Billy Hatcher
DH	Andre Dawson

The pitchers were Roger Clemens, Aaron Sele, Joe Hesketh, Danny Darwin, Ken Ryan, Greg Harris, Chris Nabholz, and Jeff Russell.

Key subs were Tim Naehring, Tom Brunansky, Carlos Rodriguez, Wes Chamberlain, Lee Tinsley, and Rich Rowland.

Now that's an exciting team! And one with an exciting future, too. Dan Shaughnessy should lick Dan Duquette's boots.

February 19—Bobby Valentine

OLKIN: Item: "New York Mets manager Bobby Valentine's MRI showed he has a torn rotator cuff." Ah, poetic justice.

HENZLER: Mat, I know what you're saying, but Bobby Valentine lost much of his own playing career due to injuries. A good career too, if the scouting reports can be believed. I'm not sure if "poetic justice" is really the appropriate term.

ZMINDA: Valentine was considered a terrific prospect until he broke his leg in a ghastly incident in 1973. I believe he was going up to catch a flyball at the wall, and as he came down his leg got caught in the chicken-wire fence, resulting in a severe leg fracture as well as some spinal damage. Really nasty stuff. He was 23 years old and never really recovered.

I always thought Valentine was somewhat overrated coming through the Dodger system (maybe Bill could speak to this), but there's no doubt the injury wrecked his chances of having a good career.

JAMES: At the time, I thought Valentine was going to be a Hall of Famer. I didn't have the MLEs system at the time, and have never gone back and reconstructed them for him, so I don't know what I'd think now.

February 19—Fun with Team Leaders

FULLAM: I was just sifting through last year's team stats when I saw that Oakland's *leading* strikeout pitcher was Carlos Reyes, who fanned a whopping 78 batters. This seemed like an absurdly low total to me—does anyone know if this is some sort of record?

MILLER: Another cool "low" leader total: Ron Oester's team-leading RBI total of 58 in 1983 for the Reds!

MOYER: Lowell Palmer led the 1973 Phillies in wins with three. (I just made that up.)

ZMINDA: Yes, and Palmer was the first player to pitch (*and* pose for his baseball card) with shades on. *That's* cool!

DEWAN: How about Ken Berry leading the White Sox in hitting in 1967 (I believe) with a .241 average!

Try to top that one.

ZMINDA: John is right, but actually both Berry and Don Buford tied for the club lead with .241 averages. The neatest thing about it is that the '67 White Sox nearly won the pennant!

DEWAN: Don is right too, but Buford's average was actually lower when carried to more decimal places (as I recall)! Not that I'm splitting hairs. . .

HENZLER: Here's the list of fewest strikeouts by team leaders since 1900. Reyes' total was the lowest by a team leader (excluding strike years) since Paul Splittorff led the Royals in 1983 with 61:

Fewest Strikeouts For Team Leader—(since 1900)

Year	Team	Pitcher	K
1902	Yankees	Long Tom Hughes	45
1930	Reds	Red Lucas	53
1924	White Sox	Sarge Connally	55
1926	Phillies	Hal Carlson	55
1933	Phillies	Ed Holley	56
1981	Cardinals	Bruce Sutter	57
1926	Red Sox	Hal Wiltse	59
1926	Orioles	Win Ballou	59
1918	Giants	Pol Perritt	60
1942	Giants	Cliff Melton	61
1983	Royals	Paul Splittorff	61
1932	Red Sox	Bob Weiland	63
1935	Braves	Fred Frankhouse	64
1946	Pirates	Jack Hallett	64
1932	White Sox	Sad Sam Jones	64

And here are the lowest RBI totals by team leaders since 1900. If you exclude the strike years, Oester's team-leading 58 RBI for the '83 Reds was actually one *more* than Dan Driessen's and Cesar Cedeno's 57 for the '82 Reds.

Fewest RBI For Team Leader—(since 1900)

Year	Team	Hitter	RBI
1981	Twins	Mickey Hatcher	37
1910	Orioles	George Stone	40
1909	Twins	Bob Unglaub	41
1981	Padres	Gene Richards	42
1910	White Sox	Patsy Dougherty	43
1981	Blue Jays	John Mayberry	43
1908	Yankees	Charlie Hemphill	44
1906	Cardinals	Jake Beckley	44
1902	Giants	Billy Lauder	44
1908	Twins	Jerry Freeman	45
1907	Cardinals	Red Murray	46
1954	Orioles	Vern Stephens	46
1981	Pirates	Dave Parker	48
1916	Twins	Howard Shanks	48
1919	Braves	Walter Holke	48

I used a minimum of 400 AB in generating this list of lowest batting averages by team leaders. Tommy Agee thus led the 1972 Mets with an average of .227. (Cleon Jones batted .245 with 375 AB; Ed Kranepool hit .269 in 327 AB).

Lowest Batting Average For Team Leader—(since 1900; minimum 400 AB)

Year	Team	Hitter	Avg
1972	Mets	Tommie Agee	.227
1967	White Sox	Ken Berry	.241
1908	Dodgers	Tim Jordan	.247
1910	White Sox	Patsy Dougherty	.248
1952	Pirates	Gus Bell	.250
1972	Padres	Nate Colbert	.250
1903	Twins	Kip Selbach	.251
1908	Twins	Jerry Freeman	.252
1965	Mets	Ed Kranepool	.253
1972	Rangers	Dick Billings	.254
1968	Angels	Rick Reichardt	.255
1994	Angels	Chad Curtis	.256
1967	Rangers	Frank Howard	.256
1943	Athletics	Irv Hall	.256
1966	Yankees	Elston Howard	.256

As I pointed out, the minimum ABs can be changed to alter the outcomes for team BA leaders. Here's what the list looks like using 300 AB as the minimum (keep in mind '81 was a strike year).

Lowest Batting Average For Team Leader—(since 1900; minimum 300 AB)

Year	Team	Hitter	Avg
1981	Blue Jays	Lloyd Moseby	.233
1967	White Sox	Ken Berry	.241
1908	Dodgers	Tim Jordan	.247
1910	White Sox	Patsy Dougherty	.248
1903	Twins	Kip Selbach	.251
1908	Twins	Otis Clymer	.253
1965	Mets	Ed Kranepool	.253
1967	Rangers	Frank Howard	.256
1910	Orioles	Bobby Wallace	.258
1943	Athletics	Bobby Estalella	.259
1972	Rangers	Toby Harrah	.259
1916	Braves	Ed Konetchy	.260
1971	Angels	Sandy Alomar Sr	.260

PINTO: The really cool thing about Ken Berry is that he did it while also starring in F-Troop!

February 20—Danny Tartabull Signs with Phillies

ZMINDA: I'm sure Danny's defensive prowess and gung-ho attitude will go over big with those Philly fans.

MITTLEMAN: You're mean (smile); aren't you going to miss him?

JAMES: Danny Tartabull in the outfield, on artificial turf. . . man, that's going to bring back memories of Greg Luzinski. Danny was a *terrible* outfielder when he was in KC 10 years ago.

FULLAM: Based on the fact that Jim Fregosi had plans to use *Pete Incaviglia* as a defensive late-inning replacement at the start of last season (for Daulton), Tartabull's glove can only be a plus.

COOPERSON: Tartabull's no Incaviglia. . .

FULLAM: He can't be *worse*, can he???

ZMINDA: Actually, he behaved himself during his season with the White Sox. But he's a brutal outfielder, and he thinks he's getting shafted on his contract. Once he kicks his first ball away and the fans start booing, well. . . it's not a pretty picture.

But being close to New York again, maybe they'll put him in another "Seinfeld" episode.

JAMES: Danny Tartabull gets stuck in an elevator with Newman. . . hey, this could work.

February 20—Mitch Williams' Comeback

GREENBERGER: Anyone know what kind of living Mitch Williams makes attempting comebacks? Does he collect real dough for it?

JAMES: Compared to you and me, or compared to baseball players?

PINTO: Bill, you mean you don't make as much money as Barry Bonds?

JAMES: Not yet, but my agent claims that Simon and Schuster promised him that I would be the highest-paid baseball writer in the world, no matter how many books I sell.

OLKIN: Is that why you quit writing books?

February 24: The Most Overrated Players in Baseball

I'm all for giving credit where credit is due. By the same token, nothing rankles me more than undeserved accolades. Yes, it's time for the Major League All-Overrated Team. (We're still looking for corporate sponsorship!)

While some of these players were good at one point in their career, others have taken advantage of their ballpark, their media exposure or the limelight provided by playing on a winner. I did not include any pitchers. (Steve Avery has taken too much abuse lately and I don't want to get on Dennis Eckersley's bad side.) I also limited the number of Colorado players to two. Without this "Rockies" rule, all eight Rockies starters would make the team. (That's what happens when you play in the best hitters' park of all time.)

C — Sandy Alomar, Jr.

How long will it take before people realize he isn't half the player Roberto is? Did folks have the same problem distinguishing Hank and Tommie Aaron? Sandy is 31 now and has played in more than 90 games in only two seasons. He established career highs of 60 runs and 66 RBI back in 1990. His career batting average is .270 and he's never drawn more than 25 walks or hit more than 15 homers in a season. Last year he threw out a slightly higher percentage of runners than average. In 1995, he was slightly below average against baserunners. Was Alomar's 1996 campaign any better than say, Charlie O'Brien's or Greg Myers'? Why in the world has Alomar made four All-Star games?

1B — Andres Galarraga

He joined the Rockies at age 32. He had not hit above .260 in any of his prior four seasons. He's now hit .315 in his four seasons with Colorado. Did he find the fountain of youth? Guess again. His road statistics for 1996 say it all: .245 BA, 15 HR, 47 RBI, .290 OBP.

2B — Mark Lemke

OK, he plays on a winner, he's had outstanding postseasons and he's decent with the glove. He's also a .248 career hitter who's never even collected 20 doubles in a season. He set a career high last year with 64 runs. (Is that something to be proud of?) He's 9-for-27 in career steal attempts. And, he won't even take one for the team (0 HBP in 3,167 career plate appearances).

3B — Terry Pendleton

He won a questionable MVP award six years ago. Since then, his average has dropped 80 points and his power has been cut in half. He's 36, having posted an on-base percentage of .290 and a slugging average of .345 in 1996. He's no longer spectacular with the leather. This isn't somebody you want at the bottom of the lineup, let alone in the middle of it.

SS — Rey Ordonez

After all the early raves, most people came down to earth about Ordonez last year. Still, many continued to compare him to a young Ozzie Smith. Everyone says he's a great defensive player. And how can you measure that with statistics? Well, how about those 27 errors (third-most among major league shortstops)? Or what about his range factor of 4.86? Five shortstops had higher numbers. You want more? Ordonez' zone rating in 1996 was .934. The league average was .935. As far as hitting goes, forget it! Ordonez knocked out 17 extra base hits and 30 RBI last year. He collected only 10 unintentional walks. He's not half the player Ozzie was, either in the field or at the plate.

LF — Moises Alou

Alou had one great year (1994), but has been nothing more than average in his other seasons. In the year of the hitter, Alou hit .281 with 21 homers, drew a few walks and had no speed. Glenallen Hill hit .280 with 19 homers in about two-thirds the at-bats. Sure, Alou knocked in 96 runs, but who didn't in 1996? Among 1996 N.L. right fielders, Alou ranked 11th in OBS (on base percentage plus slugging percentage).

CF — Darryl Hamilton

The Rangers were thrilled to acquire Hamilton before 1996. Evidently, they thought he'd actually accomplished something in his career. Last year he hit .293 with 93 runs scored. But how impressive is that considering the hitters behind him? He can hit for average, but he has no power, doesn't draw walks and no longer uses his speed.

RF — Dante Bichette

1996 Road Statistics: .253 BA, 9 HR, .296 OBP, .401 SLG. Need I say more?

DH — Cecil Fielder

Admittedly, Fielder was a great story when he came back from Japan in 1990. He also put together a fine season that year with a .277 average and 51 homers. But it's been six seasons

244

since, and he's now nowhere near that production. Fielder does one thing well—hit dingers. The problem is, he does nothing else. He has to hit a boatload of homers to help you. He has to be among the best home-run hitters in the league to be of value. He's not. His 39 last year ranked fourth among A.L. first basemen.

Still, most teams would take an extra 39 homers. But look what else this comes with:

1) A .252 average in 1996, and a career average of .256—OK for a shortstop, but among the very worst for a 1B/DH;

2) Some ability to draw walks, but not a lot—the true superstars at his position (Thomas, Vaughn, McGwire, Palmeiro, E. Martinez) all draw more;

3) Very few extra base hits aside from the home runs—he's never had more than 25 doubles in a season;

4) A poor glove at a hitters' position;

5) The slowest feet known to man.

Would you rather have Fielder than Frank Thomas or Mo Vaughn? Or Rafael Palmeiro or Mark McGwire? Or Edgar Martinez? Or Jeff Bagwell? Or Fred McGriff? Or Eric Karros? Or John Jaha? As bad a season as John Olerud had, his OBS was still higher than Fielder's. Paul Sorrento's OBS was higher than Fielder's. So was Scott Stahoviak's and Mark Grace's and Jeff King's.

— John Sasman

February 24—George and Cecil

OLKIN: Cecil Fielder says: "It meant a lot to me to have [Steinbrenner] tell me that he respected me, not just as a baseball player, but as a player."

If not a baseball player, then what? A tennis player?

MOYER: Maybe, in light of the shocking recent revelation that baseball players play cards for money in the clubhouse, he meant a card player. I also heard rumors that Cecil plays a mean piccolo. I also saw an old Cecil photo in a sandbox with a bunch of neighbor kids from the *TSN* photo files. Maybe that's what he meant, as in, "Can Cecil come out and play?"

JAMES: Sumo.

February 24—Cloning

SICKELS: With the announcement over the weekend that Scottish scientists have successfully cloned sheep, isn't it only a matter of time before some unscrupulous owner starts cloning his players? How bout a team of Alex Rodriguezes? Or Frank Thomases? If you lose a free agent, *you can just clone him*! I think there is a big opportunity here for the small market teams.

FAUST: And injuries? Ha! Even with Canseco and McGwire, Oakland wouldn't miss a beat. They could even bring back Rickey. . .

JAMES: Wait a minute! As luck would have it, we already *have* a genetic duplicate of Jose Canseco: Ozzie. Anybody want to know what Ozzie Canseco would hit in Camden Yards?

One of my favorite movies of all time—Multiplicity.

PINTO: The Canseco brothers also show that cloning won't always work. The two have exactly the same genetic makeup, yet one is a slugger and the other can't stay on an ML roster.

SICKELS: I guess the idea won't work with someone like Babe Ruth. You have to have live cells.

DEWAN: There's this mosquito who once stung Babe Ruth. He got stuck in some tree sap and the DNA was preserved. . .

ZMINDA: Hence the famous phrase, "He could hit the ball out of any park. . . including Jurassic!"

FAUST: All-injured team:

C	Sandy Alomar
1B	Mark McGwire (honorable mention to Bagwell)
2B	??
SS	tie: Kevin Elster and Shawon Dunston
3B	Edgar Martinez
LF	Rickey Henderson
CF	Lenny Dykstra
RF	Dave Justice
DH	Jose Canseco

So, who'd I miss? I can't think of a decent, chronically-injured second baseman.

CANTER: Robbie Thompson.

COUVILLON: Does Geronimo Pena count?

FAUST: Wow, he might be too injured, but then again, I let Dykstra beat out Griffey for the CF job. He does have some modest half-seasons. . .

JAMES: 2B—Brent Gates

PINTO: And now a word from the science community:

I was once a bio-chemist and know a little about cloning. The idea of cloning someone from a lock of hair or skin cell just doesn't work. We've known for quite some time that as cells differentiate in the body, the genes can rearrage themselves, so that while all cells have a full complement of chromosomes, they don't have a full complement of genes. To clone someone, you need cells before they differeniate; pregametes are probably best, but any stem cell would probably due. Once a cell has differentiated, however, you lose some genetic information.

The best example of this is in the immune response. You can make a nearly infinite number of immune resposes with a finite number of genes, because these genes can rearrage themselves, each one producing an exquisite antibody. Pretty cool.

February 25—What Pitcher Can Survive Coors?

I'm sure you saw in today's paper how the Rockies are all excited about Bill Swift's recovery from arm problems. When they signed him, they reasoned that he'd be the perfect type of pitcher to succeed in Coors Field. Since he's an extreme groundballer, the thin air wouldn't hurt him—or so the theory went. He hasn't been a world beater during his two seasons with the Rockies, although you can justifiably blame his arm problems for that. But still, after watching the Rockies play there for two seasons, we *still* don't know if Swift is the type of pitcher that can succeed there—because we really don't know *what* kind of pitcher is best-suited to work there. The Rockies, for one, sure don't seem to have any answers.

All we have are theories, none proven nor disproven. Some say you need to keep the ball on the ground to prevent the home run. Others say you need to prevent walks since baserunners are much more likely to come around to score there. Another school of thought holds that you need strikeout pitchers, since the only real solution is to keep the ball out of play entirely. Everyone seems to agree, however, that flyball pitchers don't have a prayer of surviving there.

The "groundballer" theory seems to be the most prevalent, but there's one big problem with it: most groundballers rely on breaking pitches to produce ground balls. In Colorado, the thin air means less wind resistance for *pitched* balls as well as batted balls. Breaking pitches rely on wind resistance for their movement, so they tend to flatten out in Colorado. For this reason, breaking ball/groundball pitchers may not enjoy any advantage at all there.

But enough theorizing. . . what do we actually *know?* Well, we can try to learn a thing or two from the Rockies staff. There have been 10 Colorado pitchers who have thrown 50 innings at home and on the road over the last two seasons. I've listed their home ERA minus their road ERA to find out which pitchers suffered the most:

Home ERA - Road ERA (1995-96)

Bryan Rekar	7.09
Roger Bailey	2.49
Mark Thompson	2.30
Marvin Freeman	2.22
Kevin Ritz	1.84
Armando Reynoso	0.52
Bill Swift	0.52
Steve Reed	0.06
Darren Holmes	–0.04
Curt Leskanic	–0.41

Interestingly, the list divides neatly into two groups—the top five, who suffered a significant amount, and the bottom five, who weren't hurt all that much. I'll bet you didn't expect to see Kevin Ritz in the former category. He won great praise as a "Coors Field pitcher" when he won 17 games last year, but the truth is that he doesn't enjoy any special advantage there compared to the rest of the staff. Now, let's use these two groups to test some of the theories we mentioned above.

First, the groundball theory. Swift has posted a 2.82 ground-to-fly ratio over the last two seasons, which is one of the highest figures in baseball. He shows up in the bottom group, but overall, the two groups are fairly similar in terms of groundball tendencies. Groundballers like Roger Bailey, Marvin Freeman and Kevin Ritz were hurt by the park, while flyballers like Armando Reynoso and Steve Reed weren't. Getting ground balls, in and of itself, doesn't appear to give a pitcher an advantage.

How about the walk theory? Now there may be something to this one. Four of the five pitchers in the top group walked more than 3.9 men per nine innings, while none of the bottom five exceeded that mark. Good control may be a necessity—in fact, it may be the one weakness that hurts Kevin Ritz.

Next, let's look at strikeouts. There appears to be something here as well. Despite the presence of Swift and Reynoso, the bottom group significantly out-performed the top group in strikeouts per nine innings. This, however, may be partly the result of all three short relievers appearing in the bottom group. Swift and Reynoso didn't strike out any more men than the starters in the top group, but they succeeded nonetheless. It still seems more than likely that strikeouts help.

Apart from all the old theories, there *does* seem to be one characteristic that defines the two groups: *age and experience*. Take another look at the top three pitchers on the list. When Bryan Rekar spent his first season in Coors, he was a 23-year-old rookie. Next is Bailey, who was also a rookie, age 24. Then comes Mark Thompson, who spent his first extended stay in the majors in Coors at age 24. He'd thrown only nine innings in the majors before he came to Coors.

Overall, the top five pitchers' average age in their first season at Coors was 26.6; the bottom five's average age was 29.4. The top group averaged 126 innings of previous major league experience; the bottom group averaged 402. That's a significant difference.

Taken all together, the data forcefully suggests that veteran pitchers have an easier time adjusting to Coors than do rookies. That certainly would make intuitive sense, wouldn't it? For a young pitcher, one of the biggest obstacles to success is a lack of confidence. If a pitcher hasn't yet encountered success in the majors, there may still be doubts in his mind about whether he can get hitters out. Until he has the confidence to pitch within the strike zone, he's not likely to go very far. Ironically, the best way to develop the confidence necessary for success is through *success itself*. If a pitcher gets off to a good start, he'll start to believe in himself, and his career will likely move forward from there. If a pitcher is mercilessly pounded during his first time around the league, it may kill his confidence—no matter how good his stuff is.

There is no better example of this than Bryan Rekar. He began the '95 season at Double-A, where he went 6-3 in his first 12 starts, fanning 80 batters and walking only 16 in 80.1 innings. That got him a promotion to Triple-A, where he had to deal with an extremely hitter-friendly home park. The park proved to be no obstacle, as he went 4-2 with a 1.49 ERA in seven starts. That got him promoted to the Rockies, where he became part of their starting rotation for the second half.

His '95 major league stats weren't bad, if you take the park into account. His 4-6 record wasn't anything special, but he posted a respectable 4.98 ERA. Still, that number must have been quite a disappointment for Rekar, who may have expected more from himself after dominating the minor league hitters. He maintained an excellent strikeout-to-walk ratio, and his hits-to-innings weren't bad, given the environment.

Last season, both ratios went to hell as he fell apart completely. The meltdown earned him a trip back to Triple-A, where he pitched much more poorly than he had the first time around. What happened?

Two words: Coors Field. On the road, Rekar was undoubtedly one of the best young pitchers in the league. During '95 and '96, he posted a road ERA of 3.13, with less than one hit per inning pitched and a strikeout-to-walk ratio of almost two-to-one. But at Coors, Rekar absorbed such a hellacious pounding that his confidence was completely destroyed. He allowed 114 hits and 79 earned runs in only 68.2 innings for a quadruple-digit ERA of 10.35. It's easy to see how he could have returned to Triple-A fully convinced that he wasn't good enough to make it in the majors.

The sad part is that he was more than good enough. He had an unusually hard time adjusting to Coors Field, but the ability was there, and I think he would have made it in time. He may still.

The other youngsters, Roger Bailey and Mark Thompson, haven't had quite as hard a time dealing with the thin air, but their careers have hardly taken off. Overall, it seems clear that guys who are fresh out of the minors have a harder time dealing with Coors.

It makes perfect sense to me. If I'm a rookie pitcher, my biggest fear is having one of those horrible four-inning, eight-run starts that will balloon my ERA and hasten my return to the minors. I can't imagine what it would be like if half of my starts were likely to end up like that.

Perhaps other hitters' parks also impair young pitchers' development, to a lesser extent. Is it just a coincidence that the Tigers and Red Sox have had a long-standing inability to develop pitchers? And is it also a coincidence that many of the teams that have developed a lot of young pitchers lately—the White Sox, Padres and Dodgers come to mind—reside in pitchers' parks? (The Braves are the exception, obviously.)

In a hitter's park, the veterans don't have the same worries that the kids do. They may get hit hard, but even if that happens, they know they won't be sent down. The guys who've succeeded at Coors seem to be the guys who realize that they can get hammered from time to time and still survive.

Look at Kevin Ritz. Early in his career, when he was trying to get his feet on the ground in Detroit, he posted ERAs of 11.05, 11.74, and 5.60 in consecutive seasons. Then he came to the Rockies, and in his first year with them, his ERA was 5.62. This is a guy who can deal with failure.

The point is that he survived all that. When the Rockies moved from Mile High Stadium—the most extreme hitters' park in baseball—to Coors Field—the most extreme hitters' park *in baseball history*—he didn't bat an eye. Since then, he's been their most successful pitcher, even though he's hurt by Coors more than most Rockies pitchers.

Reynoso, Reed, Holmes and Leskanic—these guys all weathered the storm at Mile High before taking on Coors, and the experience seems to have toughened them up. You tend to think of Bill Swift as someone who's enjoyed a lot of success, but over the first two years of his career, he went 8-19 with a 5.11 ERA. He knows how the canvas feels.

If Coors continues to chew up and spit out young pitchers, it will have grave implications for the Rockies' future success. Free-agent pitchers would rather retire than sign up with Colorado, so the Rockies have geared their minor league system toward developing pitchers. They've spent almost all of their high draft picks on pitchers, and they expect to have quite a few young arms coming up in the next few years. Unless the rest of their kids fare better than Rekar, the Rockies will be left high and dry—unable to develop pitchers, and unable to attract free agent pitching talent.

Their latest kid pitcher is Jamey Wright. He didn't throw enough innings last year to make the list above, but he didn't take to Coors well, either. His ERA at home was 2.71 runs higher than on the road, which would have been the biggest margin of all Colorado pitchers, except for Rekar. Scouts rave about his physical ability, but I think his mental makeup will prove to be just as important. If he can worry about his wins instead of his ERA, he'll do fine. If not, it could get ugly.

Meanwhile, the Rockies remain excited about Swift. If he's healthy, I like his chances, too—but *not* because be throws grounders.

—Mat Olkin

February 27—Spring Training

Spring training games begin tomorrow, and I'm sure most of you are as eager as I am to see the teams in action again. But do spring training records really mean anything? Are teams that play winning ball during the exhibition season likely to continue to do so once the bell rings? There's a school of thought that says it's important to win *any* time, and that a good record in spring training "builds a winning attitude." True or false?

Basically, the answer is "false." We looked at spring-training records in the 1995 edition of the Baseball Scoreboard, and found no real relationship at all between winning in the spring and winning in the regular season. Here's an update of the study, looking at spring records going back to 1988:

1988. The American League division winners in 1988 would be the Boston Red Sox and the Oakland A's. Both teams were mediocre in spring training that year: the Red Sox went 16-15, the A's 14-16. To be sure, the National League division winners from '88—the Dodgers (21-11) and Mets (19-10) *did* have excellent springs. But the best spring record of all in 1988 belonged to the New York Yankees (22-10), who would go on to finish fifth in the seven-team American League East in '88.

1989. The top won-lost percentage in the spring of '89 belonged to the San Diego Padres (18-8, .692), who would finish a competitive second in the N.L. West that year. But the *worst* spring record in '89 belonged to the Chicago Cubs (9-23, .281), who would go on to win the N.L. East. The eventual N.L. West champions, the Giants, also had a lousy spring (13-19). Over in the American League, both division titlists, the A's (19-13) and Blue Jays (21-10), would tune up for the regular year with great springs. But the Cleveland Indians had a great spring, also (19-11). . . and they went on to post a 73-89 record.

1991. Spring training started very late in 1990 because of an owners' lockout, so we'll skip that year. In 1991, the best spring record belonged the Minnesota Twins (21-10), who had finished in last place in 1990. That fall, the Twins would complete a Cinderella "worst-to-first" season by winning the World Series. Maybe that was significant in building a winning attitude. And it's possible that the Atlanta Braves, who would also go from last to first in 1991, started their turnaround in spring training, when they posted a solid 15-12 record. This seems like great evidence until we point out that the Braves had had an even better spring mark in 1989 (17-12). . . and then went on to finish last with a 63-97 record. Another note about 1991: the Toronto Blue Jays went 9-19 in the spring, but went on to win the American League East.

1992. This time the Braves had a "horrible" spring (10-19), but still went to the World Series. All the other 1992 division winners had either mediocre or lousy springs: the A's and Pirates each went 15-13, and the eventual World Champion Blue Jays went 13-18.

1993. The Blue Jays tuned up for another World Championship by posting an 11-19 record in the spring. The other division titlists that year all had good springs: White Sox 19-13, Phillies 16-10, Braves 17-11. But nobody had a better spring in 1993 than the Cincinnati Reds (18-9). They went on to finish fifth with a 73-89 record.

1994. There was no postseason in 1994 due to the strike, but none of the clubs in first place at the time of the work stoppage had had very good springs: White Sox 17-16, Yankees 12-15, Rangers 12-19 in the American League; Dodgers 15-15, Reds 12-19, Expos 10-20 in the National. The Expos, who had the worst record in baseball during spring training, had the *best* record in baseball during the regular year.

1996. We'll skip 1995, which featured another strike-shortened spring training. All the division winners would prepare for the regular year with decent springs, though two of them were right around .500: the Rangers went 19-11, the Indians 21-13 and the Yankees 16-15 in the A.L.; the Braves 16-10, Padres 20-13 and the Cardinals 15-15 in the N.L. But the best spring-training record in '96 belonged to the California Angels (21-10), who would go on to post a 70-91 record. The *second*-best spring record in 1996—would you believe it?—belonged to the Detroit Tigers (20-10).

Need we say more?

—Don Zminda

February 28: Where Have You Gone, Omar Moreno?

How can Hollywood miss such a golden opportunity? The re-release of "The Graduate" begs an update of Simon and Garfunkel's "Mrs. Robinson." We're over Joe DiMaggio's retirement. It's time to start paying homage to guys like Ron LeFlore and Omar Moreno. Who cares that neither could play a lick, these guys were stars when the stolen base was king.

Remember how it was 10 or 15 years ago? LeFlore stole 97 bases in 1980 to edge out Moreno for the National League lead. Moreno finished with 96 steals that season, his third straight 70-steal campaign. Tim Raines, of course, replaced LeFlore in the Expo outfield and swiped 71 bases in his rookie year, on his way to six straight 70-steal seasons. Around the same time, Rickey Henderson and Willie Wilson were tearing up the basepaths in the American League. Then came Vince Coleman. He stole 110 bases in his rookie year of 1985, the first of three straight 100-steal campaigns.

In fact, at the time there were big-time base stealers throughout professional baseball. Coleman, for example, stole 145 bases in 113 games in Class A in 1983. Donell Nixon notched 144 that same year in the California League. Meanwhile, Otis Nixon stole 94 for Columbus. Jeff Stone and Mike Felder added 90-plus steal seasons in the minors in 1982. Marcus Lawton (who?) swiped 111 bases and was thrown out only 8 times playing for Colombia of the Sally League in 1985. The steal disrupted the pitcher, it opened up holes in the defense, it set your offense in motion. (At least that's what everyone said.)

Fast forward to 1996. Kenny Lofton leads the American League with 75 steals. Eric Young tops N.L. players with "only" 53. What's happened to the running game? While these are fine totals, they pale in comparison to the numbers posted a few years ago. Lofton's 1996 total would have been good enough for only third in the A.L. in 1980. Young's total would have place him eighth in the N.L. in the same year. As for the minors, no one collected more than 70 stolen bases in either 1995 or 1996. There are no big-time basestealers in the majors and none on the horizon.

In fact, in just a few years there has been a dramatic drop in the number of big-steal seasons. Here is a decade-by-decade breakdown:

Top Stolen Base Seasons

Years	50+	60+	70+	80+	100+
1990-96	41	15	8	1	0
1980s	64	38	26	16	7
1970s	49	19	10	2	1
1960s	20	8	4	2	1
1950s	1	0	0	0	0

Note: Totals for 1972,1981,1994, and 1995 adjusted
for labor disruptions.

There are still three years left in the 1990s, yet it is clear that this decade will not have nearly as many big stolen-base seasons as in the prior decade. What's most amazing about the above chart, however, is not the lack of steals in the 1990s, but the flood of them in the 1980s. Look at the number of 80-plus stolen base seasons. Including the strike adjustments, there have only been 26 such seasons since 1900. More than 60 percent of those seasons were in the 1980s. And remember, it wasn't all Rickey. Six different players accounted for those 16 seasons.

The decrease in big-steal seasons puts Rickey Henderson's record out of reach for the time being. In the 1980s, it was evident that Brock's stolen base total would be surpassed. Either Henderson, or Raines, or Coleman or somebody was going to break Lou's record. Now, however, with 1,186 steals and counting, Henderson's mark is secure. Kenny Lofton, after leading the A.L. in steals for five straight seasons, has the best chance of overtaking Rickey. Still, he would need to average 75 stolen bases (his career high) until he was 41 to take over the record.

One method Bill James suggests further illustrates the strength of Henderson's mark. James likes to determine the number of seasons of league-leading performance that are needed to achieve a record. A decade-by-decade breakdown of the league-leading stolen base totals shows the safety of the stolen base record:

League-Leading Stolen Base Totals

Years	Avg. Leader	Years to 1,186
1990s	67.1	17.7
1980s	90.2	13.1
1970s	66.8	17.8
1960s	57.1	20.8
1950s	29.8	39.8

Besting Henderson is difficult even in the most conducive of times. Doing so when the stolen base isn't nearly as popular makes it almost impossible.

So, will we ever see the return of the big-time base stealers? Who knows, I'm still trying to figure out how to get Chuck Tanner digitized in with a young Dustin Hoffman. (Just think of the marketing possibilities: new music and new video!)

— John Sasman

1997 Predictions

Ethan D. Cooperson

American League

East: **Baltimore**. If Mussina returns to form and the offense comes close to last year's output, this is the team to beat.

Central: **Cleveland**. Matt Williams will ease the pain of Albert Belle's departure, and Charles Nagy is ready for his best year yet.

West: **Seattle**. With Randy Johnson and Ken Griffey Jr. healthy, and Juan Gonzalez out of the Texas lineup in April, Seattle rates the edge.

Wild-Card: **Chicago**. Albert Belle and Frank Thomas give the White Sox the edge over as many as five other contenders. Don't discount Minnesota as a dark horse.

National League

East: **Atlanta**. They don't just have Maddux and Glavine—they have Maddux and Glavine on salary drives.

Central: **St. Louis**. Filet Mignon manager, hamburger team in a ho-hum division. Their starting pitching isn't bad.

West: **Los Angeles**. A healthy Brett Butler makes them better than San Diego and Colorado. Their pitching is excellent.

Wild-Card: Florida. Like Baltimore last year, too much talent to miss the postseason.

World Series

Atlanta over Cleveland in seven games. Two deep, well-rounded teams should wage a classic battle. Atlanta's Cy Young hurlers have experienced Game Seven's in the past, so the Braves get the nod.

Awards

MVP

A.L.: **Ken Griffey Jr., Seattle**. Thomas won't win it; he plays with Belle. Belle won't win it; he's Belle. Junior hasn't won one yet, so why not '97?

N.L.: **Gary Sheffield, Florida**. With Bobby Bonilla hitting behind him, last year's N.L. slugging percentage leader (discounting Colorado players) should put up monster numbers.

Cy Young

A.L.: **Charles Nagy, Cleveland**. Was 17-5 last year, and at 30 is still getting better.

N.L.: **Ismael Valdes, Los Angeles**. The next Greg Maddux? No pitcher threw more quality starts than Valdes last year.

<u>Rookie of the Year</u>

A.L.: **Nomar Garciaparra, Boston**. Slick-fielding shortstop continues to improve at the plate.

N.L.: **Scott Rolen, Philadelphia**. On a bad team, with no pressure (because no one in Philly cares), Rolen will have a chance to shine.

<u>Kevin Fullam</u>

American League

East:

1.) **Baltimore**. With the Yanks likely to tail off, the division is Baltimore's for the taking this season.

2.) **Toronto**. The offense isn't there, but a rotation with Clemens, Guzman, and Hentgen in it sounds *awfully* good.

3.) **New York**. If Steinbrenner thinks he can rely on guys like Duncan, Strawberry, and Rogers again, he's kidding himself.

4.) **Boston**. I like Vaughn and Jefferson, but swapping Roger Clemens for Steve Avery ain't exactly a good maneuver.

5.) **Detroit**. Thank God for the Pistons, right?

Central:

1.) **Chicago**. It's not *solely* because of the acquisition of Belle—but it sure does help.

2.) **Cleveland**. If Brian Giles develops and Matt Williams reverts to his All-Star form, things could get interesting. . .

3.) **Minnesota**. With Molitor, Knoblauch, and Cordova, they've got an outstanding offensive cornerstone, but they had them last year—and they didn't win then, either.

4.) **Milwaukee**. Please tell me the Brewers aren't still planning on slapping Chuck Carr (career OBP: .318) in the leadoff slot. . .

5.) **Kansas City**. The Royals gave Mitch Williams a spring training tryout—I'm now encouraged to pick them to finish last on general principles.

West:

1.) **Seattle**. There's just *too* much offense here to pick against them. When you add in a healthy Randy Johnson, well—there's not a stronger pennant contender in the A.L.

2.) **Texas**. What will they do without Kevin Elster's 24 HRs this year?

3.) **Oakland**. They may be injury-prone, but a McGwire-Canseco reunion will put a *lot* of runs up on the scoreboard.

4.) **California**. They'll be neck-and-neck with the A's, but there aren't enough weapons here to challenge the big boys.

Wild-Card: **Cleveland**.

National League

East:

1.) **Atlanta**. They can't afford to keep their starting rotation together too much longer. . . can they?

2.) **Florida**. It'll be close, but the "Jim Leyland Cavalry" won't be *quite* enough. Keep an eye out in '98.

3.) **Montreal**. They had all of the pieces in place two years ago, but then came the strike.

4.) **New York**. Young arms or no young arms, the Mets just don't have the talent to compete in one of baseball's toughest divisions.

5.) **Philadelphia**. Still waiting for the return of Lenny Dykstra and Darren Daulton. . . And Mike Schmidt. . . and Steve Carlton. . .

Central:

1.) **Houston**. It's about time for Bagwell and Co. to taste some postseason action.

2.) **St. Louis**. The memory of their NLCS collapse against the Braves last season still lingers.

3.) **Cincinnati**. The Reds do have talent—but if they have to count on Neon Deion again, they've got problems.

4.) **Chicago**. Sure, the Cubs finally have a decent outfield, but in two years they'll need a whole new *infield*. . .

5.) **Pittsburgh**. What do you want me to say? Kevin Elster and Dale Sveum will lead the Triple-A Pirates to the Series?

West:

1.) **Los Angeles**. All of those "Rookie of the Year" awards have to start paying off sooner or later, right?

2.) **San Francisco**. Well, they still have Bonds—and they got rid of last year's squad. That's good enough for me. . .

3.) **Colorado**. Something tells me that when Galarraga's 40, he'll *still* be slugging over .500 at Coors Field—but with about a .280 OBP.

4.) **San Diego**. With Caminiti, Joyner, Finley, and Gwynn all 32 and over, the potential collective decline here looks pretty scary.

Wild-Card: **Florida**.

World Series

Seattle over Atlanta in six games.

Awards

MVP

A.L.: **Alex Rodriguez, Seattle**

N.L.: **Mike Piazza, Los Angeles**

Cy Young

A.L.: **Randy Johnson, Seattle** (Stay healthy, Randy!)

N.L.: **Alex Fernandez, Florida**

Rookie of the Year

A.L.: **Todd Walker, Minnesota**

N.L.: **Vladimir Guerrero, Montreal**

Jim Henzler

American League

East: **Baltimore**. I respect Davey Johnson's managerial ability, and the offense should continue to percolate. Can Joe Torre defy the odds two years in a row? Not likely.

Central: **Cleveland**. Yes, they'll miss Albert Belle, but Jim Thome and Manny Ramirez are ready to prove they rank among the game's elite hitters.

West: **Seattle**. Alex Rodriguez and Ken Griffey Jr. are players for the ages. When you combine them with Jay Buhner, Edgar Martinez and a *healthy* Randy Johnson, Seattle's front-line talent is unmatched.

Wild-Card: **Chicago**. Any lineup featuring Frank Thomas and Albert Belle has to be considered dangerous. Depth in the pitching staff could haunt them.

National League

East: **Atlanta**. Baseball's best dynasty since the 1971-75 Oakland A's. Few teams could consider *not* playing Andruw Jones.

Central: **St. Louis**. I thought they overachieved in 1996, and I don't think they got any better by only growing a year older. But I'm not sure any other team in this division improved, either.

West: **Los Angeles**. Great pitching, and enough hitting to get by.

Wild-Card: **Florida**. They better reach the playoffs, or Dave Dombrowski's head will roll. With a new manager, high-priced free agents and exciting young talent, who else will take the fall if they fail?

World Series

Seattle over Florida.

Awards

MVP

A.L.: **Ken Griffey Jr., Seattle**. This generation's Hank Aaron finally reaches age 27. If we could ever expect his peak performance, this would be the year.

N.L.: **Gary Sheffield, Florida**. Sheffield was 27 last year. Didn't play too badly, either. Even if he doesn't reach last year's numbers, he should at least have more runners on base to drive in.

Cy Young

A.L.: **Scott Sanders, Seattle**. A dark-horse candidate, to be sure. His elbow could blow up anytime, too. But he wasn't abused last year, he's got terrific stuff, and the Mariners should score lots of runs for him.

N.L.: **Greg Maddux, Atlanta**. Still the game's most efficient pitcher. It'll be interesting to see how the Braves' new ballpark affects their pitching staff.

Rookie of the Year

A.L.: **Todd Walker, Minnesota**. A hitting machine with a clear shot at playing time.

N.L.: **Andruw Jones, Atlanta**. Again, playing time will be the key. He needs to improve against righties, and the Braves have other options, but *no* rookie has better tools or greater potential.

Mike Mittleman

American League

East: **New York**. The loss of John Wetteland will force super set-up man Mariano Rivera to move into the closer role, leaving somewhat of a void, but the Yankees depth should help them prevail over a much-improved Toronto team as well as the pitching-suspect Orioles.

Central: **Cleveland**. The White Sox may have stolen Albert Belle away from the Tribe to form an awesome alliance with slugger Frank Thomas, but the loss of pitcher Alex Fernandez leaves them short in their attempt to overtake the still-powerful Indians squad.

West: **Seattle**. Add a stellar rotation to perhaps the league's most potent offense and you have a sure winner in the Mariners. Starters Jeff Fassero and Scott Sanders will serve as superb complements to the Big Unit in making this the team to beat going into the postseason.

Wild-Card: Toronto.

National League

East: **Atlanta**. The Marlins signed the most free agents and have improved considerably, perhaps enough to throw a scare into the Braves. However, Atlanta's starting rotation is still the best in baseball and will ensure them another postseason appearance.

Central: **St.Louis**. The Cardinals brought in nine new players and manager Tony La Russa last year and were able to win this division. They have the best outfield in the game and a top-flight starting rotation. Closer Dennis Eckersley may be good for one more year and winning this division won't be all that hard considering the competition.

West: **Los Angeles**. The defending division champion Padres are one of the oldest teams in the league and had the benefit of some career performances last year that are not likely to be duplicated. The Dodgers have the second-best pitching staff in baseball, and with their lineup stocked with superb young talent, they should move past San Diego to capture the flag.

Wild-Card: **Florida**.

World Series

Seattle over Atlanta.

Awards

MVP

A.L.: **Ken Griffey Jr., Seattle**

N.L.: **Mike Piazza, Los Angeles**

Cy Young

A.L.: **David Cone, New York**

N.L.: **Kevin Brown, Florida**

Rookie of the Year

A.L.: **Todd Walker, Minnesota**

N.L.: **Andruw Jones, Atlanta**

Steve Moyer

American League			National League		
East:			**East**:		
Boston	93-69		Atlanta	90-72	
New York	85-77		Montreal	85-77	
Baltimore	83-79		New York	81-81	
Toronto	83-79		Florida	80-82	
Detroit	52-110		Philadelphia	75-87	
Central:			**Central**:		
Chicago	96-66		Houston	91-71	
Cleveland	86-76		St. Louis	83-79	
Milwaukee	78-84		Cincinnati	82-80	
Minnesota	78-84		Chicago	75-87	
Kansas City	76-86		Pittsburgh	51-111	
West:			**West**:		
Seattle	92-70		Los Angeles	94-68	
Texas	82-80		San Diego	88-74	
Oakland	81-81		Colorado	87-75	
Anaheim	69-93		San Francisco	72-90	

Boston wins the A.L. by clubbing everyone over the head and getting just enough pitching. The **LA Dodgers** take the N.L. The Red Sox win it all. If Dan Duquette gets fired, *bet on* the White Sox.

Awards

MVP

A.L.: **Frank Thomas, Chicago**

N.L.: **Mike Piazza, Los Angeles**

Cy Young

A.L.: **Heathcliff Slocumb, Boston**

N.L.: **Hideo Nomo, Los Angeles**

Rookie of the Year

A.L.: **Frank Catalanotto, Oakland**

N.L.: **Andruw Jones, Atlanta**

Tony Nistler

American League

East: **Baltimore**. Jimmy Key for David Wells is not a bad trade-off, and Eric Davis proved last season that he still has plenty left in the tank. If Cal Ripken's move to third goes off without a hitch, this team has the offense to make big winners out of Key, Mike Mussina and, yes, even Scott Erickson. Brady Anderson won't hit 50 again, but he shouldn't need to to beat out the Yankees.

Central: **Chicago**. With a 3-4-5-6 combination capable of driving in 400-450 runs, Chicago simply has too many bats to pitch around. The South Siders' starting staff doesn't go as deep as Cleveland's does, but Matt Williams and Jim Thome can't match the production of Albert Belle and Frank Thomas. The Twins made a few moves to keep them interesting, but Terry Steinbach and Bob Tewksbury aren't enough.

West: **Seattle**. Quality left-handed pitchers are worth their weight in gold, and the Mariners are filthy rich. Lou Piniella can begin with the starting lefty trio of Randy Johnson, Jeff Fassero and Jamie Moyer and end with lefty closer Norm Charlton. Couple all that wealth with perhaps the most potent offensive lineup in the game today, and you have the makings of a club that *should* lead from wire to wire.

Wild-Card: **Cleveland**. Belle is out, but let's not forget about Williams, Thome, Kenny Lofton, Manny Ramirez, Julio Franco, Sandy Alomar. . . or John Hart and Mike Hargrove.

National League

East: **Atlanta**. The vault opened in Florida, but the Braves aren't buying all the hype. Watching Chipper Jones, Ryan Klesko, Jermaine Dye, Javy Lopez and Andruw Jones on the same field together for an entire year promises to be a treat. . . unless your name is H. Wayne Huizenga.

Central: **St. Louis**. Certainly a big part of the Cards' chances for a repeat performance in the N.L. Central hinge on the 42-year-old arm and elbow of Dennis Eckersley. The starting rotation has some youth, however, and if Ray Lankford can bounce back from rotator cuff surgery when he returns to the lineup in May (the Cards hope it may be even sooner than that), he joins Ron Gant and Brian Jordan to form a very solid trio patrolling the outfield grass. The Astros are always an intriguing offense, but the middle relief just isn't there. Besides, a pennant is a lot to ask from a first-year manager.

West: **Los Angeles**. STATS projects the starting rotation of Hideo Nomo, Ramon Martinez, Ismael Valdes, Pedro Astacio and Tom Candiotti to post a combined 70 wins. With any kind of help from the relief corps, 90 wins should be well within reach. That will be enough to take home the N.L. West pennant. Unless, of course, the Rockies learn to win on the road.

Wild-Card: **Florida**. The magic number could be 89 for the Marlins in 1997. . . one win for each million the fish shelled out in the offseason.

World Series

> **Atlanta** over Seattle

Awards

> ### MVP
>
> **A.L.: Ken Griffey Jr., Seattle**
>
> **N.L.: Chipper Jones, Atlanta**
>
> ### Cy Young
>
> **A.L.: Mike Mussina, Baltimore**
>
> **N.L.: Hideo Nomo, Los Angeles**
>
> ### Rookie of the Year
>
> **A.L.: Nomar Garciaparra, Boston**
>
> **N.L.: Andruw Jones, Atlanta**

Mat Olkin

American League

East: **Baltimore**. The Orioles are the best of a surprisingly weak division. They aren't nearly as powerful as last year, and Bordick's an offensive zero, but Benitez contributes a surprisingly solid year out of the pen. Ripken plays third without complaint.

Toronto and Clemens are both underwhelming. Cito Gaston investigates the possibility of changing his facial expression.

Mariano Rivera blows a lot of leads early in the year, and the Yanks' pitching is in shambles by year's end. Yankees fans decide that Joe Torre is a lousy manager and clamor for the return of Buck Showalter.

Central: **Cleveland**. With the deepest bullpen in baseball, the Indians edge the White Sox without a single starting pitcher winning more than 15 games. Brian Giles has a super year in LF, minimizing the impact of Belle's defection. Paul Shuey takes over as the closer.

The White Sox miss Alex Fernandez. Jaime Navarro is a disappointment, and a fifth starter still can't be found. Belle helps, but the team looks too much like the '96 Orioles.

West: **Seattle**. The Mariners become the best team in the league and win the division by 10 games. Johnson and Fassero each win 19 games. Jose Cruz Jr. quietly puts together a good year after his recall in May.

Injuries finally hit the Rangers. Benji Gil doesn't look any better the second time around. There are no youngsters to step in when the regulars go down.

Wild-Card: **Chicago**. The White Sox edge the Yankees and Red Sox before being quickly eliminated in the playoffs. After the last game, the reporters think of Belle and Navarro, and decide to skip post-game interviews. Instead, they just make up the quotes. No one complains.

National League

East: **Atlanta**. The Marlins are good, but not quite good enough. The Braves, with something to prove, play like they did in '95. Maddux reclaims his title as the game's best pitcher. Chipper Jones gets even better.

Once again, the Expos aren't as bad as everyone expected. Ugueth Urbina emerges as a star out of the bullpen. Vlad Guerrero bats .317 in 400 at-bats.

Bobby Valentine tears his rotator cuff. The Mets concede that he wasn't as good a manager as they'd thought.

Central: **Houston**. The Astros and Cardinals fight for the division title while struggling to stay above .500. On the final day of the season, they are tied, each one game over .500. The Cardinals go with Andy Benes on three days' rest, while the Astros pull Billy Wagner out of the bullpen to make his first major league start. St. Louis loses, and Houston emerges victorious.

The Pirates are bad. The Cubs are worse.

West: **Los Angeles**. The Padres have a great bullpen, but the Dodgers have the best starting rotation West of Atlanta, and LA wins by eight games. Caminiti doesn't start hitting until July.

Wild-Card: **Florida**. The Marlins easily outdistance the Expos and Padres but are swept in the first round of the playoffs. There is much finger-pointing afterward. Bobby Bonilla vows he'll never play third base again. Gary Sheffield demands to be traded. Jim Leyland wishes for the good old days with Pittsburgh and Bonds.

World Series

Seattle over Atlanta in seven. Randy Johnson loses the opener to Greg Maddux but rebounds to win Games 4 & 7.

Awards

MVP

A.L.: **Ken Griffey Jr., Seattle**. Last year some writers wanted to give him the award over Alex Rodriguez. This year Junior stays healthy, Juan Gonzalez doesn't, and the writers finally get to vote for who they want.

N.L.: Mike Piazza, Los Angeles. A one-man offense for the pennant-winning Dodgers.

Cy Young

A.L.: Kevin Appier, Kansas City. The Royals' hurler finally gets some runs.

N.L.: Ismael Valdes, Los Angeles. The Braves' stranglehold on the award is broken. Maddux has better stats, but writers are tired of voting for him.

Rookie of the Year

A.L.: Nomar Garciaparra, Boston. Edging out Todd Walker, the Red Sox' infielder claims the honors.

N.L.: Vlad Guerrero, Montreal. The Expos' slugger is the best of a strong field. Andruw Jones might have won if the Braves hadn't taken so long to deal David Justice. Scott Rolen hits for a good average and leads the league in doubles, but people expected more than 12 homers. Kevin Orie overcomes an early slump to prove that he is *not* the next Gary Scott.

Don Zminda

American League

East: **Baltimore**. The Yankees will be competitive, but I think Davey Johnson and his boys will get it done this time.

Central: **Chicago**. The Indians *could* win again, but I think the loss of Albert Belle will be too much to overcome.

West: **Seattle**. Very strong team, especially if Randy Johnson makes it all the way back. Griffey could hit 62.

Wild-Card: **Cleveland**. They'll be good, and Brian Giles will be one of the league's best rookies. But they won't be good enough.

National League

East: **Atlanta**. How can you not pick the best-managed team in baseball (including the front office)?

Central: **St. Louis**. They're old in some vulnerable places, like the bullpen, but I think they'll have enough to win this weak division.

West: **Los Angeles**. No Rookie of the Year this time, but nobody in the West can stop them.

Wild-Card: **Florida**. They won't be as good as some people think, but they should be good enough to make the playoffs.

World Series

Seattle over Los Angeles in six.

Awards

MVP

A.L.: Ken Griffey Jr., Seattle

N.L.: Mike Piazza, Los Angeles

Cy Young

A.L.: Mike Mussina, Baltimore

N.L.: Ismael Valdes, Los Angeles

Rookie of the Year

A.L.: Todd Walker, Minnesota

N.L.: Vladimir Guerrero, Montreal

STATS' Consensus Picks

American League

       East: Baltimore

       Central: Chicago

       West: Seattle

       Wild-Card: Cleveland

National League

       East: Atlanta

       Central: St. Louis

       West: Los Angeles

       Wild-Card: Florida

World Series

       Seattle over Atlanta

Awards

       MVP

       A.L.: Ken Griffey Jr., Seattle

       N.L.: Mike Piazza, Los Angeles

       Cy Young

       A.L.: Mike Mussina, Baltimore

       N.L.: Ismael Valdes, Los Angeles

       Rookie of the Year

       A.L.: Todd Walker, Minnesota

       N.L.: Andruw Jones, Atlanta

Our Favorite Games

Mike Mittleman

Game 3, 1964 World Series

Author David Halberstam wrote a superb book published last year entitled *October 1964*. The book chronicled this remarkable year, the last season of what had been one the longest dynasties held by any team in professional sports—the New York Yankees. Decade after decade going back to the 1920s right up until this period, the Bronx Bombers were the standard of excellence. In 1964, the Yankees were coming off a World Series defeat to the Dodgers in 1963 facing the upstart St. Louis Cardinals in what would turn out to be the end of an era.

As a life-long Yankee die-hard and idolizer of the Mick and his teammates, I had the opportunity to attend Game 3 at Yankee Stadium that year. A 13-year-old baseball fanatic living in New England among throngs of Red Sox fans and Yankee haters had to be there to witness what had become so dear to my life: a chance to see Number 7 up close and in the World Series. It was not my first time. Two years earlier, I attended a game in the Giants-Yankees 1962 series—my first visit to the House That Ruth Built. However, Mickey Mantle did not hit a home run for me that day. In fact, in all the times I went to regular season games when the Yankees invaded Fenway Park, Mantle never launched one into the grandstands. This left me unfulfilled and wanting of a lasting memory. After all, my brother would constantly boast about how he had attended Don Larsen's perfect game in the 1956 World Series.

I recall Jim Bouton, whose cap flew off with almost every pitch, starting for New York and battling against tough southpaw Curt Simmons. The series was tied 1-1 heading into the game and everyone figured this one to be tight and low scoring. The Yankees scored first when Clete Boyer doubled down the line sending Elston Howard home in the second inning. However, the Yankees had trouble getting to Simmons after that while St. Louis came up with a run in the fifth to tie the score.

Heading into the bottom of the ninth, Cardinals manager Johny Keane summoned knuckleballer Barney Schultz to come in and work his magic. Schultz would be facing Mickey Mantle to lead off the inning. After taking several warm-up pitches, Schultz paused to look over his defense while Mantle stepped into the left-handed hitters' box. Schultz let go of the first one and with a thunderous crack heard for what seemed like several seconds, Mantle hit a tape measure shot into the third deck in right field. The home run was glorious and dramatic. It not only won the game, but it was Mantle's 16th career World Series home run, breaking Babe Ruth's record.

The Yankees lost the World Series in seven games that year, and it was devastating. However, the memory of seeing my idol perform such a magnificent feat in such a glorious occasion will always be my favorite baseball experience and the game I most remember.

Jim Henzler

Two Cardinals Games from 1967

One bright morning during the summer of 1967, my father ignited a spark. Though the spark wasn't the type which fuels flames, it did kindle a passion within me which remains to this day. Ask him about the incident, and my dad probably wouldn't have the foggiest recollection of it. And yet the episode remains etched in my mind with the clarity of a six-year-old's perspective.

The incident was rather ordinary, really. I'm not sure why it has stuck with me all these years. But it has. On that particular morning my dad stopped me as I was headed out the door to play. He referred me to one specific section on the sports page of the *St. Louis Post-Dispatch*—the major league standings. And for some reason, those standings absolutely captivated me.

Perhaps some background might be helpful. 1967 was a special year for St. Louis baseball fans. The Cardinals had gotten off to a strong start, winning their first six games of the season. They continued to play well through the first couple months, though Cincinnati actually led the National League for all of May and the first half of June. When the Reds began to fade, the Cubs succeeded them as Cardinal challengers. By July 15, the Redbirds had mustered a three-and-a-half game lead over the Cubbies as Bob Gibson toed the rubber against Pittsburgh. But a vicious Roberto Clemente line drive cracked Gibson's leg, and threatened St. Louis' pennant chances.

Without their staff ace, the Cardinals dropped seven of their next 12 games and fell into a first-place tie with Chicago. Now *that* was a surprise. Those pesky Cubs had finished in *last* place only the year before, behind the likes of the expansion Astros and Mets. The Cubs weren't *supposed* to be contenders in 1967. But there they were, in a flat-footed tie with the Cardinals on July 24. Unfortunately for the Cubs, however, they immediately commenced what would become a patented midsummer swoon, losing 13 of their next 16. Their season, in effect, was over. The Cardinals, meanwhile, had shifted into overdrive. Just one month later, on August 24, the Cardinals had won 21 of 28 and extended their lead to a whopping *11-1/2* games over Cincinnati.

I'm guessing that sometime during this period (as a six year old, I had no real concept of dates), my father proudly showed me those National League standings, with St. Louis assuming a commanding position atop the list. And something just clicked. I may not have understood dates, but I did know my geography (something else my dad taught me) and I did know where I lived. It was just *neat* to see my city ranked ahead of all those other places I knew. Combined with an already growing fascination over the game itself, those standings just enchanted me. I'll never forget that feeling. I had a sense of the community of baseball fans in those other cities, fans who could only look with envy upon the fans of St. Louis, of which I was included.

Also in the midst of this Cardinals' surge, my mom and dad took my brother, sister and me to the very first game I can remember. Thanks to the STATS database, I can now pinpoint the exact date—August 10, 1967. The new Busch Stadium was only a year old, and the Cardinals were facing San Francisco. On the walk through the parking lot toward the stadium, I was talking about Giant outfielder Jesus Alou, whose baseball card was one of the first I owned. Alou's name, as we all know, is pronounced "Hay-zoos." But as a youngster whose reading skills were only developing, I pronounced his name as it appeared phonetically on the card—"Jee-sus." "No," my mother advised, "we only pronounce one person's name like *that*."

The seats we had were in the upper deck of right field—"Up in heaven," my mom said. Only one foul ball even came close to our section, and that was more than 20 feet away. If memory serves me, Willie Mays connected for a first-inning single—a line drive to center—the first hit I can remember seeing in person. Later, Lou Brock made a sensational diving catch after racing toward the left-center field gap. Over the radio, Cardinal broadcaster Harry Caray called the catch the best he had seen all season. (Memo to Cub fans: In my heart, I'd still like to believe that when St. Peter escorts Harry through the Pearly Gates, and God asks him to select under which team he wishes to be admitted, Harry will choose. . . the St. Louis Cardinals! You just don't take the Birds off the chest that easily, even 30 years later.) The Giants grabbed the lead, and the Cardinals mounted a late rally. St. Louis got a couple runners on, only to have Alex Johnson commit a baserunning blunder. Somehow, Johnson had ended up on third base. The problem was, another Redbird was already stationed there. "Stupid Alex Johnson," my dad muttered, and the Cardinal comeback expired.

The Cardinals eventually lost the game, 5-2, as Mike McCormick bested Ray Washburn. McCormick would go on to win the National League Cy Young Award with a 22-10 record and an ERA of 2.85. Had Gibson not been injured, it may have been a different story. Gibby did return to win three of four decisions down the stretch, including the 5-1 victory over the Phillies on September 18 which clinched the pennant for St. Louis.

It seemed as though my beloved Cardinals were destined to win it all. That feeling only intensified when they grabbed a 3-1 lead over Boston after four games of the World Series. Gibson had won Games 1 and 4, and it appeared there was no way the Red Sox could come back. That, sadly, was the foolish confidence of youth. As the Cardinals proved in 1968, 1985 and, painfully, once again in 1996, no series lead of three-games-to-one is ever safe—at least not when they're involved. Jim Lonborg stifled the Cardinal bats for his second series win in Game 5. Boston then exploded for three homers in an 8-4 Game 6 spanking.

Fortunately, I did some exploding of my own. I got sick during the afternoon of that Game 6 defeat—all over the floor of my second-grade classroom. My mom picked me up in the nurse's office, and I headed home with a case of the flu. My timing had been exquisite! I'd be able to watch the series finale at home the following afternoon. Game 7. Gibson versus Lonborg. Why can't all illnesses result in such serendipity?

The game itself was almost one-sided. Lonborg was pitching on only two days rest, and laboring. The Cardinals finally solved him with two runs in the third inning. Right around the time my mom prepared the chicken soup, Gibson, one of the best-hitting pitchers of that era, took matters into his own hands with a solo homer in the fifth. An inning later, Julian Javier's three-run clout extended the lead to 7-1. Game over. No way Gibson would blow that. When George Scott struck out swinging to end the game, Gibson had posted his fifth straight complete-game World Series victory dating back to 1964. His 1967 series stats rival any pitching performance in World Series history—27 innings, 14 hits, 26 strikeouts, 3-0 record, 1.00 ERA. Christy Mathewson's three shutouts in 1905 might be the only comparable performance.

While I'm sure I'd be a baseball fan today had the Cardinals not excelled in '67, the World Championship certainly didn't hurt. It also helped to have a dad who respected and enjoyed the game, and who cared enough to pass that appreciation on to his son. I want to thank him now for that gift. I'm reminded of the value of that gift every time I watch a game. Or check out the standings.

Ethan D. Cooperson

Game 4, 1980 NLCS

Phillies' reliever Tug McGraw called the game "a motorcycle ride through an art museum. . . you see all the pictures but afterwards you have no idea what you just saw."

One writer noted that the Houston Astrodome was dubbed the "eighth wonder of the world," and that the game it hosted on Saturday afternoon, October 11, 1980—Game 4 of the NLCS, Philadelphia vs. Houston—was the ninth wonder of the world.

Even Bill Virdon, stone-faced manager of the Astros, noted that, "Not a lot of things were new out there today. They just never happened in the same game before."

How odd was this game? First of all, consider the starting lineup the Phillies used with their backs to the wall: Mike Schmidt (48 homers, .624 slugging percentage in 1980) hitting third, with Bake McBride (9 homers, .453 slugging percentage in '80) batting cleanup. Greg Luzinski, the Phils' cleanup hitter of the last five years and the home-run hero of Game 1, was benched in favor of Lonnie Smith. *Rookie* Lonnie Smith.

For Phillies manager Dallas Green, whose club had lost consecutive extra-inning games to fall into a 2-1 hole, it was time to get desperate. In fact, the whole 1980 season represented something of a last chance for the team. After NLCS losses in 1976, '77 and '78, the sense was that Philadelphia *had* to take the next step in '80. But Houston, the confident new kid on the block, appeared to have things going its way. They had dealt the Phillies two gut-wrenching losses, and, despite having played a one-game playoff to win the West Division crown earlier that week, they could send a rested pitcher to the hill for Game 4. Vern Ruhle, who would take part in one of baseball's all-time weirdest plays, got Virdon's nod to pitch for the pennant.

For Philadelphia, their hopes rested with the left arm of Steve Carlton. If anyone could keep them alive in the series, surely Carlton—he of the 24 wins and 2.34 ERA in 1980—would be the one to do it. Carlton would be working on just three days' rest, but as the Phillies' Pete Rose said optimistically in the rubble of his team's Game 3 defeat, "They have to beat the best pitcher in the world tomorrow to win the pennant."

At a fever pitch long before the game, the Astrodome capacity crowd of 44,952 was even more charged following the pre-game appearance of Houston pitcher J.R. Richard, whose brilliant career had been short-circuited by a stroke midway through the '80 season. Still harboring hopes for a comeback the following season, Richard threw out the first pitch as the crowd roared its approval.

Through the early innings, however, Carlton kept that crowd silent. "Lefty" allowed the Astros just one baserunner through three innings, on a second-inning double by Art Howe, whom he stranded at second. The Phillies, meanwhile, had early chances against Ruhle. Garry Maddox struck out with a runner at third and one out in the second, and Mike Schmidt was retired with two on and two out in third, keeping the game scoreless. Schmidt's pop-up to first base left him 3-for-17 in the series, and ran the Phils' left-on-base count to 33. But none of that frustration would approach the *exasperation* that befell the Phillies—and all of the Delaware Valley—in the top of the fourth.

Bake McBride started the inning by punching an 0-2 pitch to left for a base hit. Manny Trillo then shot a grounder past Houston third baseman Enos Cabell for a single, putting runners at first and second with no outs. Maddox, who found himself in the middle of several critical plays in the series, was the next hitter, and after fouling off a bunt, found himself down in the count, 1-2. Ruhle came inside with a fastball and jammed Maddox, who sent a semi-line drive in the direction of the mound; what resulted was probably the most bizarre play in the Phillies' 98-year history. Ruhle reached down to field the ball, apparently scooped it up on a short hop, and threw to first to retire Maddox. Trillo and McBride advanced to second and third, as first baseman Howe walked the ball to the mound—until he saw his teammates gesturing wildly. First base umpire Ed Vargo had signaled that Ruhle actually *caught the ball*; with McBride already at third, Howe simply needed to throw to second and the Astros would have a *triple play*. Howe ran to the bag himself, as home plate umpire Doug Harvey conferred briefly with Vargo: Triple play!

Led by Green, the Phillies shot from the dugout to protest. With the inning (theoretically) over, Houston left the field as Harvey and the base umpires assembled in an impromptu conference. Writers began scrambling to look up the history of triple plays in LCS play (there had never been one). On Phillies radio, analyst Tim McCarver's "No, no, no!" drowned out play-by-play voice Harry Kalas, as soon as the triple play became apparent. But wait: Harvey broke from his meeting with the other umpires, and headed towards the first-base box seats, to confer with league President Chub Feeney. From Feeney's box, Harvey's next stop was Astros' skipper Virdon, and Virdon wasn't happy with what the umpire had to tell him. Suddenly the Astros were hopping mad, and it appeared the play had been overruled. Then Harvey advised Green of the decision, and the Phillies were none too pleased, either.

Somehow, the men in blue and the men in suits had decided on a sort of "compromise," where two outs were recorded. The play clearly should have counted for either one out or for three, and two outs seemed like the best way to split the difference. The official explanation, posted on the Astrodome scoreboard, went, "The play was ruled a catch and a double play. However time was called prior to the third out. Runner remains at second base." Of course, the runner hadn't remained at second base. . . it was one of the rare on-field decisions in baseball history that left *both* teams upset. Both sides immediately protested the game, even though, in reality, the league office had already made its ruling. On Philadelphia television, straightlaced Andy Musser called the double play "the season's most unusual play." Responded Richie Ashburn, "How about the *career* most unusual play?"

With the cloud of two protests hanging over it, the game continued, and it quickly went downhill for Philadelphia. The score was still 0-0, but now the Phillies had to feel that not only were their bats in a slumber, but fate was against them. Whereas Green had vented his frustrations at Harvey ("No bleepin' way"), Phillies fans had to feel more of a sense of despair, that it wasn't meant to be, maybe not in 1980 and maybe not ever. On the first pitch after the 14-minute delay, Larry Bowa grounded out, ending the controversial rally-that-wasn't.

Philadelphia fans also had to know that Carlton, their ace, was never the same pitcher after a rain delay. After the closest thing to a rain delay the 'Dome had to offer, Lefty wasn't sharp. And neither was his left fielder, the defensively challenged Lonnie Smith. Enos Cabell led off the bottom of the fourth with a deep drive to left that Smith backpedaled on—then appeared to lose altogether. The ball didn't even reach the fence on the fly, but Cabell got a double out of it, then moved to third on a Joe Morgan ground out. Gary Woods then walked, setting up another Smith adventure. Art Howe hit the second hard shot of the inning to left. This time the rookie caught the ball two steps from the warning track, as Cabell tagged and scored easily. Woods, the runner at first, made an aggressive play and broke for second, as Smith attempted to throw, *only to have the ball slip out of his hand and roll away.* Woods kept going around second as Smith chased the ball down, some 20 feet from where he had made the catch. And then he picked it up and threw Woods out at third base. A 7-5 sacrifice fly double play, where the outfielder throws the ball into the turf, then picks it up and throws out the runner. From the playground to the NLCS. . .

In the fifth the Astros tacked on another run, in a slightly more conventional fashion—but one no less distressing for Phillies fans. Hall of Famer Carlton gave up a booming triple to Luis Pujols (career .193 hitter) and an RBI single by Rafael Landestoy (career .237 average) through a drawn-in infield. The score was now 2-0, as the league office issued a release explaining the umpires' decision on the disputed double play, and announced that a post-game meeting would be held to rule on the protests. On Phillies' radio, McCarver pointed out that if the Astros won, they would have to hold a dry celebration until a decision was made on the protest. Down two runs, with their bats silent, the Phillies seemed to have only the slim chance that their protest would be upheld.

With Ruhle continuing to shut Philadelphia down, Carlton continued to struggle in the sixth. He walked Morgan, who was then forced at second by Woods. Lefty then walked Howe on four pitches—the last ball intentional after Woods stole second—and walked Jose Cruz unintentionally. At that point, Carlton, who had allowed one hit and no walks through the first three frames, had been touched for three hits and five walks in 2.1 innings after the fourth-inning rhubarb. The Phillies' ace was finished. With Pujols to bat with the bases loaded and just one out, Green turned to 24-year old righthander Dickie Noles. A hit would break the game open, but Noles induced Pujols to loft a medium-distance fly to right. McBride made the catch as the ever-aggressive Astros daringly sent Woods from third. A good gamble, it appeared, as Bake's throw was well up the first base line, allowing the run to score, and the other runners to advance to second and third. But little was as it appeared in this contest. The Phillies screamed immediately that Woods had left too soon. Noles stepped off the rubber and lobbed the ball to Schmidt, who didn't seem to think the Phillies' appeal would be upheld. But Schmidt trotted to the third base bag. . . and umpire Bob Engel went up with the right arm. Woods had been nailed for leaving too soon; the run did not count.

Had the umpires given one back to the Phillies, a sort of make-up after the earlier decision? Perhaps. Philadelphia owner Ruly Carpenter would later say it was "the only play [the umpires] got right" in the series. But at the time, for the Phillies and their fans, it didn't seem to matter very much. Taking away Houston's apparent third run seemed like little more than giving a man a final cigarette before he would be executed. The Phillies went down in order in the seventh. Beginning with Maddox' controversial at-bat in the fourth, Ruhle had now retired 11 of the last 12 hitters to face him, and Philadelphia was now working on 20.1 innings without scoring a run. In the last of the seventh, Houston again threatened to break the game open, again loading the bases on walks. Noles departed after passing Terry Puhl and Cabell with two outs, and Kevin Saucier walked Morgan on four pitches—the eighth walk allowed by Phils' pitching! But veteran Ron Reed came out of the pen to face Denny Walling, pinch-hitting for the embattled Woods, and induced a grounder to first base. The 3-1 putout kept Houston's lead at 2-0.

With the Astros unable to build on their lead, the 'Dome, as described by ABC-TV's Keith Jackson, became quiet, as the Astro faithful seemed to be waiting to explode. But, six outs away from the National League flag, their anticipation would turn to tension. Greg Gross led off the Phillies' eighth, and on a 1-1 pitch—just the 87th pitch by Ruhle on the day—Gross grounded a sharp single up the middle. Smith was the next hitter, and this at-bat was his chance at redemption for his defensive snafu. On a 1-2 pitch, Smith hit a grounder that normally would have been fielded by third baseman Cabell—but with Houston in a late-inning, guard-the-line defense, the ball went through. Just like in the fourth inning, the Phillies had runners at first and second with no outs. Rose was the next hitter, with Schmidt on deck. With the tying run at first base, Green called for a bunt—which Rose failed to execute. He fouled off one attempt, then pulled the bat back and took a called strike. But with the count 1-2, Charlie Hustle hit a bouncer to the right side. Smith stopped in the basepath to let the ball bounce past him, and past a diving Morgan, into right field for a hit, scoring Gross. From virtually a dead stop, Smith took off, not hesitating around second. Jeffrey Leonard, who had taken over in right field for Woods, thought Smith would be an easy out, and fired the ball to third—much too late. Seeing the play in front of him, Rose sped around first and easily beat Cabell's throw to second. A seeing-eye bouncer to the right side had turned into the equivalent of an RBI double. Now the score was 2-1, with runners at second and third, no outs. After 95 pitches, Ruhle was finished.

Now the pressure was on Houston, as Virdon brought in rookie righty Dave Smith to face Schmidt. Schmidt would finish the NLCS with just a .208 average, but in this at-bat he would make his two most important contributions of the series. After falling behind 0-2, Schmidt just got a piece of a Smith breaking ball—and fouled it at the plate, off the ankle of catcher Pujols. After hobbling around the plate, taking treatment from Houston trainers and hobbling a little more, Pujols decided he couldn't continue. Quite a problem for the Astros: Pujols was in the lineup only because their regular catcher, Alan Ashby, had suffered a rib injury. Now, Virdon was forced to use third-string catcher Bruce Bochy, who had played all of 22 games during the regular season. The change would later prove significant.

Schmidt battled Smith to a 3-2 count, then topped a grounder behind second base. Smith scored to tie the game, with Rose heading for third. Morgan fielded the ball, and inexplicably took a long look at Rose—so long that Morgan, playing with a sore arm, never had a chance to throw to first to get Schmidt. The consummate professional, Morgan had made a serious error in judgment, and not gotten an out on the play. Virdon changed pitchers again, this time turning to lefty Joe Sambito to face the left-handed McBride. As Sambito took his warm-up tosses, ABC's Cosell reminded viewers that they were "witness to one of the most wildly improbable games in recent baseball history."

More was still to come. Sambito fanned McBride with some nasty breaking pitches for the inning's first out. Manny Trillo then became the fifth straight hitter to fall behind in the count, but on a 1-2 pitch he sent a low liner to right field. Leonard came in, and much like Ruhle four innings earlier, either caught or trapped the ball. Right field ump Bruce Froemming signaled a catch, as Rose tagged and scored the go-ahead run ahead of Leonard's throw. But Schmidt, the runner at first, was sure the ball was trapped; he was standing on second, without ever having tagged up. The result: an incredulous Schmidt was easily doubled off first, but the run counted; Rose had scored before the out on Schmidt was recorded. Television replays seemed to show the ball had been trapped, but the play stood as the fourth double play in the game, the third started by an outfielder. But now Philadelphia was six outs away from forcing a Game 5.

With bullpen ace McGraw having pitched three innings the day before, Green went to Warren Brusstar to pitch the eighth. After Brusstar set Houston down 1-2-3 on just six pitches, Green let him bat in the top of the ninth, and try to close out the Astros with the Phillies still leading, 3-2. But Brusstar opened the last of the ninth by walking the light-hitting Landestoy, running the Phils' staff total to nine free passes on the day. Needing a bunt with his pitcher Sambito coming up, Virdon then turned to. . . *pitcher Sambito* to bat for himself. Sambito had a total of one sacrifice in five major league seasons, but in the crucible of the LCS he bounced the bunt in front of the plate, successfully moving Landestoy to second. How could Virdon have known? When the next hitter, Terry Puhl, lined a hit to right, Landestoy scored easily to tie the game, and the Astrodome erupted. Now the winning run was at first. Cabell was the hitter, with the dangerous Morgan on deck. Dallas Green came to the mound, most likely to call for his tired ace, McGraw. But just as Virdon had stuck with Sambito, Green left Brusstar in to face Cabell. Surely he would switch to McGraw for the left-handed Morgan—but the point became moot. Puhl took off with the 2-2 pitch, which Cabell lofted routinely to right field. Puhl never saw the ball until too late. McBride made the catch and easily doubled him off first. It was, incredibly, the fourth double play started by an outfielder in the game.

For the third straight game, the Phillies and Astros had played nine innings without reaching a conclusion. Where was the pressure now? Each team had to feel lucky to still be in the game, yet exasperated at having not already won. And each club was still fuming over umpiring decisions. For the Phillies faithful, the situation was nothing new. Their heroes had been eliminated from the 1976 and '78 NLCS's on sudden-death defeats, and had lost a critical ninth-inning heartbreaker in the '77 LCS. Would it be that surprising if it happened again?

Now in his third inning, Sambito fanned Del Unser to open the 10th. But Rose rapped a single up the middle, bringing Schmidt to the plate with the go-ahead run on first. Sambito fell behind Schmidt, 3-0, then delivered a pitch that appeared well outside—but was called strike one. Schmidt eventually flied out on a 3-2 pitch, and apparently took some ribbing from the Houston dugout. The frustrated slugger gestured towards the Astro bench, and was still shouting into the Houston dugout after reaching the Phillies' bench. Now, with two outs, Dallas Green had another decision to make. Rather than letting McBride face Sambito, who had fanned him in the eighth, Green opted for his other frustrated slugger, the benched Luzinski. "The Bull" had hit 129 homers between 1975 and '78, but had absorbed the wrath of the Phillie faithful during subpar 1979 and 1980 seasons. Here was his chance at redemption. With the count 1-0, Sambito left a fastball up, and Luzinski crushed a liner to the left field corner. Extra bases, but. . . the ball hit the fence on one hop, and caromed directly to left fielder Jose Cruz, who fired to shortstop Landestoy. The cutoff man had to take the ball on a short hop, and although he had a little trouble digging the ball out of his glove, Landestoy turned to throw home as Rose was just rounding third. The ball beat Rose to the plate, but it short-hopped Bochy. With all of 118 major league games behind the plate, the Astros' third-string receiver—in the game only because of the Ashby and Pujols injuries—did not step up to catch the throw in the air, even though he would have had time to come back and make the tag. The ball bounced away and into the runner's path, and as Bochy tried to retrieve the ball he was met by the left forearm of Rose ("I went in any way I could"), smacking him in the mouth. The Phillies again led, 4-3. Manny Trillo followed with a gapper to left-center, and the lead was two runs.

With much of the immediate pressure lifted, Green went to McGraw to close the door in the bottom of the 10th. Morgan struck out looking. Leonard flied to right. Howe sent a fly to short center, where Maddox jogged in and made the catch. Phillies 5, Astros 3, 10 innings.

278

McGraw launched into a series of jubilant karate-chop kicks on the mound, as the Phillies poured from the dugout. The incredulous Astros scratched their heads.

EPILOGUE

Of course the Phillies withdrew their protest immediately after the game, and the National League rejected Houston's protest: Philadelphia had not scored a run in the controversial fourth inning. Doug Harvey would ultimately retire as one of the most respected umpires in National League history. But on October 11, 1980. . . let's just say that Harvey & Co. met their match.

Most baseball fans with a good sense of history know what happened the next day. The Phillies and Astros went extra innings for an incredible fourth straight game. Many fans know that Game 5 was in its own right an all-time classic, the Phillies coming back despite trailing, 5-2, with Nolan Ryan on the mound in the eighth inning. Many fans will know that Houston's Terry Puhl went 4-for-6 in Game 5 to finish the series an amazing 10-for-19, but that Garry Maddox doubled in the winning run as the Phillies prevailed, 8-7, in 10. And of course the Phillies went on to their only World Series triumph by sneaking past the Kansas City Royals in six games. But ask any Philadelphia fan, ask any baseball-conscious person who lived in the Delaware Valley in 1980, what was *the* classic game of the postseason, and their reaction will tell you all about the elation, the frustration and of course the amazement of "Game Four in Houston."

Tony Nistler

Game 4, 1984 NLCS

Some baseball fans find their one true love and never stray: one player and one team who capture their heart for a lifetime. Not me. Baseball heroes and team allegiances have come and gone in my life. Fickle? Maybe.

But no less passionate.

In the late 1980s and early '90s, it was the Twins and Kirby Puckett. In the mid-'80s, the Mets of Dwight Gooden and Darryl Strawberry garnered my affections. But in 1984, my heart was with the San Diego Padres and my hero was Steve Garvey. Boy, was I in for a treat.

With a Padre banner—the one with the jolly, bat-swinging priest—tacked to my bedroom wall and nearly the entire Garvey baseball card collection displayed on my dresser, I followed San Diego while it waded through a mediocre 1983 effort and then through a wonderful '84 campaign that saw the Pads capture the National League West flag, earning the right to face the Chicago Cubs in the NLCS. However, my favorite first sacker had hit only eight home runs the entire '84 season entering the LCS—his lowest total in 11 years. In fact, he had done little at the plate in the final month and a half of the regular season, and in the first two games in Chicago, "Senator" and the rest of the Padre bats were virtually lifeless. The team quickly found itself down two games to none in the best-of-five series.

That's when they headed home. Buoyed by a surprisingly triumphant welcome by the San Diego fans, the Pads came alive in Game 3, and with a win, set the stage for what then-Padre manager Dick Williams would later refer to in his autobiography *No More Mr. Nice Guy* (Harcourt Brace Jovanovich, 1990) as "simply the best playoff game I have ever witnessed, period." And he witnessed plenty.

To this day, I'd have a hard time accusing the veteran skipper of hyperbole.

So too, would every one of the 58,354 who packed San Diego's Jack Murphy Stadium the night of October 6. The occasion was Game 4 on a pleasant Friday evening in front of a national television audience. I was one of many who sat transfixed in front of my glowing tube for 3 hours and 13 minutes—and for good reason: my team and my hero were about to work a miracle.

Cliches be damned, this was perhaps the biggest game in Padre franchise history to date. The team was in the postseason for the first time, and the last thing it wanted to do was lie down meekly in four games.

Enter Garvey. . . center stage.

Garvey was no stranger to the postseason during his days with the Dodgers—he already owned a World Series ring from 1981 and an MVP trophy from the 1978 NLCS. Little did Chicago know that he was about to add to his trophy case. After flying out to Keith Moreland in the first inning, Garvey offered a hint of what was to come when he capped a two-run third frame for San Diego with a two-out RBI double off Scott Sanderson, scoring Alan Wiggins. It was Garvey's first extra-base hit of the series. . . though it would not be his last. The Padre lead was short-lived, however. The Cubbies answered with three runs in the top of the fourth courtesy of back-to-back dingers by Jody Davis and Leon "Bull" Durham to give the visitors a 3-2 lead. The up-against-the-ropes Padres could have panicked at this point.

Instead, Garvey continued to dance with destiny.

In the bottom of the fifth, the first sacker smacked a two-out single back through the box, plating Tim Flannery and sending Sanderson to the showers with the game tied 3-3. At this point, you had to be thinking, as I was, that Garvey had used up his daily quota of clutch hits. . . but we would all be wrong.

After the Padres' Dave Dravecky and the Cubs' Warren Brusstar held their ground in the sixth, San Diego mounted another threat in the bottom of the seventh. With one out, Padres pinch hitter Bobby Brown drew a one-out free pass from Tim Stoddard. With two outs, Stoddard intentionally walked a young up-and-comer by the name of Tony Gwynn. That brought you-know-who to the plate, and Garvey delivered yet again in the clutchest of situations: another RBI single, this time to left, bringing myself and 58,000-plus incredulous spectators out of our seats and couches. The usually businesslike Garvey pumped his fists in the air. A passed ball by Davis with Graig Nettles at the plate then scored Gwynn, and the Padres suddenly found themselves staked to a 5-3 lead heading into the eighth inning.

And still Garvey was not through.

Dick Williams wasted no time trying to nail this one down, calling for Goose Gossage—he of the 25 saves and 2.90 ERA in the regular season—to hold Chicago in the eighth inning. As destiny would have it, the Goose couldn't answer the call. . . this was somebody else's game to win. RBI hits by Moreland and Davis knotted the count for the second time, this time at 5-5. If not for his passed ball, Jody Davis may well have been staring at a Cubs' lead and the LCS MVP Award. . . but this was somebody else's game—and somebody else's award—to win.

Future Hall of Famer Lee Smith entered the fray for the North Siders and shut the door on San Diego in the bottom of the eighth. The scoreboard continued to read 5-5 as the Pads and Craig Lefferts took the field in the ninth, and the Cubs proceeded to mount a threat that nearly took my breath away. A one-out double by Bob Dernier and a two-out intentional walk to Gary Matthews brought pinch hitter Henry Cotto to the plate. The rookie carried the weight of the entire city of Chicago and its 39 years (the last time the Cubbies had been to the World Series) of frustration to the plate, but Lefferts took the bat out of the youngster's hands, plunking the 23 year old to load the bases. Longtime Garvey teammate Ron Cey stepped to the plate. Together the two had patrolled the corners of the LA infield for the better part of 11 seasons, with Garvey grabbing most of the headlines during those years. But now Cey had his shot at the spotlight. . . except that this was someone else's game to win. The third baseman grounded out to Wiggins at second to end the threat and keep the score knotted at 5-all going into the bottom of the ninth.

And you better believe the entire baseball world knew that Garvey was due up third.

With Smith, whose 33 saves in '84 placed him second in the N.L., still on the mound, Wiggins led off the ninth by striking out, but Gwynn followed with a single up the middle. What happened next is usually reserved for myths and fairy tales.

Dick Williams: ". . . my thoughts were interrupted by the loudest crack I ever heard."

Tim Flannery: "The last person I saw do something like that was Roy Hobbs."

Steve Garvey: "As soon as the ball went toward the fence, everything froze in time. It was as if all sound stopped."

Jerry Coleman: "It's gone! The Padres win! . . . Oh, doctor!"

As if he hadn't already done enough for one evening, Garvey sent a Smith fastball deep into the night, where it finally landed in the bleachers in right-center. Final score: Padres 7, Cubs 5. The *Cub- Busters* (borrowed from the hit movie of the time), and the Cub-Bus*ter*, had put the final touch on a script too unbelievable for even Hollywood to concoct. If you weren't there to see it, you can just imagine the pandemonium at the Murph. If you weren't there to see it, you can just imagine the scene in my living room. If you weren't there to see it at all, I'm sorry.

San Diego would find itself down in Game 5 as well, but the team again rallied to complete one of the most improbable NLCS comebacks in baseball history. Virtually everyone still agrees, however, that the final contest will be forever lost in the shadow of Game 4.

After his blast and subsequent mobbing by manager and teammates, Garvey would say, "I love the situation. I love the challenge. And it's my pleasure to [have] come through."

And it was *my* pleasure—*our* pleasure—to have watched.

Don Zminda

Game 5, 1986 ALCS

I am neither a Red Sox nor an Angel fan, but my favorite game of all time, without question, is Game 5 of the 1986 American League Championship Series. In terms of drama on the field, few games can surpass it. This game also has to rank near the top in terms of *human* drama. Consider all the elements in play before the game even started:

1. The Red Sox, perhaps baseball's most star-crossed franchise, were trying to make it back to the World Series, which they had last won in 1918.

2. The Angels, who were in their 26th season, had never even *been* to a World Series.

3. Gene Autry, the Angels' beloved owner, had spent millions on expensive free agents in his search for a championship, only to come up empty year after year. In that sense, Autry was a dead ringer for Boston's late owner, Tom Yawkey, who had also spent millions in a fruitless attempt to buy a championship. In 1986, the Red Sox were still owned by Yawkey's widow, and both the Yawkeys and the Autrys were still looking for that elusive title.

4. It wasn't just the teams and the owners who had spent years in fruitless pursuit of a championship. Angel manager Gene Mauch, as cursed as either of the franchises matched up in this series, was trying to make it to his first World Series after 25 seasons of managing in the big leagues.

5. Two aging veterans, one on each team, were also trying to reach the Series for the first time. Don Baylor of the Red Sox, who was finishing his 16th major league season, had played in four LCS prior to 1986. Each time his team had lost. And Bobby Grich of the Angels, who had come up through the Baltimore Oriole farm system with Baylor—and who had later been a teammate of Baylor's with the Angels—had also played in four playoff series prior to 1986; like Baylor, he had always been on the losing side. For Grich, who was in his 17th major league season, reaching the World Series in '86 was especially urgent: he had already announced he was going to retire when postseason play ended.

6. The Angels entered Game 5 with a three-games-to-one lead, seemingly a sure thing . . . but Mauch's teams were notorious for blowing "sure things." In 1964, Mauch's Phillies had lost the pennant after holding a six-and-a-half game lead with only 12 games left to play. And in the 1982 LCS against the Milwaukee Brewers, Mauch's Angels had blown a two-games-to-none lead in the (then) best-of-five series—the first time that had ever happened.

The prelude to Game 5, which was held on a bright, sunny Sunday afternoon at Anaheim Stadium, was a thrilling contest the night before. The Red Sox, trailing two games to one when Game 4 began, looked certain to tie the series when they entered the bottom of the ninth with a 3-0 lead and their ace, Roger Clemens (24-4 that year) on the hill. The Sox had history on their side as well: *in more than 80 years of postseason games, no team which had entered the ninth inning with a lead of three or more runs had ever lost.* But the Angels scored three times to send the game into extra innings, then won it in the 11th on a hit by Grich. California's game-tying rally in the ninth had been given a big boost when Sox left fielder Jim Rice had lost the ball in the lights for a double, and the tying run came across when reliever Calvin Schiraldi hit Brian Downing with a bases-loaded pitch. In this series between two cursed franchises, the Angels appeared to be the ones who were blessed.

Game 4 had lasted until the wee hours, and the sellout crowd of 64,223 was still celebrating the unexpected victory when Game 5 began the next afternoon. You had to like California's chances. The Angels were going with their ace, Mike Witt (18-10), a 6'7" righthander who had stopped the Red Sox on five hits in Game 1. Boston countered with lefthander Bruce Hurst (13-8), the winner in Game 2, but Witt had one big advantage: he was working on his normal four days' rest, while Hurst had had only three days off. Witt was brimming with confidence. As he explained years later to Mike Sowell in the book *One Pitch Away*:

> It was a big, emotional game. In Game 4, we came back against Clemens, and we were riding high. Just one more game. That was what we were thinking. I had the same feelings I did the first game. I was real confident. I knew I could get them out, because I had done it before.

Witt set down the Red Sox in order in the top of the first. Hurst gave up a two-out walk to Brian Downing in the bottom half, but Downing was promptly caught stealing. Rice singled to lead off the Boston second, but Witt struck out Baylor and Dwight Evans, then got two strikes on the Boston catcher, Rich Gedman. Witt had been very successful against Gedman prior to this game—Gedman was 2-for-24 against him, according to the *Elias Baseball Analyst*—and he appeared to strike Gedman out with a curveball. But Gedman managed to graze the ball with his bat, and Angel catcher Bob Boone couldn't hold on to the foul tip. Given a second chance, Gedman promptly homered into the right field seats on the next pitch. The Red Sox led, 2-0.

Witt settled down, and the Angels began to get to Hurst, putting at least one runner on base in each of the first six innings. In the second, DeCinces led off with a double that produced no runs—but the two-bagger would indirectly have a profound effect on the game. Sox center fielder Tony Armas crashed into the fence trying to catch DeCinces' hit, hurting his ankle. Armas played a couple of more innings, then had to leave the game. His replacement was a fellow named Dave Henderson.

California finally got on the board when Bob Boone led off the third with a home run, but though the Angels threatened in every inning, Hurst nursed the 2-1 lead into the sixth. DeCinces doubled with two out, and then Grich lofted a long fly ball to the fence in left center. Henderson, who had entered the game the previous inning, appeared to catch the ball, but it came loose when he reached the wall. The ball flew out of his glove and sailed over the fence for a home run. Suddenly, the Angels led, 3-2. The crowd went wild, calling Grich out for a curtain call. Grich got so caught up in the emotions of the moment that he pumped his arm and raised his leg, like someone pulling on a train whistle.

The Angels added two more runs off Bob Stanley in the seventh; things were going so well for them that Rob Wilfong, a .219 hitter, doubled in a run. Witt had passed the 100-pitch mark late in the eighth inning, but he appeared to be in command as he took the mound for the ninth with a 5-2 lead. The crowd was beginning to celebrate, and the Anaheim police began taking their positions for the postgame festivities.

Bill Buckner led off the Boston ninth with a single up the middle, but that was no big deal; the Sox had gotten a hit in every inning since the fifth. Still looking good, Witt struck out Rice, then prepared to face Baylor, who was 2-for-26 lifetime against him at that point, according to Elias. Witt got to 3-2 on Baylor, then threw him a wicked down-and-away curveball. "A good pitch. A sharp-breaking pitch," according to Doug DeCinces. "An almost-unhittable pitch," wrote Mike Sowell. Not quite. Baylor not only got his bat on it; he slugged it over the left-field fence for a two-run homer. Wrote Roger Angell in the *New Yorker*:

> Baylor's home run, which I watched again and again in taped replay during the winter, ranks as the Feat-of-the-Month in this feat-filled October. Witt's pitch broke sharply away over the farthermost part of the strike zone, and Baylor not only got his bat on it but somehow muscled the ball in the opposite direction and out of the park.

California's lead was down to 5-4, but Witt appeared unruffled. He quickly got Evans on a pop-out to DeCinces. One out to go. "When I caught the ball Mike Witt was just 10, 15 feet away from me," recalled DeCinces. "He had come all the way over to get the ball, and he was zeroed in. You could feel it. This game was over."

Not to Gene Mauch, it wasn't. Rich Gedman was the next hitter, and Mauch had a decision to make: should Witt pitch to Gedman, or should he bring in southpaw reliever Gary Lucas and go lefty-against-lefty? Though Mauch was well aware that Witt "was our ace all year," as DeCinces put it, there were a number of factors in favor of bringing in Lucas:

1. Witt had thrown 121 pitches, including 16 thus far in the ninth inning. 2. Gedman had gone 3-for-3 against Witt thus far in the game—a home run, a double and a single, all hard-hit

balls. 3. Gedman had batted .186 against lefties in 1986, .282 vs. righties. 4. The night before, Mauch had brought Lucas in to pitch to Gedman, and Lucas had struck him out. Lucas had also struck out Gedman during a regular-season game between the two clubs.

Mauch may have had another reason for wanting to make the switch. Throughout his managerial career, Mauch was known for "sticking with the hot pitcher," often to the point of disaster. In 1964, his Phillies had blown their big lead after Mauch began using his aces, Jim Bunning and Chris Short, on two days' rest. In the 1982 LCS against Milwaukee, he had started Tommy John on three days' rest in Game 4, despite the fact that he had a two-games-to-one lead, and John had gotten hammered. Then, in Game 5, he had stuck with his best reliever, righthander Luis Sanchez, in a crucial late-inning situation against lefty-swinging Cecil Cooper. "Nearly everyone in the ballpark expected Mauch to bring in lefthander Andy Hassler," wrote Larry Wigge in the 1983 *Official Baseball Guide*. Mauch stayed with Sanchez, and Cooper came through with the series-winning hit.

After thinking it over, Mauch sent pitching coach Marcel Lachemann to the mound to bring in Lucas. Doug DeCinces and Bob Boone were dumbfounded. Said DeCinces:

> Boone and I looked at each other, and we went "Oh, shoot!" Mike Witt was so disgusted. He walked off the mound and stared into center field. I mean, here's a guy who had carried us all the way, And he was so prepared mentally and physically to get this guy out.

Despite DeCinces' comments, Witt would say later that he had no problem with the decision to take him out. "He made the right move," Witt said of Mauch. "In that spot, bringing in a lefty makes sense."

Perhaps the move made sense, but it didn't work. Lucas threw one pitch to Gedman, an inside fastball, it got away from him and hit Gedman on the forearm. It was the first time Lucas had hit a batter since 1982.

Dave Henderson, a righty swinger, was the next hitter. Lachemann came out again and brought in his top righty reliever, Donnie Moore. Again, DeCinces was incredulous. "Donnie Moore had a cortisone injection the night before," said DeCinces. "He wasn't supposed to pitch. He was *not* supposed to pitch." (DeCinces must have been having a busy day, what with both trying to play *and* manage the team at the same time. . .)

Nonetheless, in came Moore, the Angels save leader in 1986 with 21. Henderson had faced him before, and their first confrontation, in August of 1985, had eerie similarities to this game. Back then Henderson was with Seattle, and just as in the playoff game, Witt was the California starter. Even more remarkably, Witt had taken a 5-2 lead into the late innings of the '85 contest—this time the eighth—only to be relieved after giving up a two-run homer (to Barry Bonnell). On that occasion Moore had come in to face Henderson . . . and "Hendu" had belted a game-tying home run off him.

Throwing fastballs, Moore got the count to 2-2. But Henderson was starting to get a bead on Moore's heater. He fouled the two-and-one pitch straight back—a sign that he had it well-timed. "There's just absolutely no way I can come back with a fastball here," reasoned Boone. He signaled for a forkball, a pitch Moore was having trouble throwing because of his tender elbow. Moore came in with it. "A nothing forkball, BP speed, right down the middle of the plate," said a disgusted DeCinces later.

Henderson hit it out of the park for a two-run homer. Suddenly the Red Sox were ahead, 6-5. The crowd of 64,000 was totally stunned.

By rights Henderson's home run should have killed the Angels, but it didn't. . . yet another reason why this was such a remarkable game. Moore got Ed Romero for the final out of the inning, and in their half, the Angels mounted a rally against the Boston bullpen. Boone led off with a single off Stanley, and after Gary Pettis bunted him to second, the Red Sox brought in southpaw Joe Sambito to pitch to the lefty-swinging Rob Wifong. Wilfong, who had a career average of .176 against lefties, lined a single to right, and Ruppert Jones, who was running for Boone, tore around third and just beat Evans' throw with a beautifully evasive slide. Tie game again. The 64,000 fans had found their voice again.

Steve Crawford came in to pitch to Schofield. "The Little Duck" singled sharply through the infield, and Wilfong raced to third. The winning run was now 90 feet away, and there was still only one out. Best of all, the Angels had the heart of their order—Downing, DeCinces and Grich—coming up.

Sox manager John McNamara played the percentage move, issuing an intentional walk to Downing. DeCinces had been killing the ball all day—he had hit two doubles—but as he prepared to hit the Angels gave him some advice:

> I remember Gene Mauch and Reggie [Jackson] on the bench, telling me, "Just nice and easy, hit the fly ball. You can do this, you know how to do this." And then I remember the thought process, and one of the things if I could take that swing back again, I would have gone back to my aggressive style of hitting. I could drive in the run by being aggressive.

DeCinces was looking for a fastball, and when he got one on the first pitch, he took that nice, easy swing and hit a nice, easy fly ball to Dewey Evans in short/medium right field. Had a weak-armed outfielder been patrolling right, the Angels might have tried sending Wilfong home. But Evans had one of the best throwing arms in baseball, and Wilfong stayed put. "I hit it to the wrong guy," said DeCinces.

The Angels still had one more chance to win it when Grich came up to the plate. Crawford missed with his first two pitches, and the third was a borderline pitch which plate umpire Rocky Roe called a strike. Grich fouled off the 2-1 pitch, then hit a spinning liner which Crawford grabbed for the third out. The Angels had blown their golden opportunity, and it was on to extra innings.

With Moore still on the hill, the Red Sox threatened in the 10th, putting runners on first and third with one out. But Moore got Rice to hit into an inning-ending double play. The Angels had a chance of their own in the bottom of the 10th when catcher Jerry Narron, in for Boone, drew a two-out walk off Crawford. Gary Pettis, who was having a great series, then walloped a fly ball to deep left field. At first it appeared that the ball would leave the yard for a game-ending home run, or at least hit off the top of the fence; had that happened, it's likely that Narron, who was running with two outs, would have been able to score the winning run. But Rice raced back and made a great catch at the wall. The big crowd groaned in agony as the Angels were thwarted again. As Al Michaels, who was broadcasting the game for ABC, put it, "If you're just tuning in, too bad."

By now it seemed only a matter of time before the Red Sox would push across the winning run, and they did so in the 11th. Baylor, the major leagues' all-time hit-by-pitch champion, got the rally started by performing his specialty. Evans singled him to second, setting up a sacrifice situation for Gedman, who'd had only one successful sacrifice all year. Showing his rust, Gedman popped up his bunt attempt. Had it been the Angels' day, DeCinces or Moore would have caught it on the fly and started a double play; instead the ball plopped out of everyone's reach in fair territory, and all hands were safe. Henderson, fittingly, was next, and he did what DeCinces had failed to do for the Angels in the ninth: he hit a sacrifice fly to center to bring home the lead run. The Red Sox might have scored some additional runs, but Downing crashed into the left-field fence to rob Ed Romero, and Wilfong made a great stop on a smash by Boggs to record the third out. But the Red Sox had a one-run lead, and the Angels finally surrendered: Calvin Schiraldi, the Sox pitching goat in Game 4, came in and struck out Wilfong, fanned Schofield as well, then got Downing on a pop-up to Dave Stapleton in foul territory. The Angels still had a three-games-to-two lead, but the Sox jumped up and down like they had already won the series.

"Everybody felt terrible," said DeCinces of the Angels' mood as they traveled back to Boston. "All we had to do was win one game. But it was like it was over." The series resumed on Tuesday night at Fenway Park, and the Angels jumped on Sox starter Oil Can Boyd with two runs in the top of the first. But Boyd wriggled out of the jam, and the Sox came right back, kayoing Angel starter Kirk McCaskill in the third and rolling to a 10-4 victory. Mauch had a veteran with a reputation as a "big-game pitcher," John Candelaria, ready for Game 7, but by this point one had the feeling that not even the guys with wings from "Angels in the Outfield" could have saved California. Candelaria was shelled mercilessly, and Clemens breezed to a series-ending 8-1 victory.

The Red Sox, of course, would have fate turn on them with a vengeance in the 1986 World Series against the Mets. But that was little consolation to the Angels, who haven't made a postseason appearance since their '86 disaster. One could argue that the franchise still hasn't recovered from Game 5, and at least one individual *never* recovered from this game. Donnie Moore, who had given up the home run to Henderson, ended up killing himself with a .45-caliber handgun after first taking several shots at his wife. He couldn't get that pitch out of his mind, said his wife, Tonya.

Gene Mauch managed the shaken Angels to a sixth-place finish in 1987, then resigned as manager in the spring of 1988. He never managed again, though he had a brief stint as a bench coach when Bob Boone became manager of the Kansas City Royals in 1995. To his dying day, Mauch will be hounded about the managerial decisions he made in 1964, 1982 and most of all, the ninth inning of that fateful playoff game in 1986. Did he make the wrong decision? Should he have stuck with Witt? Who can say for sure? As Roger Angell put it, "Mauch's moves during Boston's ninth inning of that fifth game, when the three-run Angels lead was converted to a one-run deficit, will be a Gettysburg for tactical thinkers for years to come."

Angell's right; more than 10 years after it happened, nearly every veteran fan I know has an opinion on the subject. Here's mine: I would have done what Mauch did. I would have taken Witt out of the game, and brought in Lucas. Hopefully I wouldn't have been as cursed as Mauch and the Angels were.

Kevin Fullam

Game 6, 1993 World Series

For a native Philadelphian like myself, the 1993 baseball season was one of the greatest sports experiences of my life. Born in 1974, I was too young to appreciate the Phils' reign of terror in the late 1970s and early '80s; *my* childhood was filled with summer after summer of listening to Harry Kalas pump excitement into each and every ballgame. . . which, of course, usually happened to end in Philly losses. From 1984-92, the Phils had just one winning season (in 1986), and even *then* they weren't able to save face—not with the New York Mets topping them by over 20 games in the standings. Though I always felt baseball was magical regardless of how the hometown team fared, we Phillies fans were perennially left to deal with the painful aftermath of bungled trades, failed free-agent signings and a scarcity of minor league talent.

Hope springs eternal at the start of every baseball season, but even at the beginning of 1993, you could just *sense* that things were different in Philadelphia. Three straight wins to begin the season? We were usually surprised if the Phils had three wins by the *end* of April.

Once they got rolling, the wheels of the Phillies bandwagon would not slow down. After storming out to a 51-21 start, winning the N.L. East was an afterthought; at no point during the season were the Phillies ever seriously pressured for the division title. Though the Atlanta Braves proved to be a formidable foe in the N.L. playoffs, they soon succumbed to a flurry of late-inning rallies, defensive heroics and pitching masterpieces. And so, on came the Blue Jays. . .

After dropping two of the first three games, the Phils blew a 14-9 lead in Game 4 in what many consider to be the wildest World Series game ever played. Staving off elimination with a 2-0 shutout from staff ace Curt Schilling in Game 5, the Phillies traveled to Toronto for the pivotal contest. . .

Unlike the preceding World Series games in Toronto, an energized crowd populates the SkyDome for Game 6. The Blue Jay fans anticipate their team clinching the World Series tonight, and they want to be a part of the celebration. Both starting pitchers, Dave Stewart and Terry Mulholland, were shelled when they battled in Game 2, but as soon as Game 6 starts, there's no question as to which hurler is in command of his peak "stuff." Stewart strikes out Blue Jays arch-nemesis Lenny Dykstra to open the game, and he quickly retires the Phillies in the first after allowing a two-out walk to John Kruk.

Mulholland, on the other hand, is beset with difficulties almost from the start. The lefthander is pounded in the bottom half of the inning, as both Paul Molitor and John Olerud connect for extra-base hits to stake Toronto to an early 3-0 lead. The offensive fireworks are all the fans need to get riled up; they smelled blood at the outset of the game—now they can taste it.

Mulholland settles down over the next couple of innings, but his teammates are unable to generate much of an offensive threat. However, Jim Eisenreich finally puts the visitors on the scoreboard in the fourth when he slaps an RBI single to plate Darren Daulton.

At the first hint of Philadelphia's revival, the Blue Jays respond, as they had done for nearly the entire Series. Posting single runs in each of the next two innings, Toronto would take a sizable 5-1 lead and force Phillies manager Jim Fregosi to lift Mulholland after just five innings—his third poor postseason outing in as many starts. Soon after the Series ends, he would be traded to the Yankees for a couple of minor league prospects.

Philly's shaky bullpen had sabotaged the team's efforts in previous games, but in the sixth a hero emerges to stem the tide: Roger Mason. Mason threw two-plus innings of shutout relief work in Game 4, and tonight he appears to be on top of his game once again. The righthander is throwing hard, but more importantly, he's throwing *strikes*, a concept that had seemed to escape some of the other Philadelphia relievers. With Mason in command, the Blue Jays manage just a leadoff single by Roberto Alomar before going down in order.

Trailing 5-1 in the seventh, the situation looks grim for the Phils. Not only are they running out of time, but Stewart is doing a masterful job on the mound. However, though he has only allowed two hits and three walks on the evening, Philadelphia's patience at the plate has forced Stewart to labor excessively. After Kevin Stocker works a 2-2 count to lead off the inning, the rookie shortstop fouls off four more offerings before drawing a walk. With the 10 pitches, Stewart has now thrown 109 on the night—after little more than six innings of work.

The next batter's jersey says "Morandini" on the back, but it might as well still be Stocker at the plate. Taking a cue from his double-play partner, the second baseman fouls off a series of 1-2 sliders before stroking a line drive just inches over the glove of a leaping Tony Fernandez at shortstop. With Stocker going to third on the play, the Phils have runners at the corners with no one out.

Before the inning began, the Blue Jays were well-positioned to close out the Series; not only did they have a four-run lead late in the game, but they also lucked out in terms of how Philly's batting order was currently aligned. With the eighth and ninth hitters leading off the seventh, not only would the Phils probably come up empty in the inning, but they also would be starting off the eighth with Mariano Duncan—not Lenny Dykstra. Duncan was having a good Series with the bat, but Dykstra had been *unstoppable*. "Nails" had already scored eight runs and slammed three homers against the Toronto staff.

Now, however, Dykstra was coming to the plate with runners on base, no outs—and a bevy of sluggers coming up behind him. Blue Jay manager Cito Gaston had already started to warm up Al Leiter and Danny Cox, but Gaston is forced to keep Stewart (who was up to 115 pitches by this point) in the game to buy some more time for his relievers.

After falling behind in the count 3-1, Stewart can no longer afford to take chances with the strike zone: Dykstra, like most of Phillies, was not one to chase bad pitches—and loading the bases was an unacceptable option. Firing a fastball down the heart of the plate (his 21st pitch of the inning), Stewart can only turn and stare as the Phillies sparkplug crushes the ball into the second deck in right field, bringing the Phillies to within 5-4 and breathing new life into their hopes for survival. Exactly what Gaston *didn't* want to happen.

The SkyDome grows silent as Gaston trudges to the mound to replace Stewart. However, with the bases empty and Toronto still holding a one-run lead, the crowd seems to exhibit a nervous-but-calm exterior. One lone Blue Jay fan is fighting a losing battle as he tries to rally his fellow spectators to generate some noise. "That fellow wouldn't have to do that in Philadelphia," comments Tim McCarver. And right he is: whatever people may say about them, Philly fans have *never* been accused of failing to voice their opinion on *any* matter.

With Duncan at the plate, Gaston brings in righthander Danny Cox. Cox, who pitched with the Phils during the 1991-92 seasons, appeared in Games 3 and 5. . . and was decidedly unimpressive, allowing four walks and three hits in just three innings of work. Duncan, who was used extensively as a platoon player with Morandini during the season, has had immense difficulties with righthanders in the past—but he foils Gaston's strategy by lacing Cox' 1-1 pitch into center field for a single.

Most people assume that Cox will only face Duncan, leaving Al Leiter to greet the Phils' middle of the order, which includes left-handed hitters such as John Kruk, Daulton, and Eisenreich. However, Gaston keeps his reliever in the game—a puzzling move. Since Fregosi would obviously never pinch hit for any of his stars, bringing in the southpaw Leiter would have seemed to be a solid strategy.

With a mouthful of tobacco, a scruffy goatee and an unusual batting stance, Kruk always looks ugly at the plate. . . but here in the seventh, he's *swinging* ugly as well. After flailing and missing badly on a 2-1 slider, Kruk redoubles his efforts, but he's tempted again by another Cox slider on the very next pitch. Trying in vain to check his swing, Kruk cannot—and is promptly rung up for the strikeout.

The Blue Jays may have dodged one bullet, but the Phillies have the rest of their offense's chambers loaded with ammunition. As Cox works to Hollins, Duncan starts to dance around at first, making the veteran nervous and forcing him to keep an eye out for the potential basestealing threat. On the 2-2 pitch, Duncan takes off for second. He appears to be in trouble: the pitch is shoulder high and right down the heart of the plate—almost as good as a pitchout. Catcher Pat Borders leaps to his feet and quickly fires down to second. . . and it indeed appears to be in time, but Duncan just barely eludes the tag and is safe. On the very next pitch, Hollins smacks a ground single up the middle, tying the game at five.

Daulton is 0-for-8 lifetime vs. Cox, but here he needs just five pitches to work a walk, moving Hollins to second. Cox now has thrown 20 pitches in the inning, but he remains on the mound to face the left-handed Jim Eisenreich. Where is Leiter?

On the 1-2 pitch, Eisenreich smashes a chopper high off the plate just beyond the pitcher's mound. By the time Fernandez can field the ball, Hollins and Daulton have each advanced and Eisenreich is safe at first with an infield single, loading the sacks with still only one out.

With the left-handed hitting Milt Thompson due up at the plate, Gaston *finally* goes to Leiter—immediately prompting Fregosi to send up Pete Incaviglia as a pinch hitter. While it's easy to see why Toronto would want Thompson's defensive skills out of the game, why didn't Leiter come in to face any of the previous Phils sluggers? Perhaps Gaston didn't want to throw him up against Philadelphia's best hitters so soon after his abysmal Game 4 performance (2.2 IP, 8 H, 6 ER). Of course, coming into the game in a bases loaded/one-out situation with the score tied couldn't have made the reliever's day a whole heck of a lot easier, either.

Incavigilia, never known for his patience at the plate, jumps on Leiter's first pitch and launches it into center field. Devon White gloves the ball for the out, but the drive is deep enough to plate Hollins for Philadelphia's go-ahead run.

Stocker, batting for the second time in the inning, can't provide his teammates with any insurance runs. After flailing helplessly at a couple of Leiter offerings, he goes down on three pitches.

In the span of 20 minutes, the momentum of the game—and the Series—has completely shifted. However, even though Philadelphia's five-run outburst has enabled them to regain control of the game, one still can't help but feel that the Blue Jays were lucky to get out of the bases-loaded jam while allowing just a single run to score. Considering the strength of both clubs' hitting attacks, a one-run lead is hardly safe.

The bottom half of the seventh is uneventful, as Mason puts the Jays down 1-2-3. Seeds of doubt are starting to form in the crowd's minds: two of Toronto's best hitters, Henderson and Molitor, were retired during the inning—they may not get the chance to bat again.

Leiter remains in the game to face the Phils in the top of the eighth. Although Dykstra draws a one-out walk and steals second, Duncan and Kruk are unable to drive him home.

Surprisingly, Mason appears on the mound as the Blue Jays come to bat—his third inning of work. Fregosi has set-up men Larry Andersen and David West warming up in the bullpen, but decides instead to ride the hot arm of Mason as long as he can. After Carter is retired on a flyball to left, Fregosi strides to the mound and taps his left arm. Aha! The Phils' skipper never had any intention of staying with Mason; he just wanted him to pitch to Carter before switching to the southpaw West against Olerud.

West, like his teammate Mitch Williams, throws heat, but his accuracy is questionable at best. After failing to get a couple of borderline calls around the strike zone, West winds up walking Olerud (who is promptly replaced by Alfredo Griffin at first) on just five pitches. Out pops Fregosi again—clearly unhappy with the way events have transpired. Now tapping his right arm, he calls for the entrance of Andersen.

Most of the Phils bullpen has struggled so far in the Series, but the veteran Andersen has been one of the most reliable set-up men for Philadelphia throughout its championship season. With home plate umpire Dana DeMuth again squeezing the plate, Andersen runs a full count against Roberto Alomar. As Griffin takes off, Alomar raps a sharp grounder to Kruk at first. Kruk steps on first for the out, but it would have been a double-play ball had Griffin not bolted for second.

Fernandez slams the next pitch on the ground to Kruk as well. . . or does he? DeMuth rules that the ball made contact with Fernandez' foot, making it a foul ball. Upon closer review, however, it's clear that the baseball came *nowhere near* Fernandez' foot or leg. Instead of ending of the inning, DeMuth's call gives the Toronto shortstop another crack at the plate. This would become critically important as events progressed.

Andersen's next pitch tails inside and plunks Fernandez in the arm—this time there's no question of what happened. With runners at first and second, Ed Sprague strides to the plate. If Toronto has a weak link, Sprague is it: the third baseman, certainly no offensive powerhouse that season (.260-12-73), has gone just 1-for-15 during the Series with six strikeouts. Surprisingly, like Stocker and Morandini in the seventh, Sprague is tenacious at the plate, fouling off a series of 3-2 Andersen fastballs before drawing a walk to load the bases.

Here's where Toronto's fun ends, as Andersen retires 1992 Series MVP Pat Borders on a pop-up to Morandini. However, by cycling through their lineup, the Jays ensured that the top of their order would be waiting for whoever took the mound in the ninth. And of course, they knew all too well about the ticking time bomb the Phils were holding in their bullpen.

At the end of the inning, McCarver comments that "perhaps Fregosi should leave Andersen in to start the ninth against Henderson." Prophetic words.

Taking no chances with the prospect of more Philadelphia runs, Gaston pulls out all out the stops by bringing in relief ace Duane Ward to pitch the ninth. Ward easily shuts down Hollins, Daulton, and Eisenreich to retire the side and set the stage for the grand finale. . .

As the bottom of ninth is about to unfold, Phils' closer Mitch Williams jogs in from the visitors' bullpen. The only thing missing is the Trogs' hit song "Wild Thing" blaring from the speakers (ah, only in Philly).

Rickey Henderson steps into the batter's box. His career stats vs. Mitch: 1-for-5 with four walks. After Williams' first pitch sails shoulder high, it's pretty apparent that Henderson has absolutely *no* intention of getting his bat off his shoulders. When the second pitch sails high, Daulton takes a few steps toward the mound in an effort to calm down his teammate, but it ain't working. Henderson walks on four pitches. Fregosi starts piling more tobacco into his over-stuffed cheeks. Pitcher Curt Schilling gets ready to drape a white towel over his head. Neither he, nor many of his teammates in the clubhouse, can bear to watch.

Williams' first pitch to White is a called strike. Maybe White will have to start swinging. After Williams follows with two more neck-high balls, White fouls a few offerings out of play. Working the count to 3-2, he lines the next pitch into left-center field. There's a moment of panic when it's evident that Dykstra has lost the ball in the lights, but Incaviglia sees it the whole way and gloves it for the first out of the inning. Though it was reported that Williams seemed to be losing his velocity in his last few outings, McCarver claims that the hurler was clocked at 91 MPH during his battle with White.

Is it possible that Williams can send the Series to seven games? Molitor, the next batter, throws a huge wrench into those thoughts by lining a 1-1 pitch into center field for a single. Henderson, however, is forced to stop at second since it was unclear whether Dykstra would be able to nab the drive.

With two runners aboard, Blue Jays slugger Joe Carter steps to the plate. Carter is a notorious free-swinger, which will be to Williams' advantage; in contrast, a lineup full of nine Rickey Hendersons could probably bat around without ever putting the ball in play. After getting ahead in the count 2-0, Carter takes a called strike. For him, there is no such thing as taking *two* called strikes during an at-bat: he would now be swinging. Williams follows up with a 2-1 slider that Carter would need a golf club to hit—but he swings and misses anyway for strike two. Hungry for the strikeout, Williams takes the sign from Daulton, rears back, and releases the 2-2 pitch. . . and the roar of the crowd would soon be deafening. . .

Ever since Williams arrived on the scene at the start of the '91 season, he never lacked for support from the hometown fans. But after his Game 4 performance, during which he blew a 14-9 eighth-inning lead, just about *everyone* lost faith in the lefthander—including even a few of his own teammates. Why did Fregosi choose to bring him back in such a critical situation just two games later? More importantly, why did he match the notoriously-wild Williams against Henderson to lead off the inning? Henderson's overall on-base percentage that season against southpaws was .461—against Mitch it's arguable that total shot up to over *.500*!

The answer was obvious: Mitch was The Closer. Ludicrous or not, the fact was that there was practically no chance that Fregosi would have decided to use a different reliever—going to another pitcher at that stage in the Series would probably have shattered Williams' confidence irrevocably. Of course, surrendering the game-winning homer did the job well enough anyway. . .

No one said it better than Series hero Joe Carter: "With Mitch out there, we knew something good was going to happen (for us). And it did." Right indeed, Joe. From the moment Williams, took the mound, Philadelphia's tenuous hold on the ballgame quickly began to unravel. From talking to fans after the game, it seems that nearly every Philadelphia supporter *knew* that Mitch would blow the game. They just weren't sure how he would do it.

Why, you may ask, if I'm a Phillies fan, did I choose to highlight this game? Because, amazingly enough, I remember the seventh-inning *comeback* more than the grisly ending— and because, even though they lost, the '93 Phils appealed to me in sort of a "tragic heroic" kind of manner. I doubt if there will *ever* be another team like that one; I just wanted to enjoy the ride one more time.

Mat Olkin

Game 5, 1995 A.L. Divisional Playoffs

It has already been a playoff series for the ages, and the best is yet to come.

In the first game of the 1995 American League Division Series, The New York Yankees beat the Seattle Mariners, 9-6, before the largest Yankee Stadium crowd in 20 years. The day before, the upstart Mariners had won a one-game playoff over the California Angels to take the A.L. West title, capping a miraculous comeback in which they made up 12-1/2 games in six weeks to overtake the Angels. But in Game 1, they succumbed to New York's David Cone, who labored but survived six walks and two home runs by Ken Griffey Jr. Griffey's second homer of the game tied it at four apiece in the top of the seventh, but the Seattle bullpen gave the game away by surrendering four runs in the bottom of the inning. Yankees' closer John Wetteland was touched for two runs in the ninth but held on for the 9-6 win.

Game 2 took 15 innings to decide. The Mariners took a 4-3 lead in the seventh, but closer Norm Charlton gave up a run in the bottom of the frame to tie it up. The game remained tied until the top of the 12th, when Griffey's third homer of the series—off John Wetteland—gave the M's a 5-4 lead. Still, New York almost pulled it out in the bottom of the inning. Wade Boggs and Bernie Williams walked, and Ruben Sierra followed with a long drive to left field. Boggs easily scored the tying run, and Williams rounded third looking to score the game-winner. The ball and Williams raced to home plate, and Williams was out, thanks to a perfect relay throw. The game continued. Finally, in the bottom of the fifteenth, at 1:15 AM, New York catcher Jim Leyritz—who had caught all 15 innings—lined a two-run homer through the rain off Tim Belcher to win the game, 7-5. Belcher walked off the field, down the runway, and past a pack of cameramen. One man's videocam was running, and as he drew the losing pitcher into focus, Belcher turned and slugged him.

Randy Johnson saved the Mariners' season for the second time in five days in Game 3. Back home at the Kingdome, Seattle chased Yankee starter Jack McDowell, who'd missed more than two weeks with a pulled muscle behind his shoulder. Johnson struck out 10 over seven innings, and the Mariners lived to play another day by winning, 7-4.

Game 4 was the Edgar Martinez show. The Yanks jumped all over Seattle starter Chris Bosio for a 5-0 lead after two and a half, but Martinez brought the M's back with a three-run homer in the bottom of the third. Seattle added another run that inning, and going into the bottom of the eighth, it was tied, 6-6. The Mariners loaded the bases off Wetteland, bringing up Martinez. He launched a line drive to center field that cleared the fence for a grand slam, running his RBI total for the game to seven. The Yanks came back with two runs in the top of the ninth, but the game ended when Griffey hauled in Bernie Williams' blast at the warning track. Ten feet more, and the shot would have tied the game.

With the series tied, the Mariners called on Andy Benes to make the biggest start of his life: Game 5. In the top of the sixth, Don Mattingly—who had played for the Yankees for 14 years but had never reached the postseason—stroked a two-run double to give the Yanks a 4-2 lead. Meanwhile, David Cone had pitched seven strong innings for New York. Six more outs, and the Yankees would advance to face the Cleveland Indians in the American League Championship Series.

But the Yanks aren't quite there yet. It's the bottom of the eighth, and Cone is tiring. With one out and Junior Griffey up, he leaves a belt-high fastball over the plate, and the young Mariner deposits it in the right field seats to cut it to 4-3. The crowd erupts in cheers. Sirens blare. But the Mariners are still a run behind.

The home run was Junior's fifth of the series, tying Reggie Jackson's record for the most home runs in a postseason series (of course, Mr. October—who happens to be in attendance this particular evening—needed six full games to establish his mark in the 1977 World Series). Out in the Seattle bullpen, Randy Johnson, who had thrown 116 pitches only two days before, stands up, stretches, and picks up a baseball.

Edgar Marintez quickly bounces to shortstop, and now there are two out and no one on. Tino Martinez steps in. Cone is one out away from finishing the inning, but he's really beginning to strain. He misses with a curve, then bounces a fastball in the dirt. A curve wide of the plate runs the count to 3-0. The fans stomp and cheer. Cone finally gets a curve over, but misses with a fastball, and Tino trots to first.

Up steps Jay Buhner, a former Yankee farmhand who has blossomed since his trade to Seattle several years ago. Cone misses with a variety of breaking pitches, and then throws ball four—but Buhner can't check his swing. Unable to control his curve and slider, Cone comes with a fastball and Buhner lines it toward the second baseman, Randy Velarde. Velarde climbs the ladder but comes up a rung short, and the ball zips an inch over his glove into center field. First and second, two out. Signs in the stands read, "Refuse To Lose!"

The Yankees' pitching coach, Nardi Contreras, visits the mound. In the Yankees' bullpen, young Mariano Rivera warms up. John Wetteland is nowhere to be seen.

Pinch-hitter Alex Diaz digs in. Cone throws a curve, low.

Then Seattle manager Lou Piniella calls time. He's out in front of his dugout, pacing up and down, looking for someone. Who? He can't find him. He asks around. No one knows. Suddenly, the missing player emerges from the runway. Piniella immediately sends him in to pinch-run for Tino Martinez at second base. The young man now represents the tying run. His name is Alex Rodriguez.

Cone resumes working on Diaz. He gets him to swing over a devastating split-fingered fastball, but he still can't locate his slider, and Diaz walks to load the bases. With catcher Dan Wilson due up, Piniella goes to the last left-handed bat on his bench, utilityman Doug Strange, a switch-hitter with a .236 lifetime average.

David Cone has now thrown 141 pitches. His first slider to Strange bounces in the dirt, but Strange, who's looking fastball, jumps out front and can't hold up. Cone leaves a fastball outside, and then fires one into the dirt for ball two. As Cone goes into his windup, catcher Mike Stanley signals with his mitt—unconsciously, perhaps—to keep the ball down. The slider refuses to obey, and hangs upstairs to run the count to 3-1.

Cone snatches the return throw out of the air and takes a deep breath. The noise is rising. With everything he has left, Cone fires a fastball right down the middle. Strange takes all the way for strike two.

This is it. 3-2. This is the pitch Cone has to make. With an out here, he can end the inning with the lead intact and come to within three outs of winning the game. Ball four will tie up the game, and a hit will likely give Seattle a lead with only one inning to play. Cone takes the sign, unblinking.

He winds and deals. The forkball sticks in his hand. Strange watches it until it bounces an inch in front of his shoetops. Cone doubles over, hands on knees, both exhausted and disgusted. The Seattle bench springs to life. Strange flings the bat away and runs to first base triumphantly. Rodriguez jogs home, steps on the plate, and as the noise washes over, we have a tie game.

Now, after 147 pitches, Cone is lifted. He takes off his glove and walks to the dugout, head down. In the Yankees' luxury box, Reggie Jackson stands and applauds Cone's gritty effort. Beside him, George Steinbrenner gestures furiously. He barks objections and commands at no one in particular. No one seems to be listening.

Down on the field, Randy Johnson stops tossing and begins seriously throwing. His purpose is no longer mere psychological intimidation; this is now actual preparation.

Meanwhile, Mariano Rivera takes his warmups. The youngster has had an unremarkable rookie season, posting an ERA of 5.51 while falling out of the starting rotation. However, since manager Buck Showalter installed him as a middle reliever to start the playoffs, Rivera's been outstanding. So far, he's thrown 4.2 scoreless innings against the Mariners, striking out seven and walking no one. He gets set to pitch to Mike Blowers.

With the sacks still full, Blowers has a chance to blow the game wide open. The television announcers point out that Blowers' career average with the bases loaded is .420.

Rivera throws a fastball with plenty on it, right down the middle for strike one. Blowers fouls off another on the outside corner, thrown equally hard. Rivera finishes with one more down the middle. Blowers realizes he's watched it go by, and turns to make the long walk to the dugout. Inning over.

Now it's the ninth, but the Yanks won't die. Against Seattle closer Norm Charlton, Tony Fernandez leads off with a double off the right field wall. After an intentional walk to Randy Velarde, Piniella pulls Charlton.

Johnson enters.

"Welcome to the Jungle" blares from the loudspeaker, as the tallest, scariest pitcher in baseball takes his warmup tosses. The crowd goes nuts, screaming and bowing in mock-un-worthiness.

In 1995, Johnson enjoyed one of the most dominant seasons any pitcher has ever had. He won 18 games and lost only twice, while leading the league in both strikeouts and ERA. He was simply invaluable, not only for his effectiveness, but for his durability as well. He consistently worked deep into games, saving the beleaguered Seattle bullpen. Several times during the season, he had worked on short rest to help out the Mariners' patchwork starting staff. And finally, he had proven to be the ultimate big-game pitcher. Twice during the last seven days, he had won a do-or-die game to keep Seattle's hopes alive. The only question now is whether he can do it one more time, with only one day of rest.

The first batter he has to face is the Yankees' future Hall-of-Fame third baseman, Wade Boggs. There are very few pitchers that Boggs can't hit, but Randy Johnson happens to be one of them. Over his career, Boggs has gone 2-for-16 with eight strikeouts against the big lefty. For that reason, Buck Showalter rarely uses Boggs when Johnson is slated to pitch. In Game 3 of the Series, Showalter had even inserted a rookie, Russ Davis, to face Johnson instead. Now Boggs stands in and sizes up his opponent.

On the first pitch, Boggs, who hasn't laid down a successful sacrifice bunt all year, squares around. Bad idea. A high, tailing fastball bores in on him like a chin-seeking missile. Boggs pulls back in self-defense, and the ball deflects off his bat, inches from his head. He steps out to collect what's left of himself.

On the next pitch, Boggs squares and offers half-heartedly, pulling back to watch a fastball paint the outside corner at the knees. Strike two.

The rookie catcher, Chris Widger, signals for a slider, but Johnson knows how he wants to pitch Boggs, and he steps off. Widger gets the point. Johnson pours in a belt-high fastball, and Boggs swings through it on his way to the dugout. The Dome gets even louder.

But now, with one out, Johnson has to face one of his toughest foes in the entire Yankee lineup. Bernie Williams, their switch-hitting center fielder, is due up. He digs in batting right-handed, his strong side. During the regular season, 13 of his 18 homers have come batting righty—in a span of less than 200 at-bats. What's more, he hasn't been fazed by Johnson in the past. In 29 at-bats, he's lit up Johnson for a .345 average, the third-best mark for any player who's faced the Big Unit 20 times. The day before yesterday, against Johnson in Game 3 of the Playoffs, he drew a base on balls, singled and homered.

Johnson works carefully, missing with a slider down and away and a fastball downstairs. On 2-0, he has to come in with one. It's a good one to hit, a fastball right down the pipe, but Williams pops it up. At second base, the excitable Joey Cora looks skyward and does jumping jacks, feverishly waving off absolutely no one. He snags the pop for the second out. Randy Johnson got away with one, and now he's almost out of it. All he has to do is get Paul O'Neill.

O'Neill hates Lou Piniella. When Lou was his manager in Cincinnati, they never got along, and Piniella pushed hard for the trade that sent him to the Yankees, where he has now become one of their finest all-around players. His only weakness is an inability to hit certain types of left-handed pitchers, a fault Showalter masks well by sitting O'Neill whenever the situation calls for it. This is one such situation; Showalter has always done his best to keep O'Neill away from Randy Johnson. In the three times he's been allowed to face the Big Unit, O'Neill has gone hitless, striking out twice. When Johnson pitched Game 3, O'Neill watched from the bench until Johnson was out of the game. But now, he has to stand in; Showalter can't afford to take out one of his best hitters. Not now.

Johnson's first pitch illustrates precisely why a hitter like O'Neill can't touch him. He throws a slider directly at O'Neill's shoulder, and as O'Neill jumps back—with both feet—the ball breaks back over the plate for strike one. Unfair.

Johnson comes back with another. It rolls in, not nearly as sharp as the last, but the previous pitch had accomplished its purpose. O'Neill, bailing out, pops it off the end of his bat. Widger spins and tosses his mask. The crowd hushes, and erupts into a huge ovation when the catcher squeezes it for the third out. We go to the top of the ninth, and the Mariners have the top of the order coming up: Vince Coleman, Joey Cora, and Ken Griffey Jr.

Still no sign of John Wetteland. As Rivera gets set to face Coleman, the "Rocky" theme pumps through the stadium. Of the 57,411 people in attendance, no one seems to think the song is the least bit corny.

Rivera fires a strike, which Coleman lets pass. Another high fastball follows, and Coleman fouls it back, shaking his head afterward.

In the Yankee bullpen, a tall, lanky righthander gets up to throw. Amazingly, it *isn't* John Wetteland—it's Game 3 starter Jack McDowell, who has never before pitched relief in a major league game. He's had one day of rest since he last pitched.

Rivera works to Coleman, but the speedy left fielder has finally timed his fastball. He lines it into center field for a base hit, and the noise begins to swell once more. Nardi Contreras visits the mound to discuss how to keep Coleman close at first.

That brings up Joey Cora in an obvious sacrifice situation. He pops it foul on the first attempt, but then lays down a perfect sacrifice bunt to move Coleman to second. Now, will Showalter have Rivera pitch to Griffey? The fans clamor for it, but the answer is obvious. Junior takes his four balls and jogs to first.

Edgar Martinez leaves the on-deck circle. The TV graphic shows that against Rivera, he's 6-for-7 lifetime, with two home runs. Showalter knows this. He comes to the mound and waves in Black Jack McDowell.

Ordinarily, this would be Wetteland's situation exclusively, but things have changed. The M's have torched him all three times he's pitched in the Series, and Martinez' eighth-inning grand slam off him yesterday has sealed the deal. Edgar will not get a second chance to beat Wetteland.

Later, Showalter's decision to pass over Wetteland in favor of McDowell would be hotly debated. Some would flatly assert that Showalter deserved to be fired for this one move alone, while others would contend that the order to skip Wetteland came from a "higher" authority, high up in the luxury boxes.

Down in the seats, the place is rocking. For many years, the troubled Seattle franchise had struggled to survive in a town where support for the team was, at best, tepid. This year, as the Mariners pushed for a new stadium to replace the dilapidated Kingdome, the issue had come to a head. Just when it seemed that the Mariners might end up having to leave town, the ballclub launched its wondrous late-season pennant drive. Sporting dramatic comebacks on an almost nightly basis, the M's wiped out a huge deficit and caught the Angels at the wire to finish in a tie for first place.

During that historic stretch run, Seattle became, in the words of just about everyone, a "baseball town." Fans packed the Dome night by night, intoning the M's new mantra, "Refuse to Lose!" When the Mariners hosted the Angels for a one-game playoff to decide the A.L. West Championship, over 52,000 screaming fans packed the Kingdome to witness Randy Johnson send the Mariners to the postseason for the first time in their history. Now, they implore Edgar Martinez to deliver them into the League Championship Series.

McDowell overthrows his first fastball, and it comes in too high. His next fastball has much better location, but doesn't pack the same pop. Still, Martinez watches it to even the count at 1-1. A low heater puts Martinez ahead in the count. McDowell overthrows another fastball, and it comes in high and away. Martinez fouls it back, and winces to himself. He knows he's swung at ball three.

On 2-2, McDowell throws his first split-fingered fastball, and it isn't particularly sharp. It hangs high and away, but Martinez, looking fastball, swings over it for strike three. He glances back at McDowell. He will remember.

With two out, Alex Rodriguez digs in. After working the count even at 1-1, he pulls an outside fastball on the ground to shortstop. Fernandez fields and flips to second for the force. Perhaps someday the youthful Rodriguez will learn to take that pitch to right field, but tonight, it ends the inning for Seattle.

Before the game, television announcer Tony Kubek had asked Lou Piniella if Randy Johnson would be available tonight. "Maybe for one inning," was Lou's reply. Now, in the bottom of the 10th, Johnson has already thrown his one inning, but there's no way he's coming out now.

Ruben Sierra leads off for the Yanks. Johnson uses a few backdoor sliders to run the count to 2-2. Sierra fouls off a couple of pitches as as the crowd grows hushed. Then, Johnson snaps off a wicked slider. It starts in the strike zone, but dives into the dirt as Sierra tries to hold up. On the appeal to first, umpire Dan Morrison punches him out.

Sierra refuses to believe it, throwing both hands in the air. He glares incredulously at Morrison and takes a few steps toward first base. Morrison takes a few steps toward home and glares back. Sierra mimes the check swing and insists he only went "this" far. Showalter has to come out to save his player from ejection. The replay shows that Sierra held up, but there's one man out now.

Don Mattingly steps up for his at-bat—possibly his last as a New York Yankee. As the season has worn on, his retirement has grown from a possibility to a probability, and finally to an inevitability. In his well-respected 14-year career, "Donnie Baseball" has become the symbol of Yankee baseball, playing through pain for years with grace and dignity. Still, he's never tasted the postseason, and the drive to get him there one last time has been a huge motivating factor for his teammates during the season's closing months.

Mattingly's clutch double in the seventh had driven in two runs to give the Yanks a 4-2 lead, and it would have been a storybook ending if the lead had held. Now, he stands in against Johnson, hoping to add one more chapter to the book before it closes forever.

Johnson gets a slider over for strike one. Mattingly watches it, but doesn't bail out as the other lefties have. Mattingly's not scared of Randy; he's nicked him for a .356 average over his career. However, Johnson comes back with his best slider all day, a hard breaking ball that starts out aimed at Mattingly's numbers and ends up down and out of the strike zone. An unhittable pitch, and Mattingly waves at it to go to 0-2. Johnson follows with an identical pitch, but Mattingly restrains himself and lets it pass for a ball.

Mattingly's now seen three sliders, and when he gets another, he'll know what to do with it: stay on it, follow it out over the plate, and slap it to left field—hopefully to the spot where his seventh-inning double fell. Mattingly readies himself.

It is not to be. Johnson pours in a fastball right down the pipe, and Donnie can only watch as Widger rolls strike three back to the mound and heads for the dugout. Mattingly's been *had*, and he knows it. He drops the bat to his side, staring out in deep and dark thought. He glances at the ground, turns, and walks away.

Gerald Williams is next. A couple of fastballs run the count to 1-1, and then Williams pulls a slider foul to make it 1-2. Williams crowds the plate, hoping to reach the next slider.

There is no next slider. Johnson puts a 95-MPH fastball over the inside corner. Williams jumps back, but it's too late—he's been rung up. Johnson yells, "Got you!!!" but the only sound that can be heard is the fervent screaming of thousands of fans. Johnson has struck out the side.

Leading off the bottom of the 10th, Jay Buhner looks at a couple of fastballs to even the count at 1-1. McDowell offers a splitter that doesn't split, and Bone lines it into left for a single.

Chris Widger will now attempt to sacrifice. Showalter makes a quick trip to the mound to discuss how it should be played. Widger squares but pulls back, taking ball one. He tries again and fouls one off, and then pulls back and lets strike two pass. The rookie looks to third for the sign and blows a bubble. Two strikes; this should take off the bunt sign. But it doesn't: McDowell spins a high breaking ball, and Widger contorts himself to try to meet it gently. He does, but the ball glances foul at his feet for strike three.

One out, man on first, Doug Strange at the plate. On 0-2, Stange grounds one to the right of second base. Randy Velarde gloves and spins, Fernandez gets Buhner at second for one, and the throw to first. . . *safe*. It was very close at first.

Mike Blowers follows with a grounder into hole on the left side. Fernandez makes a nice backhand stop, spins and throws to second on the run, but Velarde can't hold the low throw. The replay shows that Strange's headfirst dive would have beaten the throw anyway—by an eyelash.

With two out and two on, Vince Coleman grounds one to the wrong man, Gold Glover Don Mattingly, who throws to Fernandez at second for the force out. As we go to the top of the 11th, announcer Tony Kubek says, "I doubt Lou Piniella would let Randy Johnson go any longer than this inning."

Mike Stanley leads off. Johnson rolls a slider outside, then fidgets with his uniform. His next pitch runs very high and away for ball two. Kubek says, "Johnson might be getting close to empty now." Another one high and away makes it 3-0. Johnson finally gets one over the plate, but it's high for ball four, a four-pitch walk to start the inning. Pat Kelly runs for Stanley. Johnson takes a deep breath.

Tony Fernandez gets a low fastball, and drops the bat on it for a beautiful sacrifice bunt. That brings up Randy Velarde.

This is exactly what Buck Showalter wanted. The Yankees' skipper is well-known for his knowledge and use of individual batter-pitcher match-ups. His awareness of each of his hitters' track records against different pitchers enables him to make more informed in-game substitutions, and greatly aids his lineup selection. By holding out Paul O'Neill against tough left-handers, he's helped O'Neill to blossom into a .300 hitter. Playing only against the pitchers they're best-suited to hit, part-timers like Jim Leyritz and Gerald Williams have made major contributions.

If you asked Showalter which hitter he'd like to send up in a big game against Randy Johnson, with one out and the go-ahead run on second base, he'd undoubtedly reply, "Randy Velarde." As Velarde gets set to hit, the following stat takes on vast importance: of all active players who have batted 20 times against Johnson, Velarde has the highest batting average—.462, 18-for-39. No one is within 100 points of him.

Piniella could order an intentional walk. He doesn't. On 1-0, Johnson leaves a hittable fastball over the plate, and Velarde comes through against Randy once more, grounding one through hole and into left field. Pat Kelly rounds third and beats Vince Coleman's off-line throw to the plate.

They've finally gotten to Randy Johnson. High-fives all around in the Yankees' dugout. Yankees 5, Mariners 4.

Showalter sends Jim Leyritz up to pinch-hit. Buck knows how badly Leyritz wants this at-bat. In May, a pitch got away from Randy Johnson, and Leyritz, who crowds the plate, tried to fend it off with his hand. The ball deflected off his hand and glanced off his face. Leyritz hit the dirt, understandably in fear for his life. However, when he realized that he hadn't been seriously hurt, he continued the dramatics, thrashing around in the dirt to great effect. The incident nearly set off a brawl, and later, Leyritz—who would be hit by seven more pitches in part-time play this season—vowed to "get even." Now is his chance.

Johnson starts him with a flat slider that rolls high and away for a ball. This obviously is not the same Randy Johnson as last inning. His slider has lost its bite, and his fastball doesn't have the same pop.

Johnson steps off. This is the time to reach back for something extra, but it's becoming increasingly doubtful that he has anything left to reach back for. However, it would soon become apparent that this is the exact moment where Johnson, incredibly, gets his second wind.

Johnson steps back up and snaps off the best slider he's thrown in the entire inning. Leyritz fouls it off. Widger likes what he saw and wants another, but Johnson shakes him off. Randy fires a fastball with "oomph," which Leyritz watches for strike two. Does he go back to the slider? No, it's another heater, knee-high across the inside corner. Leyritz watches it into the mitt, and then sees Dan Evans' right fist fire into the air.

Leyritz immediately launches into a tirade. Evans' mask comes off. Leyritz goes to throw his bat, but restrains himself, barely. "That is not a (deleted) strike!" If Leyritz gets tossed, the Yankees are out of catchers. Showalter comes out to lead him away.

Two outs, Bernie Williams due up. Piniella goes to the mound and orders the free pass. Johnson nods. Four balls later, it's first and second with two down. One more out to go, but now it's someone Johnson can handle: Paul O'Neill.

O'Neill knows he's going to get the slider, and he does, but all he can do is foul it off. Johnson gives him an even nastier one, but O'Neill takes Mattingly's approach and watches it break out of the strike zone. Johnson saw how O'Neill eyed the slider, so he comes with the fastball, the best one he's thrown all night. O'Neill, seriously behind on the ball, swings and spins out of the box, and keeps on walking. One and two; one pitch away for Johnson.

Johnson takes off his cap and inhales deeply. He looks defeated, which, in fact, he quite literally may be. He stares at the ground, thinking, fixes his hat and comes set.

He fires a high heater in on the hands, but O'Neill gets a piece of it and fouls it back. Now, the slider, but O'Neill stays on it just enough to tip it off the end of his bat.

Another deep breath for Johnson. He's now thrown him both the fastball and the slider. Widger goes through the signs, too quickly. Johnson, aggravated, steps off. He knows what he wants, and calls Widger out to tell him.

It's a fastball, down and away. O'Neill watches. It isn't Johnson's fastest, but it's the most perfectly placed pitch he could have thrown, knee-high and outside, heading for the black. O'Neill guesses "ball." He's wrong. It catches the corner, leaving O'Neill standing there with a useless bat on his shoulder and a grimace on his face.

But it's not a victorious moment for Randy Johnson. He takes one glance at the unforgiving scoreboard, bows his head and walks off.

This is it. Bottom of the 11th. One run down. Heart of the order: Cora, Griffey and Martinez. McDowell is still on the mound.

Joey Cora digs in for the biggest at-bat he's ever had. The day before, he caused a furor when he rolled a bunt down the first base line. As he charged down the line, Mattingly fielded the ball and instinctively realized that his only play was to tag Cora as he sprinted by. On the dead run, Cora fell away from Mattingly, barely eluding the tag. In the same motion, he reached out with his left arm fully extended and tagged first base. The Yankees argued long and hard that Cora had run out of the baseline, and they may have been right. It was too close to call. No one knew for sure, except the umpires, apparently, who ruled that he had not strayed far enough to be called out. The call proved to be tremendously important. Two batters later, Edgar Martinez followed with the decisive blow, a grand slam.

But Cora doesn't seem to be bunting this time. He takes the first three pitches to run the count to 2-1. Then it happens—he *does* bunt—a beautiful drag bunt toward first base, just like yesterday. Mattingly fields the roller a few feet inside the line, while Cora races to pass Mattingly before the ball gets there. He almost does. Mattingly picks it and all he can do is to try to tag Cora. Incredibly, Cora falls away, eludes the tag by a hair and tags the base safely. It's an absolute carbon copy of yesterday's play: Cora isn't an inch further outside—or inside—the baseline. Showalter argues, but Dan Morrison calls it the same as yesterday: *safe*.

The fans clamor for Junior, and this time the Yankees have no choice but to pitch to him. He's provided so many clutch home runs this year, including an astounding total of five so far in this series. But another one here would be the biggest of all. It would be the most historic moment in Seattle baseball history. This has to be on Junior's mind.

But it also must be on Jack McDowell's mind. He gives Griffey an outside fastball just off the plate, a pitch that can't be pulled, and Junior watches it for ball one. Leyritz doesn't like the call; he holds the ball for an extra instant before firing it back. McDowell's face shows he doesn't like it either.

McDowell needs a strike. He throws the same pitch, but moves it in an inch or two, just to get the call. There is no call. Junior, who just tries to meet it, gets on top of it and pounds a liner up the middle. Cora goes to third, while the noise meters go into the red.

The crowd is on its feet. The entire Seattle bench is standing. Edgar Martinez is up.

His last time up, Edgar fanned when he swung over a split-fingered fastball from McDowell.

McDowell gives him a fastball—hittable, belt-high on the outer half of the plate—but it isn't what Edgar's looking for. He lets it pass for strike one. McDowell gets the sign. He peers over his shoulder at Griffey on first base.

It's the pitch Martinez has been waiting for, the splitter, down and in. He jumps on it and drives it into left field. Cora scores to tie the game. The ball bounces four times and hits the wall. Griffey rounds second. Gerald Williams plays the carom and throws to Fernandez. Griffey rounds third. Fernandez throws to the plate. HERE COMES JUNIOR!!!

HERE COMES JUNIOR!!!

HE'S SAFE!!!

Griffey jumps up, both fists in the air, and is immediately mobbed by a swarm of jubilant Mariners. Peeking out from the bottom of the pigpile is the unmistakeable, mile-wide smile of Ken Griffey Jr.

Fireworks explode above, the crowd explodes below. Music blares. No one can hear what song it is. No one cares. Everyone dances.

Everyone, that is, except the New York Yankees. They stand motionless in the dugout, stunned.

The television people try to interview Griffey on the field. It doesn't work. Griffey manages to get across the fact that he is very happy. The man with the microphone sends it back upstairs.

Meanwhile, high up in his luxury box, George Steinbrenner stares down at the field, arms crossed, standing alone. He says nothing, but his expression leaves no doubt: *Somebody Is Going To Pay For This*.

A World Series Journal

by Craig Wright

It was about two years ago that Stan Reynolds wrote me about his being diagnosed with ALS, better known as Lou Gehrig's disease. He wrote a rather classy, wonderful letter, and I felt a call on our friendship that would be greater than anything that had gone before. Stan and I were good friends in my time in Texas, but we were not actively what you would call "close" friends. I helped introduce him to "computing" and got him started as a STATS scorer and then later as a STATS press box reporter; he introduced me to collecting "Hartlands" (little statues of select players that began back in the 1950s); we played on some softball teams together, and we enjoyed chatting at the ballpark about baseball. But it wasn't like we were in the habit of hanging out at the other guy's home, and there would be months in the offseason when we would not see each other at all.

But while we were not "close" friends, we always knew we could be—that our friendship had something special to it. After a few winter months of not seeing each other, it was always a delight to get together again and very easy to get comfortable in that way good friends have with each other. It was interesting to see that, after my move to California, we actually did stay in touch much more than I did with many others who, by the nature of our activities, would have been described as "close" friends.

I know I was especially touched when he sent me the Honus Wagner statue from the "Hartland" series, and it is the only one of my collection that I keep on my desk. It has always resonated with more than just my high regard for Wagner, whose autograph is my favorite of my collection. I've always been aware of that little nine-inch figure as a reminder of my friend in Texas.

As the playoffs started in October of 1995, it came to me that Stan— who had never seen a World Series game—might want to attend the World Series games in one of the two cities. When I felt him out about this idea, I could see I was on to something. I told him it was awfully late to try and arrange tickets, but I would give it a go. It was indeed too late to do it through my normal sources, and when I tried some of my auxiliary sources, I missed by mere hours snaring some tickets through a friend of mine. I could tell Stan was disappointed when I gave him the news, and I was also kicking myself for not being more aware and responsive to something that I felt God had given to me to do. I told him, "Next year. Stay strong; we'll go next year."

It has become very easy for my work schedule to fill up quickly, but from that day, whenever something came up that could threaten to tie me up during mid-October of 1996, I always told the client right up front that I would not be available at that time, that I was going to the World Series. I also made it a point to start very early on getting tickets and funding. This time I wanted to do it right. I wanted Stan to see the whole Series, start to finish, and I wanted his wife Kathy to be there to share this as well. That's an expensive proposition because of the extremely high airfares when you don't know where you are going until a day or so before you leave. I had it in mind that I might be able to raise the money so that the major expenses for Stan and Kathy would be covered.

I contacted STATS, Inc. about making a major contribution or doing a matching funds deal. Well, STATS has never sought recognition for their response, but I want people to know. This is the prompt e-mail I received from STATS CEO, John Dewan:

> Stan has done a wonderful job for STATS over the years. And he still continues to do so. We really appreciate everything he's done, and the least we can do is try to bring some joy to him and his family at a very difficult time.
>
> Craig, [if you can arrange the trip] STATS will cover Stan's and his wife's expenses to go to the World Series. It sounds like he has a couple of kids too. If the overall expenses to include his kids are not too high, STATS will cover the whole thing. If they're on the high side, I personally will pay his kids way.

And if you look in your 1997 *STATS Major League Handbook*, which is the flagship book of STATS' many annual books, you will find: "This book is dedicated to STATS baseball reporter Stan Reynolds, whose courage is an inspiration to us all."

Stan and Kathy felt it would be easier and probably best if the kids stayed in school. On my end, we made the decision that even though it would be a major expense to have my wife Catie come to the first couple games in New York, I wanted to be sure she got to know Stan and Kathy, and to share in what I hoped would be a special experience.

Getting tickets with handicapped access was not as easy as I had hoped. Stan can walk, but only for short distances, and it is difficult to handle many stairs. The Texas Rangers and Los Angeles Dodgers pledged to get us good seats with wheelchair access. And our seats in St. Louis would also have been very convenient, just a couple steps down from a walkway accessible by wheelchair. But with the other playoff cities, it was pretty much take the kind of seats I've gotten in other years—usually upper reserved. (Because it has gotten very expensive to attend the Series, and because I am often so busy in October, I hadn't been to a World Series in the 1990s, but I attended 40 World Series games spread over eight World Series in the 1980s. In six of the eight, I attended the Series from beginning to end.)

Adding to the problem, for the first time in my nine World Series orders, there was a screw-up in the ticket order. For Atlanta, I got the four tickets I requested, but two were in the right field corner and two were in left field. And of course, with Atlanta and New York, we were dealing with two of the older stadiums that would not have much handicapped access. Particularly in New York, I had a lot of trouble getting any advance information on the best gate to enter, where to store the wheelchair during the game, etc.

So I felt we were flying a little blind as we prepared to leave for New York. I have to admit I was feeling a lot of stress at that time, and I called a Christian Science practitioner to work with me on the thought of "harmony" for this trip. That feeling of stress began to lift when Catie and I switched planes at the Dallas-Ft. Worth airport and saw Stan and Kathy waving at us as we got on the plane to New York.

You know, sometimes we don't realize what we need most until the moment we get it. I hadn't realized what a relief it would be for me to simply see Stan and know first-hand that he was really doing all right. To put my hand on his shoulder, to talk with him, share the excitement—to know he was really there, really OK—that relaxed me like nothing else could. And indeed, from that moment, one member of our party had already gotten what he wanted most out of this trip.

I knew that in arranging everything, there had been a lot of calls between Catie and Kathy, and that they had really hit it off just talking on the phone. Together in person they were like chatty sisters. Both Stan and I enjoyed seeing them together, and we noted that there were a lot of similarities between the two. I hadn't really gotten a chance to know Kathy in Texas, and before this trip was done, she was on my list of heroes. She has such a positive approach to helping Stan and making sure that the quality of his life is compromised as little as possible. With a "can-do" attitude, patience, and early starts, we were able do just about anything we wanted.

That first night in New York may have been my favorite. I had told Catie how much I liked Stan's sense of humor and his ability to tell a good story. At dinner he nearly had Catie falling off her chair, laughing at stories about his kids and telling Mickey Rivers stories. (Stan had worked in the Rangers' clubhouse when Rivers was there, and they had become pretty good friends.) When we left to go back to the hotel, I realized my face ached a little from so much smiling and laughing.

Saturday, October 19, 1996

The next morning we quickly found out that Game 1 was rained out, so there was nothing to do but hit Manhattan and have a good time. By late morning we were at an art exhibit of Andy Jurinko's work. This was Stan's choice, and I was surprised to find that I knew this guy's work. In fact, I had a copy of his painting of Yankee Stadium in my office, and I had several "bitmaps" (computer images) of his stuff. Stan was intrigued by the latter, and it is a common practice now in our e-mail that I will attach one of my Jurinko's bitmaps to share with him. Jurinko was about halfway through his 25-year career as a painter when he became obsessed with the images of baseball, particularly from his youth in the 1950s, and that's pretty much all he has painted for the last 12 years or so.

A lot of his work in this exhibit featured head shots, including many obscure players. The 1950s was not a favorite era of mine, and I'm not that good at attaching names even to the faces that I recognize. Still, I imagine I could beat 90 percent of the fans in identifying the players covered in this exhibit, but I couldn't touch Stan, who was nailing a ton of guys that I didn't have a clue on. The larger action paintings were the most interesting, and when we got to the back of the hall, I saw a Dutch door with the top open, and looking in I could see a couple of large Jurinko paintings that were unpacked but not on display. The room was sort of a storage room and office, and when I brought Stan over to see what was in there, the guy working at the desk insisted we come in and look around. He was from the Netherlands, and I believe he was a part-owner of the gallery. He was very kind and chatted with us for quite a while. When we were leaving he came out front with us and gave us some souvenir postcards of the exhibit.

We then went down to Broadway and got tickets for the off-Broadway show "Matty: An Evening with Christy Mathewson," a one-man show on the life and writings of Mathewson. After a nice Italian dinner we were off to the play. Catie and I had actually seen this actor, Eddie Frierson, do a little show on Mathewson at a SABR convention about 10 years ago. Tonight's show was at the Lamb's Theatre, which is a historical building that was originally the Lamb's Club back in Mathewson's day, and he and manager John McGraw were in the habit of meeting there for lunch a couple times a week. After the show—which was very good and extremely accurate historically—we got to chat with Eddie, and he moaned at one point about how if he had known the Series was going to be rained out, he would have tried hard to get a ticket for Game 2, which would now be played on Monday, originally a travel date. (Naturally he was performing on the regularly scheduled nights of Saturday and Sunday.) Well, Catie needed to go back on Monday, regardless of the rainout, so we told him, hey, we have an extra ticket for Game 2. Come with us. So we made arrangements for him to meet us at Gate 4 before the game.

Sunday, October 20, 1996

We slept in and had a lazy day. Except for Kathy doing some shopping and Catie and I taking a walk, we mostly hung around the hotel, sharing pictures and visiting until it was time to go to the game. We were plenty early to make sure we could get around without fighting the crowd. Remember we are talking about 55,000 people in a ballpark originally built in 1923—when people were smaller and less concerned with convenience and personal space. But it was essentially a breeze. Where the car service dropped us off was close to what was probably the best gate for us. We easily found our way to the elevator and on up to our level. I was able to wheel Stan right out into the seat area, and then taking his time he was able to go up to our seats in the ninth row. In a bit of good fortune, Stan's view from his seat toward home plate went over the entrance from the walkway, which meant that his view would not be blocked much by people standing up at exciting moments in the game.

Storing the wheelchair was a l-o-o-o-n-g trip back down to ground level and behind home plate, where it could be stored in the Yankee Lobby. Our seats were in foul territory near the right-field foul pole. I liked these seats much better than the ones I had for my first World Series game which was right here in New York in 1981. That year I was at ground level but back in under the overhang in left field. When I got home from this Series, I looked up the date of my first W.S. game, and not only was this the return to the site of my first World Series, it was also the actual anniversary. Game 1 of the 1981 Series had also fallen on October 20th.

Stan and I were both very impressed with the sight lines from our seats. While we were up high, we felt like we were almost on top of the field, and we would be able to follow all of the defensive positioning very well. You definitely would not get this feel in a modern stadium. That's partly because they now move the upper grandstands further away from the field to eliminate some of the posts that would block views down below. And in older stadiums the aisles are narrower and rise at a sharper grade. Try this some time if you are in the upper deck of Tiger Stadium or Yankee Stadium: take a look to your left and right and see how steep the grade of the seats is. You won't see that in a modern park where the aisles are wider, and so naturally you move further away from the field with each row.

I always thought it was special that my first World Series game came in this ballpark, which is synonymous with World Series history, and I know it was special to Stan as well. The ideal for both of us would have been to see the Texas Rangers make their first World Series appearance, but when they were eliminated, Stan had e-mailed me, "Oh well, where else should a die-hard fan of the game see his first World Series but in Yankee Stadium?"

The Yankees have always been one of Stan's favorite teams, though often more for their history than an identification with the more recent teams. He quietly rooted for the Yankees throughout the Series, especially when they fell behind early, as he wanted a long series. Kathy enjoyed rooting with the crowd and so she rooted for whoever was the home team. Catie and I leaned to the Braves as they are a minor client of mine. I know that I wanted Stan to see the World Series clinched at home as there is something special about being in a crowd celebrating their team as World Champions that is vastly different from being in a crowd that is disappointed and only politely congratulating a new World Champion that got there by beating their team.

Game 1 quickly made history when, in the second inning, Andruw Jones belted a home run to become the youngest player to ever homer in the World Series. He hit it off Andy Pettitte, which made it less surprising in that he clobbered lefties during his big league trial. The next inning the Yankees brought the infield in against Chipper Jones with men on second and third. Both Stan and I felt this was way too early for this kind of move. Jones hit a hard grounder that went for a hit but could have been an out if the infield was back. It ended up being a big inning where Pettitte was knocked out of the game and Jones hit another homer, this time off righty reliever Brian Boehringer, who probably should not have even been on their W.S. roster. (Dave Pavlas was robbed of his spot for making the mistake of being an older finesse pitcher. He was a more effective pitcher than Boehringer both at Triple-A and in the majors.) In the fifth, Jones just missed hitting a third home run—again off Boehringer—as Darryl Strawberry went up above the fence to haul in his long drive. The very next batter, Fred McGriff, did homer off Boehringer to make it 9-0. The Yankees did score one run on their way to a 12-1 defeat. With the game turning quickly into a blowout, the raucous Yankees fans took to fighting in the stands. It was worse than the first night game in San Francisco of a Dodgers-Giants series. We also had a few occasions of fans running out on the field and delaying the game.

With the big lead, the Braves did not hold Strawberry on base when he reached on a fielder's choice, and I noticed that he then took an unusual baserunning stance where he simply squared off and aimed himself to second base, all set to drive off his front leg. While unusual, it also made sense, and I pointed it out to Stan. Turns out he had noticed it as well, and I remembered that it was often true back in Texas that—with all the different things that can be noticed when you are free of the TV camera's direction—we tended to notice the same little things on the field.

The winning pitcher, John Smoltz, was from my home town (Lansing, MI). The winning margin of 11 runs tied a World Series record. Including their last three games in the NLCS, the Braves had outscored their opponents 44-2 over their last four postseason games. In regard to Andruw Jones' performance, I have to laugh at the fact that he will technically still be a rookie in 1997. How many rookies have two World Series homers before their "rookie" year?

Picking up the wheelchair after the game was a real adventure. After getting past the guard at the gate to get to the Yankee lobby, it was simply too crowded to take the chair back through that narrow gate, so the only thing to do was lift it over the side barrier and then climb over. Then I had to maneuver it against the flow of the huge crowd to get to the elevator. It seems like they could find a better place to store the wheelchairs.

Monday, October 21, 1996

Last night, I woke up in the middle of the night to find Catie quietly sobbing. She was having her own thoughts about Stan and Kathy, which I won't try to interpret for her, other than her comment that she had become especially grateful for the good health of her family. I do know that one of the little pleasures on this trip was simply pushing Stan's wheelchair. When you think of all the little hardships Stan and Kathy deal with every day, it really makes you want to do something concrete to help, even in the smallest way. I told Catie what great satisfaction I found in being in charge of the wheelchair, and it sounded so good to her that like a little kid she had to try it herself. I know it sounds like Huck Finn and whitewashing the fence, but, yep, she understood.

The next morning we had breakfast together and then Catie was off to the airport and back to our children. It was the first time she had ever been away overnight from our little three-year-old Joshua. (He handled it just great, maybe even better than she did.)

I really enjoyed reading *The New York Times* sports page, which I was surprised to find was quite extensive, and, not so surprisingly, well-written. I laughed when one writer noted that with Jones' second homer, he had become the second-youngest player to homer in a World Series game—second to himself 30 minutes earlier.

We met Eddie "Matty" Frierson at the park and ended up witnessing another easy win for Atlanta. Greg Maddux pitched a superb game, and I asked Eddie if he saw any similarities between Maddux and Mathewson. Other than the exceptional control they both enjoyed, he really didn't see much connection. He did offer that, among modern hurlers, Nolan Ryan at his peak was probably the closest in exciting the fans' fervor and respect in the way that Matty did.

We knew Maddux had pitched with exceptional control in this game and gotten a lot of groundouts, but I didn't realize until I saw the next day's paper that he had allowed just one fly out and that he threw just 20 balls in his eight innings.

Both Stan and I were disappointed that manager Bobby Cox did not let him go for the shutout and instead gave Mark Wohlers the ninth inning. Maddux obviously wasn't throwing a lot of pitches. (The next day we learned he had thrown only 82 pitches.) It wasn't a save situation, and with the rainout, there would be no travel day. Atlanta doesn't have a deep bullpen. It was an odd decision in some respects, but a reliever can also go stale with too much time off. It's a tough call to make. But what about the bad karma of denying all these folks the ability to say on the day that Maddux goes into the Hall of Fame that they were there when he threw a brilliant shutout in the World Series? Geez, 82 pitches. Oh, what the heck, we'll still remember his dominance in this 4-0 game.

No one will remember years from now, but Andruw Jones nearly hit another homer. In the sixth inning he drove Bernie Williams to the wall, and it looked like the ball would have gone out if Bernie hadn't leaped and caught it, turning it into a 400-foot out. The STATS scorers are asked to note whenever a defensive play robs a batter of a home run. When I got back home and looked at the STATS record, this fly ball and Andruw's near miss in Game 1 were the only balls in this Series where the defense prevented a home run. As a hitter he is still raw in a lot of ways, but to show this kind of power as a teenager is really incredible.

Even though the Yankees were out of the game pretty early, there were no fights in our section, which made me feel better about Yankee fans, though we still had some clowns running on the field from time to time.

Tuesday, October 22, 1996

With the rainout we had to scramble a little to change our flight to Atlanta, as did a lot of people connected to the World Series, and our plane was a "Who's Who" of baseball. American League President Gene Budig was there with his wife, and I noticed she had a protective sense about her husband. I wondered if that was related to all the controversy surrounding his very poor decision in the Roberto Alomar spitting incident. I was curious to see what she would do if someone approached him about it here, but besides being held back by my sense of manners, I wasn't going to risk testing her just to satisfy my curiosity.

Stan and I had a good time recognizing all the different people waiting for the plane. There were so many that I can't recall them all. Joe McIlvaine, General Manager of the Mets, stands out in my memory, perhaps because he stands out anyway with his height and goofy hair. We saw Jeff Torborg, who was also on our flight back to New York a few days later, and Stan observed that you could tell he was a catcher from the way he walked. I saw Joe Falls, who was the big local sportswriter when I was growing up as a Tigers fan. I saw Bruce Jenkins of *The San Francisco Chronicle*, and Tracy Ringolsby of *The Rocky Mountain News* gave us a wave. Oh, and I saw the old Mets first baseman, Keith Hernandez. He wasn't on this flight but stopped by to say hello to some of his friends in line. The big highlight of my spotting familiar faces was right in front of me while I was in line arranging for the storage of Stan's wheelchair. It was Jim Murray, my favorite sportswriter of all time. He was engrossed in conversation with the guy he was traveling with, otherwise I might have intruded enough just to tell him how much I enjoyed his work over the years.

In Atlanta we got our rental car, checked into the hotel, had a light lunch and rested up before heading to the ballpark. We ended up in a parking lot that charged $20! That's the most I've ever paid at any event. Kathy checked to make sure they were not going to pack cars in like sardines, and that early folks like us would not have to wait on others before we could get out of the lot after the game. Well, when we got back to the lot after the game, we were the only car still there. Stan dryly observed, "I'm sure glad that Kathy made sure we wouldn't be blocked in."

I had no trouble selling my extra ticket at face value, and the Braves personnel were just great about helping us to our seats. They didn't have an elevator, but they had a motorized scooter to assist folks like Stan. We just dropped off the chair at their Customer Services spot, and they zipped Stan and Kathy up the ramps and they even waited until they were sure that Stan would not need further assistance in getting to his seat.

As usual, we were plenty early and I anticipated that I would be able to sit with Stan and Kathy for quite awhile before having to move to my seat way over in left field. But you know, I never had to move. Contrary to what you might think about a sellout World Series crowd, there are a few seats that will go unoccupied. They are usually single seats in upper reserved, which are held to the last minute by ticket scalpers/ticket services in hopes that they can still get a good price for what is generally an undesirable ticket. Well, God was kind enough to place one of these rare seats right next to Stan, and that was the seat I "happened" to sit in.

It was Tom Glavine versus David Cone, and both pitched quite well. Only an unearned run in the fourth kept it from being a 1-1 tie going into the eighth. But the Braves bullpen stumbled in the eighth to screw up Glavine's strong seven innings of work. They gave up three runs and the game eventually ended at 5-2.

Besides the blessing of the open seat next to Stan, the highlight of this game was glancing over at the center field scoreboard and seeing this message, "Lou Gehrig's record of 2,130 consecutive games has been broken. Now it's time to break his disease. Support ALS research." I quickly nudged Stan so he could see it before it went off the board. We never saw this message again the rest of the series. Stan likened it to the mystical scoreboard message in "Field of Dreams," the movie based on John Kinsella's enchanting book *Shoeless Joe*.

Wednesday, October 23, 1996

During the day we toured the Civil War "Cyclo-Rama," which is a historic painting from the 1880s, done in the round so you have a 360-degree view of the battle outside Atlanta. It was quite interesting, both in the sense of history and in the pioneer effort to do this kind of painting, plus the efforts to restore it and protect it. It is quite tall and far around. Maybe I didn't hear them right, but I think they said the original artists used 30,000 gallons of paint.

We then toured the Coca-Cola Museum/Exposition or whatever they call it. Atlanta is where Coca-Cola began, and they have a building dedicated to housing a permanent exhibit on the company, both past and present. I have to say that I found it quite interesting and well done.

I sold my extra ticket for Game 4 to a bellman at the hotel who was thrilled to be able to go to a World Series game without having to pay more than face value. Now that we knew our way around the stadium a bit, we were able to come up with cheaper parking that even had easier access to the park. And again we were fortunate that the seat next to Stan was open for the whole game.

And what a crazy game it was. Yankee starter Kenny Rogers had absolutely nothing working for him. He was knocked out early in the third inning after allowing five runs. Atlanta scored another run in the fifth to make it 6-0. Denny Neagle was cruising, and it looked like it would be an easy win for Atlanta, but it turned into a very weird night with the very first batter in the next inning. Yankee shortstop Derek Jeter hit a soft foul fly down the right-field line. Keep in mind we were sitting in the upper deck in right-field foul territory. We had an excellent view of where Jermaine Dye was when the ball was hit and the jump he had in going after the ball. If he had been able to keep coming in a straight line to where the ball was coming down, he not only would have had a shot at catching the ball, I think it would have been an easy play. But he couldn't go directly to the ball because umpire Tim Welke apparently didn't believe anyone had a chance at the ball and ended up right between Dye and the ball. Dye tried to get around him, but that extra time let the ball drop, keeping Jeter alive at the plate.

In Welke's defense, the umpires who work the outfield foul lines in postseason play aren't used to working from this position, which is never used with the four-man crews during the regular season. But I have a hard time excusing his blunder. He could see the first baseman and second baseman didn't have any kind of shot at the ball. Yeah, he obviously didn't realize where Dye started off or what a good jump he had on this ball, but the right fielder was the only guy he had to worry about. I know he didn't want to miss whether it was fair or foul, but this ball was in the air for some time. I think it was a pure brain lock that kept him from taking a quick glance to make sure he was not going to impede the right fielder's shot at the ball.

He was booed, but not that harshly. After all, it wasn't likely to have an impact on this 6-0 game. But it definitely did. Given a second chance, Jeter laced a leadoff single and eventually scored. Without that run, the game never would have gone to extra innings and the Braves would have won. Heck, without that run Bobby Cox probably doesn't make the first of his two controversial pitching moves for the night.

See, Mike Bielecki came in to bail the Braves out of a jam in this inning, and he was pitching about as well as a guy can pitch. He faced seven batters, walked one, whiffed four and allowed no hits and no runs . Throwing that well, and with a three-run lead, I expected that Cox would let Bielecki start the eighth inning and then replace him if he got into any trouble.

Instead, Cox went right to Wohlers, and it turned into a disastrous outing, capped off by Wohlers allowing a three-run homer to Jim Leyritz to tie the game. After the game, Cox defended bringing Wohlers in so early saying, "[Wohlers has] been in the eighth inning many times this year." Bielecki also supported Cox by saying, "I hadn't gone more than a couple innings all year."

That sounds good, but Bielecki was simply wrong, and Cox' statement was a bit misleading. Noting that Wohlers has come into the eighth inning before is not the same as having him start off the eighth. The truth is that only once the whole year had Cox asked Wohlers to get six outs to finish the game, and he blew the lead in that game, too! To do that here, with a three-run lead and the set-up man throwing the game of his life, it seems fair to second-guess this decision, and there was no second-guessing for Stan and me as we opposed the move as it happened.

When I read Bielecki's comment the next day, I thought it was pretty silly. Bielecki had made a handful of starts (five) for the Braves in the second half. Certainly he was physically capable of going another batter or two past two innings, especially when it was a very easy two innings where he had faced a lousy seven batters. When I got back home I looked it up, and in 27 percent of his regular-season relief outings he had faced more than seven batters (averaged nine in those games). And twice in the second half he pitched more than two innings in relief, including three shutout innings while facing 12 batters on July 6. Don't believe everything you read.

I also thought it was interesting that Eddie Perez came into the game in the eighth inning with Wohlers. There hadn't been a pinchhitter or pinchrunner for Javy Lopez; this was purely a defensive replacement. I think Lopez is badly underrated as a defensive catcher, but because Maddux prefers pitching to Perez, Eddie has gotten this great reputation at Lopez' expense. But it seems more likely to me that Perez is simply a better fit for Maddux' style of pitching, and who is the most dissimilar pitcher on their staff to Maddux? That would be Wohlers, and in regular season play, Wohlers has allowed 20 hits and eight earned runs in the 18.1 innings that he has thrown to Perez—far worse than to their other catchers, including Lopez.

In this game it was Perez who went away from Wohlers' 98-MPH fastball to call the slider that Leyritz belted for the three-run homer. Add in the World Series stats and Wohlers has now allowed 26 hits in 20.1 innings while throwing to Perez, and his ERA with Perez stands at 4.87, or about twice as high as with Atlanta's other catchers. Incidentally, Perez allowed another two runs in the other two innings he caught in this World Series. The switch to Perez in this game also hurt on offense. No one questions that Lopez is the better hitter, and in the bottom of the eighth, with the go-ahead run on second base, they were stuck with Perez at the plate (he hit a weak groundout).

But the oddities in Atlanta's decisions does not end there. Now we come to Cox' decision to leave Steve Avery in the game and have him intentionally pass Bernie Williams with two outs and men on first and second, which meant Avery had to face Boggs with the bases loaded. I can think of four things that motivated Cox:

- One, Williams is a switch-hitter but he is a far, far better hitter from his natural right side and kills lefties like Avery.

- Two, Bernie had hit well in postseason play and could have been seen as in a hot streak, and indeed, Cox would later cite this factor in the postgame interviews.

- Three, Bielecki and Wohlers were already used up, and McMichael had a tired arm and had just surrendered a homer to Williams the night before, so the most likely alternative out of the bullpen was the righthander Brad Clontz. Even though Williams is a much weaker hitter from the left side of the plate, like most righty sidearmers Clontz is also weaker against lefty hitters.

- Four, Avery's spot in the lineup was coming up in the next inning, and Cox would want to pinch hit for the pitcher and didn't want to waste a new reliever to get a single out.

That first motivation is one I can't argue with. It was important to avoid having Williams get a shot against a struggling lefty like Avery. But it seems to me that it would have still been better to have gone ahead and replaced Avery with Clontz and let him pitch to Williams.

Look, the second motivation above is really pretty weak. I'm not a big believer in anyone's ability to predict the continuation of a hot streak, and even the the argument for Williams being in a hot streak was debatable. Williams had hit well in the playoffs, but the Braves had handled him quite well in the World Series. He had hit a few balls hard, but at the time of this play he was just 2-for-16 in the Series. In this particular game Williams was 0-for-4 without a hard-hit ball. (He ended up hitting .167 for the Series.)

The motivation based on Clontz having trouble with lefty batters is based on a real enough factor, but you are still gaining an awful lot by simply making Williams turn around and hit lefty, which generally knocks about 70 points off his batting average (104 points in 1996). Granted, Clontz versus Williams is not an ideal situation, but isn't it better than the alternative of creating a situation where either a hit or a walk gives the Yankees the lead, and Avery is facing Wade Boggs? Avery has had a bad year and struggled with his control. He also had walked one of the four previous batters on four pitches. Boggs has one of the great eyes at the plate, and a walk will produce the go-ahead run.

It seemed an unwise trade-off to me. Cox left Avery in; issued an intentional pass to Bernie, and Avery ended up walking Boggs to give up the game-winning run. Then, Cox did a double switch so he could bring Clontz in and not have to pinch hit for him right away. Clontz pitched great, popping up his first batter (dropped for an error) and struck out the next guy to finally end the inning. But if Cox was willing to do a double switch to bring Clontz in at that time, why not do it when Avery was faced with the Williams' dilemma? With that double switch, Cox gave up the fourth motivation for that questionable intentional walk.

318

At four hours and 17 minutes it was the longest game in World Series history. The Series was tied at 2-2, and the Series would be settled in New York. With the Braves rotation for the last three games being Smoltz, Maddux, and Glavine, that more than evened up New York's edge in having the home field for two of the three final games. The Yanks had come a long way from a couple days ago when fans were writing them off in both cities. But the players were more realistic about it. I remember one of the Braves downplaying their lead after Game 2, saying, "It takes four to win. We've only got two."

Thursday, October 24, 1996

During the day, we wheeled down to the Planet Hollywood to have lunch and then wheeled over to visit Centennial Park, built to honor the Olympics, and where they had the tragic bombing this summer. I got a kick out of the Planet Hollywood, which is like a sports memorabilia bar, but with TV/Movies as the theme. They had lots of interesting stuff. They had the suit that Clark Gable wore in "Gone with the Wind," plus the suit Tom Cruise wore in "The Firm," a favorite movie of mine. They had tons of interesting small items like a bat used in "A League of Their Own" and Batman's utility belt from the TV series. My favorite item was a pair of Harold Lloyd's glasses. He was a great comedian in the 1920s who was just a wonderful athletic, physical comedian in the genre of that silent film era. He was better than Charlie Chaplin, and, indeed, in their time he was more popular than Chaplin. He has been largely forgotten because he put severe restrictions on the use of his films after his retirement, and specifically curtailed their adaptation for use on television.

Game 5 was a special moment in ballpark history. It would be the first time that a ballpark's final game would be in a World Series. I made sure to take a couple pictures of the Hank Aaron statue, which is one of the best baseball statues I have ever seen. (The Stan Musial statue in St. Louis is hands-down the worst.) Aaron didn't build this place the way Ruth "built" Yankee Stadium, but Hammering Hank is the guy who made this park "The House Where Ruth Finished Second." (I believe that is originally Furman Bisher's line.)

Inside the stadium, while we were waiting for the cart to take Stan up to our section, I saw this old man quietly waiting in his wheelchair. With his thin, lanky build, his long gnarled hands from a lifetime of work, and his unpretentious dress (jeans with suspenders, red plaid shirt, and baseball cap), he reminded me a great deal of my Grandpa Hiler, who taught me about the game and to love it. I asked this elderly gentleman if I could take his picture, and I consider that shot my best reminder of this aspect of this game, that it is the last in the history of Atlanta-Fulton County Stadium.

Well, we finally had a guy show up with the ticket to "my" seat next to Stan, but he sat elsewhere for a while so we could spend some time together until the person with his "borrowed" seat showed up. I actually didn't have to move until after the first inning had been played.

It was an extremely well-pitched game. John Smoltz allowed just four hits and struck out 10 in eight innings. The lone run to score off him resulted from an uncharacteristic misplay by

Gold Glove outfielder Marquis Grissom. The Yankees' Andy Pettitte pitched just as brilliantly, holding the Braves to four hits and zero runs in eight innings. Pettitte helped himself considerably with two fine defensive plays in the sixth. With men on first and second and none out, he charged a bunt and made a gutty, quick throw to nail the lead runner at third. This play kept the double play in order, and that is exactly what he got on the next batter, with Pettitte himself starting the double play.

After the Series, when I got back home, Catie told me the home plate umpire had done a very poor job in this game, and that it had been especially damaging to the Braves' hitters. We can't see stuff like that from the kind of seats we had, but I do remember that the third inning ended with a man in scoring position when Lemke took a called strike three on a pitch that looked incredibly low, even from left field.

In the ninth, Pettitte allowed a leadoff double to Chipper Jones. Fred McGriff hit a grounder to the right side that moved Jones to third, and Yankee closer John Wetteland came in the game. Lopez hit a hard grounder to third base, so that Jones had no chance to score on the clean play. Klesko was intentionally passed to bring the right-handed hitter Jermaine Dye to the plate. Luis Polonia pinch hit for Dye, and he put up a great battle. After fouling off six pitches, he crashed a ball into the right-center field gap. If it fell, the game was tied for sure, and it was likely that Ryan Klesko—running with two outs—would score the winning run. But the ball stayed up just enough for right fielder Paul O'Neill to make an over-the-shoulder running catch as he approached the warning track. Yankees win 1-0. What a game, but this is probably one I would have enjoyed more on TV. It may have been the best-pitched game I have seen in all the World Series I've attended, and it is hard to follow and appreciate good pitching from the kind of seats we got for a World Series.

For the first time in this Series, the Yankees were now the favorites. Some suggested it would hurt the Yankees to go back to their home park, noting that they had won all eight of their road games in postseason play this year. While it would not have surprised me to see Atlanta win two in a row with Maddux and Glavine pitching for them, I think this theory about the road victories was simply fun speculation for the fans, and that this road streak was just chance distribution. The Yankees easily could have lost two of these three games, and such streaks are generally pretty meaningless. However, I did see something in Game 5 that made me think the Braves were ripe to be taken by a lesser team.

I was greatly surprised at what I saw Chipper Jones do in the ninth when he was on third base with one out. When the ball was hit sharply to third, Charlie Hayes had to step away from the third-base line to make the play, and then take another step toward first base to make his throw. This all happened so quickly that the shortstop was a long ways from getting over to third base to help hold the runner. When Hayes started his throw to first, Jones should have been bouncing down the line a step or two, getting ready to score if there was any kind of muff at first base. It wasn't likely to happen, but you have to be ready to take whatever is given you, especially when playing another good team. Heck, you would do this in a lot less crucial situations, and this was one out in the ninth of a 1-0 World Series game! Instead, when that ball was fielded by Hayes, Jones simply gave up and started walking back to third—playing it excessively safe. Where is Billy Martin when you need him?

Now contrast that with Pettitte's go-for-broke play to get the lead runner on the sacrifice attempt in the sixth. It seems to me that the Yankees accepted their underdog role and were scrambling and battling to take advantage of every little edge they could find. The Braves were content to try and win by simply being the better, more talented team. It wasn't working.

I did end up with an interesting souvenir from the now-retired ballpark. A lot of fans were taking whatever wasn't fastened down, and a few were going beyond that. Near me in left field were a father and son who had brought a ratchet set and took out the "seat" portion of their seats and were walking out with them under their arms. Some were taking down signs, and whatever. I hadn't really thought about taking anything. I like to travel light, and it seemed better to leave such stuff to the fans who really had a tie to this ballpark. When we went to Customer Service to pick up the wheelchair, I stopped off in the bathroom nearest there. I was a little surprised to see the faucet heads were off all the sinks except one. I guessed the souvenir hunters were responsible, but I was surprised that would be something they would want or that they would be easy to remove. When I went to wash my hands I went to the sink which still had its faucet heads, and when I pushed down on the cold water push handle, it just leaned forward as if it were loose. I just lifted it up and it came right off. I thought, "Well, I guess I am meant to have a souvenir of this park," and put it in my pocket.

When I told Stan he got a real laugh out of it—especially when on our way to the parking lot we came across this woman berating this one fellow for taking a sign. I don't know if it was her favorite sign or what, but she was really cursing him and saying stuff like, "How low can you get? Stealing a sign!" Stan got a tremendous case of the giggles thinking about what she might say if she knew what I was carrying in my pocket.

Friday, October 25, 1996

After flying back to New York and getting settled in at the hotel, I stayed in to catch up on some of the work piling up on me, particularly my analysis of the minor league free agents. Stan and Kathy went into the city in hopes of seeing Julie Andrews in "Victor Victoria," but they couldn't get tickets and settled instead for "Grease." I did take a break and went out and had a Korean dinner. Turns out that Flushing (where our hotel is) has one of the largest Korean populations outside of Seoul. Very hot, spicy food; very good.

The big news in New York was that Frank Torre, the former big leaguer and big brother of Yankee manager Joe Torre, had a new heart and was doing very well after the transplant operation. He had been waiting a long time and it was getting to be a real concern whether one would be available in time. Between this and the fact that Joe Torre had never before been to a World Series in 4,200 games as a player and manager, there was a lot of talk about it being "destiny" that the Yankees win this Series.

Saturday, October 26, 1996

When I saw Stan and Kathy in the morning, they told me about a problem they had with the wheelchair. During their theater excursion, the right leg rest of the wheelchair broke off while negotiating a curb. Kathy was going out to see about getting it welded back on or replacing that part. Stan and I stayed behind and talked up a storm.

When Kathy got back, she told us that the metal was too thin to weld, but she was able to get a replacement part. I started off to the lobby to sell my extra ticket to one of the bellmen, but Kathy suggested that we offer it to the guy at the wheelchair place, that he had been real nice and helpful, and he might trade the cost of the part for the ticket. I guess I haven't explained why I hadn't been selling my extra ticket for its real value rather than face value—particularly here in New York where they are very valuable. Because I buy these tickets through the club allotments, they are traceable to me if they turn up in some illegal activity, and it would cost me future access to such tickets. Besides, it's fun when I have an extra ticket to make it available to good fans who might otherwise not be able to find an affordable ticket to the Series.

So I told Kathy to call this guy and see if he would be interested. Turns out he is a big baseball fan and was thrilled to make the trade and also offered to drive. His name is Jeff and he showed up in a car with a license plate that read something like 69METSFAN. It was just great having him along, and he was so appreciative of the opportunity. He told us he never closed up his shop so fast, and how amazing it was to have awoken that morning and gone about so much of his day without having a clue he was going to be at tonight's game. He felt certain the Yankees were going to win that night—which may relate to his background as a Mets fan. The 1986 Mets are one of only two teams that have won a World Series after losing the first two games at home.

Besides being a good fan, Jeff fit in well with our little group, thanks to his business, which makes him very comfortable with the physically handicapped. He knows the pace and anticipates things. He was also a good New York driver who knew right where he was going, and got us into the parking garage right by the Stadium.

When I took the wheelchair back down after we got to our seats, I was dreading taking it all the way over to the Yankee lobby, remembering how hard it was to pick it up there after the game. Around the elevator are these little waiting rooms where the color guard waits before the game, and where family members of the players often hang out after the game. I asked the security guard at the elevator if there wasn't somewhere around there that I could store the wheelchair during the game. She thought about it a bit, and told me I could stick it in a small unused corridor that was simply being used to store boxes. I appreciated her cooperation.

The National Anthem was sung by this little bit of a girl who has been a lucky charm for the Yankees. She sung the Anthem for them a few times, and the Yankees always won when she sang. She has a big voice for a little girl and performed with absolute confidence. Nothing about this intimidated her. I was impressed and thought she was one of the better good-luck charms, even better than John Wetteland's hat. If anyone in the future wonders about whether John changed to one of the special hats they have for the World Series, he did not. He made them sew the World Series emblem on his lucky regular-season cap.

Greg Maddux and Jimmy Key both started out well, but in the third, Maddux had his only bad inning of the Series, and it was a big one. Everything seemed to happen at once, as four hits quickly came together for three runs. In his other 14.2 innings in this Series he allowed just eight hits, one walk and zero runs. But this one inning was eventually the ballgame, as it so often is in baseball. (In support of the big-inning theory, in five of the six World Series games the winning team scored more runs in one inning than the losing team did the whole game.)

I did get one of my best laughs at the start of this inning. The Yankee fans tend to love their team, but they are profanely demanding of their heroes all the same. Paul O'Neill had played the whole Series with a painful hamstring pull, and he led off the big inning against Maddux with what looked like a possible double. As he rounded first and headed for second, the fan behind me was yelling, "Run, you gimpy Mother F_____, run!"

I don't mean to be so critical of Bobby Cox as I believe strongly that he is far above average in his managerial ability, but he sure made a lot of strange moves in this Series, and none was stranger than his decision to start Terry Pendleton against Jimmy Key in Game 2 and again in Game 6. The Braves don't pay to have me scout their own team, but this is one of the things I wrote late in the season for another team in regard to Pendleton:

> I suggest matching a lefty against him in a key at-bat. In his career, Pendleton has generally been a better hitter from his natural right side, but he has struggled so badly against lefties this year, that I am reluctant to dismiss it as chance. Perhaps something physical is hindering his right-handed swing this year. He has just one extra-base hit off lefties this year.

Yet here was Cox going out of his way to DH Pendleton against the left-handed Key. Granted, Klesko has a large platoon differential, but he's a better bet to produce against Key in this Series than Pendleton is, and especially with the edge that Yankee Stadium gives lefty power hitters. And heck, if the Braves felt it had to be a righty DH against Key, why not Mike Mordecai, who has shown some pop against lefties in his career (.472 SLG vs LHP), even though he is crummy against RHP? And maybe the Braves were too loyal to Pendleton in even having him on the postseason roster. They left themselves extremely vulnerable in the World Series for any DH games against a lefty pitcher.

Pendleton looked feeble against Key in Game 2, though he did bloop a weak pop fly that fell for a hit. And Pendleton ended up a central figure in destroying two of the Braves' best scoring opportunities against Key in Game 6. Leading off the third inning, Pendleton reached base when Mariano Duncan botched his easy ground ball. But then Pendleton was thrown out trying to steal second, a particularly poor play for a 36 year old with little speed or basestealing skill. And this play gets stranger the more you look at it. I had written the following warning for the Braves in regard to running on Key.

> . . . [Key] is very tough to run on, and the steal success rate against him is actually lower than it has been with Andy Pettitte. Solo steals of second are only 6 for the last 16 against Key (38 percent) and 2-for-8 this year (25 percent).

> Don't run on him in the first three innings! It seems Key's main strategy is to show early that he is on guard against the running game, and then he lightens up. In addition to getting 80 percent of his pickoffs in the first three innings, the steal attempts in the first three innings have had a miserable 11 percent success rate.

Pendleton was running at the top of the third inning, and there was nothing to indicate it resulted from a failed hit-and-run. Jeff Blauser did not swing at the pitch, which was called a ball, and this was not one of the counts I recommended for a hit-and-run against Key. It was extremely costly as Blauser ended up doubling, and even if Pendleton had not scored from first on that double, he would have scored on Grissom's subsequent ground ball. And if Pendleton had not used up that out with his caught stealing, then the two walks and two hits that led off the next inning would all have taken place in the third inning and plated Blauser as well. The net result was that without Pendleton's very ill-advised steal attempt, the Braves would likely have scored three runs, minimum, in the third inning, and with their later run in the ninth, won this game.

Pendleton being a poor batting match against Key hurt them a great deal when he came to bat with the Braves trailing 3-1, this time with the bases loaded and just one out. Pendleton—who grounded into a career-high 18 GDPs during the regular season—bailed out Key with a routine double-play ball to shortstop. (If it had been only a lousy fielder's choice, it would have scored a run, and the Braves' later run in the ninth would have tied the game rather than leaving them a run short.) Pendleton never did hit a ball sharply off Key in those two starts.

Besides Pendleton's play dragging them down in this game, the Braves had more problems with the umpires. Prior to the fifth inning, the scoreboard did a "This Date in Baseball History" segment which noted on this date 11 years ago that a brutal call by umpire Don Denkinger cost the Cardinals the 1985 World Championship, and if I remember right they even showed the video of the play. I glanced down on the field to see how the umpires were taking this. Ooooh, their body language didn't like it. They were all looking at the screen with either their arms crossed or their hands on their hips. But what could they say? This "replay" was history, it did not have anything to do with this game, nor was it meant to show up this crew of umpires. So, I found it ironic that in this very inning an umpire would make the worst call of this series. Marquis Grissom had reached base on a single, and on a pitch to the next batter, the ball got away from the catcher and Grissom tried to advance to second. Joe Girardi made a heck of a throw, but it was obvious to everyone in the park that Grissom had beaten the tag—except for umpire Terry Tata, who called him out. Catie could confirm by the replay at home that Grissom was safe, but even there at the park, Stan and Jeff were agreeing that the Yankees had gotten a break.

And as fate would have it, this error by the umpires again ended up being crucial to the outcome of the game. If Grissom had been called safe, then Chipper Jones, the Braves' best hitter for average, would have had the chance to hit with two outs and their fastest man on second. Instead, he was simply the leadoff batter for the next inning. He doubled. This blown call was also especially grating to me because, with their backs to the wall, Grissom was playing the kind of ball the Braves should have been playing the whole Series. He did exactly the opposite of what I criticized about Jones' baserunning in Game 5. I hated to see him unfairly penalized for doing the right thing.

Cox gave heck to Tata over his call, and as he walked off the field he said something to umpire Tim Welke, who was the umpire who kept Dye from catching that crucial fly ball in Game 4. (The newspapers also said that Cox had been unhappy with Welke's ball-strike calls when he was behind the plate.) Cox must have said something pretty bad, because Welke ejected him even though Cox was headed off the field and Welke had not been involved in this play at second base. It's rare to eject a manager in a World Series game, and under these circumstances, most umpires would have just let him keep walking unless he said a few choice magical words directed personally at the umpire. That appears to have been the case. After the game, Cox said he should have been ejected, but that he wanted Welke to know he had blown some plays.

After Jones' leadoff double in the sixth, Key got the next guy and Torre lifted him to get to the Yankees' middle relievers, who are the best in baseball. David Weathers and Graeme Lloyd each pitched one-third of an inning to get them to the seventh, and that brought in Mariano Rivera, who would be a closer for most teams in baseball. Rivera threw two near-perfect innings, walking just one batter.

In the ninth, John Wetteland came very close to blowing the two-run lead given to him. He struck out Jones, but Klesko singled, and Pendleton, now hitting from the left side, singled him to third. Polonia pinch hit and struck out. Grissom singled to make it a one-run game. Lemke hit a foul pop to third base and the defending World Champions were no more; hail the World Champions of 1996, the New York Yankees.

I do feel sorry for the Braves, but there are a lot of people to be happy for, and I'm happy for baseball as well. This is how baseball works. This is how it should work. It doesn't matter that the Braves were probably the better team. It doesn't matter that poor umpiring may have cost the Braves two games or that an improbable error by a great defensive player lost a third game by a 1-0 score. It doesn't matter that in the overall numbers the Braves hit better and pitched better in this World Series than did the Yankees. Far more than in the other sports, it is difficult for even the best baseball teams to consistently dominate in a short series.

And that's the beautiful part of this game, that you never really know how it is going to play out. After the Series, my friend Matt Gaylen idly wondered in a letter when was the last time the Braves lost four straight. I looked it up, and it was only about five weeks before the World

Series. The Braves lost four straight games from September 10 to 14 against the Rockies and Mets, and it was actually a five-game losing streak.

And for all the oddities of their loss, the Braves are far from unique in the way they were upset in this World Series. We had that reminder of that 1985 Series being decided by an obvious umpiring error. We have Bill Buckner's error on a routine grounder deciding the 1986 Series. And even though it was unusual for a team to lose the Series after outscoring the winner 26-18 overall, that was only the second-largest edge by a losing team. The old Yankee fans know exactly what that frustration is like. In 1960, the Yankees outscored the Pirates better than two-to-one (55-27) and still lost the Series.

I've experienced my share of special crowd celebrations following the World Series. The 1984 celebration in Tiger Stadium will always be a special one for me, and I was touched quite a bit by the 1987 celebration of the Twins victory, but I think this may be the one that will stick most vividly with me. When Hayes grabbed that pop foul, Wetteland quickly dropped to one knee in gratitude and then leaped into the air where he was tackled by teammates. Who knows when his feet touched the ground again. But the best stuff came after that. Totally impromptu, the celebration on the mound started to bleed down the left-field line. I don't know who really started it, but I remember seeing Cecil Fielder waving his arms and hopping up and down as he moved down the foul line, and soon the whole team was following him in a joyous victory lap around the park.

Wade Boggs, who says he is normally scared of horses, climbed on the back of the horse of a mounted policeman and rode with him around the park, waving and slapping hands with fans and other mounted policemen. When he got back to the dugout area, he ran over to home plate. Turning to the crowd behind the plate, with his cap in his hand, and taking a big windup step, he threw his arm forward in a salute to the fans. It is a scene I don't think I will ever forget.

In the stands there was all kinds of stuff flying through the air. A few hats, a lot of paper, etc. I kept my hat but I did toss several handfuls of popcorn. Stan was loving it, his eyes were just dancing, and we stayed a long, long time. As we were making way for a father and son who were heading for the exit, I told the son that he would remember this, that this was history. I eventually went down to retrieve the wheelchair, and when I backed it out of the corridor where it was stored, I turned it around and nearly hit this big guy in a Yankee uniform. It was Cecil Fielder, who had come up from the locker room to spend a few minutes with his family before heading back to the celebration. It was pretty noisy and raucous in that crowded little area, but as I went by him I leaned in and said, "Congratulations." I doubt he even heard me, but it was a first in my World Series experience.

Riding up in the elevator, it was just me and these two young black guys, maybe in their early to mid-20s. They were euphoric as we talked about the game. One guy said it was like a dream come true. I told them about what it had meant to me as a 16 year old when the Tigers won the 1968 World Championship, how that had really cemented my already strong interest and love for the game, and that I liked thinking of all the young fans out there right now who might be going through that same experience. I also told them how I was there more as just a baseball fan than a Yankees fan, and yet it was still magical for me. The guy on the left gave a little nod and said with utter conviction, "Baseball is the best game." I liked hearing that; I'd heard a few too many sentiments of this just being about New York, that the Yankees are great and everyone else sucks.

Just as we were reaching the upper level, I said, "There is another story to this Series." The doors opened and these guys just stopped as if they had all the time in the world; they weren't going anywhere until they heard this story. So I told them about my friend Stan, how one of the ties between us was baseball, and about being able to take him to this World Series. They said that was a great story and they were sorry about my friend's illness. I said, "Well, there is always hope." The guy on the right touched my shoulder and said, "And you keep that hope," and then they were gone. For me, that elevator ride was one of the great memories from this trip.

When we came down the elevator and got off at the family waiting area, catcher Joe Girardi was there and Jeff got him to autograph his World Series program. It took forever to get out of the parking lot and back across the river, but with Jeff at the helm it was stress-free. When he dropped us off at the hotel, he said, "What time should I pick you up for the parade?" We all laughed as we knew we would be long gone by the time they had the parade on Tuesday. He understood that, but he also wanted us to know that if we did stay around for the parade, he wanted to help us out by doing the driving. This made a big impression on Stan, who repeated this part of the story many times in trying to capture how much he thought of Jeff. Stan also loved Jeff's strong New York voice in rooting for the Yankees. He did have a special ability for projecting his voice when he wanted to.

At the airport we got a chance to say hello to John Blake of the Texas PR department, who had been my source for the tickets. He had felt bad that they weren't able to do any better on the tickets, and he was very happy to hear how well everything had gone. We also saw Gerry Fraley, a writer I was friendly with in Texas but whom I hadn't seen in nearly four years.

When we got close to the Dallas-Ft. Worth airport, a major thunderstorm hit the area and they had to close the airport. We had to turn around and land at Shreveport, Louisiana, where we sat on a side runway for hours. It wasn't so bad, as Stan and I played a game of "What would I do if I were a GM?" followed by a review of his impressions of individual ballplayers from his clubhouse days. It passed the time pretty well, but we were sure ready to get back home when they finally let us proceed.

Naturally I had missed my connecting flight, and my replacement flight also ended up being canceled. On the positive side, though, this gave me a chance to meet Stan's parents, and that was worth a lot. I'd never met them in my Texas days, and as brief an encounter as this was, I could see how Stan had turned out to be one of the most decent men I've ever known. And you could see how much they loved their son. When I was telling them about my experience with the two guys on the elevator, and their message of keeping that hope, I realized that his mother had tears in her eyes, but she firmly kept her face turned toward me until I was through, that she wasn't going to miss a word of this. I liked that about her. And his dad paid me the highest compliment I've had in my life—next to Catie's agreeing to be my wife. As he shook my hand he said, "I've been wanting to see what a true friend looks like."

After the Reynolds' were all off, I spent several hours at the airport as the airline shot my third horse out from under me. All told, over 250 flights were canceled that day. I couldn't get a flight until the next day. So I called Kathy, and she came and got me. The next morning Stan and I hung out together in his home talking over the trip and the future. Before we went to the airport we stopped by The Ballpark in Arlington. It did me good to see how well Stan was able to get around totally on his own, that he can still drive, and had the ability to use the little crane—and that's really what it is—to load and unload his little power scooter.

Stan told me about the upcoming golf tournament some friends had put together to raise money for some of Stan's future special needs, including computer equipment that will let him work more often from home. The baseball people from Stan's past and present were particularly generous. Guys like Eddie Robinson, Buddy Bell, Mike Hargrove, etc. Stan told me he was a little surprised to find that catcher Don Slaught had also sponsored a team or a hole. Slaught hadn't been a Ranger when Stan worked in the clubhouse; he wasn't with the Rangers that long, and it has been several years now since he played for Texas. I do know this, Don Slaught was one of my mother's favorite Rangers, and Don had autographed a ball for her out of his appreciation for her concern and prayer when he was hit in the face by a pitch many years ago. He's a good guy, and I would not be surprised to find she had also given him a little spiritual nudge on this. My sister had sent me Mom's few pieces of baseball memorabilia. When I got back from Texas, I dug out that ball and made it first in line among the little display of autographed balls in my office.

About STATS, Inc.

STATS, Inc. is the nation's leading independent sports information and statistical analysis company, providing detailed sports services for a wide array of clients.

As one of the fastest-growing sports companies—in 1994, we ranked 144th on the "Inc. 500" list of fastest-growing privately held firms—STATS provides the most up-to-the-minute sports information to professional teams, print and broadcast media, software developers and interactive service providers around the country. Some of our major clients are ESPN, the Associated Press, *The Sporting News*, Electronic Arts, Motorola, Sony and Topps. Much of the information we provide is available to the public via STATS On-Line. With a computer and a modem, you can follow action in the four major professional sports, as well as NCAA football and basketball. . . as it happens!

STATS Publishing, a division of STATS, Inc., produces 12 annual books, including the *Major League Handbook*, *The Scouting Notebook*, the *Pro Football Handbook*, the *Pro Basketball Handbook* and the *Hockey Handbook*. These publications deliver STATS' expertise to fans, scouts, general managers and media around the country.

In addition, STATS offers the most innovative—and fun—fantasy sports games around, from *Bill James Fantasy Baseball* and *Bill James Classic Baseball* to *STATS Fantasy Football* and *STATS Fantasy Hoops*.

Information technology has grown by leaps and bounds in the last decade, and STATS will continue to be at the forefront as both a vendor and supplier of the most up-to-date, in-depth sports information available. For those of you on the information superhighway, you can always catch STATS in our area on America Online (Keyword: STATS).

For more information on our products, or on joining our reporter network, write us at:

STATS, Inc.
8131 Monticello Ave.
Skokie, IL 60076-3300

. . . or call us at 1-800-63-STATS (1-800-637-8287). Outside the U.S., dial 1-847-676-3383

. . . or visit our website on the Internet at *www.stats.com.*

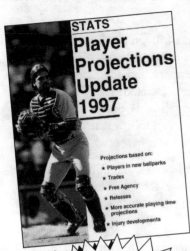 

STATS On-Line

Now you can have a direct line to a world of sports information just like the pros use with STATS On-Line. If you love to keep up with your favorite teams and players, STATS On-Line is for you. From Charles Barkley's fast-breaking dunks to Mark McGwire's tape-measure blasts — if you want baseball, basketball, football and hockey stats, we put them at your fingertips!

STATS On-Line

- **Player Profiles and Team Profiles** — The #1 resource for scouting your favorite professional teams and players with information you simply can't find anywhere else! The most detailed info you've ever seen, including real-time stats.

- **NO monthly or annual fees**

- **Local access numbers** — avoid costly long-distance charges!

- **Unlimited access** — 24 hours a day, seven days a week

- **Downloadable files** — get year-to-date stats in an ASCII format for baseball, football, basketball, and hockey

- **In-progress box scores** — You'll have access to the most up-to-the-second scoring stats for every team and player. When you log into STATS On-Line, you'll get detailed updates, including player stats while the games are in progress!

- **Other exclusive features** — transactions and injury information, team and player profiles and updates, standings, leader and trailer boards, game-by-game logs, fantasy game features, and much more!

Sign-up fee of $30 (applied towards future use), 24-hour access with usage charges of $.75/min. Mon.-Fri., 8am-6pm CST; $.25/min. all other hours and weekends.

Order from  Today!

Use Order Form in This Book, or Call 1-800-63-STATS or 847-676-3383 or e-mail: info@stats.com

Bill James Fantasy Baseball

Bill James Fantasy Baseball enters its ninth season of offering baseball fans the most unique, realistic and exciting game fantasy sports has to offer.

You draft a 26-player roster and can expand to as many as 28. Players aren't ranked like in rotisserie leagues—you'll get credit for everything a player does, like hitting homers, driving in runs, turning double plays, pitching quality outings and more!

The team which scores the most points among all leagues, plus wins the World Series, will receive the John McGraw Award, which includes a one-week trip to the Grapefruit League in spring training, a day at the ballpark with Bill James, and a new fantasy league named in his/her honor!

Unique Features Include:

- **Live fantasy experts** — available seven days a week

- **The best weekly reports in the business** — detailing who is in the lead, win-loss records, MVPs, and team strengths and weaknesses

- **On-Line computer system** — a world of information, including daily updates of fantasy standings and stats

- **Over twice as many statistics as rotisserie**

- **Transactions that are effective the very next day!**

"My goal was to develop a fantasy league based on the simplest yet most realistic principles possible. A league in which the values are as nearly as possible what they ought to be, without being distorted by artificial category values or rankings...."

\- **Bill James**

All this, all summer long...for less than $5 per week!

 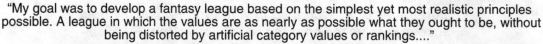

Bill James Classic Baseball

Joe Jackson, Walter Johnson, and Roberto Clemente are back on the field of your dreams!

If you're not ready to give up baseball in the fall, or if you're looking to relive its glorious past, then Bill James Classic Baseball is the game for you! The Classic Game features players from all eras of Major League Baseball at all performance levels—not just the stars. You could see Honus Wagner, Josh Gibson, Carl Yastrzemski, Bob Uecker, Billy Grabarkewitz, and Masanori Murakami...on the SAME team!

As owner, GM and manager all in one, you'll be able to...

- "Buy" your team of up to 25 players from our catalog of over 2,000 historical players (You'll receive $1 million to buy your favorite players)
- Choose the park your team will call home—current or historical, 63 in all!
- Rotate batting lineups for a right- or left-handed starting pitcher
- Change your pitching rotation for each series. Determine your set-up man, closer, and long reliever
- Alter in-game strategies, including stealing frequency, holding runners on base, hit-and-run, and much more!
- Select your best pinch hitter and late-inning defensive replacements (For example, Curt Flood will get to more balls than Hack Wilson!)

How to Play The Classic Game:

1. Sign up to be a team owner TODAY! Leagues forming year-round
2. STATS, Inc. will supply you with a catalog of eligible players and a rule book
3. You'll receive $1 million to buy your favorite major leaguers
4. Take part in a player and ballpark draft with 11 other owners
5. Set your pitching rotation, batting lineup, and managerial strategies
6. STATS runs the game simulation...a 154-game schedule, 14 weeks!
7. You'll receive customized in-depth weekly reports, featuring game summaries, stats, and boxscores

Order from  Today!

Use Order Form in This Book, or Call 1-800-63-STATS or 847-676-3383 or e-mail: info@stats.com

STATS Fantasy Hoops

Soar into the 1996-97 season with STATS Fantasy Hoops! SFH puts YOU in charge. Don't just sit back and watch Grant Hill, Shawn Kemp, and Michael Jordan—get in the game and coach your team to the top!

How to Play SFH:
1. Sign up to coach a team.
2. You'll receive a full set of rules and a draft form with SFH point values for all eligible players - anyone who played in the NBA in 1995-96, plus all 1996 NBA draft picks.
3. Complete the draft form and return it to STATS.
4. You will take part in the draft with nine other owners, and we will send you league rosters.
5. You make unlimited weekly transactions including trades, free agent signings, activations, and benchings.
6. Six of the 10 teams in your league advance to postseason play, with two teams ultimately advancing to the Finals.

SFH point values are tested against actual NBA results, mirroring the real thing. Weekly reports will tell you everything you need to know to lead your team to the SFH Championship!

STATS Fantasy Football

STATS Fantasy Football puts YOU in charge! You draft, trade, cut, bench, activate players and even sign free agents each week. SFF pits you head-to-head against 11 other owners.

STATS' scoring system applies realistic values, tested against actual NFL results. Each week, you'll receive a superb in-depth report telling you all about both team and league performances.

How to Play SFF:
1. Sign up today!
2. STATS sends you a draft form listing all eligible NFL players.
3. Fill out the draft form and return it to STATS, and you will take part in the draft along with 11 other team owners.
4. Go head-to-head against the other owners in your league. You'll make week-by-week roster moves and transactions through STATS' Fantasy Football experts, via phone, fax, or on-line!

Order from  Today!

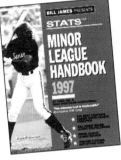

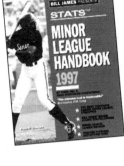
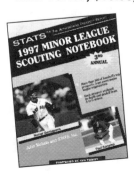

Bill James Presents:

STATS 1997 Batter Versus Pitcher Match-Ups!

- Complete stats for pitchers vs. batters (5+ career AB against them)
- Leader boards and stats for all 1996 major league players
- **Item #BP97, $14.95, Available NOW!**

STATS Baseball Scoreboard 1997

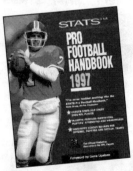

- Lively analysis of all the hottest topics facing baseball today!
- Easy-to-understand charts answer the questions fans always ask
- Specific coverage for each major league team
- **Item #SB97, $18.95, Available NOW!**

STATS Pro Basketball Handbook 1997-98

- Career stats for every player who logged minutes during 1996-97
- Team game logs with points, rebounds, assists and much more
- Leader boards from points per game to triple doubles
- **Item #BH98, $19.95, Available September 1997!**

STATS Pro Football Handbook 1997

- A complete season-by-season register for every active 1995 player
- Numerous statistical breakdowns for hundreds of NFL players
- Leader boards in a number of innovative and traditional categories
- **Item #FH97, $19.95, Available NOW!**

Pro Football Revealed:
The 100-Yard War (1997 Edition)

- Profiles each team, complete with essays, charts and play diagrams
- Detailed statistical breakdowns on players, teams and coaches
- Essays about NFL trends and happenings by leading experts
- **Price: $18.95, Item #PF97 , Available July 1997!**

STATS Hockey Handbook 1996-97

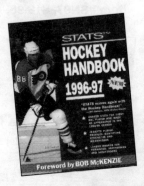

- A complete season-by-season register for every active 1996 player
- Numerous statistical breakdowns for hundreds of NHL players
- Leader boards in numerous innovative and traditional categories
- **Item #HH97, $17.95, Available NOW!**
- *STATS Hockey Handbook 1997-98*
  Price: $19.95, Item #HH98, Available August 1997

STATS, Inc. Order Form

Name_____

Address_____

City_____ State_____ Zip_____

Phone_____Fax_____Internet Address_____

Method of Payment (U.S. Funds Only):
❏ Check   ❏ Money Order   ❏ Visa   ❏ MasterCard

Credit Card Information:

Cardholder Name_____

Credit Card Number_____ Exp. Date_____

Signature_____

BOOKS (STATS publications now include free first class shipping)

Qty.	Product Name	Item Number	Price	Total
	STATS Major League Handbook 1997	HB97	$19.95	
	STATS Major League Handbook 1997 (Comb-bound)	HC97	$21.95	
	STATS Projections Update 1997	PJUP	$9.95	
	The Scouting Notebook: 1997	SN97	$18.95	
	The Scouting Notebook: 1997 (Comb-bound)	SC97	$20.95	
	STATS Minor League Scouting Notebook 1997	MN97	$18.95	
	STATS Minor League Handbook 1997	MH97	$19.95	
	STATS Minor League Handbook 1997 (Comb-bound)	MC97	$21.95	
	STATS Player Profiles 1997	PP97	$19.95	
	STATS Player Profiles 1997 (Comb-bound)	PC97	$21.95	
	STATS 1997 BVSP Match-Ups!	BP97	$14.95	
	STATS Baseball Scoreboard 1997	SB97	$18.95	
	Pro Football Revealed: The 100 Yard War (1997 Edition)	PF97	$18.95	
	STATS Pro Football Handbook 1997	FH97	$19.95	
	STATS Basketball Handbook 1997-98	BH98	$17.95	
	STATS Hockey Handbook 1996-97	HH97	$17.95	
	STATS Hockey Handbook 1997-98	HH98	$19.95	
	Prior Editions (Please circle appropriate year)			
	STATS Major League Handbook '90 '91 '92 '93 '94 '95 '96		$9.95	
	The Scouting Report/Notebook '94 '95 '96		$9.95	
	STATS Player Profiles '93 '94 '95 '96		$9.95	
	STATS Minor League Handbook '92 '93 '94 '95 '96		$9.95	
	STATS BVSP Match-Ups! '94 '95 '96		$3.95	
	STATS Baseball Scoreboard '92 '93 '94 '95 '96		$9.95	
	STATS Basketball Scoreboard/Handbook '93-'94 '94-'95 '95-'96		$9.95	
	Pro Football Revealed: The 100 Yard War '94 '95 '96		$9.95	
	STATS Pro Football Handbook '95 '96		$9.95	
	STATS Minor League Scouting Notebook '95 '96		$9.95	

MULTIMEDIA PRODUCTS (Prices include shipping & handling charges)

Qty.	Product Name	Item Number	Price	Total
	Bill James Encyclopedia CD-Rom	BJCD	$49.95	
	STATS On-Line	STON	$30.00	

SEASON FINAL & YEAR-END REPORTS (Prices include shipping & handling charges)

Qty.	Product Name	Circle Format				Price	Total
	Season Final Report	Paper	3 1/2" disk	5" disk	Mac	$12.95	
	Lefty/Righty Report	Paper	3 1/2" disk	5" disk	Mac	$19.95	
	Stolen Base Report	Paper	3 1/2" disk	5" disk	Mac	$34.95	
	Defensive Games by Position	Paper	3 1/2" disk	5" disk	Mac	$9.95	
	Catcher Report	Paper	3 1/2" disk	5" disk	Mac	$49.95	
	Relief Pitching Report	Paper	3 1/2" disk	5" disk	Mac	$49.95	
	Zone Ratings/Outfield Arms Report	Paper	3 1/2" disk	5" disk	Mac	$99.95	
	End of Season STATpak	Paper	3 1/2" disk	5" disk		$9.95	
	Team(s):						
	STATpak Subscription	Paper	3 1/2" disk	5" disk		$29.95	
	Team(s):						

FANTASY GAMES & STATSfax (STATSfax prices reflect the monthly charge for service)

Qty.	Product Name	Item Number	Price	Total
	Bill James Classic Baseball	BJCB	$129.00	
	How to Win the Classic Game	CGBK	$16.95	
	Classic Game STATSfax	CFX5	$20.00	
	STATS Fantasy Hoops	SFH	$85.00	
	STATS Fantasy Hoops STATSfax—5-Day	SFH5	$20.00	
	STATS Fantasy Hoops STATSfax—7-Day	SFH7	$25.00	
	STATS Fantasy Football	SFF	$69.00	
	STATS Fantasy Football STATSfax—3-Day	SFF3	$15.00	
	Bill James Fantasy Baseball	BJFB	$89.00	
	Fantasy Baseball STATSfax—5-Day	SFX5	$20.00	
	Fantasy Baseball STATSfax—7-Day	SFX7	$25.00	

1st Fantasy Team Name (ex. Colt 45's):_____ _____

   What Fantasy Game is this team for?_____

2nd Fantasy Team Name (ex. Colt 45's):_____ _____

   What Fantasy Game is this team for?_____

NOTE: $1.00/player is charged for all roster moves and transactions.

For Bill James Fantasy Baseball:

Would you like to play in a league drafted by Bill James? ❏ Yes ❏ No

---

TOTALS

	Price	Total
Product Total (excl. Fantasy Games)		
Canada—all orders—add:	$2.50/book	
Order 2 or more books—subtract:	$1.00/book	
(**NOT** to be combined with other specials)		
IL residents add 8.5% sales tax		
Subtotal		
Fantasy Games Total		
GRAND TOTAL		

STATS, Inc. 8131 Monticello Avenue Skokie, IL 60076-3300

All books now include free 1st class shipping!
Thanks for ordering from STATS, Inc.